Yugoslav Folk Music

NUMBER 9 IN THE NEW YORK BARTÓK ARCHIVE
STUDIES IN MUSICOLOGY

THE NEW YORK BARTÓK ARCHIVE

Benjamin Suchoff, *Trustee*

The Béla Bartók Archives:
History and Catalogue

Rumanian Folk Music
I Instrumental Melodies
II Vocal Melodies
III Texts
IV Carols and Christmas Songs (*Colinde*)
V Maramureş County

Turkish Folk Music from Asia Minor

Béla Bartók Essays

Yugoslav Folk Music
I Serbo-Croatian Folk Songs (with Albert B. Lord)
II Tabulation of Material
III Source Melodies: Part One
IV Source Melodies: Part Two

Yugoslav Folk Music

VOLUME ONE

Yugoslav
FOLK MUSIC

Volume One

Serbo-Croatian Folk Songs
and Instrumental Pieces
from the MILMAN PARRY COLLECTION

by BÉLA BARTÓK
and ALBERT B. LORD

Edited by BENJAMIN SUCHOFF

with a Foreword by GEORGE HERZOG

STATE UNIVERSITY OF NEW YORK PRESS

1978

Published by
State University of New York Press
Albany, New York 12246

Printed in the United States of America

Library of Congress Cataloging in Publication Data

Bartók, Béla, 1881–1945.
Yugoslav folk music.

(New York Bartók Archive studies in musicology; no. 9)
Vol. 1 originally published in 1951 by
Columbia University Press, New York,
which was issued as no. 7 of its
Studies in musicology.
Includes bibliographies and indexes.
CONTENTS: v. 1. Serbo-Croatian folk songs and
instrumental pieces from the Milman Parry collection.
1. Folk-songs, Yugoslav—History and criticism.
2. Folk-songs, Croatian—History and criticism.
I. Lord, Albert Bates, joint author.
II. Suchoff, Benjamin.
III. Herzog, George, 1901–
IV. Series: Béla Bartók Archives.
Studies in musicology; no. 9.
V. Series: Columbia University studies in musicology; no. 7.
VI. Title.
ML3590.B32 784.4′9497 78-8188
ISBN 0-87395-383-5

TO THE MEMORY OF

MILMAN PARRY

Editor's Preface

WHEN Hungary signed the Treaty of Trianon on June 4, 1920, almost three-quarters of its territory and two-thirds of its inhabitants were distributed among Austria on the west, Rumania on the east, and the newly created national states of Czechoslovakia on the north and Yugoslavia on the south. This circumferential dismemberment allotted the Burgenland, with its German majority and basically Croatian-Magyar minority, to Austria; Slovakia and Ruthenia, each with a large Magyar minority, to Czechoslovakia; Transylvania[1] to Rumania, from Maramureș in the north to and including parts of the Banat in the south; and Croatia, Slovenia, Bácska, and part of the Banat, with Croat or Serb majorities and essentially Magyar-German minority, to Yugoslavia.[2]

One of the far-reaching effects of the treaty was the curtailment of field trips in formerly Hungarian territories by Hungarian ethnomusicologists. As Bartók put it,

> But no one is allowed to take phonographs across the frontier, neither one way nor the other! They wouldn't even let me bring my own notebooks through! The most I could hope for would be to procure some special permits from heaven knows how may different authorities, and that only after I don't know how many weeks of running around for them! No, the curtain has been drawn over that work . . . [phonograph cylinders] would be confiscated at the border.[3]

The impact of this "drawn curtain" on Bartók, hardly measurable by the foregoing laconic lines, can be reliably assessed in terms of his ethnomusicological objectives. Fifteen years before, in 1905, he had set out to "collect and study Hungarian peasant music unknown until

[1] An enclave of more than a half-million Székely, Hungarians who lived in the eastern part of Transylvania.

[2] The port of Fiume, on the northeast Adriatic coast, was given to Italy.

[3] *Béla Bartók Letters,* ed. János Demeny, English trans. Péter Balabán and István Farkas, rev. Elisabeth West and Colin Mason (London: Faber & Faber, 1970), hereafter cited as *Letters;* letter to Ion Bușiția, May 8, 1921, pp. 153–55.

then," impelled by an earlier examination of Hungarian "folk music" which led to the discovery that "what we had known as Hungarian folk songs were more or less trivial songs by popular composers and did not contain much that was valuable."[4] At that time Bartók's interest in folk song concerned his own activity as a composer, he was seeking a basis on which to develop a compositional style with Hungarian roots. Significantly, and in order to determine the morphological aspects of autochthonous Hungarian folk music, Bartók decided to base his investigation on scientific method; on the spot phonograph recording and transcription by ear would make possible the subsequent extraction of accurate data for analysis. But Bartók soon realized that there are foreign elements in the peasant music of Hungary; indeed, the next year he collected folk music in Slovak villages and, beginning in 1908, in Transylvanian Rumanian ones, in order to test his newly formed hypothesis that a kinship or reciprocal influence existed between the folk music of linguistically differentiated peoples living within the borders of old Hungary.

> Such adopting of [Hungarian] melodies cannot be avoided among neighboring countries. Of course it is only a person very familiar with the musical folklore of both countries who is able to see his way through this chaos. For this reason my opinion is only temporary and can be settled only after I have collected in many more regions.[5]

During these first years of folk music exploration Bartók was able to "rejuvenate" his compositions by means of the pentatonic and modal configurations in the music he encountered in the peasant village. But his compositions were so negatively received by Budapest audiences, in comparison to the welcome given his first book-length essay on folk music[6] by Bucharest scholars, that in 1912 he decided to withdraw from the artistic scene and devote himself primarily to ethnomusicological activities, for he was by now well aware that a vast treasure of musical folklore was at hand or awaited unearthing in the field, that this ma-

[4] *Béla Bartók Essays,* comp. and ed. Benjamin Suchoff (London: Faber & Faber, 1976), hereafter cited as *Essays.* The quotation is taken from essay No. 52, "Autobiography" (trans. Richard Tószeghy).

[5] *Bartók Béla levelei,* ed. János Demény (Budapest: Zeneműkiadó Vállalat, 1955), hereafter cited as *Lev.,* III. Letter to Ion Bușiția, August 14, 1909 (trans. Elma Laurvik).

[6] *Cântece poporale românești din Comitatul Bihor* (*Ungaria*) [Rumanian Folk Songs from Bihar County (Hungary)], Bucharest: Academia Română, 1913. The collection, inadequately titled, contains instrumental pieces (Nos. 292–362) among the 371 melodies.

terial had a value far beyond compositional utilitarianism, and that he himself already was one of a small band of pioneers in the newly established discipline of comparative musicology. Bartók the artist thus turned Bartók the scholar. The new objective, one which he followed with untiring energy and unwavering integrity until the end of his life, was that

> Systematically scientific examination of the morphological aspects of folk music material (consisting first of grouping the material according to certain methods, and then, of describing the typical forms and structures which will appear in a material thus grouped) will enable us to determine clearly the types and to draw various conclusions concerning the transformation, migration of the melodies, their connection with foreign materials, etc.[7]

Although the greater part of Bartók's avocational time and attention was addressed to the collection and study of Slovak and Rumanian folk music (he had been appointed professor of piano at the Budapest Academy of Music beginning in 1907), he nevertheless found it necessary to consider the folk music of Yugoslavia. It seems reasonable to conclude that Bartók's turn toward South Hungary stemmed from his brief collecting trip in Nagyszentmiklós (now Sânnicolaul Mare, Torontal County, Rumania), the place of his birth, in January, 1910. Among the instrumental pieces recorded there was a peasant flute (*fluer*) melody which the performer said was a Serbian dance melody.[8] In addition, Bartók collected forty-eight vocal melodies, of which more than a third contained refrain lines of a type to be found outside of the Banat (that is, southwestern Hungary which contains Rumanian villages near Serbian and Slovene territories).[9] One of the songs had a peculiar heterogeneous character, as if it were "a foreign body in the bulk of the Rumanian material."[10] Then Bartók apparently compared its melody

[7] *Essays,* No. 7, "On American and British Folk Music Material." (English text in Bartók's autograph.)

[8] See melody No. 252 and its Note in Béla Bartók, *Rumanian Folk Music,* ed. Benjamin Suchoff, Vol. I (The Hague: Martinus Nijhoff, 1967). Published in three volumes (I: Instrumental Melodies; II: Vocal Melodies; III: Texts) and hereafter cited as *RFM* (I, II, or III). See note 21, below, for details concerning *RFM,* IV and V.

[9] Unlike the Rumanian double refrains, which alternate in melody-stanza pairs, the Serbo-Croatian type occur always in the same melody stanza. In addition the Serbo-Croatian refrains may contain Turkish words (invariably unintelligible to the singer); the Rumanian do not. See *RFM,* III, lxxix–lxxx.

[10] Melody No. 394c. in *RFM,* II, 494. See also p. 22 for Bartók's discussion of Class *B* (*tempo giusto*) melodies.

with the Yugoslav folk songs collected by Fr. Š. Kuhač and there found three variants;[11] in fact, he was at first pleased with Kuhač's transcriptions, commenting in 1912 that the melodies "are correctly notated as well as ordered according to the text. It is regrettable that the work has been expanded by the addition of wholly unnecessary piano accompaniments. . . . we need to supplement Kuhač's collection which lacks extent."[12]

During March and November, 1912, therefore, while collecting in the Banat counties of Temes (now Timiș, Rumania) and Torontal, Bartók sought, found, and recorded several Serbian folk musicians in the villages of Temešmonoštor (now Mănăștur) and Sárafalva (now Saravale, formerly Sarafola), respectively. He collected and subsequently transcribed twenty-one instrumental and vocal pieces (see note 33, below, for additional information concerning this Serbian material). Probably on the basis of this small number of melodies, apparently the only Serbian folk music transcribed from phonograph recordings up to that time, Bartók revised his opinion of Kuhač's contribution. Thus, in 1919, Bartók complained in print that the folk music collections published by Yugoslavs were jotted down by amateurs and that systematic classification of the material, like that of Western Europe, was carried out almost exclusively according to the texts.[13] Later, in a lecture given in the United States in 1940, Bartók elaborated on the problem:

> Eight or ten years ago, if we wanted to examine the Serbo-Croatian material, we found ourselves up against a few obstacles. The available material consisted of about 4,000 tunes, for the most part in pre-war [World War I] transcriptions made by ear, without the aid of an Edison phonograph or gramophone.—Subtleties of execution and ornamentation can scarcely be studied at all in this material, since they [the subtleties]are lacking in these rather amateurish transcriptions; but at least types and classes could be established.—The Serbo-Croatian scholars never used recording instruments, for reasons unknown to me.[14]

[11] Nos. 601–03 in Vol. II of Kuhač's anthology *Južno-slovenske norodne popievke* (Zagreb, 1878–81).

[12] *Essays,* No. 22: "Comparative Music Folklore."

[13] *Essays,* No. 23: "Music Folklore."

[14] *Essays,* No. 25: "Some Problems of Folk Music Research in East Europe." (English text in Bartók's autograph.) In regard to early field recordings made in Yugoslavia, see the editorial preface to Vol. III of the present publication.

Bartók managed to continue his accumulation of the incredibly rich Slovak and Rumanian materials well into 1917. As if in anticipation of the forthcoming political and economic conditions that were to terminate his field trips, beginning in 1914 he produced a number of small piano and vocal compositions based on folk music and, more importantly, composed theater music in the form of the ballets *The Wooden Prince* (1914–16) and *The Miraculous Mandarin* (1917–18). The earlier ballet was produced in Budapest in 1917; its success marked a change in attitude towards Bartók's compositions. The next year his Second String Quartet (1915–17) and his opera *Bluebeard's Castle* (1911) were performed: a contract with the publishing house of Universal Edition, Vienna, followed on July 4, 1918.

> After these promising beginnings there followed, alas! the complete political and economic breakdown of 1918.
>
> The sad and troubled times that followed for about a year and a half were not conducive to serious work.
>
> And even today [1921] conditions are not such as would allow us to think of continuing our studies in musical folklore. They are a "luxury" we cannot afford on our own resources. Political conditions are another great impediment. The great hatred that has been worked up makes it almost impossible to carry out research in parts of countries that once belonged to Hungary.[15]

The "drawn curtain" previously referred to prevented Bartók from personal contact with South Slavic folk music, and he therefore turned to the collections made without the aid of the phonograph, published by Kuhač, Kuba, Bosiljevac, Kačerovski, Đorđević, and Žganec.[16] He needed source material in the 1920s, for comparative purposes, during the preparation of three major studies for publication: *A magyar népdal*, that is, *The Hungarian Folk Song* (1924, also published in German in 1925 and in English in 1931), *Melodien der rumänischen Colinde* (completed in 1926, revised and published in 1935), and *Slowakische Volkslieder* (completed in 1928 and published posthumously).

There is only brief mention of Yugoslav material in Bartók's monumental book on Hungarian folk song: genuine Rumanian melodies are nearer to Yugoslav tune types than they are to Hungarian ones, and

[15] See note 4, above.

[16] See Bartók's description of published and unpublished source materials on pp. 22–27, below.

South Slav peasant music shows no similarity to the Old Hungarian *parlando-rubato* pentatonic melodies of eight or twelve syllables.[17] Later, in 1926, Bartók was able to say that Rumanian carols ending with a half-cadence can most plausibly be traced back to South Slavic influence, since the terminal half-cadence as well as certain scale patterns, diffused in Rumanian areas, play a predominant role in Yugoslav music.[18] Expressed in another way, the same year, Bartók wrote:

As to the main musical dialect of the Rumanians [of Alba, Hunedioara, Bihor, the Banat], I think it must have come into existence under Yugoslav influence. Unfortunately I do not know Serbian folk music well enough to support my opinion, but I do know this much: in Serbian folk music the most characteristic structure is the F major hexachord in which g^1 serves as final tone and half-cadence, and in which the first, third and fifth tones are the main degrees of the scale. Exactly the same scale is widespread among the Banat Rumanians. In Alba and Hunedioara, as the result of the tonal shift upward one step, the fourth and sixth degrees replace the third and fifth as the main ones. Out of the latter structure arose the Lydian hexachord in Bihor, with first, fourth (natural), and sixth main degrees.[19]

In his book on Slovak folk song Bartók mentions that the construction of the Slovak bagpipe is almost identical with that found in Hungarian, Rumanian, and Serbian regions, and moreover, that the Serbian bagpipe has small bellows.[20]

In addition to his ethnomusicological writings, including smaller pieces published in various international journals, Bartók undertook concert tours as a pianist, and he began composing piano works for the purpose. In 1926, for example, he produced four important works: the First Concerto, the Sonata, *Out of Doors,* and the Nine Little Piano Pieces. Serious difficulties with the publishers of his folk music studies

[17] *A magyar népdal,* pp. xxii–xxxiii. By means of comparative studies, after he had collected Turkish folk music in Anatolia in 1936, Bartók determined that the so-called Old-Hungarian folk music style can be traced back to the sixth or seventh century A.D. (see Introduction to Part One in Béla Bartók, *Turkish Folk Music from Asia Minor,* ed. Benjamin Suchoff [New Jersey: Princeton Univ. Press, 1976]). The so-called New-Hungarian style, which arose in the nineteenth or eighteenth century, differs from the old in terms of form (rounded or architectonic) and scale (modal and modern major and minor).

[18] *Colinde,* p. xxiv.

[19] *Lev.,* III, p. 164, letter to Emil Riegler-Dinu, June 4, 1926. The description of the scale appears as music notation in Bartók's original letter (trans. Elma Laurvik).

[20] *Slowakische Volkslieder,* Vol. I (Bratislava: Academia Scientiarum Slovaca, 1959), p. 64.

—circumstances that were to plague him throughout his life—interfered to a certain extent with other creative and scholarly activities well into the 1930s. Nevertheless, in 1932 he decided to rework his entire Rumanian material, revising old notations and making entirely new transcriptions of some of the recorded melodies. The ultimate purpose of this task was to produce a series of volumes that would supplement his 1923 publication, *Volksmusik der Rumänen von Maramureș,* revise the melodies of the 1913 Bihor study (*Chansons populaires du département de Bihar*) and those of the *Colinde* (whose manuscript, its publication long delayed, was still in the hands of Oxford University Press in London), and add thousands of other Rumanian vocal and instrumental melodies that he had gathered between 1908 and 1917.[21]

Bartók's re-examination of his Rumanian material, coupled with a statistical survey he had made of aspects of Žganec's 1924 publication of Međumurje[22] melodies, may have prompted him to consider writing a documented comparative survey of all the East European musical folklore that he had investigated up to that time. Taking advantage of newly opened opportunities in radio broadcasting, on November 21, 1933, Bartók gave a lecture on the Budapest Radio entitled "The Influence of Hungarian Folk Song on Neighboring Folk Music," which he illustrated with piano and recorded examples and which in 1934 appeared, "appropriately enlarged," in printed form—including 127 music examples in Bartók's autograph—under a somewhat different title.[23]

Before we proceed further with our historical narrative, let us pause momentarily and briefly discuss the portion of Bartók's outstanding treatise that applies to Yugoslav material. In the closing chapter, entitled "The Folk Music of the Serbo-Croatians and the Hungarian Folk Music," Bartók states that he had reviewed and classified about 2,500

[21] See note 8, above. Vol. IV of *Rumanian Folk Music* is the revised edition of *Colinde,* entitled *Rumanian Carols and Christmas Songs,* and Vol. V, also a revised version, is entitled *Maramureş County.* Both volumes, edited by the present writer, were published in 1975 by Martinus Nijhoff, The Hague.

[22] Or Mur Island (Muraköz in Hungary), a triangle of land, about 795 sq. km. in area, between the Mura River, the Drava River, and the old Austrian frontier. The reader interested in a description of and studies about former Hungarian territories should consult C. A. Macartney's excellent book *Hungary and Her Successors: 1919–1937* (London, 1937).

[23] *Népzenénk és a szomszéd népek népzenéje* (Hungarian Folk Music and the Folk Music of Neighboring Peoples). Budapest: Béla Somló. Also published in French in Vol. II of *Archivum Europae Centro Orientalis* (Budapest, 1936), pp. 197–244.

melodies collected in Croatia, Slovenia, Dalmatia, and in Bosnia and other regions inhabited by the Serbs, for the most part from the collections of Kuhač and Kuba. He goes on to aver that there is hardly any connection between these melodies and the Hungarian material. But in Žganec's Međumurje collection of 636 melodies Bartók found that a total of sixty-six per cent of them were either Old-Hungarian (190), New-Hungarian (158) or other Hungarian "dotted" rhythm types (41). The most remarkable fact is that so many borrowings were made from the Old-Hungarian tune types, and Bartók goes on to note with surprise that there is a greater proportion of Old-Hungarian pentatonic melodies in Žganec's Yugoslav collection (thirty-three per cent) than in Bartók's Hungarian material (nine per cent).

There can be no doubt of the Hungarian origin of the pentatonic tunes of Muraköz [Međumurje]; on the one hand they are completely identical with the old Hungarian melodies propagated throughout Transdanubia, on the other hand no similarity between these tunes and the others of the Serbs and Croats can be found. It would truly be an exaggeration to concede that melodies of this type had been propagated from the region of these two districts, throughout the Hungarian linguistic territory, and as far as the Székeley-inhabited region of Transylvania.

Bartók concludes the chapter with the plea that, since the Croat collection constituted one of the most important sources for study of old Hungarian melodies, one of the most urgent tasks ahead should be the publication of the "universal anthology" of the more than ten thousand Hungarian folk songs collected thus far, so as to provide "convincing testimony of the ancestral origin of the most important part of the Hungarian folk songs."

Whether the lecture, the resulting publication, or a combination of various factors was responsible for Bartók at long last achieving his cherished desire to devote himself to ethnomusicology as his principal vocation is uncertain. In September, 1934, he moved from his piano studio at the Budapest Academy of Music to a small room on the first floor of the Academy of Sciences: his commission from the ministry was to work on folk music.[24] Bartók immediately set out, by means of correspondence, to remedy two deficiencies in his quest to circumnavigate

[24] *Letters,* p. 238. Letter to Imre Deák, March 5, 1935.

the varied seas of foreign stylistic character that surround the Hungarian island of musical folklore. One of them, the influence of Bulgarian rhythmic patterns, will only be lightly touched, since this aspect of musical style is perhaps best examined within another context. The other, the matter of Serbo-Croatian autochthonous material, seems to have been approached through contact with Vinko Žganec and Ludvik Kuba.[25]

In what appears to be the first[26] in a series of letters between Bartók Žganec, the former asks,

> How is the collecting activity proceeding in Yugoslavia at present? Could I study phonograph recordings somewhere? Is the phonograph used at all? Are there anywhere any major (unpublished) collections, noted down and in a state suitable for study in Zagreb or Belgrade for instance? Is any major publication planned? I would be very interested to see such material, not from the Hungarian point of view, for, as one can see from Kuhač's and Kuba's great (Bosnian and Hercegovinian) collection (published in Sarajevo), with the exception of the items from Muraköz, there are hardly any points of contact. But it is with Rumanian folk music that I would like to compare it as thoroughly as possible; for I suspect, especially in the music of the Rumanians in the Banat, a strong Southern Slav influence; what is more, I even think that the music of the Rumanians in the Bihor region came into existence as the result of the crossing of pentatonic and Southern Slav melodies.

After discussing certain performance peculiarities he has noted in the Kuhač and Kuba materials, Bartók mentions that he would like to determine whether the so-called Bulgarian type of rhythm occurs in the Serbo-Croatian linguistic territory. The letter concludes with a postscript indicating that Bartók can "only understand the [Croatian] folk texts, but the literary language, hardly."[27]

On the same day Bartók mailed the recently published "booklet containing my radio talks" to Žganec; a few weeks later it was "returned from the Yugoslav frontier, stamped 'ZABRANJENO, INTERDITE'! I don't suppose the frontier guard read the booklet; it rather seems he has imposed an intellectual blockade."[28] Another copy, with a dedica-

[25] See note 16, above.

[26] Bartók may have previously requested Žganec to send the second volume of Međumurje material (published in 1925), which contains 264 religious folk songs.

[27] *Letters,* pp. 229–33, letter of October 27, 1934.

[28] *Letters,* p. 236, letter of November 7, 1934.

tion, probably sent out at the same time, was received in Prague by Ludvik Kuba. Bartók also sent a letter to Kuba, probably containing the same or similar lines as those in his letter to Žganec, since Kuba responded that "It will be a great pleasure to meet you in Prague and to cooperate with you in scholarly matters."[29] When the two met in Prague, during the last week in November—Bartók performed his Second Piano Concerto with the Czech Philharmonic Orchestra on November 28—it was decided that Kuba would correct his published material from Bosnia and Hercegovina, and send an edited copy, together with unpublished songs, for Bartók's use.[30] Not until May, 1938, was Kuba able to complete the work: "It was no easy task to extricate these 160 vanished songs from my fifty-year-old notes, and I would not have undertaken this if you, dear Master, had not shown such keen interest in them. No wonder that it took such a long time."[31]

Other than information concerning source materials, Bartók's contact with Žganec was hardly fruitful. The correspondence between them, during 1934–36, which included shipments of Bartók folk music publications, seems to focus on Bartók's candid references to the lack of melodies from Serbo-Croatia collected on phonograph records.

I am surprised to read in your letter that Kuhač has still 4,000 unpublished melodies. These are surely in some library where they can be studied, aren't they? In my opinion it would be better not to publish these, Kuhač's notations being very defective, but rather to use the money thus earmarked for new collecting activity, namely, collecting organized scientifically with all kinds of equipment (phonograph!).[32]

Toward the latter part of 1935 Bartók revised his earlier notations of Serbian melodies collected in the Banat in 1912, and sent a copy to

[29] *Documenta Bartókiana,* ed. Denijs Dille, Vol. III (Budapest: Akadémiai Kiadó, 1968), p. 171, hereafter cited as *DocB,* III. Letter of November 8, 1934, Prague. Trans. Richard Tószeghy. According to Dille (p. 172) a facsimile of the first and last pages of Bartók's letter to Kuba, unavailable at the time of this writing, appears in Stanislaw's biography *Ludvik Kuba, Kniznise Hubednich Rozhledi* (Prague, 1963), pp. 192–93.

[30] *DocB,* III, 178–79, letter from Kuba, November 16, 1935.

[31] *DocB,* III, 222, letter of May 24, 1938. Kuba was then more than seventy-five years old. Bartók's regard for this material is evident by the fact that he brought it with him when he emigrated to the United States in 1940.

[32] *Letters,* pp. 239–40, letter from Bartók, July 3, 1935. It seems reasonable to conjecture that Bartók was subtly attempting to suggest that Žganec—a lawyer in the city of Zombor (formerly Hungarian territory)—might be able to arrange for a subsidy or at least official permission for him to undertake a collecting trip in Yugoslavia.

Žganec.[33] The latter's response, dated, April 22, 1936, may have been their last communication.

> The extremely interesting music material of the book [*Musique paysanne serbe et bulgare du Banat*], that you collected with so much affection, gratified me exceedingly. I showed it to my friends, and all of them were amazed by the precision of your notation. Such accuracy as revealed by you is something new in the realm of folk music collecting.
>
> As soon as I shall have the leisure I intend to write a detailed and long review of this book and will mail it to you.[34]

Any lingering thoughts Bartók may have had about the possibility of still visiting Yugoslavia to collect folk music were diverted by negotiations leading to an official invitation, during the same month, to lecture in Turkey on "les méthodes d'étude sur la musique populaire en général, et les éléments principaux de votre Ecole tout particulièrement."[35] At long last, at age fifty-five, Bartók achieved international recognition of his twin attainments. Since he was asked also to compare Hungarian and Turkish folk music, and since he managed to widen the purpose of his visit to include the collecting of Turkish peasant music, he plunged into the study of Turkish folk music in general and the language in particular. Following a busy concert schedule that spring, moreover, was the June invitation from the Basel Chamber Orchestra to write a composition to commemorate its tenth anniversary. The work, Music for Strings, Percussion, and Celesta, was completed in September, the Turkish lectures were drafted and mailed to Ankara in October, and on November 2 Bartók left Budapest for Istanbul.

Bartók broadcast the results of his activities in Turkey in a lecture given on the Budapest Radio on January 11, 1937, which was later published in booklet form.[36] Comparing Turkish and Serbo-Croatian materials, he found that "rain begging" songs are generally known by the Turks, and that the songs correspond in text and melody to Yugoslav songs used for the same purpose: their melodies are similar to the nursery rhymes and children's playsongs of the Hungarian, Slovak, or

[33] See pp. xxxi–xxxii and Appendix II, below.

[34] *DocB,* III, 191–92.

[35] *DocB,* III, 190, letter from the president of the Ankara Halkevi, April 14, 1936. It is not clear whether the word *école* refers to Bartók as ethnomusicologist, as composer, or perhaps as both.

[36] *Essays,* No. 20: "Folk Song Collecting in Turkey."

other Western European nations. Although he collected only ninety tunes, he found that twenty per cent of them were similar to the Old Hungarian music, a statistic that takes on great significance when it is considered that the Old-Hungarian tune type, other than in its borrowed form, cannot be found among the Yugoslavs.

In September Bartók prepared a report of the work done at the Academy of Sciences in connection with the publication of the comprehensive collection of Hungarian folk songs.

> We have been engaged in preparing these for the press since September, 1934. During this time I have revised the transcriptions of all the phonograph cylinders, 1,026 in number. Meanwhile, Kodály has selected all relevant material from what is already in print. We have copied, and partly systematized, the song material—necessary for purposes of comparison—of the neighboring peoples of Hungary (Bulgarian, Serbo-Croatians, Slovaks, Poles, Ukrainians).[37]

The report goes on to estimate that the material would be ready for the printer by the end of 1940. But the political events beginning in 1938 interrupted this plan as well as dashing whatever hope may have remained of a collecting expedition to Yugoslavia or elsewhere. The nazification of Europe, including his Vienna publisher, hardened his resolve to leave Hungary.

> I would like best to turn my back on the whole of Europe. But where am I to go? And should I go at all before the situation becomes unsupportable, or had I better wait until the chaos is complete?[38]

Bartók found the answer to his dilemma—by means of Serbo-Croatian musical folklore!—during his concert and lecture tour in the United States in April and May, 1940. A few days after his lecture at Harvard University on April 22, on problems of East European folk music research (see page xii, above, for his original remarks on Yugoslav material, which he later revised), a letter arrived from Albert B. Lord, who had attended the lecture, advising Bartók that, contrary to the latter's assumption that there are no recorded collections of Yugoslav folk music, a fairly large collection of recordings (made in Yugoslavia

[37] *Letters,* pp. 262–63, letter to the secretary-general of the Hungarian Academy of Sciences, September 14, 1937.

[38] *Letters,* pp. 275–76, letter to Dorothy Parrish [Domonkos], February 8, 1939.

by the late Professor Milman Parry of Harvard, from June, 1934, to September, 1935) was on hand; that a description of the collection would be mailed to Bartók; and that Bartók, while in New York, should meet George Herzog and Samuel Bayard, the two other scholars interested in the musicological aspects of the Parry collection.[39]

Bartók's concert at Columbia University on May 1 provided him with the opportunity to discuss the possibility of a future position there with Herzog, Douglas Moore, and Paul Henry Lang, all professors at Columbia.[40] Moore, newly appointed as chairman of the music department, offered to investigate the chances of obtaining a grant from the university's recently established Alice M. Ditson Fund (set up for "the aid and encouragement of American musicians"); Herzog and Lang were to look into the possibilities of Bartók transcribing the heroic songs from the Parry Collection at Harvard (working, however, under Columbia's auspices), which had not been previously examined and whose transcription was needed as illustrative music material for Lord's planned book on the textual aspects of those songs.[41] Also at this time Bartók's new publisher, Boosey and Hawkes, serving in a managerial capacity as well, was arranging for another, more extensive, concert tour of the United States by Bartók in the 1940–41 season.[42] Bartók therefore returned home that summer to make his preparations for the

[39] Letter in the New York Bartók Archive of the Estate of Béla Bartók (hereafter cited as NYBA), April 23, 1940. Dr. Lord, also a Harvard professor, accompanied Parry on the expedition (see Lord's editorial preface to *Serbocroatian Heroic Songs,* Vol. I [Harvard University Press, 1954] pp. xiii–xvi, 3–6).

[40] On May 17 Bartók wrote to Dorothy Parrish (*Letters,* pp. 282–83) that "There are plans (excepting concertising) to make it possible to me (and to my wife too, of course) to stay here longer, perhaps for several years. I am not authorised to give details, but I hope these plans can be turned in reality."

[41] Douglas Moore, "Bartók at Columbia," *The Long Player* (New York), October, 1953, p. 16. A letter from Bartók to Moore (copy in the NYBA correspondence files), dated May 2, states: "I certainly was glad to have the opportunity to meet you personally and to have a quiet talk with you, which was extremely interesting for me. Unfortunately, I cannot change my plans, which I explained in my letter to Dr. Nicholas Murray Butler [then President of Columbia University]." The letter to Butler (copy in the NYBA correspondence files), dated the same day, states that Bartók must return to Hungary "to save my life work: the collection of many records of Hungarian folkmusic. . . . I intend to return to the United States at the end of October 1940 and then will stay several months."

[42] In a letter from Ralph Hawkes, head of the company, to Bartók, dated August 22, 1940 (copy in the NYBA correspondence files), a postscript reassures him that an attempt would be made, during September and October, "to find a spot for you as Professor for a season or so," in accordance with Bartók's wishes.

possibility of permanently leaving Hungary. Although his economic future—in a foreign land—surely must have then seemed precarious, the opportunity of at long last coming into contact with recorded autochthonous Serbo-Croatian musical folklore provided Bartók, now fifty-nine years old, with the strength to take this bold step.

> The reason for inviting me here (apart from the fact that it would help me personally) was so that I could accomplish certain research work, that is, to study and transcribe this incomparable material on Yugoslav folk music. It is, in fact, this work which brought me here (as far as work is concerned, without taking into consideration my own feelings): material such as this can be found no where else in the world, and (apart from some Bulgarian material) this is what was so badly lacking to me over in Europe.[43]

Hardly had Bartók and his wife, Ditta Pásztory-Bartók, disembarked in New York on October 30, 1940, when they set out on a recital and lecture tour of the United States. The following year, in February, came the good news of his appointment, until June, as visiting associate in music at Columbia University. And on March 27 he began work on the transcription of the folk epics on the Parry Collection recordings which had been sent down from Harvard for the purpose.[44] Certain recordings also contained lyric songs, and when Bartók heard them he realized that the songs could serve as the basis for undertaking a definitive study of Serbo-Croatian musical folklore.

> This unique collection of over 2,600 phonograph records—to my knowledge the only collection of Yugoslav folk music on acoustical recordings—contains a very large mass of epic song accompanied by the gusle, a primitive one-string instrument. The style and musical treatment of these heroic songs is probably as close to that of the Homeric poem as any folk music style found today may be. While from the historical, literary, and musicological point of view this material is invaluable, from the musical-esthetic point of view the lyric songs or "women's songs" and the instrumental pieces in the collection are more rewarding. The epic songs are carried by a mode of chanting which, while on the whole simple, varies somewhat from region to region and singer to singer. The chant itself is undoubtedly part of old European folk heritage, but the gusle accompaniment occasionally shows parallels with Arabic melodic

[43] *Letters,* p. 306, letter to his elder son, Béla II, June 20, 1941.
[44] *Letters,* p. 299, letter to Béla Bartók II, April 2, 1941.

treatment—probably due to an influence during the long Turkish occupation.
There are two ends in view according to which the collection ought to be studied. One is the transcription into music notation of the most important samples of the epic material, to be incorporated into its literary and textual study at Harvard University. The other is the transcription of the other materials in the collection, for an inclusive picture of Yugoslav folk music. This latter could well result, as you once suggested, in a book on Yugoslav folk music. I estimate that transcribing those parts of the collection which are the most important in these two respects would take a year's time, not including my work during the current semester.[45]

At the time Bartók wrote the foregoing lines, negotiations were in process by his concert management for a professorial appointment elsewhere as well as concert bookings for the following season. To Bartók's great pleasure his request for extension of the Columbia appointment was granted on May 5, and for a full academic year, thus offering the possibility of completing his work on the Parry Collection. Concurrent with his study and transcription of this material was the classification and, in a number of cases, revision of the published and unpublished Serbo-Croatian melodies which he had worked on in Europe and brought to the United States. And a third project, begun at this time and concentrated on during the summer, was the study and preparation of his Rumanian folk music material for publication.[46]

On October 27 Bartók's examination of the Parry material had progressed to the stage where he felt capable of writing "a short paper on the result of my research-work at Col. Univ. for publication somewhere."[47] The paper, "The Parry Collection of Yugoslav Fok Music," was later printed in the *New York Times,* on June 28, 1942 (Bartók's emended form of the article appears as *Essays* No. 21). In November plans were made but not realized for Bartók to join with Herbert Halpert, a student of George Herzog, in "recording some of the Serbian material in Indiana" during Bartok's concert tour that month.[48] Re-

[45] NYBA correspondence file, letter to Douglas Moore, April 18, 1941.

[46] See *RFM,* III, p. viii; see also Agatha Fasset, *The Naked Face of Genius* (Boston: Houghton, Mifflin Company, 1958), p. 121.

[47] NYBA correspondence files, letter to Douglas Moore.

[48] NYBA correspondence files, letters to Bartók from Stith Thompson, dated November 18, 1941, and George Herzog, dated November 24.

turning by train from Los Angeles in December Bartók wrote the following lines to the Kodálys in Budapest, which summarize his Columbia experiences during 1941:

I am busy in an annex of Columbia University, in Herzog's phonogram archive. Its equipment is excellent. It is almost as if I were continuing my work at the Academy of Sciences, only under changed circumstances. Even the premises are just as elegant. [. . .] But I would like to revert to the Parry Collection. He chose his singers exceptionally well; nearly all of them sing in a peasant style. Kuba was right: word- and syllable-interruption are a general habit; the "heavy" melismata are characteristic (not consisting of lighter tones but of fully-weighted ones)—Kuba pointed to that, too, somewhere. I came upon a strange ballad performance: "Free" stanzas, that is, the stanza contains A, B, and C types of sections; the first section is A, the next three, 4 or even more sections, varying unsystematically, return to A or (preferably) B, in any case C appears only in the last section (possibly in the penultimate one, too); the stanza ending occurs on the text pause (end of the sentence). It somehow brings to mind the Rumanian pentatonic "free" stanzas of Szatmár [Satu-Mare] County and adjacent regions (which the Székely had also adopted in a 5-section form), though there is no connection between the text and the stanza.

The notation of the heroic poems makes an awfully monotonous impression at first, but the more time one devotes to them the more one becomes familiar with them. Thus I am now already searching with great pleasure the lesser and greater individual or some other divergences amidst the uniformity. One could write a whole book on this way of making music. It is almost incredible that up to now I hardly had an idea that this last vestige of folk minstrelsy still flourishes in our neighborhood.[49]

Bartók's "short paper" on the Parry Collection, probably completed before the end of December, was ready for presentation on January 20, 1942, to a member of the Ditson Committee, who was brought by Douglas Moore to meet Bartók "and, if possible, to hear one or two of the records upon which you have been working."[50] Apparently the purpose of the visit was related to Moore's subsequently successful attempt to obtain a further grant from the Ditson Fund to

[49] NYBA correspondence files, letter to Zoltán and Emma Kodály, dated December 8, 1941.

[50] NYBA correspondence files, letter from Moore to Bartók, dated January 13, 1942. A holographic draft and two corrected, typescript versions, originally titled "The Milman Parry Collection of Serbo-Croatian Folkmusik" [*sic*], are in the NYBA MS files.

underwrite the expense of a book on Yugoslav folk music, that he had earlier suggested Bartók should write (see note 45). For Herzog, in a note written to Bartók the next week, suggested that they, Paul Henry Lang, and "the man from Columbia Press" should meet "to discuss the details."[51] A few days thereafter Bartók was gratified to learn that his appointment at Columbia would be extended until the end of the year, and, on March 15, Bartók wrote a lengthy technical memorandum to Albert B. Lord concerning their future collaboration on the planned book. Not quite three months later Bartók was able to write that he was working on two projects: "Rumanian Folkmusic of Transylvania and Banat (in preparation): about 2400 melodies, introduction, etc. Serbo-Croatian Folkmusic (in preparation, going to be published soon by Columbia University Press): 80 melodies, very detailed introduction (containing examination of some general aspects of the problems connected with research work in folk music)."[52]

Bartók's use of the word "soon" was overly-optimistic, even though he devoted the entire year to research. He was slowed by parallel study of the Rumanian material; a task made necessary in order to determine the reciprocal influences, if any, between the Banat Rumanians and the Serbo-Croatians. Realizing, too, that classification procedures of the two materials had much in common, he soon perceived that he could therefore prepare their introductory studies more or less parallel with each other. Thus the findings for *Rumanian Folk Music* vocal melodies provide the data for the conclusions to be found further below (p. 86):

> At a time when the Serbo-Croatian material was not yet well-known to me, I inclined toward attributing the preponderance of four-section melody structures (many of them heterometric) and the frequent use of refrains in the Banat area to Serbo-Croatian influence.
>
> This hypothesis, however, proved to be wrong, since four-section structures are found mostly in western Serbo-Croatia, and even there the greater part of them are of foreign or urban origin. Besides, their characteristics considerably differ from those of the Rumanian structures. Therefore, no foreign influence can be determined concerning their existence in the Rumanian material—for the time being. The same can be said about the frequent use of refrains in the Banat area, though the Serbo-Croatians use them lavishly, too.

[51] NYBA correspondence files, letter dated January 28, 1942. See also Moore's memoirs in *The Long Player* (note 41, above).

[52] NYBA correspondence files, letter to Dr. Anson, dated June 1, 1942.

But, somehow, their character and placing within the latter material show a considerable difference and can scarcely be brought into connection with their frequent appearance in the former.[53]

In December Bartók reported that "I have finished [the book on Serbo-Croatian folkmusic] in October," although the Preface is dated the following year, February, 1943.[54] But the true labor pains connected with the birth of *Serbo-Croatian Folk Songs* were yet to come, nor was its father destined to see the offspring. As Bartók was later to put it, writing in similar figurative style, "The gestation of the elephant is nothing in comparison with the time needed [. . .] to give birth to this book—provided that it will not miscarry in the meanwhile."[55] The profuse documentation related to editorial problems, during the period of 1943–1945 and for more than five years after Bartók's death, clearly indicates that—to borrow from an old adage—there were too many cooks involved in an attempt to prepare a recipe whose ingredients were couched in a language and symbolic representation hardly comprehensible to other than its inventor.

On the one hand was the matter of collaboration by mail with the co-author, Albert B. Lord, which included questions about the texts, their translation, and even production problems on text–melody conformity. On the other hand were those aspects of interpretation and subsequent typesetting or engraving of Bartók's explanatory material and his transcriptions—the latter surely being the most complicated ethnomusicological notations published up to that time!—which involved Herzog, Lang, music autographers, and editorial specialists. Rather than dwell on this subject, whose abundant documentation would require chapter-length narration, let us move on to examination of sources.

THE SOURCES

Although Bartók had transcribed 80 of the 205 Serbo-Croatian songs and all but one of the 16 instrumental pieces of the Parry Collection,

[53] *RFM*, II, p. 18.

[54] NYBA correspondence files, letter to Wilhelmine Creel, dated December 31, 1942. Bartók adds that "All this was a rather tiresome work (and my struggling with the English language) but very interesting indeed."

[55] NYBA correspondence file, letter to Victor Bator, dated August 11, 1944.

he limited publication to the 75 vocal melodies that form the music examples of the 1951 edition of *Serbo-Croatian Folk Songs*.[56] In the present edition the withheld songs (Record nos. 9–10, 338, 342, 1538b) and instrumental music (R. 335–37, 341, 343–44, 379, 385–91, 1473, 2937) are published in Appendix I (below, pp. 430–450) in facsimile of the holograph, all to provide the reader with examples of Bartók's work methods in folk music transcription and, of course, to augment the fund of reliably transcribed (that is, on the basis of phonographic recordings) Serbo-Croatian material—especially the instrumental kind.[57]

Music.—By 1941 Bartók was confident enough of his skill to produce a duplicate copy of his first trial by means of carbon paper. The twin drafts contain only these melodies: Nos. 7, 12b.c., 20, 27e., 28a.c., 29 (carbon copy), 32 (carbon copy), 33, 34 (carbon copy), 35, 36, 39b., 41, 42, 44a.b.[58] Excepting a few cut up pieces, the MS consists of 21 $\times$ 35cm. sheets of bond paper (without watermark) on which are crudely-drawn music staves containing Bartók's pencilled notations. Corrections, additions and improvements appear in both copies, in ink and red crayon (the carbon copy also has pencilled notations here and there).

The MS construed to be the second draft, since it was used by Bartók in the determination of melodic order and of variants, contains the first melody stanza of the 75 published vocal melodies (with the exception of Nos. 1 and 28b. which are without music notations) and two, subsequently discarded variants (R.3142–4=var. No. 6 and R.3235–8= var. No. 9). The melody stanzas now appear in the form of principal tones, but not fully skeletonized, with their underlying text portions. This draft apparently was written on three different occasions: pencil, india ink, blue-black ink. Melody numbers are in green crayon, here

[56] Bartók's papers indicate that he did not transcribe the remainder, approximately 125 songs, for the following reasons: about 40 of them already had been transcribed by Samuel Bayard; about 30 were unusable, since the informant was an old woman whose wavering pitch precluded exact transcription of her output; and other songs were either the same melody sung to different texts or recited instead of sung. It should be mentioned, too, that Bartók may have transcribed all of the instrumental pieces; the omitted transcription, however, was not among the MS.

[57] A concordance of record–melody designations is given in Appendix I.

[58] The drafts include the mentioned instrumental and withheld vocal melodies. The NYBA code numbers are 116A and 116B (numerical designation the same as that written by Bartók on the envelope containing the MS), and the location of the remaining two-thirds of the MS is unknown.

and there altered with ink, and variant information is in red. Like the first draft the staves are hand ruled in pencil or carbon copy, on bond paper sheets 21cm. wide and about 10cm. from top to bottom (the length of the pieces, cut from larger sheets, varies with the number of staves—from one to four—on each leaf). Cassification and performer's data are entered throughout the MS; here and there are Bartók's comments in English and Hungarian.[59]

The reason for the carbon copy of the first draft becomes evident when it it considered that Bartók apparently did not prepare a fair copy of his transcriptions for use by the copyist, Wolfgang Weissleder. The corrected, pencilled version seems to have been used instead, and the carbon copy—not always similarly improved!—was held by Bartók in the event of loss of the original MS.[60]

Bartók selected five Parry Collection songs as illustrations, in the form of diapositive slides, for use in his 1941–1942 lecture-recital tour. He had melody Nos. 12a.b., 14, 28c., and 41 copied by a professional autographer for that purpose, and they differ slightly from their counterparts in the published book.[61]

The skeleton form of the Parry melodies is a separate draft, notated by Bartók in india ink on 24-stave music paper and then cut up into individual pieces. Text syllables and improvements are added in blue-black ink, and in one case (No. 9) the unusual key signature of one flat, *A*-flat, as its sole component is circled in red crayon. A few comments are added in pencil, for the most part instructions to the copyist where to place the skeletonized melodies.

The final copy is, of course, the music examples autographed by Wolfgang Weissleder on master sheets. Peripheral material, in the form of slips cut from the same kind of transparent paper and containing Bartók's corrections and additions, most of them typographical

[59] Melody Nos. 2 and 3, written in ink, have skeleton forms of their melody sections (perhaps as a trial run?). Almost all of the pieces also have pitch indications and M.M. marks. (This draft is reproduced in facsimile at the end of Vol. IV.)

[60] The *Serbo-Croatian Folk Music* file of Columbia University Press shows that Bartók dealt directly with Weissleder until the latter delivered the complete music examples, at varying intervals, to the Press (the last twenty-five leaves on June 28, 1944).

[61] The autography is different from Weissleder's notations. The lecture was a revised version of his earlier (1940; see note 14, above) one on "Some Problems of Folk Music Research in Eastern Europe." A facsimile of the slide of melody No. 12b. appears in the editor's article "Computer Apllications to Bartók's Serbo-Croatian Material," *Tempo* (London) No. 80, Spring, 1967, plate facing p. 17.

in nature, can be considered as a kind of authorial draft for proofreading purposes.[62]

Text matter.—Three drafts of Part One to *Serbo-Croatian Folk Songs* were among Bartók's papers on Yugoslav folk music material. Each draft also contains Notes to the melodies, tabulations, and music notations used to illustrate the text matter.

The first version was written on two occasions: Introduction in india ink, corrected in pencil by another hand, with red crayon markings; then the remainder of the text matter in blue-black ink, with Bartók's pencilled corrections as well. The entire draft is written on the reverse side of letters to Bartók, advertising circulars, and other pieces of mixed size. The Notes to the melodies are sketched on slips cut from the mentioned materials or from mailing envelopes.

The second version, written in blue-black ink on bond paper, was intended as the fair copy for typesetting purposes. Hardly a line of this version is without copyreader's insertions in red crayon,[63] a number of pencilled additions appear here and there in Bartók's or George Herzog's autograph, and there are also several editorial improvements written in ink on slips of paper which are clipped to various pages of the draft. The Notes to the melodies form part of the draft, and the tabulations and music illustrations are included as separate pieces—for the most part Ozalid proofs of master sheet originals.

The third draft is a typescript carbon copy prepared by Columbia University Press and sent to Bartók on July 17, 1944. It contains Bartók's improvements in blue-black ink, pencil, red and green crayon, and there is another set of Ozalid proofs of the tabulations and music illustrations. Except for a few typographical errors the corrected draft is identical with the published version of the text matter.[64]

It is not difficult to assess the impact Bartók received when he first saw the "mutilated" fair copy and then compared it with the typescript version. Writing from Saranac Lake (New York), where he spent the summer, he acknowledged receipt of the drafts and his gratitude to the editor and George Herzog for the editing.

[62] Comparative survey of the two materials, by way of spot checks of Bartók's profuse, multifarious entries, indicates that his improvements were incorporated into the final copy.

[63] By Ida M. Lynn, editor for the Columbia University Press.

[64] Bartók corrected the original form of this draft, of course, and returned it to the publisher for typesetting purposes.

To see how you worked and changes you made is extremely profitable to me for two reasons: first to see how a serious editing, going into the minute details, is done; and second, to improve my English (though it is already much better than it was two years ago when I wrote this work).[65]

But his true feelings about the matter, mentioned further above (p. xxvi), are quite different.

The Columbia Press people disturbed me. They sent me the proofread text of the Serbo-Croatian book. The editor is very painstaking, cannot see the book from the many letters. Herzog . . . has excellent ideas and protects me from the encroachments of the editor.[66]

The same complaint, written a few weeks later, is augmented with the following details: "For a month I have been brooding over semi-colons, colons, and I have drafted hundreds of new counter-proposals. We shall fight the battle in October."[67]

The third use of the word "disturbed" is found in Bartók's letter to his publisher, Boosey and Hawkes, dated September 12, 1944, in connection with his plans for that summer: "Yes, this long delay should account at least for a big symphony or a deterioration in my conditions. Unfortunately neither the former, nor—fortunately—the latter is true." Bartók goes on to explain the problems he had to deal with in correcting the Serbo-Croatian MS and the "bickerings" he had with the music autographer.[68]

In addition to the material described above are numerous pieces and fragments having to do with the first draft. Written in ink, pencil, and red crayon, there are jottings, statistical calculations, tabulations, music examples, performer's data, and so forth, all on the reverse side of what had been letters, circulars, and envelopes sent to

[65] NYBA correspondence file, undated draft of a letter to Ida M. Lynn. The editor acknowledged receipt of a second version of this letter on August 9, 1944: "I am very glad that you are pleased with the editing and the retyping. . ." Bartók's letter also informs the editor that the copyist, Wolfgang Weissleder [who was in Saranac Lake at that time], was correcting the music examples.

[66] See note 55.

[67] NYBA correspondence file, letter to Elizabeth and Paul Kecskeméti, dated August 22, 1944. The letter, in Hungarian, appears in English translation in *Letters* (pp. 333–34).

[68] NYBA correspondence file. The letter is addressed to the editor, Hans W. Heinsheimer. It should be noted, however, that Bartók's plans included work on the third volume, the poetic texts and their introductory study, of *Rumanian Folk Music*. See the present writer's discussion in that work, pp. vii–x (publication details are in note 8, above), and the related correspondence in *Letters,* pp. 334–342.

Bartók. There is also a glossary of Hungarian equivalents of Serbo-Croatian words in the Parry Collection songs, compiled by Bartók according to record number.[69] And, finally, there is a collection of letters from Albert B. Lord, and Bartók's memoranda and draft replies concerning this correspondence or the collaboration of the two men with regard to Part Two of *Serbo-Croatian Folk Songs.*

CORRECTIONS AND ADDITIONS TO THE REPRINT

As mentioned above there are but few discrepancies between the corrected third draft of the text matter and the published version, and they are for the most part typographical in nature. These errors have been corrected, and updated bibliographic references have been added to the marginal notes and the Bibliography (p. 93, below).[70]

Six music examples required emendation:[71] No. 1, addition of syllabic and range designations; Nos. 2, 28b.c., correction of range designation; No. 49, addition of range designation; and No. 51, downward extension of the first bar line.

THE APPENDICES

Appendix One is a facsimile reproduction of the vocal and instrumental melodies transcribed by Bartók from the Parry Collection, which he withheld from publication, and which were editorially compiled from MS 116A and 116B (description on p. xxvii and its marginal note).

Appendix Two is a facsimile reproduction of the twenty-one Serbian vocal and instrumental melodies from Bartók's annotated copy of his

[69] Included here are three pages of equivalents, in Hungarian, English and French, for words Bartók transcribed from the Parry heroic song, "The Captivity of Đulić Ibrahim," during his work on that material (publication details are in note 39, above).

[70] Lacunae on p. 25 were filled in on the basis of data appearing in *Folklore musical* (Paris, 1939), pp. 210–220. See also John Weissmann's listing of errata in his review in *Journal of the English Folk Dance and Song Society,* VII/I (December), 1952, p. 45. The reader is advised that Weissmann's tabulation of "Correct compass" is, excepting melody Nos. 2 and 49 (copyist's slips!), an erroneous compilation and should be ignored. Bartók's range designations are based on the skeleton form (the principal tones) of the melody, that is, the true structural form that serves as the basis for classification and comparative purposes.

[71] Bartók checked the corrected music examples before the copyist delivered them to the publisher (see note 60).

"Musique paysanne serbe (No. 1–21) et bulgare (No. 22–28) du Banat. Budapest, 1935."[72]

Appendix Three is a facsimile reproduction of Bartók's holographic list of Serbo-Croatian refrains, which he placed in Vol. III (pp. 625–640) of *Rumanian Folk Music* for comparative purposes (see p. xi, above).[73]

In his description of published and manuscript collections of Serbo-Croatian folk melodies (below, pp. 22–27) Bartók refers to the "Tabulation of Material" which he completed in July, 1942, as a supplementary (appendix?) part of the MS of *Serbo-Croatian Folk Songs*.[74] In view of the length of the "Tabulation" and the need to provide it with descriptive and explanatory apparatus to facilitate scholarly use, the "Tabulation of Material" has been placed in Vol. II of the present publication.

The source melodies whose morphological data provided Bartók with the basis for constructing the "Tabulation of Material" (p. 25, below) are published in facsimile form in Vols. III–IV of this publication.

SOME RELATED MATERIALS

One of the outcomes in the expansion of *Serbo-Croatian Folk Songs* to the four-volume *Yugoslav Folk Music* is the enrichment of Bartók's work by providing it with related materials in the form of discursive matter and illustrative music examples. The annotation or even the listing of the quite substantial number of folk music sources and literature published in Yugoslavia, for the most part subsequent to the completion of Bartók's studies, necessitates delimitation of this chapter to such more closely related materials as Vinko Žganec's collection of Hungarian-influenced Croatian folk melodies (see Bartók's commentary on p. 24, below); Yugoslav folk tunes in Bartók's synoptic tabulations of variants, published here for the first time; Yugoslav folk music sources in Bartók compositions; and selected publications

[72] The complete work, reproduced from the MS in the Budapest Bartók Archivum, appears in *DocB*, IV (1970), pp. 221–244.

[73] See note 8, above, for publication details.

[74] On p. 25 of the first edition the following sentence—deleted in the present publication—appears: "Since the publishing of this "Tabulation" did not seem feasible, it has been deposited at the Music Library of Columbia University for the use of readers interested in details."

which review, annotate, or have been modeled after *Serbo-Croatian Folk Songs*.[75]

THE ŽGANEC MATERIAL

In the editorial discussion on pp. xv–xvi, above, a description is given of that part of Bartók's essay, "Hungarian Folk Music and the Folk Music of Neighboring Peoples," which deals with Serbo-Croatian folk music in general and Vinko Žganec's collection of Croatian melodies from the Međumurje region in particular. Fig. 1, a facsimile of the last page of music examples from that essay (see note 23, above, for publication details), shows Bartók's holographic extract of melody Nos. 516, 296, 373, 354, and 91 from Žganec's collection.[76]

In his October, 1934 letter to Žganec (see p. xvii and note 27, above) Bartók lists those of the former's 639 published melodies which are taken over from ancient pentatonic Hungarian tunes:

6-syllable lines:	339–40 | * 55, 57–61, 63–72, 115, 414 | 126, 382b, 240–241 | 246, 254, 320, 215 | 314, 457 | 131, 256, 315 | 161–162, 166 | 207, 318 | 208, 210, 213 | 290, 299, 333–335 | 222–226 | 332 | 168, 198 | 394 | 113 | 181, 177–180 | 182–193, 197, 137–140, 204–206, 214, 247–251, 176 | 172–175, 321, 284, 66, 526–527 | 149–150, 152–156, 167, 252–253 | 209, 211–212 | 157 | 146–148 | 406–407 | 56, 74, 412 | 164, 135, 316, 382a, 127, 397, 319 | 516, 518 | 142–144, 227
7-syllable lines:	* 107, 109, 111 | 390 | 237–238 | 108 | 341, 343–344 | 349, 375 | 194–195 | 464, 476–478, 416 | 388
8-syllable lines:	255, 469, 356, 323 | 262–264, 325, 291, 485–486 | 265–267, 269 | 289, 300 | 420, 438 | 292, 295–296 | 430, 239 | 293–294 | 493–494 | 563–564
9- and 11-syllable lines:	373, 501, 358, 297
Kolomejka-like:	11, 413 | 89, 92–93 | 87, 45

* The pentatonic nature, or rather the Hungarian origin, of the two groups marked with an asterisk is still doubtful

[75] See the editorial preface to Vol. III of the present publication for additional commentaries on other related materials.

[76] Not shown are Nos. 181, 169, 293 and 194 (Bartók Nos. 2d, 9c, 51c and 60c) which are Croatian variants of Székely (see note 1, above) ancient or recent Hungarian folk songs. Bartók's comments on the music examples in Fig. 1 appear on p. xvi, above).

Fig. 1 Croatian folk songs from the collection of Vinko Žganec

Five melodies from Žganec's collection—Nos. 278, 131, 264, 337 and 501—were fitted with piano accompaniments and placed as Nos. 12.–16. in *Südslawische Volkslieder,* a collection of folk songs from Slovenia, Croatia, Serbia, and Bulgaria, edited by Heinrich Möller as part of the *Das Lied der Volker* series of folk song publications.[77] Bartók's analysis of these five melodies indicates that 13., 14., and 16. are Hungarian pentatonic melodies, and 15. is actually one-half an art song.[78]

Möller No. 8. is an arrangement of *Čekat ću ga,* a Croatian variant of the German folk song *Es klappert die Mühle.* Other variants, the editorial commentary indicates (p. 16), are sung in Slovenia, Bosnia, and Dalmatia. Bartók lists six variants in "Tabulation of Material" No. 853 (see in Vol. II of the present publication), and in Fig. 2 (below) notates sixteen variants which stem from the following sources:

1. The German source melody
2. Kuhač 601; see also "Tab. of Mat." 853a.–f. (Kuhač 602–603, Đorđević Nar. Pev. 177/2, Kačerovski 60, Kuba IX/36)
3. Hungarian variant
4. *Rumanian Folk Music,* Vol. II, No. 394a. (village of Leheceni, county of Bihor)
5. Idem, 394b. (Saravale, Torontal)
6. Idem, 394c. (Sânnicolaul-Mare, Torontal)
7. Đorđević Juž. Srb. 41 (Skoplje)
8. Idem, 263 (Ohrid)
9. Stoïn I/3242 (Bjeloradčiško)[79]
10. Idem, I/3163 (Lomsko)
11. *RFM,* II, 444h. Decănești, Bihor)
12. Idem, 444j. (Tășad, Bihor)
13. Idem, 444b. (Satchinez, Timiș)
14. Đorđević Pred. Srb. 448; see also "Tab. of Mat." 886a. (Idem, 344, Kačerovski 22, Kuba B.H. 120)

[77] Apparently fourteen volumes were brought out between 1923 and 1929 by B. Schott's Söhne, Mainz. The reader should note that Möller's *Ungarische Volkslied* volume, the twelfth in the series, was severely criticized by Bartók as "utterly unsatisfactory from both the scholarly and from the artistic point of view" (see *Essays,* No. 29: "Gypsy Music or Hungarian Music?," p. 208). In fact there were polemical exchanges between the two men in 1931 and 1932 (see publication details in *Essays,* pp. 540–544).

[78] Bartók arranged his MS collection of the Žganec published material in four envelopes marked 130, 131 (pentatonic and *kolomejka*), 132 (isometric), and 133 (New-Hungarian type).

[79] Vassil Stoïn, *Chansons populaires bulgares de Timok à la Vita* (Sofia, 1928).

Fig. 2 Synoptic tabulation of foreign variants of the

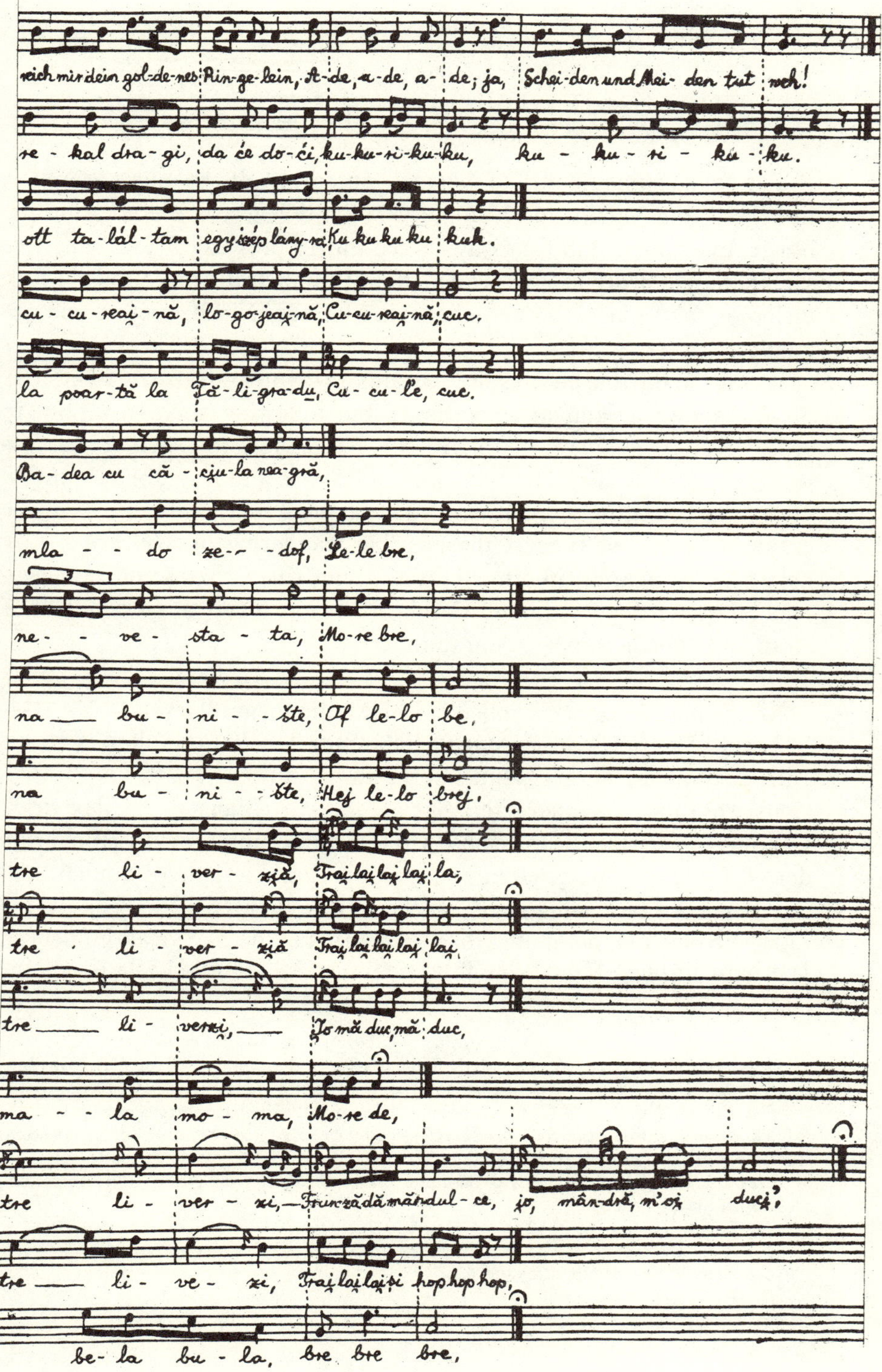

German folk song *Es klappert die Mühle,* by Béla Bartók

15. *RFM,* II, 444e. (Ginta, Bihor)
16. Idem, 444d. (Idicel, Mureș)[80]
17. Kuba XII/42 (Šabac)

The calligraphic quality of Bartók's autograph of the music examples in Figs. 2 and 3 point to his apparent intention to use the notations as illustrative material in his essay "Race Purity in Music," following this sentence: "In order to give readers an idea how transformations of folk melodies take place through their wanderings, I will quote some examples."[81]

In Fig. 3 Bartók notates six variants of another German folk song. Staff 2 shows a Hungarian variant; the following staves contain, in order, Kuhač 1446; Kuba B.H. 16; Đorđević Pred. Srb. 333; *Rumanian Folk Music,* II, 397; and *RFM,* V (Maramureș County), 36.[82] The listing of village names in Bartók's first draft of the music examples seems to suggest the possible wandering of *Mariechen*—by means of Hungarian intermediation!—south to Croatia and Hercegovina, then northeast through Serbia to the Transylvanian counties of Arad and (northernmost) Maramureș.

Returning to Žganec's collection of Međumurje folk songs, Nos. 51, 192 and 255 appear in *European Folk Song* by Walter Wiora.[83] In his Introduction the author points to the three tunes as possessing "capricious rhythm . . . characteristic of the Croatians . . ." (p. 8).[84] In point of fact this "capricious" rhythm is nothing else but Hungarian dotted (syncopated) rhythm and is not a characteristic of autochthonous Croatian folk song style. Indeed Bartók, in his analysis of the Žganec collection, points to No. 51 (Wiora 48/2d) as Slovak influenced [perhaps through Hungarian intermediation? The tune has a 6-syllable

[80] In the first draft of this synoptic tabulation Bartók indicates that *RFM,* II, variants 444a.c.f.g.i.k. are also related. This draft, on Parchment Brand (Belwin Inc., New York) music paper, was probably notated in 1941 or 1942.

[81] See *Essays,* No. 5, p. 31, where Bartók subsequently changed this sentence to indicate that one example—the *Rákóczi March*—would be cited (in narrative form). It seems reasonable to conclude that Bartók would have also used the music examples in a set of three hour-long lectures he was planning on Hungarian, North Slav and Rumanian, and South Slav folk music.

[82] See Bartók's comment in "Tab. of Mat." 1021c.

[83] No. 4 in *Anthology of Music* (edited by K.G. Fellerer). Cologne: Arno Volk, 1966.

[84] See melody Nos. 48/2d, 50b, and 68c.

Fig. 3 Synoptic tabulation of foreign variants of the German folk song *Mariechen sass auf einem Stein,* by *Béla Bartók*

isometric and isorhythmic structure rhythmically identical to melody Nos. 56b., 60 and 61 in Bartók's *Slovak Folk Songs* publication[85]].

European Folk Song employs the synoptic tabulation of melodies format to display variant relationship of Croatian, Macedonian, and Serbian folk songs—collected by Kuhač and Đorđević—which are also listed in "Tab. of Mat."[86]

BARTÓK ESSAYS

In the historical narrative above (p. x f.) a number of Bartók's essays on comparative music folklore are cited. It is appropriate to present here the salient features of those Bartók writings which underscore or elaborate on his findings or which shed additional light as the result of his work in Yugoslav ethnomusicology.

"Some Problems of Folk Music Research in East Europe," previously mentioned (p. xx, above) as a lecture given by Bartók at Harvard University and subsequently revised, presents an illustrated discussion of Dalmatian part-singing in major seconds.[87] Concerning this and other types of part-singing in Yugoslavia, Bartók comments that they are due to Western influence, because "the folk music of the neighbouring Germans of Carinthia and Styria is almost exclusively polyphonic." He discusses possible reasons for the fact that the so-called imperfect cadence at the end of melodies is characteristic for about half the Yugoslav materials he examined—a performance peculiarity not to be found in very old Yugoslav folk music. A third important point Bartók makes is with respect to the origin of the "oriental" scale (with an augmented second) which occurs frequently in Yugoslavia and Bulgaria: he believes it can be assumed that this type of scale originally was unknown to the Yugoslavs and that it was imported into the Balkans perhaps by gypsies or others who were in turn affected by Arab-influenced Turkish art music.

Bartók also refers to Dalmatian part-singing style in one of the series of lectures he gave at Harvard in 1943. After discussing Dalmatian chromaticism (see also p. 65, below), Bartók concludes with this observation:

[85] Published by Academia Scientiarum Slovaca, Bratislava, in 1959 (Vol. I) and 1970 (Vol. II). The third volume is in preparation.

[86] For example, "Tab. of Mat." 34, 60a., 1136, 1273e., 1588a.b. and 1807.

[87] See *Essays*, No. 25, p. 189; see also p. 63, below.

When I first used the device of extending chromatic melodies into a diatonic form, or vice versa, I thought I had invented something absolutely new, which never yet existed. And now I see that an absolutely identical principle exists in Dalmatia since Heaven knows how long a time, maybe for many centuries. This again proves that nothing absolutely new in the world can be invented; the most unusual-looking ideas have or must have had their predecessors.[88]

In "The Parry Collection of Yugoslav Folk Music" (publication details on p. xxiii, above) Bartók extends the brief description he gives on p. lxii below, including comments on the heroic songs that make up the bulk of this collection. In order to provide the reader with an insight of Bartók's technique in transcribing an accompanied Serbo-Croatian heroic poem, Fig. 4 displays the first page of the twenty-six he notated of "The Captivity of Đulić Ibrahim."[89]

BARTÓK COMPOSITIONS

Figs. 6 and 8 illustrate the ways in which Bartók employs Yugoslav folk music sources (Figs. 5 and 7) in his composed works.

No. 40 ("In Yugoslav Mode") from *Mikrokosmos*[90] perhaps owes its genesis to Kuhač 1484: note that the piano piece and the folk song have identical ending phrases. Bartók describes his composition as ending on a half-cadence and in imitation of Yugoslav bagpipes.[91]

No. 39 from 44 Duos for Two Violins is a thematic replication of the tune Bartók collected from a Serbian *tambura* player in 1912.[92] Compare the simple peasant performance with Bartók's ingenious contrapuntal treatments.

[88] *Essays,* No. 46 (III), p. 383. Other mention of Yugoslav folk music in *Essays* can be located by means of its Index (pp. 557–567), under such headings as Cadence, Chromaticism, Dalmatian (etc.) Folk Music, and place names.

[89] See in Parry and Lord, *Serbocroatian Heroic Songs,* pp. 437–462 (Bartók's notes to the transcription follow on pp. 463–467). Compare Fig. 4 with melody Nos. 7 and 34, below.

[90] A large-scale, basically pedagogic work for piano, consisting of 153 pieces and 33 exercises (in six volumes), composed between 1926 and 1939. Copyright 1940 by Hawkes & Son (London) Ltd.

[91] Bartók's comments on this and other *Mikrokosmos* pieces appear in B. Suchoff, *Guide to the MIKROKOSMOS of Béla Bartók* (London: Boosey & Hawkes, 1971).

[92] Copyright 1933 by Universal Edition, Renewed 1959. Copyright and renewal assigned for the U.S.A. to Boosey & Hawkes Inc. See Bartók's description of the *tambura* on p. 239 (Note 27e.**), below. The complete transcription appears as No. 7 in Appendix II, below.

NO. 4. THE CAPTIVITY OF ĐULIĆ IBRAHIM

Fig. 4 Bartók's transcription (first page) of a *gusle*-accompanied Serbo-Croatian heroic song, from *Serbocroatian Heroic Songs* (Harvard University Press, 1954)

In his Sorbonne dissertation John Downey calls attention to Bartók's use of major seconds "à la Dalmatian" and ternary structure in the second movement of Concerto for Orchestra (Fig. 9).[93] There are other structural similarities between this theme and Yugoslav folk melody. Fig. 10, a tune from the Kuhač material, clearly shows the similarity between the Bartók-invented theme and the Yugoslav folk song: isometric melodic structure; heterometric (a b c) rhythmic structure; ternary (A B C) content-structure; identical range (*1* – *8*); secondary caesura on the fifth degree of the scale, main caesura on the third degree; and melodic contour in which the first two sections describe a parabolic shape and the last melody section descends diatonically.

Yet another borrowing, in this case of scalar structure of the Serbo-Croatian material in general (see Bartók's discussion on pp. 59–61, below), is use of the Phrygian mode—transposed to F and G as a simultaneity. The typically Bartókian "neutral tonality" effect resulting from thematic bimodality is furthered by use of the major third at the main caesura (Fig. 9, m. 95). Note, too, that the theme is harmonized with anhemitone tetra-, penta-, and hexachords (that is, whole-tone scale fragments)—a vertical treatment of melodic octave-segments—and that the total impression, as generated in the lowest part (m. 90), is C as principal tone leading to the dominant (m. 98) in approximation of a "Yugoslav" cadence.

REVIEWS

Seven reviews of *Serbo-Croatian Folk Songs,* all appearing between 1952 and 1954, were available for analysis in terms of corrigenda or addenda that might be presented here as a means of improving, clarifying or providing supplementary data for the morphological aspects and resultant conclusions in Bartók's study.

The first published review apparently was that by Yury Arbatsky in the March, 1952 issue of *Notes* (Music Library Association), pp. 288–289. The reviewer believes that, with the exception of melody No. 1, the Parry folk songs "bear some of the characteristics of the Gypsies, who in the Balkans are conspicuous carriers of Western civili-

[93] *La Musique populaire dans l'oeuvre de Béla Bartók* (Paris: Centre de Documentation Universitaire, 1966), pp. 159–161.

Fig. 5 *Gusle*-accompanied folk song from Kuhač's published collection, *Yugoslav Folk Songs,* Vol. IV (Zagreb, 1881)

Fig. 6 Bartók's holograph of No. 40, "In Yugoslav Mode," from *Mikrokosmos* for Piano (NYBA MS 59 PID1ID2)

zation," particularly in the *gusle* and *tambura* performances. Arbatsky disagrees with the use of skeleton notations which "may satisfy the demands of Occidental science, but not one Balkan musician would recognize in it his own melodic patterns." He also states that Bartók's comparison of singers' characteristics (par. 1, p. 89, below) is in error, that Bartók did not understand that performers sing with more ornamented notes and in a more exaggerated *parlando* rhythm in the fall than in the winter.

On the basis of other music examples recorded in the fall—Nos. 1, 34 and 35—the reviewer's assertion is untenable: these melodies reflect "simple rural performance" to the extent that Bartók found it unnecessary to provide them with skeleton forms. The review closes with the statement that "the scientific method applied by Béla Bartók is so impressive that this book must be considered an absolute necessity for everyone remotely connected with folk music."[94]

Charles Seeger, on the other hand (*Journal* of the American Musicological Society, Vol. V, No. 2, pp. 132–135), finds the addition of skeleton forms of the melodies a wise procedure for "first reading or classificatory purposes" as well as for the use of less well-trained musicians who would probably not be able to read the full transcriptions which present "nuances of the most minute and fleeting delicacy." Seeger then goes on to the subject of Bartók's transcription techniques with respect to intonation and rhythm, which the former labels a "mixed symbolic–graph writing" in which there is a closer definition of existing symbols and invention of additional ones, a lengthy presentation which seems to have been designed as the reviewer's case for use of "electronic-mechanical graphing devices that would mediate between the acoustic graph and the 'hopped-up' varieties of ordinary music notation." Seeger concludes that Bartók's work is a model and that it "sets a standard for publications in the English language in this field."

In his review of *El cancionero popular de la provincia de Madrid*[95]

[94] In a communication to the *Journal* of the American Musicological Society, Vol. 5, No. 2 (Summer), 1952, pp. 150–151, Arbatsky supplements Bartók's discussion (see below, pp. 61–62) of the peculiar scale formation of a minor pentachord with lowered fifth degree: "In Istria and its surroundings there exists a native wind instrument, the *sopelo* or *sopilo,* which may be regarded as the main exponent of the above-mentioned scale."

[95] Volume One (Materials), by M. G. Matos, was published by the Spanish Institute of Musicology in Barcelona, 1951. Seeger's review of this work appears in *Musical Quarterly,* Vol. XXXIX, No. 2 (1953), pp. 289–293.

Fig. 7 Extract from Bartók's holograph of a Serbian instrumental dance piece (complete transcription in Appendix II, below)

Fig. 8 Portion from Bartók's holograph of No. 39, "Serbian Dance," from 44 Duos for Two Violins (NYBA MS 69 VVFC1)

edited by Marius Schneider and José Romeu, Charles Seeger criticizes the methods and procedures of collection, study and publication, particularly the "single, skeletal model-stanza versions of the sort conventionally printed in popular anthologies for general use, without indication of variant detail . . . Granted that skeletal notation has a very practical use, does not scientific study benefit from such thorough writing out of all detail and the whole song, as was done in the Bartók-Lord *Serbo-Croatian Folk Songs?*" The review not only prompted a sharp reply from Schneider (*Anuario Musical,* IX, 1954) but also a critical review of *Serbo-Croatian Folk Songs* as evidence in partial de-

Fig. 9 Bartók's holographic piano reduction of the theme for two muted trumpets, from the second movement of the Concerto for Orchestra (NYBA MS 80 TPFC1).[96] The two caesura symbols (M. 92, 95) are editorial additions

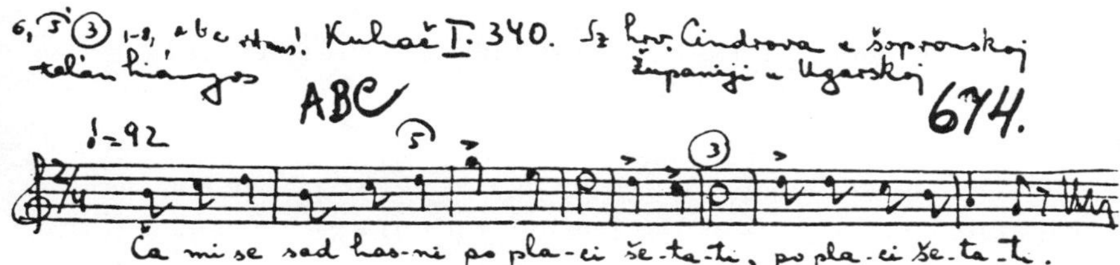

Fig. 10 Kuhač 340 ("Tab. of Mat." 674) from Bartók's collection of Yugoslav folk music materials

fense of his editorial work (*ibid.*, pp. 257–259).[97] The reader having thus been forewarned of the circumstances underlying Schneider's critique, the following annotations are offered.

Reviewer states that "Bartók affirms that in Europe there do not exist songs of pure syllables without determined or logical significance," and the former points to the *lelo il lelo* of the Basques. Referring to p. 9, below, we find that Schneider has quoted Bartók out of context: the latter specifies *Eastern* European folk songs as having "almost without exception full word meaning (or at least pretend to have one)."

Reviewer emends Bartók's assertion that part-singing in major seconds is "entirely unknown in folk music anywhere," excepting Dalmatia and Bulgarian territory (pp. 65, 73, below), by indicating its ex-

[96] Copyright 1946 by Hawkes & Son (London) Ltd.

[97] On p. 257 Schneider states (trans. from the Spanish): "As for Seeger's criticism, we reject it; and to have better orientation on the present state of modern folkloric studies, we earnestly recommend our criticism of Bartók's *Serbo-Croatian Folk Songs* as well as our contribution in honor of Kodály" [Budapest, 1943].

istence in "Oceania, Melanesia, Cambocha, Portuguese Guinea, East Africa, Estonia, and in the medieval liturgy of Milán."

Reviewer objects to Bartók's consideration of narrow range as a characteristic trait of ancient Serbo-Croatian or Slavic music, claiming that narrow range constitutes a peculiar style of ritual music in higher cultures and therefore does not represent a primitivism; moreover, that it is diffused world-wide. The reader, however, should note this statement, made by Bartók after countless hours devoted to analysis of a substantial body of Yugoslav folk music materials: "My hypothesis is that originally only narrow range, probably two-section, melodies existed in the Serbo-Croatian material. As foreign (western) influence arose, a gradual extension of range . . . could have occurred" (p. 60, below).

Reviewer objects to Bartók's attribution of pentatonicism in a few examples of Serbo-Croatian folk songs to the past Turkish occupation, claiming that the pentatonic scale is a phenomenon of evolutionary character: "The Serbo-Croatians are not a primitive people who should have awaited the arrival of the Turks to acquire so ancient a scale. Moreover, if the Serbo-Croatian melodies of pentatonic character indeed had a Turkish origin, to prove it, it would have been necessary [for Bartók] to compare them with similar Turkish melodies." This peculiar assertion by reviewer is mystifying in view of the list of specific Turkish variants given by Bartók on p. 55, below.[98]

Mention has already been made of John Weissmann's review (note 70, above) which was of value in determination of typographical errata in the first edition of *Serbo-Croatian Folk Songs*. He supports Bartók's hypothesis concerning Turkish influence on Serbo-Croatian melodies, in view of the centuries-long Turkish domination over that region, and he suggests that tetra- or pentachordal melodies in certain positions might be related to the tonal system of the ancient Greeks.

Josef Brožek and Cvjetko Rihtman have co-authored two reviews of *Serbo-Croatian Folk Songs*. The very brief English "précis" in the

[98] As the final word on this review, the reader may be interested to know that the reviewer opens his critique (p. 257) with an apparent endorsement of "simple and congenial notation without electric recording, that an individual could do with the songs of his country." This procedure is diametric to that followed by Bartók who explains the necessity for field recording on p. xii, above (see, especially, *Essays,* No. 3: "Why and How Do We Collect Folk Music?").

Journal of the International Folk Music Council (Vol. V, 1953, p. 69) probably preceded the lengthier, substantive discourse in the periodical *Bilten Instituta za Proucavanje folklora* (No. 2, 1953, pp. 407–410).[99] The Serbo-Croatian review, after a detailed presentation of data about the Parry Collection, Bartók as composer, and the transcription technique (a simpler form is suggested), recommends delimitation of inquiry to "careful ordering of a larger number of examples of the same rhythmic base, performed by various singers, from one chosen area. Insignificant changes which can be established only among individual cases [and which are personal idiosyncrasies of the singer] should not be considered . . . [only] melodies which carry the characteristic general qualities of musical practice in a fixed context, and not those which accidentally fall in that area, should be included."[100] Reviewers indicate that Milman Parry was guided toward selection of skilled singers rather than "good" ones: the former burden their songs with ornamentation and rhythmic aberration, generally ignore the texts, contaminate their songs with different content, and generally try to avoid singing the simple and well-known songs of local origin. Indeed, they prefer to exhibit their knowledge of lesser-known songs which sometimes are good, old ones but more often are of foreign origin: the result is frequently renditions with faulty or completely unclear texts.

"Good" singers are village peasants[101] whose performance emphasizes the role of rhythm which is thus more exactly fixed than intonation. Vocal color is calculated on the basis of its effect out-of-doors —resulting in an unattractive effect at close quarters—which leads to unavoidable vowel deformation.

Reviewers offer the following comments on the poetic texts:

[99] In the English review the closing statement reads: "The monograph is one of the most important contributions to the musicological analysis of Yugoslav folk songs . . . It is not, however, as Professor Herzog suggests in the foreword, the 'first systematic discussion of Yugoslav folk music.'" A footnote lists Kuba (Prague, 1923), Širola (Zagreb, 1940), and Vasiljević (Belgrade, 1950) as predecessor studies. This statement is not to be found in the Serbo-Croatian review.

[100] Bartók's response to this recommendation might well have been: "The primary considerations should be purely scientific: all melodies still in circulation should be collected, regardless of their artistic attributes (*Essays,* No. 1: "Hungarian Folk Music").

[101] The reviewers indicate that Parry recorded his informants in small Moslem towns where the singing is explicitly soloistic and much closer to the tempered scale than peasant performance; moreover, the fact that the singers are all Moslems seems to infer that Parry had a predetermined orientation. See, however, Bartók's evaluation of Parry's choice of informants on p. lxiv, below.

Text 26: It is difficult to explain the song in this form, as recorded in Gacko. But it is from Zvornik, which goes: Pod Skočićem trava potrvena,/ potrle je zvorničke spahije . . . [Under the trampled grass of Skočić,/ The Zvornik spahi trampled it . . .] Since Skočić is a small village south of Zvornik, interpretation of the song's meaning presents no problem.

Texts 16a, 17, 29: The case is similar for these texts as well as for those listed below. These three are, however—relatively speaking—given in the best way despite the fact that they stem from Montenegro.

Texts 47 and 48: Serbian origin: in the first song the beginning is changed to "Oj Omere" instead of "Oj Jovane."

Text 24: From Slovenia: the melody, otherwise very simple in syllabic structure and without decoration, is recognized therefore with greater difficulty.

Texts 4, 21b., 52: Asker melodies, with folk text, which were originally sung by Turkish soldiers and then soldiers in general.[102]

Texts 39a., 42, 50: These cannot be considered folk songs at all.[103]

Texts 10, 41, 48: Line 7 of the first one should read: "Bogom brate, tuđa jabandžijo" [Goodbye, brother, I am a stranger]; line 3 of the second should read: "Što u dvoru žubor stoji, ko se veseli?" [What babble is in the courtyard, who is celebrating?]; and line 2 of the third should read: "Samo jedna ruža kalemljena" [Only one rose garlanded].

Reviewers present detailed information concerning the willing absorption of Eastern (Turkish, Arab, Persian) music by small-town Moslems under Turkish rule (to which many primitive instruments bear testimony, such as the *šargiya, saz, tambura, daulbaz, zile, borije,* etc.), and that the Moslem peasant population also gladly accepted this small-town culture. Thus a relatively small part of the Moslem peasantry has retained the more primitive but older traditions which demand use of the *gusle:* it is incontrovertible that anyone who had adopted the small-town style of singing would know how to sing along with the *gusle.*

Reviewers state that Bartók, not having the necessary material at his disposal, failed to observe a very important fact in Bosno-Hercegovinian musical ethnography: "singing with the *gusle* is not in the least an

[102] See Bartók's Note to melody No. 52 (p. 244, below).

[103] See Bartók's Notes (pp. 242–244, below) in which he indicates the probability of urban origin of the three songs.

isolated phenomenon as regards tonal material. In fact it is precisely the characteristic chromaticism of the scales as well as the no less significant characteristic relationship between the *gusle* and the voice—a relationship in very close connection with the tradition of polyphonic singing of the second category[104]—that is found exclusively in the villages of Bosnia and Hercegovina. These two important characteristics are convincing proof that peasant singing and singing with the *gusle* belong to the same musical tradition, to the same common origins."

Lajos Vargyas' review was published in the October, 1952 issue of the now defunct journal, *Uj Zenei Szemle* (Budapest, Vol. II, No. 10, pp. 10–12), more than fifteen years prior to the publication of Bartók's *Rumanian Folk Music* study. If Vargyas had had access to the Rumanian material, he might have revised or deleted this portion of his review:

> . . . we may hardly accept the somewhat mechanical explanation by Bartók[105] that the imperfect cadence system is a foreign borrowing and originated from the truncating to one-half of some more advanced songs (of course, in some primitive phase) . . . we are far more entitled to take into consideration peculiarities originating out of internal development . . . rather than distortion of well-known, more advanced phenomena. In our opinion the imperfect cadence in the ending of Yugoslav melodies is a variant of the tonal characteristic of East European musics, wherein the compass is often lower by one note than the final tone.
>
> This assumption is all the more competent in view of the melodies in this volume being close to a part of the Rumanian songs of Bihor [County] concerning tonality and compass.

Vargyas' assertion is rebutted in *Rumanian Folk Music,* Vol. II, pp. 16–18, in Bartók's discussion of musical dialects of Rumanian regions. In the Banat area adjacent to Serbo-Croatian territory, dia-

[104] Reviewers refer to C. Rihtman's article on polyphonic forms in the folk music of Bosnia and Hercegovina, published in the (unavailable) preceding issue (Vol. I, 1951) of the same journal. But a definition of "second category" polyphonic singing is also given by Rihtman in his "Yugoslav Folk Music" essay in *Grove's Dictionary,* Vol. III of the Fifth Edition, p. 416: "The practice of polyphony may be divided into two fundamental categories: (1) forms in which the upper voice takes the lead while the lower is of secondary importance; (2) forms in which the leading voice from time to time goes below the accompanying voice. The forms of the second category are found only in the central mountainous regions (among herdsmen) . . ."

[105] A marginal note here reads: "Our editorial staff does not fully agree with this part of the article."

tonic scale fragments, consisting of an F major or minor pentachord with the second degree (g^1) as final tone, are a characteristic: "therefore, we have every reason to believe that their presence . . . indicates Serbo-Croatian influence." The minor pentachord with augmented fourth is also encountered in the Hunedoara-Alba dialect "probably as an infiltration from the Banat area." Bartók then refers the reader to *Serbo-Croatian Folk Songs* [see pp. 60–61] for more detailed explanations on the frequency of occurrence of these diatonic scale fragments—"(about fifty per cent)"—in the Serbo-Croatian and Bulgarian material.

Reviewer then supplements Bartók's delimitation of polyphonic singing in parallel seconds to Dalmatia and some Bulgarian examples by mentioning the discovery of the Soviet musicologist, Victor Belaiev, "of instances of parallel polyphony in seconds in medieval Russian music relics."[106]

It is indeed fitting to conclude this chapter with a brief résumé of Birthe Traerup's study, *East Macedonian Folk Songs,*[107] since its musical part is modeled closely after Bartók's methodology in *Serbo-Croatian Folk Songs*.

The subheading of the study is "Contemporary Traditional Material from Maleševo, Pijanec and the Razlog District," eastern Macedonian territory, and the work is "intended to be a link in a larger investigation of fok music in Macedonia and the immediatey adjacent areas." After an extensive introduction, which includes historical data, related literature, and a summary of findings with respect to musical and textual characteristics of the material, the morphology of the East Macedonian folk song material (70 melodies) is given: Rhythm (verse structure and rhythmic structure of the melodies), Melody (scales, intervals, ornamentation, and polyphony), and Form (text strophe and musical strophe). The transcriptions, which follow Bartók's notational

[106] Bruno Nettl's *Folk and Traditional Music of the Western Continents* (New Jersey: Prentice-Hall, 1965) has, in the chapter on Eastern Europe, a section on polyphony (including bibliographic and discographic references) in the Slavic countries and the Caucasus (pp. 96–101). Walter Wiora's *European Folk Song* (publication details in note 83, above) has a number of music examples in the section on part-singing (pp. 86–89).

[107] Published by Akademisk Forlag, Copenhagen, 1970, the book is the second in the *Acta Ethnomusicologica Danica* series.

techniques (some exceptions: exclusion of bar lines in *parlando* pieces, inclusion of scale patterns at the beginning of each music example[108]), are presented next and immediately followed by the poetic texts and their translations.[109] Scholarly apparatus of substantial extent forms the third part of the book: data concerning the singers and places, subject classification of the texts, glossary, list of refrains and interpolations, alphabetical and chronological lists of the texts and translations, bibliography, map of the area, and photographs.[110]

In one sense the title of the present four-volume publication is not original: YUGOSLAV FOLK MUSIC was the working title and is found as the reference heading on the Columbia University Press letters to Bartók, from 1941 to 1945. This title was also used by Albert B. Lord and by George Herzog, and the available documentation indicates that it was not until 1949, when the front matter of *Serbo-Croatian Folk Songs* was sent to the printer, that the latter title was adopted. Other factors, however, were more substantive in the decision to rename this expanded edition. First, the valid criticism of Rihtman and Brožek (see note 99, above) that the title of the Bartók and Lord book implies that its content covers the entire Serbo-Croatian language area, whereas the main thrust is with respect to the musical folklore of Bosnia and Hercegovina. Second, the addition of source melodies in Vols. III–IV and instrumental melodies in Appendix I and II in this volume has resulted in a publication that—in accordance with contemporary ethnomusicological publication practice in Yugoslavia—calls for a geographic rather than language-area generic title.

Acknowledgement is made to the following persons who provided various types of materials or assistance: Béla Bartók II, Maja Basioli,

[108] Bartók prefaced his Arab transcriptions (*Zeitschrift für Musikwissenschaft,* 1920) with similar patterns.

[109] A section on text content closes the author's Introduction (pp. 21–22).

[110] A particularly admirable tabulation of melismata extracted from *tempo giusto* melodies is given on pp. 59–60, ordered according to skeletal rhythmic patterns in 2/4, 4/4, 3/8, 5/8, 5/16, and 7/8 meters. As might be expected, the author found that "Bulgarian" rhythm (*aksak* or asymmetrical measures in quintuple and septuple meters) is "immensely typical" of Macedonian *tempo giusto* melodies.

The reader will find additional, less-closely related materials in the editorial preface to Vol. III of the present publication.

Editor's Preface

Jerko Bezić, Jozef Brožek, George Herzog, Walter Kolar, Barbara Krader, Kenneth Lohf, Norman Mangouni, Berkeley Peabody, Radmila Petrović, Dragan Plamenac, Cvjetko Rihtman, Stanley Sadie, Eleanor Suchoff, Stith Thompson, Richard Tószeghy, Valens Vodušek, and Henry Wiggins.

Grateful recognition is made here of the contributions of the Columbia University Press, publisher of *Serbo-Croatian Folk Songs* in 1951; Martinus Nijhoff, The Hague, publisher of *Rumanian Folk Music;* Macmillan, London, publishers of *Grove VI;* Fodor's Modern Guides, publisher of the map of Yugoslavia on front and back endpapers; staff members of the Budapest Bartók Archivum and of the Duquesne University Tamburitzans Institute of Folk Arts; and, of course, the State University of New York Press.

A special expression of thanks is tendered to Edith Pásztory-Bartók (Mrs. Béla Bartók) for her support which has enabled the fruition of her husband's original plan, one he was destined never to see: the unified publication of his study of Parry Collection materials with his broad spectrum, innovative morphological index of Yugoslav folk song. For it was the latter work that provided the foundation for *Serbo-Croatian Folk Songs* and, subsequently, the present publication.

BENJAMIN SUCHOFF

New York

Foreword

MILMAN PARRY, Homeric scholar at Harvard University, had the inspired thought that if we wanted to form a picture of the genesis of the great Homeric chants and how they were performed, we should observe the life of folksong where it has best survived to the present day, on the Balkan peninsula. The heroic epic songs of Yugoslavia, the so-called "men's songs," come nearest in that region to the type of tradition which was probably the foundation of the Homeric epics. So Professor Parry made in the thirties prolonged collecting trips to Yugoslavia and with the assistance of Dr. Albert B. Lord gathered a vast collection of songs, especially in the jagged mountains of Bosnia, Hercegovina, Montenegro, and South Serbia. In addition to the epics, many "women's songs"—lyrical songs—were collected; these are less outstanding in the historical and literary perspective, but their melodies have a wider musical appeal than the chant tunes of the epic poems. In order to make a lasting record of the songs in the form in which they are actually performed and to make their study possible also from the musical angle, the expedition recorded a large number of songs on disks. But soon after his return to this country, Mr. Parry died, in a tragic accident. Research on the music of the collection was for a long time hampered by the unavailability of a real connoisseur of the folk music of eastern Europe. This need was remedied when the late Béla Bartók came to this country.

Béla Bartók is known to the musical world as one of the foremost composers of our time, and one whose creative inspiration was deeply rooted in folk music. In his earlier works, especially, he often uses a vocabulary inspired by the clear spirit of folk melodies, while later the folk elements became more and more integrated and absorbed in his own personal idiom, which they helped to expand. His settings of Hungarian, Slovak, and Rumanian tunes and dances, produced over a long span of years, reflect an intimate familiarity with this material. Time and again he came back to the challenging problem of translating it for the musical audience of the city, and he evolved a variety of solutions. But it is less well known that Mr. Bartók was also a devoted student of folksong, indeed, an international authority in this field. Much of the folk music incorporated into his creative work was entirely unknown until he discovered it, in the course of laborious collecting trips to villages off the beaten track, to places that were "behind the back of God," to use a Hungarian phrase. The intensive cultural and national renaissance in Hungary at the onset of the twentieth century awakened a strong interest in folk life and folklore. The patient search conducted by Mr. Bartók and his colleague, the composer Zoltán Kodály, soon revealed that what had been accepted as Hungarian national music, through the effusive Rhapsodies of Liszt and Brahms which followed in the wake of the sparkling "alla Ungharese" movements by Haydn and others, had little to do with the folk themselves. It was merely an inflated elaboration of the popular entertainment music of the town, propagated by the Hungarian gypsies. But the countryside still possessed an entirely different body of old melodies, simple and sturdy, practically unknown in the Hungarian cities. It was a situation much like that in this country when the ballads of New England and of the Southern Mountains had to be "discovered" for a public nurtured on Stephen Foster.

Under the influence of the Hungarian peasant tunes, Bartók and Kodály, in the first decade of the century, began to develop a new national school of composition. But the regional confines were soon transcended, especially by Bartók. His scholarly interests also expanded, to embrace the folk music of the nationalities surrounding the Hungarian island. On his last recording expeditions the search for peasant music took him as far as Turkey and Algeria. Thus, by the time he came to this country, shortly before the war, the experience and the detailed knowledge of Eastern European folk music which he had amassed was equaled by no one. It was most fortunate, then, that through the warm interest of the Music Department at Columbia University arrangements could be made with Harvard University for the musical study of the Parry Collection to be delegated to him. On his part, it gave him deep satisfaction that while he was finding his roots in a new country, which he knew chiefly as a modern technological civilization, he could once more immerse himself in a musical dialect from one of those regions of Europe where old rural culture has not yet fully disappeared. This book, appearing posthumously, is one of the results of this work.

Mr. Bartók's contributions to our knowledge and understanding of folk music are the fruits of an indefatigable activity and industry. In the days of the cylinder phonograph he preserved, on records or by writing them down by ear, thousands of folk melodies. To their collating and study he devoted a scholarship so painstaking and minute that it is not easy to fathom how he could have found the time and the energy for it, in the midst of a fully creative life as composer, pianist, and teacher. The monumental corpus of Hungarian folk music which he prepared with Mr. Kodály was to have been published by the Hungarian Academy of Sciences, when the war intervened. He was the author of the monograph *Hungarian Folk Music*, a model of methods of analysis, and of basic investigations on Rumanian and Slovak folk music, besides many shorter studies and theoretical articles. In a territory charged with old political, national, and cultural aspirations and tensions, these writings are distinguished by an objective and international outlook—one important essay traces the cross-influences between Hungarian folk music and that of the neighboring peoples. He liked to stress the fact that there are no true folksongs in this region that express national prejudices or antagonisms of the peasant groups, and he felt that such attitudes were kept alive artificially by official cliques and school-taught songs. He took equal pride in being a citizen of the world, taking an interest in music the world over, and in being a member of a particular national culture, for the music of which he had the special attachment of one born in a small town, not too far from the "soil."

A combination of creative musical genius of the very first rank with persevering and detailed scientific activity is rare. Bartók looked upon the tasks and responsibilities of the collector and of the composer as entirely distinct. Those of the collector, he felt, were to gather and present the material exactly and faithfully, without any patronizing emendations or collated versions of the sort which were current in Europe and are still popular in this country. In his settings of folk melodies he often submitted also the notations of the tunes as they were recorded from the folk singers, so that the reader could compare the two and see the material in its pristine form. Characteristically, perhaps, he gave no opus numbers to those compositions which were based chiefly on folk tunes. At the same time Mr. Bartók manifested some of the same traits both as composer and as scholar: integrity of purpose, a complete lack of capacity for compromise, subordination of the subjective element to what he felt were the dictates of his material, and a careful workmanship with regard to details which, no matter how large the framework, was so exacting as to result almost in self-abnegation. He made it his task to acquire an intimate familiarity with the general folklore of the national group in which he worked and sufficient knowledge of the language for the arduous task of recording and studying thousands of song texts.

It is, perhaps, characteristic of his mode of workmanship that in order to provide the general observations in this book of seventy-odd melodies with a broader basis, Mr. Bartók made a systematic analysis and a melodic index of thousands of Yugoslav melodies, practically all that have appeared in print so far. Also, in his introductory essay he has presented a unique and searching discussion of the difficult problems of notation, classification, and analysis in the study of folk music. In his methods, Bartók was influenced by the so-called Finnish school of folklorists, who attempted to cover their national folklore systematically and in great detail. The large amount of material which they amassed called for developing effective techniques for analyzing, classifying, and indexing tunes, and these have been used fruitfully in the study of Eastern European folk music. Thus, detailed consideration is given in this book to matters such as the metric structure of the text and its relation to the tune, the structure and tonal range of the melody, and various other features. Musical rhythm is treated more briefly, since its patterns in Yugoslav folk music are free, very rich, and even diffuse; the basic structures are overlaid by a free, rubato performance and luxuriant ornamentation. But the details of this ornamentation and of the plastic fluctuations of time and of intonation were caught and notated by the author, as in his other transcriptions of folk melodies, with an exactitude practically photographic. This was possible only for a musician with an unusually discriminating and well-trained ear.

Doubts have been raised about the value and the reliability of this type of notation, since no musical notation can supplant for the reader the actual auditory experience and many small details of delivery vary in a truly alive folk tradition from performance to performance, even by the same singer. But a simplified notation, which is the alternative, robs a folk melody of its true flavor; it unavoidably introduces subjective judgments as to what is important and what may be dispensed with, so that at least for scientific purposes only a detailed and faithful notation is satisfactory. It can be combined, however, with a simplified picture of the melody, as is done here by means of the skeleton notations. The more exact transcriptions expose the construction of a melody in microscopic detail, but to follow it along places a demand on the reader, whom the author envisaged as a serious student. Much of the discussion, too, couched in a formulistic style, calls for work before pleasure. It may be kept in mind, however, that this is the first book written by the author in English; the publishers felt that his personal style and organization should not be altered appreciably after he could no longer authorize changes. Many of the findings in this study are of interest primarily to the specialist, but it is of more general interest in that it is the first systematic discussion of Yugoslav folk music. (The standard collection of Yugoslav folk melodies published in the eighteen eighties by F. X. Kuhač has many of the faults of the early folksong collections, and excellent recent compilations, such as those of V. R. Djordjević, contain little musical analysis.) The student of folksong and folk music will find this method of analysis full of suggestive leads, and the frequent comparative remarks on folk music are very valuable. The general reader will be rewarded by the interesting melodies and poems.

South Slavic folk music has an especial appeal. This may well be due to the contrast between the essential simplicity of its basic materials and the pulsing quality of life achieved through an abundance of expressive devices, including the ornamentation. This ornate treatment is partly due to an old, general European mode of folk singing; partly, no doubt, to the various Oriental influences which impinged on the Balkan peninsula, the Turkish domination being only the latest. This mixture of simplicity and of artistic elaboration pervades also the poetry, as may be seen in the decorative arrangements and repetitive patterns in the second part of the book. While the latter was planned so as to be subordinated to the musical study—detailed treatments of the literary side of this tradition will be published separately—yet we are given here a full and valuable background for the musical analysis; a picture of the recording expedition at work and of the singers, a collection of annotated authentic texts which will be welcomed by the specialist, and translations which are as pleasant to read as they are unpretentious and faithful to the original songs. Studies devoted to the heroic epic poetry in the Parry Collection of Harvard University and its music, on which Mr. Bartók worked intensively, will appear in the future. Meanwhile, this book represents an important addition to the study of South Slavic folklore and to our knowledge of the rural culture of southeastern Europe; it is a modest memorial to a great artist and a sympathetic scholar.

Indiana University GEORGE HERZOG

Preface

THE MAIN OBJECT of Professor Milman Parry's journeys to Yugoslavia in 1934–35 was to study, to collect, and to record as many as possible of the Serbo-Croatian heroic poems still in existence. He recorded about 350 heroic poems, collected from 90 different singers in 23 villages, on some 2,200 double-faced disks. His interest was not limited to this type of poem only. He recorded also: approximately 205 Serbo-Croatian so-called "women's songs," on about 210 double-faced disks; about 14 in a Macedonian-Bulgarian dialect, on 9 double-faced disks; about 30 Turkish and 11 Albanian songs, on about 40 double-faced disks; and 16 instrumental pieces on 8 double-faced disks. The Parry Collection, including the amazingly large number of heroic poems, towers high above all other recordings of Serbo-Croatian folk music in the world, being larger than all the rest combined.[1]

This publication is based on part of the Serbo-Croatian "women's songs," which I was privileged to transcribe and to study in 1941 and 1942, under the auspices of Columbia University and with the permission of Harvard University, the owner of the Parry Collection.

Two hundred songs are not many to represent an area as large as the Serbo-Croatian linguistic territory. However, their importance is enhanced by the fact that every song, regardless of its length, has been recorded in full—a procedure not very often used in recordings of Eastern European folk music, for various reasons (such as the high costs and lack of time). From this point of view the Parry Collection ranks above all European collections known to me; these generally do not contain more than the first three or four stanzas of the longer folk poems.

The material published in this book is based upon transcriptions of recordings of Serbo-Croatian folk music and is, in this respect, the first publication of its kind.[2]

[1] According to the statements in *Folklore musical,* Institut International de Coöperation Intellectuelle, Paris, 1939, pp. 205–9, these consist of: 466 (probably single-faced) disks, 348 cylinders, and 150 other *enregistrements* (we do not know what kind of enregistrements they are, since disks and cylinders are separately mentioned) scattered in several European countries. Hereafter this publication will be cited as *Folk. mus.*

[2] According to *Folk. mus.,* pp. 210 ff., where no clear mention is made of material published on the basis of records.

Preface

The records are excellent, on the whole. The singers, with a few exceptions, were very well chosen. Their performance, especially concerning the timbre of voice, tone production, and ornamentation, is absolutely natural and exactly what we should expect from peasant singers whose performance is not yet marred by urban influences.

I feel privileged to have had the opportunity to make this study. It is a part of a larger investigation which was undertaken under the auspices of Columbia University in 1941–43 and was based on the extensive Parry Collection of unique materials on Yugoslav folk song and folk music deposited at Harvard University. I wish to express my appreciation to all those who helped me in this research. Harvard University gave its full co-operation by making the records and texts available, and by giving its permission to publish the results in the present book. Mr. Albert B. Lord, who participated in the late Professor Parry's collecting trips in Yugoslavia and after Parry's death carried on some of his research, gave assistance in many ways, and contributed the section on the texts, including an introduction and texts and translations of the poems. The Archives of Primitive Music, Department of Anthropology, Columbia University, furnished duplicates of the original recordings, so that the latter were saved from the damage due to the wearing down attendant on the laborious process of transcription into musical notation. I am obliged to Dr. George Herzog, of the Archives of Primitive Music, for his helpful assistance, including going over the manuscript. Credit is due to Mr. Wolfgang Weissleder for the great care he exercised in producing the excellent music copy. The Columbia University Press co-operated in every way in its task of producing a publication somewhat burdened with technical detail. Above all, however, I am indebted to Professor Douglas H. Moore, the Department of Music, Columbia University, and the Ditson Fund, whose active interest made the study and its publication possible.

New York
February, 1943

BÉLA BARTÓK

Contents

Introduction to Part One

METHOD OF TRANSCRIPTION

THE TRANSCRIPTION of recordings of folk music should be as true as possible. It should be realized, however, that an absolutely true notation of music (as well as of spoken words) is impossible because of the lack of adequate signs in our current systems of notation. This applies even more to the notation of folk music. The only really true notations are the sound-tracks on the record itself. These, of course, could be magnified, photographed, and printed instead of, or with, the usual notation. But this complicated procedure would not be of much use, in view of the all-too-complicated nature of the curves in the tracks. The human mind would not be able to translate the visual signs into tones. It must have as visual impressions conventional symbols of drastic simplicity in order to be able to study and to categorize sound phenomena. These symbols are what we call "notation" of music. When applying them to the transcription of folk music, we may add supplementary diacritical signs, in smaller or larger numbers, devised for our special purposes, in order to represent certain phenomena which occur in and are characteristic of folk music.

In spite of these additional signs, the current notation, when used to transcribe folk music, has intrinsic limitations. These limitations, however, can be overcome to a certain degree, according to our purpose and to our well-weighed choice. Our choice will take into consideration the perceptive abilities of the human mind and their limits.

In transcribing folk music only two dimensions can be assumed: pitch (as the vertical one) and the rhythm (as the horizontal one). The consideration of the third dimension, having relation to intensity and color of sound may well be discarded. We have no adequate signs for marking intensity (except for the well-known but too-general signs of dynamics) and no signs at all for tone color (timbre). Fortunately, change of intensity is no important factor in folk music (at least that of Eastern Europe), the performer's intention being to achieve evenness. And if the performance is nevertheless anything but even, this results from purely mechanical factors. Notes sung in high pitch sound louder; those in lower pitch, softer. Very rarely, indeed, do we hear single notes accentuated intentionally by the performer (and then more frequently in instrumental music than in vocal melodies) or groups of notes produced purposely with changes of dynamics. In such cases, of course, the conventional signs for dynamics must be used. Creation of new signs for color would be not only too complicated but also probably useless; the reader could never catch the right idea of the color, however elaborate the signs or description used. In this regard, in addition to a few descriptive words, all that can be done is to refer the reader to the record itself. So we must impose exactness only with regard to pitch and rhythm.

Eastern European folk music is generally based on the diatonic system of our art music. Exceptions are few; rather obvious among them is the music of the Serbo-Croatian heroic poems. The reader must bear in mind, however, that the intonation (that is, placement of pitch) of the respective degrees (whether altered by accidentals or not) is much less exact than in art music.[1] Nevertheless, these deviations, since they show a certain system and are subconsciously intentional, must not be considered faulty, off-pitch singing. This is the essential difference between the accidental off-pitch singing of urban amateurs and the self-assured, self-conscious, decided performance of peasant singers.

The first problem with which we have to deal is with what degree of exactitude we shall transcribe these deviations in pitch. My method is as follows: if the deviation is perceptible enough, arrow signs above the notes are used. An arrow pointing downward means lowered pitch, almost reaching the quarter tone below; pointing upward it means raised pitch, not quite or almost reaching the quarter tone above. These arrows may be used in conjunction with both flats and sharps, too, where they will be valid as long as are the accidentals themselves. Some special signs could conceivably be used for differences of exactly one quarter tone. They were almost never employed here because of the great difficulty in determining by ear whether the difference is exactly a quarter tone or only approximately. Obviously these arrows and comparable symbols used by others are signs of approximate value, and are, perhaps, the only practical means to be used concerning pitch deviations in Eastern European folk music.

[1] It has been shown that even the intonation of trained professional singers is seldom absolutely exact.

As a matter of fact, a system has been established and instruments invented which enable us to measure the vibrations of each scale degree of a given melody. The system is the "cent" system. In this system every tempered half tone is divided into 100 equal cents, and it is possible to express every tone in cents instead of its number of vibrations. In many cases, especially in melodies with typical tone deviations of degree, such measurements would give highly interesting and mathematically exact data about the deviations, as well as about their constancy. Some musicologists, for example, Erich von Hornbostel and Idelsohn, frequently used this procedure. I am sorry to say that I never had occasion to use it myself.

Other special signs for certain phenomena connected with pitch are the various types of *glissando*.[2]

The second problem is the degree of exactness to be used in transcribing the rhythm of folk melodies. Here, again, it must be borne in mind that an absolutely rigid rhythm never prevails even in so-called "rigid" dance rhythms.[3] Whether it be the latter or the so-called *parlando-rubato*, free rhythm, with which we often have to deal in Eastern European folk music, limits must be set to the exactitude of rhythm transcriptions. As a general rule, the deviations in "dance rhythm" which are not noticeable to the trained observer in playing the records at ordinary speed should not be heeded. They are scarcely perceptible when playing the records at even half speed. A certain limit should be set even for transcribing deviations which become rather noticeable when magnified by this procedure. This limit should correspond to the ability of the human mind to perceive differences of rhythm. Speaking in practical terms, it is about the value of a sixty-fourth at a speed of 120 beats per minute. For example, if the singer performed an eighth dotted four times instead of a quarter note, it would be best to ignore this very slight deviation. Even for an eighth dotted three times it is perhaps more advisable to write a quarter note with a half-circle over it.[4] The same limit to exactness can be set when dealing with *parlando-rubato* melodies. Of course, their irrational rhythmic formulas can by no means be called "deviations," since these melodies never present regular rhythmic patterns from which to deviate.

[2] See explanation of signs, p. 91.

[3] The same can be said of art music performances.

[4] This half circle is used to denote a slight shortening of value; see explanation of signs, p. 91.

It is advisable to use the ordinary time-signature in rigid dance rhythm only, when no deviations need to be introduced into the transcription at all. If deviations occur, then the general time signature may be inclosed in parentheses, and no changes in signature need to be introduced. Changes in time signature are to be used only when the change does not result from an occasional deviation, but is an essential rhythmic feature (alternation of different measures). In transcriptions of *parlando-rubato* performances no kind of time signature should be used, for such a device would give the reader little help, and it would only bewilder him to find in almost every measure different and most unusual signatures, such as 11/16, 15/16, 31/32.

Summing up, the transcriptions of records of folk music and their publication ought to be, as far as the described limits permit, in the manner of a so-called *Urtextausgabe* (that is, critically revised edition, in which the texts are presented according to the presumed intentions of the author or composer). In other words, nothing should be changed by the transcriber except those parts in which the performer made an obviously unintentional mistake. In critically revised editions of higher art works, obvious mistakes of the author or composer appearing in the autograph or in the (authentic or nonauthentic) first edition must be replaced by the form which we have sufficient reasons to believe is in accordance with his original intention. This, of course, must not be done without referring to and carefully describing the mistakes and misprints or without ample explanations concerning the editor's reasons for the change. Similarly, absolutely unintentional mistakes made by the performers of folk music should not be entered in the published transcriptions. For instance, if when starting on a certain note the performer's voice fails or slips so that he or she has to try again to reach the note, the results of this mischance should not be entered, much less published. The same applies when he or she drifts into a wrong pitch, but becoming aware of it, stops, and begins the whole period again. However, off-pitch notes which were not corrected by the singer, periods or bars sung (exceptionally) some degrees higher or lower than they obviously should be, excess syllables (with the corresponding notes, of course), even if seemingly added accidentally, should be transcribed and published or at least mentioned. Syllables, notes, and rests evidently omitted by accident should not be restored by the transcriber, and so forth. In some such cases, however, marginal notes may refer to the supposedly correct form. In any case, every change introduced by the transcriber should be mentioned and explained (except the unintentional errors described above).

Some scholars may have a different opinion on this subject and would perhaps include these slips and failures in the transcription as characteristic of certain singers or areas. Even so, I am against including them, for (1) they show on the records, and whoever wants to study them may find them there; (2) I consider these imperfections analogous to physical abnormities and should prefer, as far as possible, to keep apart well-shaped melodies from unintentional desultory forms.

However, in connection with this whole question, it may be borne in mind that decisions as to the cause of deviations on the part of the singer are often difficult to reach and can be made only on the basis of very intensive experience. A false judgment can change the picture of what the performance was and what the singer intended. Thus, when in any doubt at all, an alternative method may be used, by giving in the transcriptions what the investigator thinks was intended, but giving in notes all changes and errors, obvious or not, so that the reader can evaluate them as he wishes.

SETTING OF BARS[5] *AND CHOICE OF VALUES*

Both problems, although they do not interfere with truthfulness in the notation, are rather important. The right setting and choice will help greatly in understanding the structure of the melodies and will make for greater consistency in editing. Some scholars say bars should not be used in *parlando-rubato* melodies. Probably their point is that in these melodies no regularity of rhythm can be observed and that therefore the periods must not be divided into measures, since measures refer to certain regularities of rhythm. However, when we consider the original meaning of the bar (it means an articulating accent on the value following the bar), then we can easily acquiesce in the setting of bars in these periods. We can, moreover, appreciate them as very useful means of giving a clear idea of the articulation of the melody. Their place should be determined generally by the metrical structure of the text line, in the case of vocal melodies. In a style in which the meter is based on syllable count, lines of eight syllables with *4 + 4* structure may have bars after the fourth and

[5] "Bar" will be used in this book in its original meaning, that is, to signify the vertical lines dividing the piece into small parts; "measure" will signify the part between two bars.

the eighth syllables, respectively; those with *3 + 2 + 3,* after the third, the fifth, and the eighth syllables, and so forth. If we accept this as a basis for the determination of rhythmic structure of the melody, it will be extremely important to have the text in front of us when transcribing the melody. If the transcription of a recorded text is missing and if we cannot make out the text by listening to the record, we may be unable to determine even the periods of the melody, much less the sub-periods (measures). In transcriptions of *parlando-rubato* melodies bars are used for the above purpose, and broken bars are added to measures which are rather complicated and of considerable length, in order to indicate subdivisions of the measure. Of course, any other sign (comma, short line, short double line, and so forth) in place of continuous or broken bars will serve the purpose as well. It would be desirable, however, for as many editors as possible to reach an agreement concerning the use of uniform signs.

In melodies having a more or less rigid dance rhythm or a rhythm that sounds like a *parlando-rubato* rhythm, but is actually the transformation of an originally rigid rhythm, the use of bars is generally accepted. The metrical structure of the text lines is here too, the reliable basis in determining the place of the bars. In some special cases, however, we must partially abandon this basis and follow the rhythmical pattern of the melodies of rigid rhythm (for instance $\frac{4}{4}$ 𝅗𝅥 ♩ ♩ | 𝅝 | 𝅗𝅥 ♩ ♩ | 𝅝 |, in spite of having *2 + 2 + 2 + 2* as the metrical structure of the text lines; see music example No. 21) or the "declamatory"[6] accents of melodies in *parlando-rubato* rhythm.[7]

The structure of the melodies should be determined by the structure of the text; that is, the single sections (in German, *Melodiezeile*) of a given melody may be expected to correspond to the respective lines of the text (or of the stanza). This seems obvious, since the sections of melody and text generally tally with each other. However, in some cases found in Eastern Europe, especially in Serbo-Croatian folk melodies, the structure of the melodies seems at first hearing to contradict the respective portions of the text. Without the text at hand, one might very often be misled by some peculiar features of the melody (rests, climax notes, repeats) and might determine its structure erroneously, that is, in contradiction to the text structure (for example, our No. 14).

[6] "Declamatory" means here: conforming to the rhythm and inflections of the language as applied to the melody.

[7] This occurs chiefly in the Yugoslav heroic poems.

Introduction to Part One

It may be asked whether musical structure should be determined on the basis of extramusical factors. An affirmative answer is dictated by the following facts. The texts of Eastern European folk songs have almost without exception full word meaning (or at least pretend to have one[8]); texts consisting entirely of meaningless syllables do not exist (as is possible in primitive folk music). The primary purpose of the performers is to convey this meaning to the listener; the melody is a secondary factor and serves only to facilitate this conveying, to decorate the procedure, and to enhance the impression. Of course, they cannot do without melodies; texts of folk songs are never performed independently of singing. The sentences and periods in an Eastern European folk song text always correspond with its metrical sections and subsections; overlapping does not occur. Considering this fact and the previously mentioned psychological factor, we must admit the necessity for a very strict correspondence between the structure of the melody and that of the words. Obviously the end of the sentence or period in the text marks the end of the corresponding section of the melody as well.

As to purely instrumental melodies, generally those in rigid dance rhythm do not offer much difficulty, in view of the usually decisive rhythmical performance, on one hand, and the clearly symmetrical structure of the periods, on the other hand. In some cases, however, intricacies appear; for instance, when a constant "counter rhythm" is applied by the solo player on the second and fourth eighths of a 2/4 measure, as a substitute for the counter beats of an imaginary accompanying second instrument. In this case the listener may misinterpret these counter rhythm accents on the upbeats for downbeats. Only a very careful examination or eventual comparison with variants will enable us to eliminate this misinterpretation—that is, wrong placement of the bars.

Less frequent are instrumental dance melodies in which the periods contain repetitions of phrases of irregular length, for instance, $2/4\ \underbrace{a\ b\ |\ c}\ \underbrace{a\ ||\ b\ c}\ |\ d\ e\ ||$.[9] Almost invariably the listener is tempted to interpret the *a b c* as a 3/4 bar and thus the whole period as 3/4 *a b c* | *a b c* | 2/4 *d e* ||. Re-examination is likely to reveal that examples of this kind are nothing but 2/4 melodies with "shifted" rhythm in their phrases.

[8] This may happen in certain kinds of jesting texts, where frequently words are used with no sense at all, to imitate the sound of a foreign language, and so forth.

[9] Each letter stands here for a 1/4 value.

Much greater difficulties present themselves in determining the bars and the structure of instrumental *parlando-rubato* melodies. No guidance is given by text lines; accents in the performance are often misleading. If a vocal variant is at our disposal, these difficulties, of course, disappear. If there are no such variants for comparison, we may find some guidance through comparison with instrumental variants, or with other instrumental (or vocal) melodies of the same type, or through examination of the structure of the melody itself. In extreme cases, however, the position of the bars and the determination of the structure will remain matters of guesswork.

Another problem is the choosing of the values most suitable for transcribing a set of melodies. When editing single melodies, it matters little which values are used if extremes (unusually long or unusually short values) are avoided. Very long values make the transcription look too heavy; very short ones render it difficult to read. But if one works on a set of melodies belonging to the same or to kindred types, one obviously should try to attain a certain consistency in choosing the value units. It is regrettably inconsistent (but unfortunately rather frequent in amateurish publications) to transcribe melodies of similar rhythm and the same tempo in values differing in the proportion of 1 to 2; for instance, $\frac{4}{8}$ ‖: ♪ = 100 ♫♫ | ♫♫ :‖ used for some of the melodies, $\frac{4}{4}$ ‖: ♩ = 100 ♩♩♩♩ | ♩♩♩♩ :‖, for others. One must bear in mind that everything, even the slightest detail, in any publication of folk music should be in accordance with well-weighed principles, for the establishment of which the editor should be able to give his reasons.

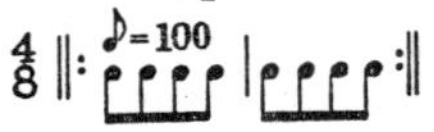

There would be no particular difficulty in choosing the value units, had the melodies of a certain type and of similar rhythm everywhere the same tempo. The facts, however, show that the tempo of melodies of the same type (especially of vocal melodies) is subject to great variation, even when performed by the same singer. The variation may exceed the double, or the half of a certain supposed standard tempo. The problem arises whether we ought to keep strictly to the values chosen for the standard tempo and change only the M. M. figure or whether we ought to set upper and lower limits and, in case the tempo passes these limits in some of the melodies, to change the values (using half or double values). Both procedures have their conveniences and inconveniences, therefore no absolute preference can be given to either of them; our decision should always be governed by the specific circumstances.

The *parlando-rubato* melodies present more difficulties in connection with the value choice. The best method seems to be as follows. By listening to the melody several times, we aim to catch the prevailing (most characteristic) length of the notes in the melody and to choose the value best suited for it. Once this is done, according to our judgment, all the values which differ from the prevailing one have to be measured and expressed by corresponding values.

In many instances even the prevailing lengths are not constant, that is, they change from section to section. In such cases, it is preferable to change the M. M. figures from section to section rather than adhere rigidly to the value established in the first section. In other words, it is preferable in such cases NOT to express the deviations in the subsequent sections in proportion to the standard value of the first section. For example, if the prevailing values of the first section are eighths and those of the second, dotted sixteenths, M. M. ♪ = 150, it is much more preferable to use eighths, M. M. ♪ = 200, in the second section. This procedure of giving each section and stanza its own metronome value is imperative when by adhering to the original M. M. figure the changes could be expressed only by too-complicated value signs, for example, a sixteenth dotted three times, or a quarter note tied to a thirty-second.

If we neglect this precaution, it may well happen (as it sometimes happened to me) that arriving at the first section of the second stanza we are compelled to use completely different values for exactly the same note lengths, for instance a quarter note in the second stanza instead of an eighth, which was used in the first stanza, although both note values have in fact the same metronomic length. These are the general requirements which help to obtain consistency in the notation of values.

In addition, there are some problems concerning details. For example, a triplet of three eighths is almost equivalent to three dotted sixteenths. Substituting one for the other for the sake of a clear, more legible notation means, of course, neglecting the difference of a thirty-second note. In my opinion this type of very slight deviation from exact notation is admissible in *parlando-rubato* melodies, especially when a 1/4 note is not slower than M. M. 100 (that is, 𝅘𝅥𝅰 = M. M. 800). The rhythmical formulas ♪♩♩ (3) and [musical notation], or the formulas [musical notation] and [musical notation], have exactly the same value. Their application should depend entirely upon the individual case—in making a choice our purpose should be to attain the clearest and most legible reading. One thing, however, should be avoided—the arbitrary interchange of these formulas without any reasonable cause. This last problem, of course, belongs already to the orthography and aesthetics of transcription.

Signs in the current notation which have a more or less vague meaning (the hold, the trill sign, the mordent, comma, and so forth) should never be used; instead of the hold and a comma, the exact measurement of the value, and instead of embellishment marks, the exact pitch of the ornamental tones should be used in the notations. Perhaps only four exceptions are permissible: the use of a wavy line above the note (for the *vibrato*), of semicircles for slight lengthening or shortening (see p. 91), and of the short grace-note. An attempt exactly to measure the duration of the latter would be unnecessary hairsplitting. As a general rule, the quarter note is suggested for values of approximately M. M. 50-130 duration; the eighth for approximately 100-200 duration. This suggestion does not pretend to be anything but a broad principle, as has been indicated already by the fact that these suggested figures show a certain overlapping. Deviations from this rule are therefore unavoidable, and each exceptional circumstance is to be dealt with on its own merits.

CERTAIN PECULIARITIES APPEARING IN THE PRESENT PUBLICATION

I always use beams instead of the old-style flags for a succession of notes sung to different syllables;[10] to melismatic groups (that is, to different notes sung to the same syllable) I apply a slur. The usage of flags (or hooks) in vocal music, still prevalent in our day, may have historical and logical foundations. However, sticking to this usage in folk music purely because of tradition is, in my opinion, rather senseless. A profusion of these hooked notes, especially when they have mixed values, are decidedly confusing to the eye. Moreover, if hooks are used, articulation remains unexpressed; [musical notation] and [musical notation], although they have different meanings,

[10] Z. Kodály applies the same method; and we both (as well as A. Schönberg, from his Op. 18 on) use it also in our original vocal works.

become undistinguishable if hooks (♪♪♪♪) are used. I cannot afford to discard the valuable advantage in articulation afforded by the other method.

As to key signatures, only such sharps and flats should be used which refer to degrees actually occurring in the melody, and which are valid throughout the whole melody. It happens frequently, even in recent and serious publications, that accidentals of the key signature refer to degrees which are not contained at all in the melody. The usage of such accidentals in the key signature is senseless and ludicrous. This unjustified habit is probably the result of a major-minor complex—a sad inheritance from the nineteenth century. According to this complex, the only existing possible and permissible scales are the major and the minor scales of the higher art music of the last two centuries, and every other scale has to be projected on these two scales and considered as an accidental deviation from them. People obsessed by this wrong theory forget that even J. S. Bach used the Dorian key signature when he meant to write in the Dorian mode.

The consistent employment of the above-described and only permissible procedure sometimes leads, of course, to rather peculiar key signatures; for instance, *b*♭ *c*♯, or *a*♭ *e*♭, or *b*♭ *a*♭ *d*♭ *c*♭! However, there is a practical advantage in this procedure; the reader perceives at a glance which scale is used in the melody.

PITCH OF MELODIES

In principle, melodies ought to be published in the original pitch as sung or played by the performers. In practice, however, we have to make a compromise in order to attain certain goals. One of these goals is to make the survey of the material as easy as possible. The most suitable method by which to attain this is to transpose all the melodies to one pitch, giving the melodies a common "tonus finalis"; to place them, so to speak, over a "common denominator." In collections where this method is used, one glance at a melody is frequently sufficient to determine its relationship to others. If we indicate, in addition, the original pitch of the *tonus finalis* by some procedure (see explanation of signs, p. 91), we fully comply with the requirements for recording the original pitch. Nevertheless, some scholars stick obstinately to the original pitch in publishing folk music, in spite of the many inconveniences it presents. For instance, approximately half the melodies may bear key signatures crowded with accidentals, at times each accidental decorated with arrows for pitch deviations. What procedure shall be followed, however, if the performer gradually changes the pitch during the performance? Let us state an example: the last note of the first stanza of a melody is a quarter tone or a half tone higher, in comparison with the first tone, than it should be; the same happens in the second stanza, and again in the third stanza, and so forth. (See music example No. 6c and other pieces sung by the same singer.) These changes are introduced GRADUALLY, NOT SUDDENLY at a certain point in the stanza. Therefore it is not possible to transcribe any of the stanzas consistently with the original pitch; one has to resort to explanations in footnotes, thus breaking the principle cherished by these scholars. This obviously shows that their principle cannot be followed with consistency. Incidentally, these gradual changes must not be regarded as off-pitch singing; probably they are characteristic of certain regions (for example, in the Rumanian-inhabited parts of the Banat district[11]) and therefore are to be observed with meticulous care.

METHODS IN SYSTEMATIC GROUPING OF FOLK MELODIES

Unfortunately, most editors of folk music have not used any musical principles in grouping; the need for it did not even occur to them. They group their material either according to texts or according to geographical units (villages, districts), or they simply do not group them in any way. The first large collections grouped according to systematic principles derived from the characteristics of the music itself were published by the Finns;[12] others were later published by the Ukrainians.[13]

There are two predominant principles which differ in purpose and partially in method. According to the first, the "lexicographical," a more or less rigid system is to be used (similar to the one used in lexicons and dictionaries) in order to make it possible to locate each melody by comparatively simple mechanical means. This has its advantages; its disadvantage consists in the fact that frequently variants (sometimes even

[11] See Bartók, *Rumanian Folk Music* (The Hague: Martinus Nijhoff, 1967), Vol. II, Nos. 15c, 67f, 176e, 198a, 202g, and others.

[12] Ilmari Krohn and others.

[13] Philaret Kolessa and others.

slightly differing variants) will have to be placed far from each other. This disadvantage is even more disturbing when it comes to melodies that belong to the same style, origin, or stock. Thus, in this grouping a given melody may be easily located, but the reader cannot very well get an idea of the different styles, structures, and even of variant groups prevailing in the material.

The system according to the second principle, which I would call "grammatical," groups all melodies belonging to the same family, or being of similar structure and representing the same style, as near each other as possible, and presents all members of the variant groups together. In order to attain this object, a rather complicated grouping system must be constructed and used, a system having all the elements of the lexicographical system intercrossed by various and numerous additional elements. A systematically grouped collection based on this system offers rather clear boundaries between the single melodic styles, structures, and families. In addition, one can locate single melodies, but in order to be able to do so one must have some previous familiarity with the material and a thorough knowledge of the rather complicated grouping system.

The question is, which is of higher importance—to be able to locate melodies easily and almost mechanically or to get a clear idea of their relationship? I am in favor of the second objective, the "grammatical" principle, in spite of its imperfections. For it has imperfections, as well as any other conceivable system. (Perfect systems for grouping can never be invented.) Therefore the system used in the present work (as well as in all my recent publications) is based on this principle.

When creating a system, various aspects of the melodies have to be considered: (1) section structure (a "section" being a portion of the melody corresponding to one line of text); (2) metric structure (metric units such as feet or the number of text syllables in each section); (3) rhythmical character (for example, free rhythm, called *parlando-rubato* or, in short, "*parlando*"); (4) melodic structure (referring to the final notes of the sections, or other significant melodic features); (5) range (*ambitus*); (6) scale system; (7) form, or content structure (referring to the content of the single sections); and in addition various subaspects, which cannot be enumerated here.

According to the lexicographical system the order of importance of these aspects is approximately as follows: 1, 4, 2, and 5 (3, 6, and 7 are rarely considered in the Eastern European material). According to the grammatical system: 1, 2, 3, 4, 5 (6 and 7 are rarely considered).

In order to simplify matters, symbols consisting of figures, letters, and the like, are to be devised and used (a procedure more or less similar to the one established in mathematics). For instance:

□ indicates a principal section of a melody, in general
[2] indicates a specific section of a melody, having a^1 as final note
] indicates a section preceding the principal one, in general
v] indicates a specific section preceding the principal one, having d^1 as final note
[indicates a section following the principal one, in general
[♭3 indicates a specific section following the principal one, having b^1♭ as a final note.

6, (that is, 6 followed by a comma) indicates an isometric stanza structure with 6 syllables for each section

7, 7, 8, 7, indicates a heterometric stanza structure with 7 syllables for the first, second, fourth section, and 8 for the third section

VII–5, a range from f^1 to d^2; and so forth (see description of grouping system, p. 28)[14]

For instance, *11,* 1] [5] [5 *1–8,* A B B A is the figure and letter symbol of a well-known Hungarian type of melody, comprising hundreds of specimens.

A general rule must be heeded in connection with the second grouping system: variants should never be scattered in different classes (subclasses and so forth), whatever the difference in their structures. If some or all the variants of a group differ in structure, these differences should be carefully examined; preference should be given to the structure which seems to be more ancient or simpler or prevailing, and so forth; melodies of this selected structure should be put at the head of the variant group, and the whole group put into the class (or subclass and so forth) indicated by the structure of this dominant variant.

Another rule (not without exception) in grouping melodies is to proceed from lower pitch or figures to higher pitch or figures. In doing so, figure and letter symbols are of great help.

[14] See explanation and enumeration of symbols on pp. 90–91.

Introduction to Part One

THE PROBLEM OF VARIANTS

To assemble all variants is not as easy as it may seem to a layman. Even if we succeed in locating all of them mechanically or by memory, it remains to be determined when a melody ceases to be the variant of a kindred melody. There remains primarily the question: What characterizes a melody as a variant of another? I should say that variants are melodies in which the pitch relation of the various principal tones to each other shows a certain similarity; or, in other words, in which the contour line is entirely or partly similar. But even on this basis immense difficulties will present themselves when we deal with hundreds or even thousands of melodies belonging to a characteristically homogeneous style. In such a long chain of melodies, in which each of two neighboring melodies can be considered beyond any doubt and at first sight as a variant of the other, and the first one in the row is so entirely different from the last one that it should not be called a variant, one has to break up these melodies into two or more separate groups. Where shall one group end, where shall the new group begin? Which of the more or less similar melodies shall be considered variants; which not? Again subjective decisions will have to guide us in the solution of all these questions.

ORNAMENTS (GRACE NOTES)

Two or more notes of different pitch sung to one syllable constitute ornaments in vocal melodies. Usually one of the notes in an ornament group can be regarded as the principal one (the one which would remain if the ornament group were stripped of the ornamental notes), and the rest as supplementary ornamental notes. The latter are frequently sung with a much lighter tone emission and ought to be transcribed with small note heads, in order to distinguish them from the heavier principal tone. In some areas, however, especially of Serbo-Croatia, ornamental groups with equally heavy tones and with sharp, definite rhythmic and melodic patterns are more frequent. I should call them "heavy" ornaments. Compared with the performance of Hungarian, Rumanian, Slovak, and probably the Ukrainian melodies, the Serbo-Croatian folk melodies (probably Russian and Greek folk melodies, too) are characteristically rich in heavy ornaments. As the heaviness or lightness of ornamental notes is an important characteristic of various territories, it is obviously important to discriminate between them in the notation by using full-size and small notes. Unfortunately, in many of the published collections no discriminating means are used.

It is rather difficult, of course, to find the principal tone in a heavy ornament group. Comparing variants and examining upbeat and down-beat relations may give useful hints for solving this problem.

OBJECTIVITY AND SUBJECTIVITY IN TRANSCRIBING AND GROUPING FOLK MUSIC

Evidently objectivity is what we must strive for. This is the ideal, an ideal which, however, can never be fully attained. Objectivity could be furthered by the use of more accurate measuring devices but in practice they would probably prove too complicated and the results would certainly be too cumbersome for the reader. If we do not employ such means, our eyes and ears serve as measuring apparatuses—rather imperfect apparatuses. Thus, through our imperfect senses many subjective elements will get into our transcriptions, rendering them that much less reliable. This applies especially to the most minute details of the performance (very short grace notes and the like); divergences in the perception of these details are not only frequent among well-trained transcribers, but even in transcriptions made by the same person. For one reason or another, it very rarely happens that the same person has transcribed twice the same piece of folk music. But when it happens, these double transcriptions, especially if separated by some period of time, are very valuable documents—the differences between them (while they concern mostly only slight and unimportant details) will indicate the degree of reliability of the transcriber in question.

Even if we do employ objective measuring instruments for determining pitch and speed, there are no imaginable implements to guide us in making the judgments which enter into our determination of structure, range, and scale of folk music. Laymen will say: "Why implements? Nothing is simpler; look at the last note of each section, count the syllables of each, and so forth, and you will have established structure, range, and scale." Few persons know, indeed, how many intricacies enter into the solution of these questions and provide hundreds of occasions for subjective judgments. A few examples: The last note of a section or even of the melody is not always the structural "final" note (*tonus finalis*). In a style in which the metric system is based on syllable count, the number of syllables does not always correspond to the number of the structurally essential syllables. Sometimes certain sections or portions of the melody are repeated; we have to determine whether these are STRUCTURALLY ESSENTIAL repeats (that is, whether they are independent portions which enter into the structural form) or nothing but casual or playful *ad hoc* repeats. A melody in rigid dance rhythm is sometimes performed in free *parlando-rubato* rhythm, but it should, nevertheless, be grouped as if it were in rigid rhythm. Sometimes it is difficult even to determine the boundaries of a single section.

There certainly are established rules and a tradition for deciding these issues, but they are not always applicable. There, again, we must turn to subjective judgment for aid. Needless to say, on these questions the difference of opinion between scholars is even greater than on those of a purely technical nature.

VARIABILITY IN FOLK MUSIC

I want to call the reader's attention to one of the most conspicuous features of folk music, namely, its continuous variability. This has been said so often that it has almost become a truism. Nevertheless, since laymen still persist in believing that folk melodies are something rigidly established and unchangeable, it is pertinent to stress over and over again the fallacy of this belief.

Some linguists assert that each uttered sound of speech is a unique phenomenon which has never occurred in the past and will never occur again in the future. At first hearing, this seems to be a bewildering statement. However, one will be more inclined to take it as an evident fact if one considers a parallel and more obvious phenomenon which does not even need to be proved; everyone will agree that each individual of every living species of animals or plants is a unique phenomenon. The same is true concerning folk melodies—a given performance of a folk melody has never occurred before and will never occur again in exactly the same way. We must not say or think that a folk melody is what it appears to be in a given performance; all we can say is that THEN AND THERE, AT THE TIME OF THAT PERFORMANCE, it proved to be such.

Some believe that the essential difference between art music and folk music is the continuous variability of folk music as against the rigid stability of art music. I agree with this statement, but with a qualification: the difference is not one of contrast, but one of degree—that is, the performance of folk music shows an almost absolute variability, while art music varies in a far lesser, sometimes in only an infinitesimal degree. We must realize that even performances of the same work of art music by the same performer will never occur twice in absolutely the same way. Of course, the NOTES of art music—because of their fixation by notation —must never be changed, whereas in folk music even notes are subject to change. And yet, if we reconsider well the first part of this statement, we see that even some of the notes in art music are subject to change: I mean the particles of embellishments (notes of trills and the like).

This eternal changeableness gives life to music, be it folk or art music, whether the changes are considerable or scarcely perceptible. These intrinsic characteristics of music seem to be in contradiction with the contemporary trend of producing music more and more by mechanical means, according to which music would be compressed into a frozen and never-changing form.

In closing these introductory remarks, may I point out to the reader once more their leading idea: that although perfection cannot be attained in transcribing and classifying folk music, we must always endeavor to approach an ideal of perfection, an ideal which in itself is still but dimly perceived. We should never tire of improving and changing our methods of work in order to accomplish this task as well as is humanly possible.

Morphology of the Serbo-Croatian Vocal Folk Melodies

SEVENTY-FIVE "women's songs" (in Serbo-Croatian, *ženske pjesme*) are published in this book in fifty-four variant groups.[1] With few exceptions, no selection has been made, could not even be attempted since when the material was compiled for this publication the remaining one hundred(approximately)[2] songs were not yet transcribed.

What are "women's songs" in Serbo-Croatian folk poetry? Almost all songs except the "heroic poems" (called also "*gusle* songs," because they are to be performed with the accompaniment of the one-stringed *gusle*). They are sung without instrumental accompaniment and as a rule, though not invariably, by women, hence the designation.[3] The text of most of these songs consists of ten-syllable lines, although lines of seven, eight, nine, and more than ten syllables may also occur. As to their subject matter, they have lyric or ballad texts, the latter generally with ten-syllable text lines. There are, however, a few "ballads" among the women's songs of our collection which have eight-syllable lines and a peculiar stanza structure (Nos. 20, 34–36; see pp. 65–66). It is not quite certain whether these should be regarded as women's songs, for they were all sung by men and are distinguished from the bulk of the women's songs by their strange stanza structure.[4] Some of the "women's songs" were sung with instrumental accompaniment (with *tambura:* music examples 27a, 44b, 39b, and even with *gusle*, examples 7, 34). The singers are, however, in all these cases, men.

[1] Referred to by number and letter, the letters indicating variants of a given basic melody.

[2] There are, in addition, about thirty songs sung by an old woman (*Đula Dizdarević*) whose performance was not reliable concerning pitch and could not be studied for musico-scientific purposes.

[3] We do not know whether this designation is of rural origin, or whether it has been introduced by the early Yugoslav scholars. See Part Two, pp. 247–249.

[4] For more details on this subject, see p. 254.

Morphology

COMPARISON OF THE MATERIAL PUBLISHED IN THIS BOOK WITH SOME OTHER AVAILABLE MATERIAL

Seventy-five melodies are a rather limited number. They would give a somewhat narrow view of the Serbo-Croatian folk melodies if published without any reference to other Serbo-Croatian material. Therefore, I deem it necessary to include a general survey of the most important published collections of Serbo-Croatian folk melodies as a background and to treat the pieces of the Parry Collection against this background. Fortunately, the main published collections of Serbo-Croatian folk melodies, the grouping of which I began some years ago when still in Europe and concluded in the United States, were at my disposal. Some unpublished melodies from a collection made by L. Kuba and some from my own collection have been added to the printed ones.

The following collections have been incorporated into this survey.

PUBLISHED COLLECTIONS

1. Bosiljevac, Š. *Album bosansko-hercegovačkih pjesama* (Folk Songs from Bosnia and Hercegovina). Zagreb, St. Kugli. Fifty melodies. Cited as "Bosiljevac."[5]
2. Bušetić, Todor. "Srpske narodne pesme i igre s melodijama iz Levča" (Folk Songs and Folk Dances from Levač). Beograd, 1902. *Srpski Etnografski Zbornik,* III. Eighty-eight melodies. Cited as "Iz Levača."
3. Đorđević, Vladimir. *Srpske narodne melodije; Južna Srbija* (Serbian Folk Melodies; Southern Serbia). Skoplje, 1928. Four hundred and twenty-eight melodies. Cited as "Juž. Srb."
4. —— *Srpske narodne melodije* (*Predratna Srbija*) (Serbian Folk Melodies from Prewar Serbia). Beograd, 1931. Six hundred melodies. Cited as "Đorđević."
5. ——*Narodna pevanka* (Folk Song Book). Beograd, 1926. Approximately three hundred and eight melodies. Cited as "Đorđević Nar. Pev."
6. Kačerovski, B. *U kolo* (Round Dance). Sarajevo, J. Studnička & Co. Eighty-seven melodies. Cited as "Kačerovski."
7. Kuba, Ludvík. "Pjesme i napjevi iz Bosne i Hercegovine" (Songs and Melodies from Bosnia and Hercegovina), *Glasnik Zemaljskog Muzeja u Bosni i Hercegovini,* XVIII (1906), 183 ff., 354 ff., 499 ff.; XIX (1907), 103 ff., 273

[5] Citations are always by the number of the melody, except item 5; for this latter work page citation had to be used, the melodies not being numbered there.

ff., 405 ff., 629 ff.; XXI (1909), 303 ff., 581 ff.; XXII (1910), 513 ff.; Sarajevo. Nine hundred and sixty-five melodies. Cited as "Kuba, B. H."

8. —— "Slovanstvo ve svých zpěvech" (The Slavs in Their Folk Songs). Pardubice, Poděbrady, Praha, 1884–1929. Vol. IX, sixty-four Croatian melodies; Vol. X, sixty-one Dalmatian melodies; Vol. XI, seventy-one Montenegrin melodies; Vol. XII, sixty Serbian melodies; Vol. XIII, sixty Bosnian and Hercegovinian melodies; Vol. XIV, thirty-one melodies from "Old" Serbia (that is, the southern part of Serbia [north of Macedonia]). Cited as "Kuba IX," and so forth.
9. Kuhač, Fr. Š. *Južno–slovenske narodne popievke* (Yugoslav Folk Songs). Zagreb, 1878–1881. One thousand six hundred and twenty-eight melodies. Cited as "Kuhač."
10. Manojlović, Kosta. "Muzičke karakteristike našega juga" (The Musical Characteristics of Our South), *Sv. Cecilija* (Zagreb), V (1925), 138 ff.; VI (1925), 174 ff. Approximately twenty melodies. Cited as "Manojlović."

MANUSCRIPT COLLECTIONS

11. Kuba, Ludvík. The continuation of "Pjesme i napjevi iz Bosne i Hercegovine" (Songs and Melodies from Bosnia and Hercegovina), not published in *Glasnik Zemaljskog Muzeja u Bosni i Hercegovini*, going from No. 966 to No. 1125. One hundred and sixty melodies. Cited as "Kuba, B. H., *MS*." in Tab. of Mat., otherwise without *MS*.
12. Bartók, Béla "Serbian Folksongs from the Counties of Torontal and Temeš" (in prewar Hungary, now Rumania). Five melodies. Cited as "Bartók." Published in Appendix II, below.

The data on published collections are mostly in accordance with the statements of the semiofficial bibliography of Serbo-Croatian folk music, in *Folk. mus.* (pp. 210 ff.) Item 4, however, has been omitted there, apparently by an oversight, although it is one of the most important collections of Serbo-Croatian folk melodies; the numerical indications of the respective volumes in item 8 are missing; and different numbers of melodies are given for items 4, 8, and 9; in items 1, 6, and 10 no figures are given for the number of melodies. The only Kačerovski publication mentioned in *Folk. mus.* has as title *Bosanske sevdalinke za klavir;* we are not sure whether it is identical with his *U kolo*. As to Manojlović, it is uncertain whether the publication used by me is identical with the one cited in *Folk. mus.* as *Muzičke karakteristike našega juga*.

There is a large collection not included in the material as enumerated above, although it has been at my disposal, that is, Dr. Vinko Žganec, *Hrvatske pučke popijevke iz Međumurja* (Croatian Folk Melodies from the area between the Rivers Mura and Drava, at their confluence), Zagreb, 1924. I had well-weighed reasons for the omission. This area consists of about three hundred square miles, formerly belonging to Hungary proper. The material collected there by Dr. Žganec, 638 melodies, a rather considerable number for such a small area, shows an overwhelming Hungarian influence—about two-thirds of them are borrowings from the so-called "Old" and "New" Hungarian musical stock (as I pointed out in "La Musique populaire des Hongrois et des peuples voisins," in *Archivum Europae Centro-Orientalis*, Budapest, 1936); and even the remaining one-third have a more or less international (or more correctly "inter-Central-East European") character. Therefore I prefer for the time being to exclude them from the above detailed material; they would only add many foreign traits to the Serbo-Croatian stock and would change the proportion between autochthonous and foreign components too much in disfavor of the former.

As to the material enumerated under items 1–10, I had to leave out (*a*) the few instrumental pieces contained in some of the publications; (*b*) the melodies deriving from territories outside Serbo-Croatia (that is, the Slovenian[6] and the Bulgarian melodies in item 9); (*c*) the Macedonian melodies deriving from an area which is clearly marked as Bulgarian, ethnically as well as linguistically, on maps dating before 1914[7] (most of items 3 and 10, and some of 5 belong to this category); (*d*) melodies of lower art music (urban music of a certain artificial kind which never could have been sung by rural people), to be found mostly in item 9.

A number of songs are not Kuhač's own collection, but are taken from older manuscripts or printed collections. Some of the same sources are used in item 5, thus it happens that the same melody appears in

[6] Serbian and Croatian are practically the same language; the two designations are due to historic reasons, and signify political, religious, and cultural differences. The Serbs adopted the Greek Orthodox religion, the Cyrillic alphabet, and a cultural orientation towards the south-east; the Croats, the Roman Catholic religion, the Latin alphabet, and a cultural orientation toward the west. The Slovenian language, however, is unanimously regarded as an independent language by linguists, though closely related to the Serbo-Croatian.

[7] There are differences of opinion regarding the language of this area, the Serbo-Croats asserting that it is an archaic form of Serbo-Croatian, the Bulgarians declaring it a Bulgarian dialect. Two facts, however, seem to be clear to neutral observers: first, that it is not Serbo-Croatian; second, that it is closer to the Bulgarian than to the Serbo-Croatian language.

different publications and in exactly the same notation.[8] Most of the melodies in Kuba XIII are published in item 7 as well. We find in item 5 some melodies of (the later published) item 4. These duplicate melodies will, of course, count as single ones.

Having made these exclusions, the following number of melodies remain for our purposes: 49 in item 1; 75 in item 2; 30 in item 3; 560 in item 4; 143 in item 5; 50 in item 6; 1,116 in items 7 and 11; 255 in item 8; 1,162 in item 9; 4 in item 10; 5 in item 12; total, 3,449.[9]

A "Tabulation" of this material has been made, containing in the first column the current number in the grouped material, in the second the number in the original edition, and in the remaining columns, the respective symbols. The "Tabulation" appears in the second volume of the present publication. Hereafter the "Tabulation" will be referred to as "Tab. of Mat."

Materials not available to me were, according to *Folk. mus.*, as follows.

PRINTED MATERIAL

Širola, B., and M. Gavazzi. "Obredne popijevke" (Ceremonial Songs). *Narodna Starina,* Vol. XXV. Zagreb, 1931. Twenty-six melodies.[10]

Kuba, L. "Narodna glazbena umjetnost u Dalmaciji" (Folk Music in Dalmatia). *Zbornik za Narodni Život i Običaje Južnih Slavena,* Vol. III–IV. Zagreb, 1898, 1899.[11]

Dobronić, A. "Ojkanje." *Zbornik . . . ,* Vol. XX, pp. 1–25. Zagreb, 1915.

Catinelli-Bevilacqua-Obradović, *Juzno slavjanske pučke pesme* (Folk Songs of the South Slavs), Beč, 1849. Twenty-five melodies.

Stanković, K. *Srbske narodne pesme* (Serbian Folk Songs), Beč, 1862. Twelve melodies.

Some other titles are cited without the number of melodies; some of the melodies in these collections have been reprinted, however, in items 5 and 10.

[8] Kuhač even had the misfortune to publish unintentionally one of his songs twice—in two different places and with two different numbers (Nos. 851 and 871).

[9] All this material will be referred to as "published material," for brevity's sake, although 11 and 12 are still in manuscript.

[10] This is, however, not mentioned in *Folk. mus.*

[11] Only the second part of this article was at my disposal, therefore, I could not include its melodies in the list of Published Material. Besides, some of them are included in Kuba X. The others, not included anywhere, represent such important data that I could not disregard them. The article will be quoted later as "N. g. u. D." (see p. 61).

UNPUBLISHED MATERIAL

There are about 2,900 melodies in various, probably private, depositories.[12] Therefore it can be stated that our material for comparison comprises little less than half of all melodies existing in notation.

Items 1 and 6 are rather amateurish publications, which have no scientific claims at all. The most important publications are items 9 (Kuhač), 7 and 8 (Kuba), and 3 and 4 (Đorđević).

The oldest of these is Kuhač's collection, made probably in the sixties and seventies of the nineteenth century. He seems to be rather mediocre as a transcriber of melodies and as an observer. In addition, he could not resist the then prevailing fashion of publishing many hundreds of folk melodies with piano accompaniment—sheer waste of time and space, even if the accompaniment were better than it is. The customs of his time may be his excuse, although his Czech contemporaries K. J. Erben, Fr. Sušil, E. Peck, and Fr. Bartoš, whose works Kuhač as a Slav should have known, rejected this nonsensical method. Their publications are on a much higher level than that of Kuhač in every respect.

The next explorer, in chronological order, is L. Kuba, a Czech painter and well-trained musician, who did his research work on Serbo-Croatian territory around the turn of the century. His work towers high above that of Kuhač, and his contribution of ca. 1,400 melodies to the stock of collected Serbo-Croatian folk music material is indeed invaluable, in spite of some idiosyncrasies in his notation. He has a keen sense of observation for certain very characteristic phenomena which almost entirely escaped the attention of Kuhač (line or syllable interruption, "swallowing" the last syllable of a line). In his largest publication, published in Sarajevo (without his consent and collaboration, he says), he tried to group the material on the basis of musical features; in this case, on the basis of scale structures. This material consists of 1,125 melodies, 965 of which have been published. The remaining 160 melodies are still in manuscript. These

[12] There are rumors that unpublished material collected by Kuhač exists somewhere and that it is almost as extensive as the published collection. The *Folk. mus.* gives the following rather obscure information on this question (p. 204): "Fr. Kuhač a recueilli un nombre imposant d'airs populaires: ses œuvres complètes publiées en partie seulement sont si nombreuses—leur seule énumération remplirait une brochure—que leur publication intégrale constituerait un corpus de quelque 8,500 pages, grand in –8, sans compter les 3,700 pp. in folio de ses sept livres *in folio* (dont 4 publiés) de la Collection *Južnoslovenske Narodne Popievke.*" This would mean about 1,200 unpublished melodies.

he kindly placed at my disposal in the summer of 1938 by sending me a copy thereof in his own handwriting.

Đorđević, who made his research apparently in the first decades of the twentieth century, obtained excellent results. His collections, items 3 and 4, seem to be the best publications so far. The very short collection by Manojlović is approximately on the same level. Item 5, of Đorđević, however, seems to have been intended for the general public and therefore complies less with scientific demands than do the other two.

The modest publication by Bušetić is on the whole good, in spite of the indirect transcription of the melodies. He was not a musician; he learned the melodies from the peasants and later asked a musician (Mokranjac) to do the notation from his own singing.

In all these publications names and data concerning singers, dates of notation (with rare exceptions), and so forth are completely missing. Some of them (items 1, 5, and 6) do not even give the names of the villages from which the melodies are derived. All these circumstances, as well as the fact that the notations therein were made by ear alone, must be kept in mind when evaluating their reliability.

SYMBOLS AND FORMULAS

Before being grouped, melodies shall be brought to a common denominator. For this purpose they will be transposed in such a way that they get a common *tonus finalis* (final tone). As such, g^1 appears to be the most suitable (see p. 13).

To facilitate the grouping work, the following system of symbols has been devised.

1. For scale degrees:

have as corresponding symbols:

Accidentals will be placed before the symbol ($\flat 3 = b^1\flat$). Auxiliary symbols for designation of caesura (the original conception of caesura, that is, the point between melody sections,[13] will be extended to cover the final note of a given melody section, except, of course, the last one):

[13] A portion of a melody corresponding to an entire text line, or to its repeated fragment or fragments (see p. 8), will be called a "melody section."

□ designates the main caesura; ⌋, the one preceding it; ⌊, the one following it. Therefore, 4⌋ [♭3] ⌊4 means a melody of four sections having c^2 for final tone in the first and third sections, b^1♭ in the second (main) section (mus. ex. No. 41); [♭3] ⌊1 means a melody of three sections having b^1♭ for final tone in the first (main) section, g^1 in the second (mus. ex. No. 18); 4⌋ [2] means a melody of three sections having c^2 for final tone in the first section, a^1 in the second (main) section (mus. ex. No. 22); [VII] means a melody of two sections having f^1 for final tone in the first section (mus. ex. No. 6). The same degree-symbols are used to designate ambitus (range); for example: *VII–4* for a range from f^1 to c^2 (mus. ex. No. 5); *1–8* for a range from g^1 to g^2 (No. 28c).

2. For syllable numbers: italicized Arabic figures, each followed by comma; *8, 5, 8, 5,* means a melody of four sections, its first and third with eight syllables, the second and fourth with five (mus. ex. No. 41). For isometric melodies (melodies with sections each having the same syllabic number, contrasting with heterometric melodies having sections of unequal syllabic number) the use of one figure will suffice. In case of the splitting of text lines (see p. 37), an additional figure in parenthesis indicates the syllabic number of the original proper text line: (*10*) *10, 6, 10, 6,* means that the text of the six-syllable melody section is a portion of the original ten-syllable text line. In some melodies one (sometimes two) of the sections is composed of two metrically equal (so to speak, "twin") parts; these will be regarded as "double" sections (that is, virtually as one section). This circumstance will be indicated in the formula by having two (equal) figures connected by the plus sign: *8, 8, 8 + 8, 8,* or *5, 8 + 8, 5,* the first one for a four-section melody with the third section double, the second formula for a three-section melody with the second section double (for instance, the melody quoted from Kuba on p. 62).

3. Similarity or difference in the content of the sections will be indicated by small-capital letters—the same letter for similar content, different letters for different content: A A B A means a four-section melody in which the first, second, and fourth sections are the same, the third different. Some special symbols used in connection with the small-capital-letter symbols are as follows.

A^5 (A^4, A^3), a fifth (fourth, third) higher than A.

A_5, a fifth lower than A

A_v, a variant of A (that is, A slightly changed)

A_s (s = *sequentia*), A one degree lower

A^s, A one degree higher.

A_s A_{ss} A_{sss}, A repeated three times in a downward sequence.

4. For isometric yet heterorhythmic melodies (heterorhythmic = of unequal rhythm; isorhythmic = of equal rhythm) small letters will be used. The same letter indicates the same rhythm; different letters, different rhythms: a a b a, a b a b, a a b c, and so forth, symbolize heterorhythmic four-section melodies.

5. For symbolizing the proportion of syllabic figures in heterometric melodies, the letter *Z* will be used in two (resp. three) sizes; *ZZ𝒁Z* indicates the metrical structure of any four-section melody in which the syllabic number of the first, second, and fourth sections is equal and lower than that of the third section. Thus, this same formula may indicate either *5, 5, 6, 5*, or *5, 5, 7, 5*, or *6, 6, 8, 6*, or *8, 8, 10, 8*, and so forth, syllabic structure; *𝒁Z𝒁*, either *10, 6, 10*, or *10, 8, 10*, or *8, 6, 8*, syllabic structure; the formula for this last type but with one double section will be: *𝒁Z + Z𝒁*. Here we shall restrict ourselves to these few examples and must refer to the "Tab. of Mat.," where the reader will find tabulated all the *Z* formulas occurring in this material.

The melodies will be grouped, successively, according to the following five principles.

(a) Determination of the sections, that is, the number of sections in each melody. It will be seen that our material has five classes: class *A*, melodies with one section; class *B*, with two sections; classes *C* and *D*, with three sections; class *E* with four sections; class *C* contains melodies with the main caesura at the end of the first section; class *D*, at the end of the second.

(b) Determination of the length, or rather the proportionate length, of the section. The length of a section is determined by the number of corresponding text syllables. We find that some of the melodies have sections of equal length (isometric structure); others have sections of unequal length (heterometric structure). On this basis we shall divide the *B*, *C*, *D*, and *E* classes each into two subclasses: I. Isometric melodies; II. Heterometric melodies.

(c) Further grouping of subclass I melodies according to the length of the section. This gives us groups in which each melody section of the song has *a*) five syllables, *b*) six syllables, *c*) seven syllables, *d*) eight syllables, *e*) nine syllables, *f*) ten syllables, *g*) eleven syllables, *h*) twelve syllables in each melody section, and so forth. (Class *A* will be divided into groups in the same way.) The groups of subclass I will be further divided according to the rhythmic structure of the sections into two subgroups: 1. isorhythmic (all sections having the same rhythm), 2. heterorhythmic (two, three, or four different rhythms for the sections). Here small letters will be used as symbols (as mentioned under Section 4 of Symbols and Formulas, p. 29). Subgroup I. 1. is further divided according to the metrical structure of the section rhythm; more natural or frequent metrical structures will precede complicated ones. For example: $4 + 4 = 8$, precedes $3 + 2 + 3 = 8$, (the latter marked in this book as 8b, [14]); $4 + 2 = 6$, precedes $2 + 4 = 6$; and so forth.[15] Subgroup I. 2., is divided according to the small letter formulas, and after having established for the latter a certain order of succession: a a b a, a a a b; a a b b, a b a b, a b b a; a a b c, a b a c, a b c b. The grouping of subclass II is a much more complicated task. It follows the proportionate length of each section. In order to facilitate the procedure we will use the Z symbols (as mentioned under Section 5 of Symbols and Formulas, p. 29), the heterometric melodies will be grouped according to their formulas. The order of the formulas is to be seen in the "Tab. of Mat.," pp. 39–50, 56–79, 103–135. Melodies with identical Z formulas will be grouped according to the first syllabic number and then the second: *5, 5, 6, 5,* will be placed before *5, 5, 7, 5,*; this before *6, 6, 7, 6,* and so forth.

(d) Divisions and subdivisions of the subgroups are formed according to the final tone of each section (caesura), the number and bracket symbols (shown under section 1 of "Symbols and Formulas," pp. 27–28) being used in this connection. The order of succession is determined by the following rules: (*a*) the lower tone will precede the higher; (*b*) melodies are grouped first according to the final tone of the ☐ (that is, main) caesura (this gives us divisions), then according to that of the preceding], and finally to that of the following [caesura (these give us subdivisions). For example: 2] [1] [2 (mus. ex. No. 40) is placed before 4] [♭3] [4 (No. 41).

[14] *b* stands here for "Bulgarian," since this metrical structure is very characteristic for Bulgarian folk-poem texts.

[15] Throughout this book, and in the tables also, an arabic numeral with a comma after it is used consistently as the symbol for the syllable number of a metric line.

(e) If in a subdivision several melodies show identical symbols, they are grouped, according to their range, into "families." Therefore *VII-♭3* comes before *VII-4*, and the latter before *VII-5* (or *6*); but *VII-4* (or *-5*, or *-6*) comes before *1-2* (or *-♭3*). Should "families" with identical symbols (including range symbols) appear, their order will be arranged according to the circumstances, since so far no systematic method for these has been established. It would lead too far afield to give detailed indications about these; it may suffice to mention two of them. In this material melodies with more lower tones are placed before those with fewer lower tones. For certain types of melodies in another collection, that is, in my "Rumanian Folk Music", a more complicated system was devised.[16]

PROBLEMS CONNECTED WITH GROUPING

1. The Serbo-Croatians use 5, 6, 7, 8, 9, 10, 11, 12, 13, and 14 syllabic text lines proper. It is not difficult to recognize and determine them. Two questions, however, arise. The first concerns the thirteen-syllable line. Shall we consider it as a single line, or as two lines, that is, *8, 5,*? Disregarding the melody, these thirteen syllables constitute metrically without any doubt one single line. Their melodies, and analogies in the comparable material of some north Central-Eastern European peoples, lead us to divide such lines, when applied to melodies, into two lines; for example, *8, 5,*.[17] To quote an example, the most frequent melody-stanza structure connected with such a line is *8, 5, 8, 5,* (some others are *8, 5,* □ and *8, 5, 5,* □ [); yet not more than one *13,*] □ [(= [*8* + *5*] × 4) stanza structure exists in the Serbo-Croatian material.[18] The other question concerns what shall be regarded as one text line when parts of the text lines are repeated, for example, when the ten-syllable line appears

[16] See the respective melody groups in Vol. II of said collection, Nos. 53–134, and also the respective description of the system.

[17] In publications consisting only of texts, in which texts are stripped from their melodies (as, for instance, in Part Two of this book) such lines may be either unbroken, as thirteen-syllable lines, or broken up into two lines, one eight-syllable and one five-syllable line.

[18] "Tab. of Mat." 1354 (Kuba IX, 2). In the Hungarian material, apart from *8, 5,* and *8, 6,* text lines, there are real thirteen- and fourteen-syllable text lines, four of them forming a thirteen (or fourteen)] □ [melody-stanza structure. A 4 × *14* syllable stanza structure is represented by six melodies in the Serbo-Croatian material: Tab. of Mat. 1355 (Kuhač 1122), 1356 (Kuhač 1385), 1358a. (Iz Levča 22), 1361 (Kačerovski 6), 1363 (Kuhač 86), 1364 (Kuba XIV, 17).

in a fourteen-syllable form as a result of a repeat of its first four syllables? We shall regard these fourteen syllables as two lines (*8*, *6*,), the first of them formed by the repeated first four syllables of the original dekasyllabic line, and the second by the remaining fifth to tenth syllables.

2. The next problem concerns the occasional text refrain syllables.[19] What shall be regarded as a text refrain? The application of the generally known definition, "recurring phrase or line especially at the end of stanzas," will not be satisfactory if we have to decide what shall be the lower limit of the number of refrain syllables. Three kinds of refrains exist: the content has a certain relation to the content of the text lines proper; the content has no relation to them, yet has a definite sense; the refrain has no recognizable sense at all. The length of types 1 and 2 will generally be not too restricted; type 3, however, may present as short a form as one-syllable or two-syllable words. According to my opinion, a limit must be set: one syllable added in the guise of a refrain should never be called a refrain; two syllables having the same function may or may not be a refrain, according to the given situation.

Syllables of refrains, or of additions in the guise of a refrain, although they do not belong to the text lines proper, are an essential part of the text and are to be included in the syllable count of the text. This will not be the case with nonessential additions of one or two (sometimes even more) syllables; they are "nonessential" because their use is most frequently not constant, though in some cases they may appear as such. Thus, they are not to be counted when establishing the syllable number of the sections. The most common of the nonessential syllable additions, and very easily recognizable as such, is the interjection *Ej* (*Hej*, *Aj*, *Haj*, *Oj*, *Hoj*) at the beginning of a line, for example: ♩ ♩ (Mi-la) is changed into ♩ ♫ (Aj, mi-la)[20] (music example No. 9, 1st St., 2d section).[21] More difficulty is caused by other, generally two-syllable, additions, put into various places (end of a line or between the metrical parts of a line). These are very characteristic of the Serbo-Croatian and Bulgarian folk songs. The most common are the following three: *more* (interjection having no specific

[19] About Serbo-Croatian refrains see more details in *Rumanian Folk Music,* Vol. III, lxxix–lxxxi and 625–640. [See also Appendix III, below.]

[20] It is frequently used in Slovak folk songs; somewhat less frequently in some types of Hungarian folk songs; even less often in Rumanian; and very rarely in Turkish material. In this publication these additional syllables are marked by the sign ⌴.

[21] Our music example No. 31d presents a very strange case: the repeat of the first essential text syllable is substituted for *Oj* (*Ru-*, *ružnu* instead of *Oj*, *ružnu,* and so forth).

sense), *aman* (Turkish, "mercy, favor"), *džanum* (from *canĭm*, Turkish, "my soul"). It is not always easy to decide whether they are really nonessential additions or not. We shall consider them nonessential when they appear, so to speak, cursorily, in a more or less hurried way, on comparatively short tone values; especially when transforming an original ♩♩ into ♫ ♩ 𝅗𝅥 (– –, dža-num), and the like. When, however, they appear on heavy tones of longer values, in repeats or cumulation (that is, when the corresponding part of the melody seems to be an integral portion of the melody), then they are to be regarded as essential syllables. In the first case their use is more or less inconstant; they may be dropped from the following stanzas and reappear again. In the second case their constancy elevates them to the rank of a refrain.

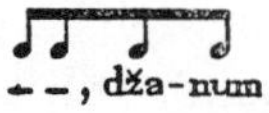

3. Is the succession of the various points of view, based on the supposed importance of the various aspects of the melodies and indicated on pp. 15–16, completely satisfactory? So far I have accepted it as satisfactory, otherwise I should have chosen a different one. What I want to point out is this: perhaps later investigators will discover some other points of view or will give a different interpretation to the degree of importance of the already established aspects. The range, for example, as an aspect of the melodies, is placed here at the very end of the rank. However, there are a certain number of melodies of a rather limited range (*VII–1*, *VII–♭2*, *VII–2*, *1–2*, *1–♭3*) which seem to be in very close relation to each other, although their features established on the basis of the remaining aspects are rather different (see pp. 52–54). One would almost be tempted to separate them from the rest of the melodies and treat them as a special class. This procedure, however, would destroy the unity of the grouping system, that is, would intermingle two contradictory systems. Besides, the transition from these narrow range melodies to those with wider range is not at all sharp; the separating of the former from the latter would be arbitrary in many instances.

4. Instead of dividing the melodies into two-, three-, and four-section melody classes, and then these single classes into isometric and heterometric subclasses, one could first divide them into an isometric and a heterometric class and then divide the two classes into two-, three-, and four-section melody subclasses. This order of succession would also be justifiable.

5. The last problem concerns the occurrence of repetition of given sections in the melody. We must determine whether the repeat is an

essential structural feature (A A), or whether it is but a result of some individual whim. In many instances it is not so easy to determine this. Sometimes wearisome comparisons with related melodies will lead to the right decision; sometimes tradition will give valuable indications.

6. Finally I must mention in this chapter a negative feature, the absence of scale aspect as a determining factor in the grouping system. Many people who attribute great importance to this factor will be surprised by the statement that it cannot be used at all as such in the Serbo-Croatian material, as well as in some other Eastern European material, because of its inconstancy. The pitch of certain degrees, especially that of a^1 and b^1, is subject to such fluctuation, even in the performance of a single person, that sometimes it is impossible to determine whether the scale purports to be a minor or a major scale. Neutral degrees are abundant; they themselves may be fluctuating in intonation. Variant groups representing three or four different scales are frequently found.[22] Besides, the overwhelming majority of the Serbo-Croatian material shows only scale fragments, that is, a pentachord or tetrachord or even less, due to the very restricted range of the majority of the melodies (see pp. 52ff.). For instance, what kind of scale could a "scale" of g^1 $a^1\flat$ degrees be called![23] All this does not mean that aspects of the scale should not be investigated; it means it cannot well serve for grouping purposes. More important than scale is the relation between range and final tone, for example, a range of *VII–4*, with main accents on the f^1, $a^1(\flat)$, and c^2 tones and with final tone g^1, is very characteristic of Serbo-Croatian and Bulgarian folk music (see pp. 52–53).

GENERAL CHARACTERISTICS OF THE SERBO-CROATIAN FOLK SONGS

STANZA STRUCTURE IN THE TEXTS

When we proceed from Slovakia[24] and Hungary toward the southeast, that is, to Rumania, we perceive a rather peculiar change. The texts of folk

[22] "Tab. of Mat." No. 123 has in the l. variant (Đorđ. 173) f^1 g^1 a^1 $b^1\flat$, in m. (Đorđ. 153) f^1 g^1 $a^1\flat$ $b^1\flat$, in o. (Đorđ. 301) $f^1\sharp$ g^1 a^1 $b^1\flat$, in v. (Iz Levča 72) g^1 a^1 $b^1\flat$ $c^2(\sharp)$ d^2.

[23] In grouping the folk-song material of some other peoples, for example, the Hungarians, the scale aspect may become a determining factor in some cases, though even then it will be less important than the range aspect.

[24] Here and in the following text, "Slovakia" stands for "Slovakia and Moravia," for brevity's sake (Moravia is situated between Bohemia and Slovakia); "Rumania" stands only for

songs in the first-mentioned two countries present almost without exception[25] decided stanza structure (that is, a more or less symmetrical, recurring structure of two, three, or four text lines) connected with the use of rhymes; the text stanzas are predominantly composed of four lines, corresponding to the four sections of the melody; a substantial part of those melodies which are not sung except on special occasions (weddings, harvests, and so forth) have no special group features.[26] In Rumania, suddenly, the text-stanza structure disappears (except in songs of urban or semirural origin) though rhymes are still in use; the four-section melody structure is not predominant, since a rather important part of the material has a three-section and a not negligible part a two-section structure; the melodies divide into primary classes according to the different occasions at which they are sung, each of these primary classes having their specific musical characteristics.[27] Going farther south, that is, to Bulgarian and Serbo-Croatian territory, we find again unequivocal changes: no more text-stanza structures and no rhymes (except in songs of urban or semirural origin); two-thirds of the Serbo-Croatian melodies have two-section or three-section structures, much of the remaining third—with four-section structures—is of urban, semirural, or foreign origin. Here, as against the Rumanian material, no primary musical classes would result from a grouping of the melodies according to their function. All melodies, however, have stanza structure. When we use the expression "text stanzas" or "absence of text stanzas," we refer to the form of the texts stripped from the melody. If the lines of the song text keep a symmetrical, recurring arrangement, then obviously there exists a text stanza structure (which generally tallies with the melody stanza). But if, stripped from their melodies, they present no regular arrangement and only structurally independent text lines remain, it would be senseless to call them text stanzas. In the latter case the single text lines will be adapted to the

those parts of that country which belonged to Hungary before the first World War. The folk music material of this region is fairly well known from various publications, whereas the very rich material of the remaining sections of the country is stored on records, for the time being, in various museums of Rumania, not having been published yet (with very few exceptions).

[25] As an exception, the texts to the Hungarian mourning songs may be mentioned: improvisations based on certain patterns with text lines being rather in prose or reminding us of free-verse structure, having no rhymes at all.

[26] At variance with this rule, the melodies of the Hungarian mourning songs, children's plays, and winter-solstice songs, as well as of the Slovakian children's plays and some harvest songs, and so forth, have distinctive characteristics.

[27] Songs performed on certain occasions will be called "Ceremonial."

melody stanzas in various ways, being originally probably only one text line in various forms of repeats to a given melody stanza.

All folk poetry of Western Europe, Slovakia, Hungary, and perhaps Ukrainia has texts in stanza structure; absence of text-stanza structures is, however, characteristic of Rumanian, Serbo-Croatian, and Bulgarian folk poetry.[28] The folk song editors of the latter peoples clearly perceived this phenomenon and accordingly published their text material, when stripped from the melodies, without breaking it up by stanza subdivisions. The first impression created by these facts is that text stanza structures originated in Western Europe, perhaps in its urban poetry, and then spread gradually towards the East, pervading Slovakia and Hungary, and that absence of text-stanza structure has its origin in the Near East, perhaps in the ancient Greek folk poetry (as for instance in the ancient Greek heroic poems). Such an assumption, however, is at variance with the result of investigations in Turkey. My rather short research work in middle and southern Asia Minor and that of others has shown that the Turkish folk poetry knows no other form but a very definite text-stanza structure, with rhymes and generally with four-line stanzas. This obviously could not be ascribed to Western European influence; evidently it belongs to the nature of the ancient Turkish folk poetry of central Asia. Therefore the Hungarian text-stanza structure of the so-called "Old" Hungarian melodies may not be considered as of Western European origin; it is, indeed, a remainder of Old Turkish cultural influence.[29]

It remains an open question for the time being whether the absence of text-stanza structures in the folk poetry of the above-mentioned peoples has its origin in the ancient Greek folk poetry or in some other sources.

MELODY-STANZA STRUCTURES

As has been pointed out, almost three fifths[30] of the Serbo-Croatian material belong to the two-section and three-section melody class. Com-

[28] This is probably true concerning Greek and Great-Russian folk poetry, too.

[29] Hungarian folk poetry has also some other traits in common with Turkish folk poetry; the whole old stock of the Hungarian melodies originates from an old Turkish musical culture of central Asia, as recent discoveries prove. See B. Bartók, ***Turkish Folk Music from Asia Minor*** (New Jersey: Princeton University Press, 1976), pp. 38–41, 196, 200–202, 204–208, 211–212).

[30] Ca. 2,000 (ca. 1,200 two-section and ca. 800 three-section melodies) out of ca. 3,450.

ing from Hungary and Slovakia, we carry with us the idea that two-section or three-section melodies are generally fragments of some known or unknown four-section melodies; this seems to be justified by the comparative rarity of these shorter structures there and because investigations based on comparison within the material show that some of them ARE IN FACT fragments of longer structures. This assumption cannot be maintained when we get farther to the southeast, especially to Serbo-Croatian (and Bulgarian) territory. Even there we may find that shorter forms are fragments of longer ones; the great bulk of the two-section and especially of the three-section melodies, however, are evidently independent formations. In dealing with this question we run into some difficulties. For instance, repeats of both sections of a two-section melody or of only one of them are frequent. If we regard these as structurally essential repeats, then the melody in question will have to be considered as a four-section or three-section melody. Comparisons and analogies may guide us in deciding this question.

Isometric structures are overwhelmingly common in the Hungarian folk melodies, in both the so-called "Old" and the "New" styles (in the latter, original isometry is frequently transformed into heterometry). The same is true regarding Rumanian folk melodies, except the so-called *Colinde* (winter-solstice songs)—and some melody structures of the Banat area adjoining the Serbo-Croatian territory to the north. The apparently oldest part of the Slovak melodies and the Turkish melodies have the same trend. The Serbo-Croatian melodies, however, have a leaning toward heterometric forms; as a matter of fact, the structures most characteristic for Serbo-Croatian folk melodies are heterometric. This trait, among others, draws a sharp line between the autochthonous melody classes of the Hungarians, Rumanians, and Turks on the one hand and the Serbo-Croatians on the other. And it is this trait which is in innermost connection with a most peculiar treatment of the text lines—the splitting of the isometric text lines in order to make them applicable to heterometric melody stanzas.[31] A similar phenomenon has not yet been observed elsewhere, or only sporadically, as far as I know, except in the Bulgarian material which has many traits in common with the Serbo-Croatian.[32]

[31] This feature has been already observed and mentioned as an outstanding characteristic by B. Širola in his article in *Zenei Lexikon* ("Music Lexicon"), Budapest, 1931, under *Szerb-horvát-szlavon zene* ("Serbo-Croatian and Slovenian Music"), Pt. II, p. 557, col. 2. Incidentally, there are cases in which line fragments are applied to isometric melody stanzas, too.

[32] A sharp line can hardly be drawn between the folk music of these two peoples.

Before describing this most important characteristic *in extenso*, I must give a short survey of the metrical peculiarities of the various text lines. Serbo-Croatian and Bulgarian folk poetry (as well as Hungarian, Slovak, Ukrainian, Turkish, and, in a different way, Rumanian[33]) uses text lines having metrical attributes which are based on the recurrence of syllable groups as metrical units, according to fixed schemata; the first syllable of these units always bears a verse accent which DOES NOT NECESSARILY TALLY with the spoken word accent. This syllabic verse structure completely disregards the natural or positional length of the syllables. A SPECIAL FEATURE IS THE ABSENCE OF UPBEATS.[34]

The main schemata are as shown on page 39. The order of the syllable-group schemata in each section (marked with *a*), *b*), and so forth) indicates their frequency, proceeding from the more frequent ones to the less frequent.

There are rarely more than fourteen syllables; when found at all, they are usually in urban texts.

According to Dr. R. Jakobson's investigations[35] there are certain rules concerning the metrical structure of the dekasyllabic line in the Serbo-Croatian heroic poem, *4* || *4* | *2*, g)1. The principal rule deduced by him states: the main caesura never divides a word (that is, the fourth syllable of the line must be the last syllable of a word and the fifth of a line the first of a word). The secondary caesura (after the eighth syllable) does not follow any rule in the cutting of words, although the corresponding musical section has a *4* + *2* structure almost without exception. This Jakobson rule applies on the whole to the dekasyllables of the lyrical and other texts as well, therefore, no further investigations are needed concerning these. I tried to examine, however, the simple lines b)1., c)1., d)7., e)1., e)2., f)1., h)1., and i)2. in a certain number of melodies (that is, in Đorđević and in our music examples), with the following results:

in e)1. *8* syllables = *4* || *4*, the caesura never cuts into a word (in 139 texts of Đorđević, and in 13 of our texts);

in d)1. *7* syllables = *4* || *3*, the caesura never cuts into a word (48 Đorđević, 1 of our texts);

[33] The Rumanian folk poetry shows only eight- and six-syllable text lines proper (that is, refrain text lines excluded).

[34] Some exceptional examples for upbeats exist in the Serbo-Croatian heroic poem texts and in the Rumanian material.—See also p. 80.

[35] R. Jakobson, "Über den Versbau der serbokroatischen Volkepen," *Archives Néerlandaises de Phonétique Expérimentale*, Amsterdam, 1933, Vols. VIII–IX.

Morphology

Table 1

Metric Schemes of the Lines

Simple Lines

a) *4* syllables (very rare)

b) 1. *5* syllables = *3* || *2*[a]
2. *5* syllables = *2* || *3*
3. *5* syllables = *4* || *1*

c) 1. *6* syllables = *4* || *2*
2. *6* syllables = *3* || *3*
3. *6* syllables = *2* || *4*

d) 1. *7* syllables = *4* || *3*
2. *7* syllables = *3* || *4* (rare)
3. *7* syllables = *2* | *3* || *2* (only one example: Tab. of Mat. 816)

e) 1. *8* syllables = *4* || *4*
2. *8* syllables = *3* | *2* || *3*[b]

f) 1. *9* syllables = *4* | *2* || *3* (rare)
9 syllables = *3* || *4* | *2* (rare)

g) 1. *10* syllables = *4* || *4* | *2* (very frequent)
2. *10* syllables = *4* || *3* | *3*
3. *10* syllables = *5* || *5*[c]

h) 1. *11* syllables = *4* | *4* || *3*
2. *11* syllables = *4* | *2* || *4* | *1*

i) 1. *12* syllables = *4* | *2* || *4* | *2*[d]
2. *12* syllables = *4* || *4* | *4*
3. *12* syllables = *4* | *3* || *4* | *1*

Composite Lines

j) 1. *13* syllables = *4* | *4* || *5*[e]
2. *13* syllables = *3* | *3* || *4* | *3*

k) *14* syllables = *4* | *4* || *4* | *2*

[a] The double line indicates the position of the main caesura, the single line of the secondary.
[b] The scheme *e*)2. is very frequently found in Bulgarian, less often, but still frequently, in Serbo-Croatian material.
[c] *g*)3. is, in fact, a doubled five-syllable line and becomes a ten-syllable line only if connected with such a melody-section.
[d] *i*)1. probably is a doubled six-syllable line, though this is not always discernible.
[e] Group *5* in *j*).1. may be subdivided as the five-syllable lines, *b*) 1.–3.

in h)1. *11* syllables = *4* | *4* || *3,* neither of the two caesuras cuts into a word (11 Đorđević, 3 of our texts);

in e)2. *8* syllables = *3* | *2* || *3,* the main caesura never cuts into a word, the secondary seldom.

The proportion concerning the secondary caesura is: in 71 Đorđević texts, approximately 2 percent of the text lines have a wordcut at the secondary caesura. The words in the respective text portion are mostly *2* + *3* syllable words (the musical structure remains, nevertheless, *3* + *2*); in three text lines *4* + *1* syllable, and in one single line *1* + *4* syllable words; in all five texts in our collection, neither the main nor the secondary caesura cuts into a word.

In b)1. *5,* = *3* || *2,* and c)1. *6,* = *4* || *2,* there is no prevailing rule for the placement of words, since *3* + *2, 2* + *3, 4* + *1* in b)1., and *4* + *2, 3* + *3, 2* + *4* in c)1. are intermingled without any regularity, although there is a slight tendency toward *3* + *2* in b)1., and especially toward *4* + *2* in c)1. For the remaining few formulas no positive results could be obtained because of the scarcity of examples; two f)1. *9,* = *4* || *2* | *3,* and one i)2. *12,* = *4* || *4* | *4,* which were at our disposal show no wordcuts at the caesuras.

If we extend our examination of the rules and absence of rules in the 5- to 11-syllable lines, we perceive certain parallels. The six-syllable lines seem to possess exactly the same metrical qualities as the second half of the dekasyllable (syllables 5–10); the eleven-syllable lines may be considered an extension of the *8,* = *4* || *4* syllable lines or of the seven-syllable lines; the five-syllable lines show a certain analogy with the first half of the *8,* = *3* | *2* || *3* syllable lines (although the latter has much more regularity):

<table>
<tr><td></td><td>no rule</td><td></td><td></td><td>permanent rule</td><td></td><td></td></tr>
<tr><td>10, = 4 ||</td><td>4 | 2</td><td rowspan="2">};</td><td>8, =</td><td>4 || 4</td><td rowspan="3">};</td><td>8b, = 3 | 2 || 3</td></tr>
<tr><td>6, =</td><td>4 | 2</td><td>11, =</td><td>4 | 4 || 3</td><td>5, = 3 || 2</td></tr>
<tr><td></td><td></td><td>7, =</td><td>4 || 3</td><td></td></tr>
</table>

The composite text lines of *13* (= *8* + *5*), *14* (= *8* + *6*), and *15*(*8* +*7*) syllables were examined only in our collection. The components show the same rule or irregularity as the corresponding simple lines: *8* and *7* invariably with word limit at the caesura; *5* and *6* irregular. In *13,*=*8* + *5* there is a tendency for *4* + *1* in the five-syllable part (word limit between the fourth and the fifth syllables, the fifth syllable representing a one-syllable word of a certain weight; for example, mus. ex. No. 43, melody St. 1–6). This is evidently called forth by the rhythm of the corresponding portion of the melody which is very frequently ♫♩♩ | 𝅗𝅥 ‖ .

The same rules concerning the cutting of words are observed in Bulgarian, Slovakian, Czecho-Moravian, and Ukrainian folk song texts. But if we turn to the Hungarian texts, we see that although there is a tendency toward ending words at the caesura points in seven-, eight-, and eleven-syllable lines, there are so many exceptions that we cannot assume the existence of established rules. This irregularity is still more prevalent in Turkish texts. What is the explanation of this phenomenon? One possible guess—at least concerning the *8,* = *4* || *4* lines—is that these were generally sung to *parlando-rubato* melodies, where the caesuras are less marked than in melodies with rigid rhythms. The weak point of this guess is that it does not very well apply to the *7,* = *4* || *3* and *11,* = *4* | *4* || *3* syllable lines, which are generally sung in rigid rhythm.

There remains another possible guess, a linguistic one. Both the Hungarian and the Turkish languages are agglutinative languages and therefore are apt to use comparatively longer words (especially the Turkish in its agglutinated infinitives and participles) than the inflecting Slavic languages.[36]

The Rumanian text lines, based on a somewhat different metrical system, cannot be used for comparison.

The aforementioned splitting of text lines will occur at one of the caesural points (marked with | and ||, the latter for the main caesura).[37] The separated line fragment is repeated at various places, according to the structure of the melody. Hundreds of combinations exist.[38]

The addition of refrain lines to the isometric text lines proper is another means of making the texts adaptable to heterometric melodies. This course is common and rather well known in the folk-song material of other

[36] See more details in *Turkish Folk Music,* pp. 200–201.

[37] There are rare although very curious, almost baffling exceptions: No. 446 and 1396 of "Tab. of Mat." (Kuba XI. 5, 11, Đorđević 207, 251 and Kuba XI. 19. B. H. 853, 854); the latter has: Pošeta-, | pošetala!

[38] Such line fragment repeats may well be distinguished from refrains proper. The fact that A—in our case a refrain—may be interchangeable with B—in our case the repeat of a line fragment—does not result in a development of similar features in A and B. Indeed, refrains and text-fragment repeats are actually antithetical features: the first represents never changing repetitions, the second ever changing repetitions. The use of the first involves repeats occurring not within the melody stanza but permanent during the whole piece (that is: not changing from melody stanza to melody stanza). In the first case parts of the main text operate; in the second, text parts which do not belong to the main text.

peoples, therefore I shall not dwell upon its description. Instead, I shall give a short tabulation of the combinations which are the result of text-line splitting and occur more than once. Frequently the two procedures are combined, that is, refrains are added AND the lines are split. In Table 2 schemata showing such combined procedures are also included. The table refers to the printed material and to our group of songs.

TABL

<table>
<tr><th>Syllables of the permanent text-lines</th><th>One-Section Melodies</th><th>☐ Isometric Melodies</th><th>☐ Heterometric Melodies</th><th>] ☐ Isometric Melodies</th><th>☐ [Heterometric Me</th></tr>
<tr><td>(7)</td><td>1.)
11,=4+7‖
[two]</td><td>2.)
10,=7+3|7+3‖
[five]</td><td></td><td></td><td></td></tr>
<tr><td>(8)</td><td></td><td>3.)
12,=8+4|8+4‖
[two]</td><td>6.)
12,8,=4+8|8⟧
[three]</td><td></td><td></td></tr>
<tr><td>(8b)</td><td></td><td>4.)
11,=8+3|8+3‖
[two]</td><td>7.)
6,5,=3+3|5⟧
[two]

8.)
8,5,=8|5‖
[two]

9.)
11,8,=8+3|8⟧
[four]</td><td></td><td>18.)
8,8,5,=8‖8|5⟧
[or (2r.)+3]
[two]</td></tr>
<tr><td>(10)</td><td></td><td>5.)
6,=4+2(1.–2.)|6‖
[two]</td><td>10.)
8,6,=4+4|6‖
[sixteen]

11.)
10,6,=10|6‖
[twenty-three]

12.)
7,10,=7|10⟧ (sic!)
[two]

13.)
8,10,=4+4|10‖
[five]

14.)
8,10,=4+(r.4)|10‖
[six]</td><td>17.)
6,=4+(1st r.2)⟧4+(2nd r.2)|6‖
[two]</td><td>19.)
10,10,6,=10⟧10|6⟧
[two]

20.)
8,6,6,=4+4‖6|6⟧
[twenty-nine]

21.)
8,6,6,=4+(r.4)‖6|6⟧
[two]

22.)
10,6,6,=10⟧4+(r.2)|6⟧
[two]

23.)
10,8,6,=10⟧4(1.–4.)+4(1.–4
[four]</td></tr>
<tr><td>(11)</td><td></td><td></td><td>15.)
8,7,=8|4(5.–8.)+3‖
[three]

16.)
8,7,=4+4|7⟧
[two]</td><td></td><td></td></tr>
<tr><td>Total of types</td><td>1</td><td>4</td><td>11</td><td>1</td><td>6</td></tr>
</table>

Morphology

Explanation:—The first figure (in parentheses) gives the syllable number of the (isometric) text lines. The second figure or figures (each followed by a comma) give the syllable number of the melody sections. Then follows the schema showing the treatment of the text lines, by splitting them up and repeating the fragments. The signs | or || indicate the end of the sections. The underlined figure or figures indicate the entire

ODY STANZA STRUCTURES

□ Heterometric Melodies	] □ [Isometric Melodies	] □ [Heterometric Melodies	Total of types
			2
			2
		29.) 6,5,6,5,=3+3|5||3+3|5|| [nine]	6
=4+(1st r.3)|4+(2nd r.3)||10|| [two])=10|6||10|| [thirteen] ,=4+4|6||10|| [nine]	28.) 14,=4+10|4+10||4+10|4+10|| [two]	30.) 10,10,13,13,=10|10||(r.7)+6|(r.7)+6|| [two] 31.) 8,6,8,6,=4+4|6||4+4|6|| [thirty-nine]	18
.,=8|3+3||11|| [two]		32.) 8,6,8,6,=8|3+3||8|3+3|| [eight] 33.) 8,7,8,7,=4+4|7||4+4|7|| [four]	5
4	1	5	33

main text line which can either fall within one melody section or may be distributed over two sections. The not underlined figure or figures preceding an underlined figure indicate the syllables of a repeated line fragment which appear before the entire main line and have been taken from its first syllables. The not underlined figure or figures following an underlined figure indicate the syllables of a repeated line-fragment appearing after the entire main line and taken from its last syllables. If these line-fragment syllables are taken from a different portion of the main line, this circumstance is shown by figures in parentheses which immediately follow and show the position of the syllables in the main line (that is, "*10*|| *4* (*1.–4.*) + *4* (*1.–4.*) | *6* ||" means that after the entire main line [*10*] its first four syllables are twice repeated).

Refrain syllables are put into parenthesis and bear the discriminating letter *r*. The number of melodies or variant groups in which the schema occurs is indicated in brackets. The combinations which occur only once are enumerated in Appendix I of "Tab. of Mat."

Relations between some of these schemata can easily be discovered. For example, 11.) (*10* | *6* ||) may be considered as a shortened form of 25.) (*10* | *6* || *10*), or 25.) as an enlarged form of 11.); a similar relation exists between 32.) and 4.); 32.) is the double of 7.), 31.) of 10.), 33.) of 12.).

Some interdependence appears between the figures of the first column and some of the schemata, too: 31.) originates from (*10*) text lines, 32.), however, from (*11*), although the syllabic symbol for both is the same: *8*, *6*, *8*, *6*,.

Some of the schemata have an influence on the musical content of the melody sections, inasmuch as the repeated text fragment carries with itself the repeat of the respective section fragment of the melody. This happens for instance in almost all melodies of schema 25.). The melody-fragment may be repeated either without any change, as in melodies having the same final tone in sections 1 and 2, or with a change of cadence (that is, of the final tone).

This leads us to the description of an extremely strange group of schemata (not quoted in Table 2) most characteristic for Serbo-Croatian melody-stanza construction. In this group the arrangement of the text line fragments runs parallel to that of the melody-section fragments, that is, the former are determining factors of the melodic content structure, and originate a rather peculiar form of melody stanza. The syllabic symbols of the most frequently occurring structure of this kind are (*10*) *4, 6, 6, 4,* , the symbol of the melodic content-structure A B B A (or some variants of this). The sign ⏝ means one text line. That is, a dekasyllable (*4* || *6*) is sung to the first half of the melody, and then the same dekasyllable is sung to its second half, this time, however, in inverted order: first comes the portion of the line standing after the main metrical caesura (syllables 5–10), and then follows the portion preceding it (syllables 1–4). The repeat of syllables 5–10 and 1–4 coincides with the repeat of the respective portions of the melody section, either without essential changes or in a more-or-less altered form. Therefore this peculiar treatment of text lines is an originator of a melody-content structure. Most of the less frequent structure schemata of this kind are in relation to the afore-described one, being its abbreviation or extension; a common characteristic for all these is the placing of the repeat of the first text syllables (that is, of the first metrical unit) at the end of the melody. In view of their importance it appears useful to enumerate here all instances of these structures, published elsewhere and in this book:

34.)[39] (*10*) *4, 6, 6, 4,*: Kuhač, 540, 736, 795, 892, 1208; Kuba B. H.. 193. 208, 295, 339, 349, 360, 406, 429, 493, 499, 702, 716, 723, 724, 872, 873, 875, 928, 1003, 1093–1096; Kuba, IX, 52; XI, 1, 30, 31, 36, 51; Đorđević, 365, 450, 483; Đorđević Nar. Pev., pp. 29 (second melody), 108 (second melody), 186 (second melody); Bosiljevac, 16, 37; our examples 31 a.b. c.d., 32, 33.
[42 + 6 melodies in 15 + 2 variant groups.]

35.) (*11*) *4 + 4 + 3, 3, 4,*: Kuba B. H., 392.

36.) (*13*) *4 + 4 + 5, 4,*: Kuba B. H., 480.

37.) (*8*) *4 + 4, 4 + 4, 4,* (A + A, A + A, A and A, A(v), B / *8, 8, 14,*): Đorđević, 546; Kuhač, 879, 880, 881.

38.) (*8b*) *5 + 3 + 3, 5,*: Kuhač, 660; Kuba, B. H. 467.

39.) (*8b*) *5 + 3, 5,*: Đorđević, 307.

[39] This and the following similar numbers continue the numbering from Table 2.

40.) (*8b*) *3 + 5, 3*,: Kuhač, 1271.

41.) (*8*) *2 + 2 + 4, 2*,: Kuhač, 1069.

42.) (*10*) *2 + 8, 2*,: Đorđević, 305.

The overwhelming majority of these extremely characteristic melody types come from Bosnia, Hercegovina, and Serbia; this is one proof of the assertion that these territories—and in addition Montenegro and Old Serbia—are the real sources of autochthonous Serbo-Croatian folk songs. It is significant that Kuhač contributed to this type a comparatively small number of melodies (eleven, as against thirty-one from Kuba and nine from Đorđević); it looks as if he neglected in his research, for mysterious reasons, to investigate the areas richest in aboriginal material.

Schemata 10.), 11.), 20.) and 25.) of the heterometric two- and three-section melodies are still more numerous in the above-mentioned areas, and a great majority come from there. They must, therefore, also be regarded as characteristic Serbo-Croatian melody types. The number of melodies is as follows:

10.) (*10*) *8, 6*,: 4 melodies from Kuhač, 31 from other collections, in 16 variant groups

11.) (*10*) *10, 6*,: 4 melodies from Kuhač, 46 from other collections, in 23 variant groups

20.) (*10*) *8, 6, 6*,: 4 melodies from Kuhač, 57 from other collections, in 29 variant groups

25.) (*10*) *10, 6, 10*,: 9 melodies from Kuhač, 68 from other collections, 9 among our music examples; in 13 variant groups

Total: 21 melodies from Kuhač, 204 from other collections, in 81 variant groups

Here, Kuhač's contribution is even smaller!

It seems that the original procedure was to use only one text line (one composite text line in structures like in *8, 5, 8, 5*, or *8, 6, 8, 6*, and so forth) for the entire melody stanza: the text line, or its parts, being repeated as many times as was required by the melody stanza. This procedure is still used in the majority of cases. Later, however, it became the fashion to use a given text line only once. The two kinds of procedure frequently get mixed, and in this case the repeats or nonrepeats of a text line by no means follow established patterns, but seem rather due to the impulse of the moment. This appears clearly when pieces are recorded twice by the same singer: the place of text line repeats is not the same on the two records (see the last Note to mus. ex. No. 12a., p. 234).

PRINCIPLES OF FORM CONSTRUCTION

No form construction occurs in one-section melodies. In fact, most of these (Nos. 1–35 of "Tab. of Mat.") may be fragments of structures of more than one section which have not yet been discovered. New material will no doubt clarify many of these cases (for example, since the "Tab. of Mat." was completed it has been discovered that our mus. ex. No. 17 is a complete two-section form (A A_v) of No. 34 (Đorđević 8) in the "Tab. of Mat."). Nevertheless, the statement that one-section melodies do not exist would not be true: our music example No. 1 seems to be such a melody, because one section is repeated (as long as the text lasts) WITHOUT CHANGES THAT WOULD LEAD TO GROWTH OF FORM. This is so although there are two-section melodies which are so similar to this example that they may well be considered variants of this one: "Tab. of Mat." No. 146 (Đorđević 168, 183, 211) and No. 310 (Kuba B. H. 319, 321, 825). One must keep in mind, however, that because of the imperfections in the notation, the real form of the melodies frequently is not sufficiently clear in transcriptions made by ear.

Two-section melodies are frequently created by repeating a section, with minor changes (A $A_{(v)}$ from A). This structure is especially characteristic of Serbo-Croatian autochthonous melodies. There are various devices for effecting a change in the second section. The simplest is to prolong the rest at the end of the second section, whereas the two sections remain essentially identical (mus. ex. No. 8, 10, 16a).[40] The published collections do not disclose this method, because the collectors neglected to measure even approximately the rest at the end of the stanzas. Without recording melodies nobody could ever discover this rather peculiar principle of form building.

Another method, always connected with the first one, consists of a slight change in the second section at any place except the last tone; for example, changing a 4/4 ♩♩♩♩ bar into 3/4 ♩♩♫ (mus. ex. No. 17) or interpolating a rest somewhere (mus. ex. No. 14).[41] This method, too, is

[40] The same method is sometimes used in order to differentiate the two halves of four-section melodies (Nos. 37, 38).

[41] The same method is sometimes used in order to differentiate the two halves of four-section melodies (Nos. 40, 49).

fairly typical. A third method, connected with the first also, consists of changing the $\boxed{\text{VII}}$, $\boxed{(\flat)2}$, $\boxed{(\flat)3}$, $\boxed{4}$, and so forth, final tone of the first section into final tone 1 in the second section. This procedure reminds us of the method used in the construction of periods in art music. A fourth device is seen in many melodies in which no repeat occurs, the second section having an entirely new content (A B) (mus. ex. Nos. 3, 5, 7). This structure is less characteristic. Finally, there are melodies in which the content of the two sections is similar—the position of the second, however, is one degree lower or higher (sequential structure A A_s or A A^s; for example, "Tab. of Mat." 161 (Kuhač 550), 229 d. (Kuhač 470); 1081 (Kuhač 1319). This structure is of western origin; the melodies are of urban or foreign derivation and frequently only fragments of longer sequential structures.

Table 3 shows the content structure of two-section melodies in the material (including the melodies in this book). In this table groups *7,*| *8b,* | *10,* | *11,* | *12,* | and *10, 6,*| deserve special attention as containing the largest number of A $A_{(v)}$ structures. The last of these is related to another typical form, the three-section form *10, 6, 10,* (see p. 46, above); this explains the frequency of the A $A_{(v)}$ structure in it (45, against 5 A B) (see Table 3, p. 49).

Isometric three-section melodies will show an enlargement of the above-described structural principles. We shall not dwell upon the structure A B C, less interesting from the point of view of form-developing methods. A B $B_{(v)}$ structures in isometric □ ⊏ melodies and A $A_{(v)}$ B structures in isometric ⊐ □ melodies may be interpreted as derivations from A B; A A $A_{(v)}$ as derivations from A $A_{(v)}$, or inversely. The very rare A B $A_{(v)}$ (in four melodies) may be brought into relation with four-section A B $A_{(v)}$ B structures.

The statistical data are as follows (including the melodies in this book):

Of 57 isometric □ ⊏ melodies, 16 have A B C; 31, A B $B_{(v)}$; 3, A $A_{(v)}$ A; 3, A B A_v.

Of 105 isometric ⊐ □ melodies, 28 have A B C; 50, A $A_{(v)}$ B; 13, A A $A_{(v)}$; 1, A B A_v.

The less frequent A $A_{(v)}$ A and A A $A_{(v)}$ seem to be the most characteristic; in fact fourteen of them come from Bosnia, Hercegovina, and Serbia.

TABLE 3

	Syllables of the Sections	A B	A $A_{(v)}$	Sequential Structure	A^3A	A^5A	Total
Of 898 □ isometric melodies	5,	14	1	...	...	...	15
	6,	30	22	13	...	...	65
	7,	22	22	...	...	1	45
	8,	132	69	3	1	...	205
	8b,	34	54	6	2	...	96
	9,	2	3	...	...	...	5
	10,	131	148	3	...	...	282
	11,	29	44	...	...	...	72
	12,	5	26	...	...	...	31
	13,	...	1	...	...	...	1
Total		399	390	25	3	1	818
Of 192 □ heterometric melodies with Zz structure	8, 5	9	5	...	...	...	14
	8b, 5,	3	1	...	...	...	4
	8, 6,	53	7	...	...	...	60
	8, 7,	19	4	...	...	...	23
	10, 6,	5	45	...	...	...	50
	All others	25	16	...	...	...	41
Of 66 □ heterometric melodies with zZ structure	7, 11,	9	2	...	...	...	11
	8, 10,	17	10	...	...	...	27
	8, 12,	6	...	...	...	...	6
	All others	9	13	...	...	...	22
Total		155	103	...	...	...	258

Beyond any doubt some of the heterometric □ ⊏ structures are Western European, especially the groups 2)2.–6., 11. of "Tab. of Mat." (pp. 64–66): of 59 examples, there are 28 from Kuhač, 3 from Kuba IX, XI, that is, probably more than the half came from the western parts of Serbo-Croatia. Structures showing complicated syllabic proportions (groups 3)2.–6. of "Tab. of Mat.," pp. 67–70) probably are of foreign origin, too; the same may be said about melodies of similar structure in class ⊐ □.

Syllabic structures *8, 5, 5,* | *8, 6, 6,* | *8, 7, 7,* | and *10, 6, 6,* |, mostly, of course, with A B $B_{(v)}$ content structure, may be regarded either as enlargements of *8, 5,* | *8, 6,* | *8, 7,* | and *10, 6,* | or as shortened forms of *8, 5, 8, 5,* | *8, 6, 8, 6,* | *8, 7, 8, 7,* | and *10, 6, 10, 6,* |.

Heterometric examples in class ⊐ □ contain more autochthonous structures. The most important of these is the already mentioned syllabic structure *10, 6, 10,* (p. 46), mostly with A A_v B content structure. Of 75 melodies belonging to only 14 variant groups 6 have: A A_v, A_{v2}; 3 have A B C; 65 have A A_v B (Kuhač contributed 11 melodies).

The most popular melodies belong to this group: No. 983 of "Tab. of Mat." comprises 36 variants (in our melodies 5 more: No. 27); No. 984 has 11 (in our melodies 3 more: No. 28); No. 989 has 8 variants. All the 175 melodies come from the above-described "autochthonous" territories, except for Kuhač 703 (from Bačka) and 1510 (from Croatia).

Among the other structures, *8, 8, 5,* | *8b, 8b, 5,* | *8, 8, 6,* | *8, 8, 7,* | and *10, 10, 6,* | seem to bear a relationship to the corresponding four-section structures which is quite similar to that between the afore-mentioned four groups in class □ ⊏ and the latter.

It might be well to mention at this point some data concerning the main caesura tones in the two- and three-section melodies: about 34 percent have [1], 17 percent [♭2], 16 percent [(♭)3], and 14 percent [VII]; the other 17 percent are split between [V], [4], [5], and so forth. The preponderance of the four lower degrees, first mentioned, is in close connection with the narrow range of the melodies, see pp. 52–53.

The class of four-section melodies offers the greatest number of borrowed foreign melodies, especially the heterometric subclass. The rich contribution of Kuhač to these classes, especially to the isometric one, is rather significant: of approximately 550 melodies, 280 are from Kuhač. An important part of these melodies come from the western portions of the Serbo-Croatian territory. Only a few of these will be described here.

Some ten-syllable isometric melodies (No. 1310 of "Tab. of Mat.," comprising 20 variants, 15 of them from Kuhač) seem to be "heroic-poem" motifs, misrepresented and wrongly squeezed into a form of four or more sections by editors. Thus, perhaps they should not have been included in the analysis of the nonheroic material. However, while the guess that heroic motifs are involved may be well founded, it is not sufficient basis for omitting this group.

The group of melodies with syllabic structure *8*, *5*, *8*, *5*, (about 125) may as well be regarded as 13-syllable two-section isometric melodies (see p. 31). Several musical reasons, however, speak for splitting the 13 syllables into two parts (*8*, *5*,) and considering them, at least musically, as individual sections.[42] The relation of this structure to simpler structures has been already mentioned on the previous pages. A remarkable feature is that their texts seem to be of urban origin, in many instances even with text-stanza structure and rhymes, whatever rural aspect their melodies may have (mus. ex. Nos. 39a.b., 40, 42, 45). On the whole, in spite of their large number, they do not belong to the characteristic Serbo-Croatian types.

More typical is the group of *8*, *6*, *8*, *6*, especially (*10*) *8*, *6*, *8*, *6*,. The former comprises 38 melodies, the latter 85, and in this, of course, the characteristic splitting of text lines appears. For their relation to simpler structures see the previous pages.

The syllabic structures *8*, *7*, *8*, *7*, and (*11*) *8*, *7*, *8*, *7*, are represented each by 19 melodies (in 16 and 7 variant groups), of which, of course, the latter is more characteristic.

The reader may bear in mind that the syllable structures *8*, *5*, *8*, *5*, | *8*, *6*, *8*, *6*, | and *8*, *7*, *8*, *7*, | are very well known from the material of the neighboring peoples. Structures 11., 13.–16. bis. of "Tab. of Mat." (pp. 127–30) which are related to the afore-mentioned 2)2.–6., 11. (p. 50), are certainly of foreign origin, as well as the latter.

The reader may be reminded that the groups 20.–24. of "Tab. of Mat." (pp. 132–35), with their more or less artificial syllabic structures, are probably of urban origin. In addition, many of them are represented by

[42] See footnote 17, p. 31.

a single melody; this circumstance makes it doubtful whether they ever lived a prolonged life, at least in the form in which they were notated. For, as long as only a single example of a certain peculiar structure is known, doubts concerning its authenticity are well founded; one never knows whether this or that particular feature may not be due, perhaps, to some fault in the performance (imperfect remembering, haphazard changes, and so forth), even if it is taken for granted that the collector has not introduced any arbitrary changes.

Our investigation has followed the principle of proceeding from the shortest structures to the longest. This was imperative because of the almost overwhelmingly greater number and importance of the shorter ones. It may be mentioned as an evidence of the great difference between Serbo-Croatian material on the one hand and Hungarian and Slovak on the other, that the investigation of the material of the latter peoples must proceed in the opposite direction. There the four-section structures are in overwhelming majority, and the three- and two-section structures are accessories only.

RANGE (AMBITUS)

At first glance one discovers a great preponderance of the comparatively narrow ranges. Here follows Table 4, enumerating the most important range formulas. Only range formulas from *VII* upward are separately quoted, the rest being less important.[43] Accidentals are omitted: *VII–3*, *VII–♭3*, *♯VII–♭3*, are merged in *VII–3.*

The formulas form two parallel groups, those with VII as the lowest tone, and those with 1 (see Table 4, p. 53).

This table shows that (*a*) more than two-thirds of the material has a range between *VII* and *5*; (*b*) almost half of these, that is, one-third of the material, has a range of *VII–4* or *1–4* —a pentachord or a tetrachord in a certain position; (*c*) there is a very marked descending trend in both groups; the range is widening toward the class of the four-section melodies, that is, toward such melody types as were collected mostly in the western parts of the Serbo-Croatian territory (a rich contribution by Kuhač).

Among the less common range formulas the extra-narrow *VII–1*, *VII–2*, *1–2*, and *1–3*, comprising 181 melodies, deserve special attention

[43] These may be studied in Appendix II, of "Tab. of Mat."

Table 4
Range

Range	I One-sect.	II □ Iso-metric	III □ Hetero-metric	IV □⊏ Iso-metric	V ⊐□ Iso-metric	VI □⊏ Hetero-metric	VII ⊐□ Hetero-metric	VIII Special	IX ⊐□⊏ Iso-metric	X ⊐□⊏ Hetero-metric	Total
I–1 to VI–10	2	51	19	8	6	26	15	...	76	129	332
VII– 1	...	3	1	...	1	...	...	...	...	...	5
VII– 2	4	33	14	...	...	3	5	...	2	4	65
VII– 3	4	110	51	1	8	32	11	9	10	17	253
VII– 4	5	189	41	10	20	88	84	14	66	138	655
VII– 5	...	80	23	4	12	41	31	3	58	139	391
VII– 6	...	8	3	...	7	8	8	...	36	57	127
VII– 7	...	15	1	2	3	1	18	...	24	32	96
VII– 8	...	...	...	...	...	1	7	...	10	18	36
VII– 9	...	...	...	...	...	...	...	...	1	...	1
VII–10	...	...	...	...	...	...	...	...	...	1	1
1– 2	1	3	3	...	...	2	...	...	...	...	9
1– 3	7	59	9	2	4	6	...	7	1	7	102
1– 4	18	119	57	2	9	39	8	10	24	31	317
1– 5	3	103	36	12	18	43	17	7	62	83	384
1– 6	1	38	6	5	10	20	13	...	58	66	217
1– 7	...	15	2	6	5	9	11	3	27	23	101
1– 8	...	1	...	7	4	6	2	6	38	35	99
1– 9	...	1	...	...	...	2	...	...	9	4	16
1–10	...	...	...	1	...	1	...	...	4	1	7
1–11	...	...	...	...	...	...	...	...	1	...	1
Total	45	828	266	60	107	328	230	59	507	785	3,215

for the following reasons: (*a*) most of them come from the "autochthonous" territories, especially from Serbia (Đorđević); (*b*) the greater part of them are ceremonial songs (hay-gathering, harvest, Lazarus's day, cradle songs, and so forth); (*c*) although they belong to different groups with various stylistic aspects, they seem to be the remnants of a unified and ancient style; see also p. 60.

This group of narrow range melodies, in spite of their comparatively small number, is very important. In the Slovak material many supposedly very old ceremonial songs have melodies of a similar narrow range.[44] Most of them are four-section melodies, but some have three- or two-section structure. Their primitivity seems to indicate an archaic origin. Are these narrow range melodies in both materials, perhaps, the remnants of a common ancient Slavic style? Unfortunately we do not have for this theory proofs as convincing as there are for the common origin of the Old Hungarian-Turkish melodies.

Other illustrations of such primitive style are found in a different region, in the narrow range Arabic peasant melodies, as the following example shows;[45] it is a wedding song from the vicinity of Biskra (Algeria), sung by two women about twenty-five years old, in June, 1913. The author's collection; transcription from record, which was later lost. The second song quoted for comparison is No. 388 from Kuba, B. H. ("Tab. of Mat." No. 165b.). Both may be compared with our mus. ex. No. 2.

It remains an open question whether there is a connection between the narrow range Serbo-Croatian and the narrow range Arabic melodies.

The rather rare wide range melodies *VII–8*, *1–8*, *1–9*, (151) also deserve attention, especially when connected with [8] [♭3] [♭3], or] [5] [

[44] See Bartók, *44 Duets for 2 Violins*, Universal Edition, Vienna, 1933, Nos. 11, 33. Reprint by Boosey & Hawkes, New York.

[45] There is an essential difference between Arabic peasant (rural) and urban music!

caesura, or A^5B^5A B content-structure, or with a fragment of such structures. These structures are characteristic of the Old Hungarian-Turkish (rural) style, therefore, should indicate either Hungarian or Turkish influence. The Hungarian alternative is not probable: the few examples of this type are found in the center of the autochthonous Serbo-Croatian areas, not in the northern border territory, and they seem to have no connecting link with the Hungarian territory. On the other hand, the centuries-long Turkish occupation may well be responsible for a rural Turkish origin.[46] These rare melodies would be the only vestiges of Turkish influence on Serbo-Croatian folk melodies. A detailed enumeration follows; the first number refers to the "Tab. of Mat."

657 (Kuba B. H. 194): *10,* [5] [5, *1–8,* A B B_v.

696 (Kuba B. H. 249, 250): *8,* 5] [♭3], *1–8,* A B C; Turkish var.: *Turkish Folk Music from Asia Minor,* No. 7, with *8,* 4] [5] [4, *1–8* structure, from Avlĭk (Kadĭrlĭ vilajet); Hungarian var.: *Hungarian Folk Music,*[47] No. 17, with *8,* 5] [♭3] [4, *1–8* structure.

828 (Kuba XII. 18): *12, 8, 8,* [5] [1, *1–♭10,* A B B;—Turkish var.: *Turkish Folk Music from Asia Minor,* No. 17 a.b., with *11,* 8] [4] [♭3, *1–♭10* structure, from Kara Isalĭ (Seyhan vilajet).

1217 (Kuba B. H. 196): *8,* 1] [1] [1, *1–8,* A B B C; Hungarian var.: *Hungarian Folk Music,* No. 8, with *8,* 1] [1] [5, *VII–8* structure.

1231 (Đorđević 116): *8,* 4] [1] [1, *1–7,* A B C D; Hungarian var.: *Hungarian Folk Music,* No. 10, with *8,* 4] [1] [1, *1–8* structure.

1247 (Kuba B. H. 1010, 1017; Đorđević Nar. Pev., p. 10, first melody; our mus. ex. 36): *8,* [♭3] [♭3] [♭3 or ♭3] [1] [♭3 or ♭3] [VII] [VII; with *VII–7,* A B B C, or with *1–8,* A B C B; Hungarian var.: *Hungarian Folk Music,* No. 14, with *8,* ♭3] [♭3] [♭3, *1–8* (with *d*♮) structure.

1268 (Đorđević 113): *8,* 7] [5] [♭3, *1–8,* A B C D; Turkish var.: *Turkish Folk Music from Asia Minor,* No. 3, with *8,* 7] [♭3] [7, *1–♭10* structure, from Tüysüz (Seyhan vilajet), Hungarian var.: *Hungarian Folk Music,* No. 19, with *8,* 7] [♭3] [♭3, *1–8* structure.

[46] The reader may keep in mind that there is an essential difference between rural and urban Turkish music, too. The former is of Central Asiatic origin, its main characteristics being wide-range four-section melodies, pentatonic scale structure (or one derived from pentatonic) and "descending" contour-line of the melody.: The urban Turkish music derives, on the contrary, from Arabic urban music, showing some unessential adaptations.

[47] Bartók, *Hungarian Folk Music* (London: Oxford University Press, 1931).

1269 (Kuba B. H. 110, 1049): *8,* 8 $\boxed{5}$ ♭3 or 8 $\boxed{\flat 3}$ ♭3; *1–♭9,* A A_vB C; Turkish var.: *Turkish Folk Music from Asia Minor,* No. 16, with *11,* 7 $\boxed{4}$ ♭3, *1–9* structure, from Hüyük (Çorum vilajet).

1270 (Đorđević Nar. Pev., p. 153, first melody): *8,* 8 $\boxed{5}$ 4, *1–8,* $A^5B^5A_vB_v$.

1291 (Đorđević 176): *8b,* ♭3 $\boxed{4}$ ♭3, *1–8,* A A_vB C; Turkish var.: *Turkish Folk Music from Asia Minor,* No. 14, with *11,* 4 $\boxed{4}$ 5, *1–8* structure from Tüysüz (Seyhan vilajet).

1313 (Kuba B. H. 186, 220, 224–27): *10,* ♭3 $\boxed{VII}$ 2, *VII–7,* A B C B_v; Hungarian var.: *Hungarian Folk Music,* No. 69, with *10,* 8 $\boxed{VII}$ ♭3, *VII–8* structure.

If we extend the study of these melodies to include the Bulgarian material, another theory suggests itself for explaining their presence in the Serbo-Croatian material. For in the former there are 278 melodies of this type, that is, with wide range, pentatonic scale-structure, "descending" contour-line of the melody; this means 3 percent of all the Bulgarian material available in print (which is a little less than 10,000 melodies), whereas the above-mentioned Serbo-Croatian 21 melodies of the same type represent not more than about 0.6 percent of the investigated Serbo-Croatian material.

There were, and still are, many purely Turkish settlements in Bulgaria; in Serbia-Croatia, none. This circumstance may account for the fact that there are proportionately six times more such melodies in the Bulgarian material than in the Serbo-Croatian. The question arises whether the presence of those 21 melodies in the latter is not due rather to an infiltration from Bulgaria than to a direct Turkish influence.

Besides this obviously Turkish influence, some rare melodies are actually borrowed from the so-called New-Hungarian material. These melodies penetrated into the stock of Bosnia and Hercegovina in fragmentary form (except the last example). There are eight of them in the printed collections (the first number in the single items of the following list refers to the "Tab. of Mat."):

(1) 596 (Kuba B. H. 410), (2) 1364 (Kuba B. H. 199), (3) 1392a.b. (Kuba B. H. 23 and 24), (4) 1751 (Kuba B. H. 281), (5) 1333 (Kuba XIII 12), (6) 1342 (Kuba XII 45), (7) 859 (Bosiljevac 36), (8) 1809a.b. (Kuba B. H. 20 and 19).

Their Hungarian variants, reduced to the fragmentary form which the borrowed melodies show, are as follows:

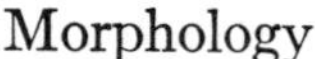

1st (and 4th) section [2d and 3d missing]

3d section

4th (and 1st) section [2d missing]

1st (and 4th) section [2d and 3d missing]

1st section

2d section

3d section

4th section of the Hungarian variants; missing in the Serbo-Croatian variant

3d section

4th (and 1st) section [2d missing]

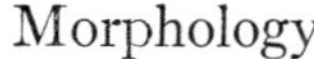

The missing sections in the Hungarian variants are as follows: in (1) and (3) unknown; in (2) and (5) similar to the third section, but with d^2 as final tone; in (4) as given after the melody; in (7) similar to the first section, but one fifth higher. In (4) the Serbo-Croatian text has the senseless refrain *rindiri baba*—a distortion of the Hungarian original, for "my sweetheart has curly hair." Our music example No. 49 probably belongs also to this group.

A possible explanation for this borrowing lies in the occupation of these areas by Hungarian troops between 1878 and 1918. In the last quarter of the last century Hungary's younger generation were already neglecting the "old style" Hungarian-Turkish melodies and fully adopted the "new style" which began to flourish at about that time. Therefore, old-style melodies could not have been taken over from these troops.

Another possibility is the infiltration of *Međumurje* material saturated with "New-Hungarian" melodies (see p. 24) into Bosnia and Hercegovina; this, however, seems to be less probable.

As a negative feature there must be mentioned the absence of the so-called "long-drawn" melody in the Serbo-Croatian (as well as in the Bulgarian) material (see p. 77, footnote 77). We know this melodic style, which originates without any doubt from Persian-Arabic sources, from the Ukraine, Rumania (Maramureș and all territories of prewar[48] Rumania),[49] Turkey (only a few specimens), Persia, Iraq, and Algeria (Djelfa). So there is a gap in the continuity of the spread of this type in the south-northern direction (Bulgarian and Serbo-Croatian territory), another gap in its spread in the east-western direction (Syria, Egypt, Tripolis, Tunis). That the type exists in Serbo-Croatian territory is not very likely, since even Kuba, whose eagerness, zeal, and ability in collecting folk music is well known, could not discover any trace of it. Either it never existed in this territory, or it must have died out before the end of the last century.

SCALES (cf. pp. 52–56)

Owing to the preponderance of narrow-range melodies, scales extending over an octave (either diatonic, seven-degree scales, or "defective" anhemitonic pentatonic scales) are comparatively rare in the Serbo-Croatian material (at variance with the Old Hungarian-Turkish and New-Hungarian material). The majority of melodies have a diatonic scale fragment consisting of the first four, five, or six degrees of an *f* major or minor (or some other variety)[50] with the second degree (that is, *g*) as final tone (the pitch given according to our system of transposition).

It must be emphasized that this is not a Dorian or Aeolian scale on *g*, turning at times to its lower seventh (*VII* = *f*). The difference is this: the first has *f a*(♭) *c* as main (accentuated) degrees, the two latter, *g b*(♭) *d*. Before the final tone of such a melody (appearing as accentuated tone only at the end) is reached, anybody would interpret its degrees as the

[48] "War" means "First World War."

[49] The Hungarian so-called *Rákóczi nóta* (Rákóczi song) from which the "Rákóczi March" originates, seems to belong to this type, too.

[50] For example, with minor third and augmented fourth, or minor third and diminished fifth.

pentachord (or tetrachord, hexachord) of a major or minor scale. Where this scale is common, the peasant singers, with a steady feeling for pitch, have a subconscious sense of modal octave-segments, even when they are presented as fragments, such as a pentachord or tetrachord. If they sing in succession two melodies, the first of which has a normal major, minor, or Dorian scale, and the second the above-described kind of scale ending on the second degree, they will sing them with one degree difference in pitch, that is, the second melody will be performed a whole tone lower.[51] Why do we not transpose these melodies ending on the second degree of the scale so that the final tone becomes a^1, as some editors have done? The only answer is that deviations from the principle of setting the final tone in g^1 would lead to confusion and to lack of consistency in our system of transposition.

In narrow range melodies the characteristics of this scale will, of course, disappear. It is spread over Bulgarian areas and appears in some Rumanian areas[52] also. The Hungarian material does not have it.

Much speculation may be indulged in concerning the antiquity of this scale. My hypothesis is that originally only narrow range, probably two-section, melodies existed in the Serbo-Croatian material. As foreign (western) influence arose, a gradual extension of range and borrowing of major or minor pentachord melodies could have occurred. While these melodies were in the process of infiltration, a change took place: the feeling for ending a melody became shifted, and the roles of the perfect and the imperfect cadences were exchanged. One tentative explanation for this phenomenon would be that Western European four-section melodies generally have the imperfect cadence at the end of the second section (the end of the fourth section, that is, the end of the melody, presents, of course, a perfect cadence). On the other hand, there is a marked trend among the Serbo-Croats (and among some other peoples, too) to borrow only fragments from foreign melodies, especially if in their feeling the melodies are too long. Accustomed to two-section structures, the borrowing of the first half of the foreign melodies with the imperfect cadence

[51] They will observe other modal relations as well. The melodies in this book do not contain examples, but in *Rumanian Folk Music,* Vol. II, there are several very enlightening demonstrations for this phenomenon, for example:

No. 301, in Mixolydian mode, with final tone *b*, and No. 270, in Aeolian mode, with final tone $c^1\sharp$, both performed *attacca* by the same two women;

No. 321 in Dorian mode with final tone *b*, and No. 124a. in Phrygian mode with final tone $c^1\sharp$, both performed *attacca* by two other women.

[52] Especially in the *Banat* area.

would suit their musical sense. Such incomplete structures, with the imperfect cadence, may have spread over the territory and, developing various characteristic structures, led to new formations. The imperfect cadence, however, remained unchanged.[53] If this were true, the melodies with "final stop on the second degree" would be later developments.[54]

There is another scale, a major scale, represented by melodies mostly of western origin, with the final stop on the third degree. There is a difference between this and the Phrygian modal scale, which is analogous to the difference between the two afore-mentioned scales: the main degrees in the first are $e^1\flat$ g^1 $b^1\flat$ ($e^2\flat$); in the latter, (d^1) g^1 $b^1\flat$ d^2.

Augmented second intervals occur frequently in the minor scale, with the final stop on the second degree, as $a^1\flat$ $b^1\natural$, and in the normal minor as $b^1\flat$ $c^2\sharp$. Whether they are signs of oriental (Arabic) influence (perhaps through Turkish mediation) is still an unsolved problem.

A very peculiar scale formation is the above-mentioned $f^1 g^1 a^1\flat$ $b^1\flat$ $c^2\flat$, not very common (for example, Đorđević, 236), and the still less frequent $g^1 a^1(\flat)$ $b^1\flat$ $c^2 d^2\flat$ $e^2(\flat)$ f^2 (our mus. ex. No. 36).[55] The former is intermediate between the diatonic and the "chromatic" scales. In spite of the small number of these "chromatic" melodies, a complete list of them is given here, which includes also the examples in Kuba's article N. g. u. D. (p.

[53] There is at our disposal an example of a rather recent borrowing of a melody which shows that this hypothesis is not as fantastic as it may seem, perhaps. See the Hungarian melody (6) on p. 58, its second and third section with a^1 as final tone. The Hungarian variant has of course g^1 (first degree) as final tone of the entire melody; the Serbo-Croats, however, took over only its first and second sections; therefore, this borrowed fragment has a^1 (the second degree) as final tone.

[54] There are examples of variant groups in which some of the variants have their final stop on the second degree, some on the first degree. Closer examination of these examples will perhaps help to solve this question. For example,

"Tab. of Mat." No. 158 a.–g.: Đorđević Nar. Pev. p. 77, second melody, Kačerovski 40a), Bosiljevac 47, Kuhač 878, Kuba B. H. 581 and 913 have imperfect cadence, Kuhač 877, perfect;

"Tab. of Mat." 177 a.–d.: Đorđević Nar. Pev. p. 24, first melody, Iz Levča 23, Đorđević 449 have imperfect cadence, Kuba B. H. 175, perfect;

"Tab. of Mat." 810 a.–c.: Kuba B. H. 817, 818 have imperfect cadence, Kuba B. H. 439, perfect;

"Tab. of Mat." 1002 a.–h.: Kuba IX, 3, Kuhač 653 a)b), 1083 have imperfect cadence, Kuhač 1039, 1040, 1099 and Đorđević Nar. Pev. p. 69, second melody, perfect;

"Tab. of Mat." 1010 a.–c.: Kuba B. H. 507 and 688 have imperfect, Kuhač 178, perfect;

"Tab. of Mat." 1440 a.b.: Kuba B. H. 578, has imperfect, Kuhač 1129, perfect;

"Tab. of Mat." 1591 a.–c.: Kuhač 1111 b) has imperfect, Kuhač 408, Kačerovski 4 b), perfect;

"Tab. of Mat." 1693 a.b.: Kuba B. H. 41 has imperfect, Kačerovski 68, perfect.

[55] The Rumanians know the former, especially in their Songs of Mourning, the latter in some of their *cântec* ("song") melodies. Both are entirely lacking in the Hungarian material.

25) because of their importance; after the enumeration No. 62 is quoted entirely. Whole note in the scales means final tone; f^1 in parenthesis, that this tone appears only in the lower part of two-part songs.

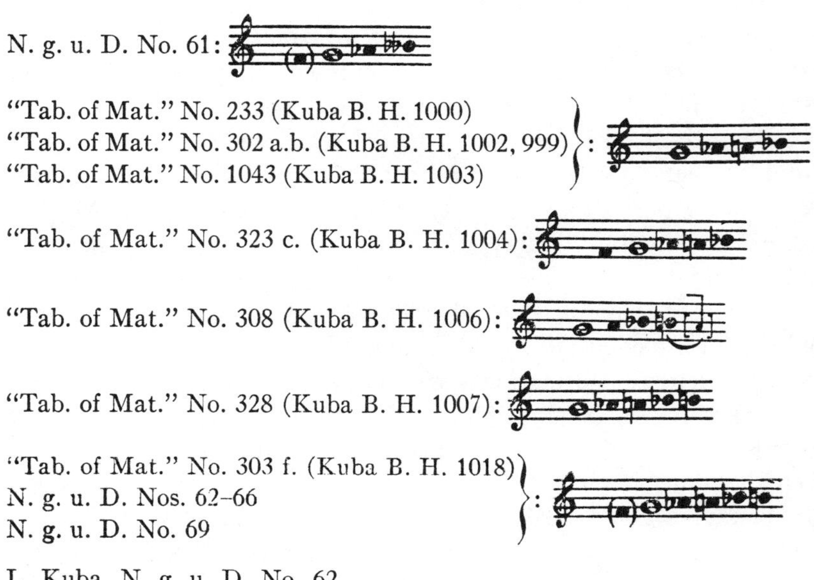

L. Kuba, N. g. u. D. No. 62.

U. Zagvozdu; đevojke.

The second example represents an Arabic chromatic melody from my own collection, the third a Dalmatian two-part melody in chromatic style (see p. 72).[56]

[56] By courtesy of Professor George Herzog, the owner of the Dalmatian record (transcribed by Bartók).

From Tolga, Algérie, June, 1913; sung by men. Text is missing. The dashes below the notes are not tenuto marks; they stand for a syllable each.

♩ = 104

Two sopels

rallentando - - - - al ♩ = ca.77

Two voices

Oj, ja-vo - re, zelen bo-re, Oj, ja - vo - - re,— ze - - len bo - - - - re,—

Z 2104, Z 2041–2042a (a), Dalmatia.

As we see, these "chromatic" scales are narrow range scales; the melodies have very few ornamental tones. Chromatic changes affect the second and third degrees, both appearing as naturals and flats in the same melody (except in one case, where only the third degree has both forms). One may get the impression that our current notation is inadequate for these scales: the use of flats and naturals in connection with the same degree implies a certain interdependence of the two and could mean here that the flat degree is a "colored" transitional form of the same natural degree, leading to another degree through the colorization (chromatization); that is, that the two forms differ only in "color," but not concerning their function and degree. Yet this is not the case with these melodies: it appears that the single tones, whether or not they show the same degree position through the inadequate notation, are treated as independent tones, $a^1\flat$ and $b^1\flat$ having nothing in common with $a^1\natural$ and $b^1\natural$, respectively; each tone is used as an independent degree. Therefore these scales ought to be regarded rather as a segment—a kind of pentachord—of a twelve-hemitone scale; but, of course, with a fixed tonality because of their ever recurring, never changing final note.

As to the example quoted from Kuba's article (see p. 62), it is a clew to very significant findings. It has many variants, all of them in diatonic scales and generally with the same text or with text variants. These are as follows: ("Tab. of Mat." 835) Kuhač 979 (from Istria, the closest variant), 977, 978, 980, 981, Kuba X, 40, B. H. 556, 557; Slovak variants: Slovenské Spevy[57] I, 194, III, 36, 62, 286; Moravian variants: Peck[58] 121, 183, 209; Černík[59] 69, 282; Sušil[60] 780a). Hungarian variants (rather remote): Bartók *Hungarian Folk Music*, No. 299 a.b.c.

This proves that the Serbo-Croatian melodies in question are borrowings from northern foreign material and that Kuba No. 62 has simply been adapted to that peculiar "chromatic" scale. A similar process of adaptation is perceived in the case of "Tab. of Mat." 303 f. (Kuba B. H. 1018) when we compare it with the rest of the variants in the same group (Kuhač 250, 251, Kuba X, 34, B. H. 387, 391). If we try, as an experiment, to spread the remaining 14 "chromatic" melodies over a diatonic scale, that is, changing the succession $g\ a\flat\ a\natural\ b\flat\ b\natural$ into $g\ a\natural\ b(\flat)\ c\ d$,

[57] *Slovenské Spevy*, Turčianky Svätý Martín, 1880, 1890, 1899, Vols. I–III.
[58] E. Peck, *Valašské národné písně*, Brno, 1860.
[59] J. Černík, *Zpěvy Moravských Kopaničárů*, Praha, 1908.
[60] Fr. Sušil, *Moravské národné písně*, Brno, 1859.

most of them will appear in this new and artificially widened garb as very well-known diatonic melody types. Therefore this "chromatic" system is not a separate independent system, with new melody formations; it is rather a transformation of the diatonic pentachord (or tetrachord), the medium range diatonic pentachord having been compressed into a narrower range "chromatic" pentachord (if one is permitted to call the latter a pentachord). The same chromatism appears in those two-part songs of Dalmatia in which the interval between the parts is generally a major second (see below, p. 72, and second example on p. 63). It has not yet been discovered in any other European territory or in northern, central, or eastern Asia; certain types of narrow range Arabic rural melodies, however, show a slight resemblance to it (see first example on p. 63).

These scales remind us of the chromaticism in the heroic song motifs. Either their origin is to be sought in the influence of that chromaticism, or both their chromaticism and that of the heroic song motifs are, though perhaps independently of each other, due to Arabic or other Eastern influence. Decisive answers to these questions cannot yet be given.

RHYTHM FORMATION

The largest part of the published material is unreliable in this regard, and therefore must be excluded from our investigations. Furthermore, all rhythm formations found in four-section melodies of probably foreign (Slovak, Hungarian, and so forth) origin will also be discarded as an irrelevant incumbrance. Therefore, the results of investigation are based mainly on the seventy-five melodies included in this book.

For purposes of analyzing rhythm formations, melodies shall be stripped of all embellishment tones, and the remaining skeleton form shall be used as a basis for investigation, as shown in most of the melodies published in this volume, below the first stanza.

The scarcity of real *parlando-rubato* rhythm is remarkable. Because of their peculiar "free stanza" structure, a small group of melodies with this rhythm gain a certain importance. The melody sections of these consist mainly of ♫♫|♫♫‖, some of the eighths sometimes prolonged. Their "free stanza" structure is based on the text: its "chapters" (portions having more or less rounded content and no constant number of lines) will determine the melody stanzas, one text chapter corresponding to one melody stanza (see mus. ex. Nos. 20, 34–36).[61] This melody stanza contains three (No. 20) or four (Nos. 34–36) more or less different patterns of sections which may be repeated irregularly; the last, however, generally does not appear except at the end of the stanza. The text lines are not repeated (as is the case in heroic poems) except the last line of the stanza in Nos. 20, 36 (both sung by the same singer, Meho Jarić). No. 35 presents a rather fragmentary form of two or three sections in its stanzas, except the first stanza. If we strip these melody stanzas of the repeats caused by the text stanza, there remains a normal four-section or three-section melody. Thus, the music has essentially an extended four-section or three-section structure. Such subordination of the melody stanza to the longer text chapters is rather peculiar and deserves fullest attention. No trace of it can be discovered in the published collections, where the editors tried to squeeze every melody into a two- three- or four-section form.[62] So few examples of this feature occur in the collection that it is impossible to ascertain whether it is an individual and haphazard formation or a wide-spread usage. In the latter case, the discovery of this phenomenon would be exclusively due to Professor Parry's method of recording songs in their entirety.

The rest of our group consists mostly of melodies in *non-parlando*, fixed rhythm, though sometimes the rhythm may appear to be somewhat flexible or, more rarely, may take the aspect of *parlando* rhythm. Examining the various rhythmic patterns found in this material, we start by assuming the pre-existence of simple original rhythmic patterns as follows:

a)

1.) ♫♫ | ♫♫ | for 8-syllable lines

2.) ♫♫ | ♫♫ | ♩ ♩ | for 10-syllable lines, or the same patterns with double values

3.) ♫♫ | ♫♫ | ♫ ♩ | for 11-syllable lines

We see a) 1. in No. 1; Nos. 16 a. and 29 have the same with double values and extended to twelve-syllables (♩♩♩♩ | ♩♩♩♩ | ♩♩♩♩ |).

[61] The second stanza of No. 20 presents an exception inasmuch as its last repeated line is not the last line of the respective text chapter.

[62] Some signs in the Bulgarian published collections seem to indicate that a kind of free stanza structure exists in the Bulgarian material, too. See also *Rumanian Folk Music,* Vol. II, pp. 25–26.

Then we proceed to determine what kind of changes happen to these simple patterns. We shall see that usually only their first two measures are subject to changes of any consequence. The main variations are as follows:

b)

1. No. 2
2. No. 7
3. IIa No. 8 a, b.
4. IIa No. 10
5. IIa No. 19

---

c)

1. No. 9
2. No. 11
3. No. 14
4. No. 16 b.
5. IIa No. 18
6. No. 17

d)

1. No. 3

2. No. 39 b. (a.: rubato)

3. No. 43, 44 a. b.

4. No. 45 (rubato >)

5. No. 47

---

e)

1. (var.) No. 6 a. b. c.

2. (var.) No. 12 a.–e.

3. (var.) (var.) (var.) (var.) (var.) No. 26, 27 a.–e., 28 a. b (28 c. : rubato)

4. No. 40

5. No. 41

6. No. 51

7. No. 30

f)

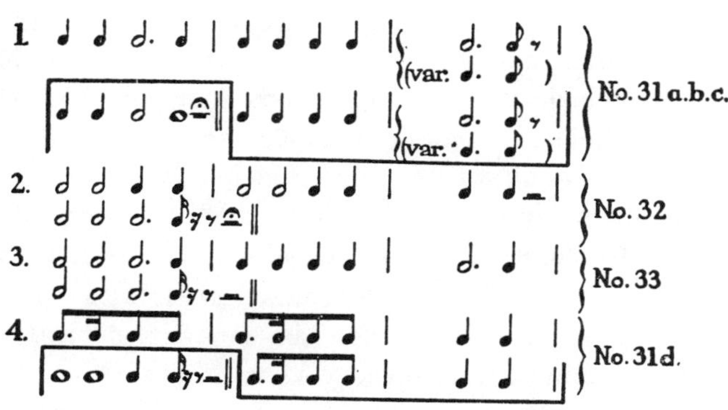

---

g)

1. No. 4

2. No. 5

3. No. 22

Group *b*) consists of patterns in which the value of one eighth (or quarter) note in one or both of the first two measures is doubled. The doubling may affect any one of the four eighths (or quarters). Variety of rhythm is attained by placing the change on different notes in the two measures (2. No. 7, both sections), by using the device in only one of the measures (3. Nos. 8 a. b.; 5. No. 19), and, finally, by using a different pattern in the second section (2. No. 7; 5. No. 19).

Group *c*) consists of patterns in which the values of the second measure in the first section are doubled. This appears clearly in 4. 5. 6. (Nos. 16 b., 17, 18). In 1., 2. (Nos. 9, 11) there occurs a quadrupling of the value of the first and second eighths in the second measure: changed to ; in 3. (No. 14) becomes . As to the second section, it has either the rhythm of the first section with a slight change (3. 6., Nos. 14, 17), or an altogether different pattern (1. 2. 5., Nos. 9, 11, 18).

In group *d)* there are patterns which use the combination of 𝅗𝅥 ♩ and ♩ 𝅗𝅥 (or ♩ ♪ and ♪ ♩) rhythms, in one or in both measures of the first section; the combination may be either the same or different in the two measures. Heterometric stanza constructions appear in 2.–5. (Nos. 39b, 43, 44 a. b., 45, 47). The rhythm in the first measure of the shorter second and fourth sections is built on the same principle in 2.–4.

Group *e)* contains rhythmic patterns in which the four values of the first measure in the first section are articulated as *3* + *1* instead of the common *2* + *2* division, showing the characteristic ♫♩ ⁝ 𝅗𝅥 rhythm or some variation of it; the last section (in two-section or three-section melodies) has the almost unchanged original rhythm (*a*)2. in double values), the second section of three-section melodies is simply a repeat—rhythmically as well as melodically—of the second and third measures of the first section (1. 2. 3.). In patterns 4.–7. the structure of the second and third (fourth) sections differs somewhat.

Group *f*), with melodies belonging to those with "special structure" (pp. 44–46), show first lines in which the first or both the first and the second bars are transformed from ♩ ♩ ♩ ♩ into ♩ ♩ ⁝ 𝅗𝅥. ♩ or 𝅗𝅥 𝅗𝅥 ⁝ ♩ ♩ (in 4., however, ♫♫ into ♩. ♪♫). No special comment is needed for this group. The same can be said concerning group *g*), in which the 8b, metrical line appears.

As the reader may note, great rhythmical variety is attained by the use of comparatively simple means.

PART-SINGING

Here follows a complete list of two-, three-, and four-part songs from the printed material and the Parry Collection.

Kuba B. H.	*"Tab. of Mat."*	*Number of Parts*
337	500 a.	2
338	500 b.	2
456	283 a.	2
474	752 c.	2
829	1553	2
1005	115 b.	2
1006	308	2
1019	285	2
1018	303 f.	2

Morphology

Kuba IX	*"Tab. of Mat."*	*Number of Parts*
3	1002 a.	2
5	321 g.	3
7	1162	3
8	690 a.	3
15	1296	2
16	588	2
21	473 b.	3
23	1372–73	2
46	610 e.	2
49	1891	2
52	1024 a.	2
Kuba X		
12	624	2
13	1506 f.	2
14	249	4
22	743	2
23	1381 c.	3
24	227	3
33	229 c.	2
43	1486	3
45	1093	3
48	1154	3
54	383 b.	3
59	1758	2
Kuhač		
370	487	2
1088	1729	2
1470	485 a.	2
Đorđević		
218	498	2
570	508	2
Bartók		
. . .	1020 a.	3
. . .	1223	2
Our Mus. Ex.		
1	. . .	2

This list shows that part singing occurs mostly in the northern and western border territories and in Dalmatia. Some of the two-part songs have simply a drone in the lower part, following the rhythm of the melody (mus. ex. No. 1). The majority of the part songs have adopted the simpler harmonies and intervals of Western European art music (melodies having a scale with final stop on the second degree receive a regular imperfect cadence of tonic-dominant chord progression at the end). A peculiarity in their performance was pointed out by L. Kuba.[63] It consists of the following usage: the main part—representing the melody proper—enters singly; the other parts join later, sometimes in the middle of a measure or even of a word. Data on the spreading of part singing and the extent to which it was considered "obligatory" in these border territories are very scarce. I learned from my Serbian peasant singers in the counties of Torontal and Temes, now in the Rumanian Banat area, that if several persons gather and want to sing they instinctively take to part singing. If an outsider asks them to sing in unison, they may do so, but they will not feel at their ease.[64]

However, in Dalmatia, besides the "normal" part singing, there is an extremely peculiar kind of "two-part" singing—in major seconds. L. Kuba devotes one part of his afore-mentioned article to a detailed description of it.[65] There are available (or at least there were before the Second World War) some commercial disks with such two-part songs of Dalmatia.[66] Listening to those records, one may hear the major seconds sometimes "degenerate" into minor thirds. Nevertheless, since these deviations seem to be more or less due to chance, this kind of performance may be called "part singing in major seconds."[67] It is used, at least in Dalmatia, in connection with chromatic-style melodies (see p. 64).

[63] In his article N. g. u. D., second part, pp. 1–6 (see also "Tab. of Mat." 1223, a melody recorded by Bartók).

[64] I obtained similar information from the Rumanian inhabitants of a near-by village, Nagyszentmiklós (Sânnicolaul-Mare), the only village where Rumanians SPONTANEOUSLY cultivate part singing, probably as a result of Serbian influence (see *Rumanian Folk Music,* Vol. II, 34–35).

[65] Pp. 12–15.

[66] Readers who are interested are referred to the following disks: Edison Bell Z 2104, Z 2041–42; Z 2105, Z 2043–44; and others in the same series, issued in Yugoslavia. For the transcription of the first one, see p. 63.

[67] A proof for this is found in the instrumental preludes on the commercial disks, which for technical reasons invert the melody played on two *sopela* (a kind of oboe), that is, there appear minor sevenths instead of major seconds. These minor sevenths are never changed into any other interval.

It is difficult to determine the origin of the normal as well as the major-second part singing. An intrinsic feature of peasant song melodies is their performance in unison. However, three great centers of part singing in Europe are exceptions: *a*) the German southeastern regions, *b*) the Great-Russian, and *c*) the Serbo-Croatian northwestern border territory—all three sections having normal part singing except Dalmatia. Does this usage originate in Western European[68] art music? This is possible, since the means used in both art music and peasant music are similar. So far, however, no evidence establishing this origin exists.

Explanation of part singing in major seconds is even more difficult. Analogous phenomena are entirely unknown in folk music anywhere, according to our actual knowledge.[69] Is it a transformation of a kind of normal part singing, or does it originate in the antique style of an extinct art music? Or perhaps the major seconds are simply "compressed" normal thirds. The latter theory seems to be the most acceptable explanation, since this part singing in major seconds is closely connected with the "chromatic" style melodies. And if the chromaticism of the latter is the result of a horizontal compression of diatonic scale segments, then the major seconds could be interpreted as having resulted from a vertical compression of thirds.

PECULIARITIES OF PERFORMANCE

Ornamental tones.—The ancient looking narrow-range melodies, the dance melodies, the *parlando-rubato* melodies to eight-syllable text lines with free stanza structure, and many melodies of foreign origin are comparatively poor in ornamental tones, and therefore differ little in their performance from most melodies in the material of neighboring peoples to the north and west. It is quite different with the other melodies, especially in the "autochthonous" areas. There we find an abundance of ornamental tones, the majority constituting "heavy" ornaments. These are, as pointed out on p. 17, ornament groups (melismatic groups) of equally heavy tones, with clear-cut, definite rhythmic and melodic patterns.[70] When we look at the skeleton form of the melodies as given in this book below the first melody stanza of most melodies, we get the picture of rather

[68] "Western European" is used in an extended sense, including German territories.

[69] Except in a few examples from Bulgarian territory.

[70] See our Nos. 2, 10 b (two examples of simpler ornaments), Nos. 4, 6 c., 10 a., 11, 12 e., 18, 22, 27 b., c., 28 c., 31 c., 41, and many others; the last is exceptionally rich.

simple, less appealing melody formations. Reading the melody as it was actually performed, we get the impression of having an incredible wealth of melodic design before us.

The Rumanian material of certain areas (for example, the Bihor area), is rich in heavy ornaments, too. There is, however, a difference between the latter and the Serbo-Croatian. The ornament tones in the Rumanian material usually lead from one principal tone to the following one, filling out the gap between intervals with a succession of degrees. Or they embellish the principal tones by circling around them or by giving them a sharper pulse (similar in effect to the mordents and inverted mordents). They are only accessories, having no individual patterns or life. The ornament tones in the Serbo-Croatian material, on the contrary, are formations of very expressive patterns and of a marvelous variety. These patterns deserve special study. Unfortunately, even an attempt at this would lead too far afield in this book.

L. Kuba grasped the peculiar character of the heavy ornaments at the very outset, and in some of his papers he emphasized their distinctive significance long ago.

Line-, word-, and syllable-interruptions.—In this paragraph we again come to an extremely characteristic feature of the Serbo-Croatian (and Bulgarian) folk melodies, that is, the line-, word-, and syllable-interruptions effected by shorter or longer rests, not for articulation's sake, but for decorative—one might almost say for expressive—purposes. This astonishing custom will invariably deceive even the best-trained musicians when they first listen to this kind of interruption. They will without fail interpret the rests erroneously, that is, as section caesuras.

There is a peculiar usage, at least in the Gacko area, of putting an extremely long rest at the end of the melody stanzas.[71] This rest, however, serves a decorative as well as an articulating purpose. As for the non-articulating rests, there are three kinds, referred to above; the difference between line interruption and word interruption, however, is not essential, because the length and the placement of the words used in the text line will determine whether there will be a line interruption or a word interruption.

[71] Since the Parry Collection contains very few samples from other areas and the earlier collectors never measured the rests between melody stanzas, we do not know the geographical extent of this usage.

Line (or word) interruptions have been observed by the editors of the printed material in 105 melodies (generally not in the first melody section):

74 by Kuba (two of them have two interruptions, the first of which takes place in the first melody section; three of the simple interruptions appear—as an exception—in the first melody section also);

27 by Đorđević (two of them with double interruptions, the first of which is in the first melody section);

4 by Kuhač (one double, the first of them in the first melody section);

15 melodies of our collection have it also: Nos. 5, 9, 11, 14, 15, 21 a. b., 22, 23 a. b., 24, 30, 40, 41, 47, 49. Of the latter, Nos. 5 and 14 have two interruptions, the first of which occurs in the first section; No. 14 deserves special attention because of the peculiar and exceptional mode of placing the interruptions, and because of the shifting of the first one, in some stanzas.

From this description it may be seen that interruptions generally avoid the first melody section. The placement of an interruption is not at all connected with the metrical structure; as a matter of fact, an interruption may appear following any of the syllables. Interruptions following the first or preceding the last syllable of the section are especially misleading, because generally there are no rests between the sections. For example, the melodic stanza of "Tab. of Mat." No. 1163 b. e. g. has the pattern *6, 6,* $\underbrace{1 \text{-'-} 5}$, *6,* (that is, it has the interruption after the first syllable of the third section). Inexperienced listeners, however, will assume the syllable structure to be *6, 7, 5, 6,* instead of *6, 6, 6, 6,*. Similarly, "Tab. of Mat." No. 788 d. g. h., with pattern *8,* $\underbrace{5 \text{-'-} 1}$, *6,* (interruption before the sixth syllable of the second section), will be interpreted as *8, 5, 7,* instead of *8, 6, 6,*.[72] In some cases the interruption is no intrinsic ingredient of the melody, as is shown by variant groups in which some of the variants have no interruption (variant a. of No. 1163), while others have it. One of our examples (No. 14) shows a shifting of the interruption in the first melody section from one syllable to another in some stanzas of the same song.

The less frequent syllable interruption has been observed in:

16 melodies by Đorđević (one has it in the first melody section);

[72] See, in addition, the respective examples in this collection.

2 by Kuba (one has two interruptions, the first of them in the first melody section);

1 by Bosiljevac (two interruptions, the first of them in the first melody section);

and in 1 melody in this book: No. 28 c.

The comments given for the line interruptions apply equally to the syllable interruptions.[73]

Analyzing the material of the neighboring peoples, we find that both kinds of interruption are known on Bulgarian territory as well as on Serbo-Croatian. They occur in a considerable number of Rumanian melodies, the interrupting rests, however, are less decisive, shorter, and therefore they do not give an impression of being used for decorative purposes, but rather as a mode of taking breath. On the whole, their use seems to be due to Yugoslav influence. The Hungarians and Turks do not know them at all.

In this connection a very important discovery has been made on Slovak territory. In a village in Zvolen County one single melody was found, in 1916, which has a PERMANENT syllable interruption on the fifth syllable of the last section.[74] It is a very ancient looking six-syllable four-section cradle song. Considering the apparently very great age of the melody, and the spontaneity with which all singers of the village, old or young, performed this song in the same way, we are fully satisfied that this interruption is a remainder—perhaps the only one on the entire North-Slavic territory—of an extremely ancient usage. Even on the basis of this single case, it is perhaps not too daring to submit the hypothesis that this phenomenon is an Old-Slavic usage, which although almost extinct among the Northern Slavs, still flourishes in Yugoslav territories.

Swallowing the last syllable of a section.—This has been observed in 20 melodies by Kuba and in 1 by Kuhač, the swallowing affects the last syllable of the last section in these 21 melodies;[75] in 2 melodies collected by Bartók ("Tab. of Mat." 39 d., 1259 b.); and in 3 in this collection: No 3, (the swallowing at the end of each stanza), No. 16 a., and b. (the swallowing occurs, however, after the third syllable of the second section in 16 a., and at the end of the second section in 16 b.).

[73] Readers who are interested in further details are referred to the last column of the "Tab. of Mat." Line- (word-) interruptions are marked there as *4* -'- *6* (= *10*); syllable interruptions as *4* + [5.] + *1* (= *6*), [5.] stands for "fifth syllable of the section, interrupted."

[74] Published in B. Bartók, *Five Village Scenes* (Vienna: Universal Edition, 1927), No. 4.

[75] More details in the last column of "Tab. of Mat."

This feature is known in the Bulgarian material, too. The same phenomenon is even more frequent in the Rumanian material.[76] The Hungarians of Transylvania have it, too, probably as a feature due to Rumanian influence. We have no data about its existence anywhere else. Its purpose is not quite clear. Its use, however, is by no means the result of a haphazard or individual mannerism; the performers employ it in the most deliberate way.

Clucking sounds.—There are two kinds of this manner of singing—(1) deliberate and (2) incidental. Clucking sounds deliberately used for ornamental purposes are all of extremely short duration and have a kind of a falsetto color produced by a peculiar technique of singing. They are very rare in the printed material, or to be more exact, they disappear there under cover of a common trill sign. Their only known precise transcription is shown in our music example No. 1; the variant of Kuba quoted on p. 231 has the trill sign as a substitute. To do Kuba and the other collectors justice, it should be mentioned that it is almost impossible to attain an exact notation of these strange sounds without studying them on records. Serbo-Croatian scholars seem to know this peculiarity very well; according to them it is spread over a certain part of Dalmatia. The Rumanians use somewhat similar sounds in their so-called "Cântec lung" (long-[drawn] song).[77] They are entirely lacking in the Hungarian and the Slovak material.

2. The other type of clucking sound is the result of a physiological process, of a certain function of the sound-producing organs when they are used to their fullest extent, that is, in "full-tone" singing (see mus. ex. Nos. 12 b., 15, 19, 23 a., 27 d., and others; 12 b. is exceedingly rich in such sounds). These sounds are never used wilfully, and they appear either at the end of a tone or before it is attacked. They may appear as a phenomenon accompanying full-tone singing in the practice of any of the peoples of central and southeastern Europe. In spite of their unintentional nature, they ought to be carefully observed and transcribed, for they give a peculiar color to the performance.

Both kinds of clucking sounds appear mainly—in some areas exclusively—in the performance of female singers; both are missing in the published collections.

[76] See *Rumanian Folk Music,* Vol. II, Nos. 534 b., 639 a.c., and others.

[77] *Ibid.,* Vol. II, No. 613 a.–h., and *Rumanian Folk Music,* Vol. V (Maramureş County), Nos. 23a.–h.

Emphatic rendition of syllables.—The most frequent means of achieving this effect in the Serbo-Croatian style is to split a vowel into two or more identical vowels by interpolating one or more *h* sounds (mus. ex. No. 12 b.). The use of these dividing *h* sounds is generally accompanied by some happenings in the melody, too—either a clucking sound appears when *h* is introduced, or a change of degree, or both.

This kind of emphatic performance has been observed by Kuba (B. H. 111, 472, 534, 600) and by Kuhač (955). The same mannerism occurs in the Turkish material[78] and in Arabic art music. In the latter, rather long ornament groups with accented tones sung to the same syllable account for it. In the former, its use is probably due to an influence of Arabic urban music. Perhaps this is true concerning the Serbo-Croatian emphatic performance, also. It is, however, possible that it originated in some usage of Western art music that disappeared long ago.[79]

Another means of achieving emphatic performance (perhaps of jocular character?) is to interpolate meaningless syllables such as *gi-ga-ga, go-gi-go,* either inserted between the broken-up particles of the vowel or simply added to the unbroken vowel. Unfortunately our collection contains only one example (No. 54); since this has been recorded only once and has an undeterminable structure, no conclusions can be drawn from it. The printed collections contain 15 examples, 11 observed by Kuba, 2 by Kuhač, and 2 by Đorđević:

"Tab. of Mat."	*Kuba B. H.*
265 d.	257
572	152
809	969
869	3
890	824
905 d.	583
1023	475
1619 e.	117
1826	987
1878	34

[78] See *Turkish Folk Music from Asia Minor,* Nos. 20, 24.

[79] The Hungarian designation "hehhentés," still in use a century ago, for melismatic groups in art music, is significant; the *h* sounds in this onomatopoetic word point to a possible use of *h* sounds in the performance of those groups.

and in addition Kuba N. g. u. D. No. 64.

"Tab. of Mat."	*Kuhač*
905 e.	1101
1084	590

"Tab. of Mat."	*Đorđević Nar. Pev.*
867	p. 86, first melody
1755 bis	p. 15, first melody

The purpose and character of this kind of emphasis is not clear. According to our present knowledge the device is absolutely unknown elsewhere.

"Stuttering" entrance of words.—This is a rare phenomenon, observed in three melodies of the published material: "Tab. of Mat." 627 (Đorđević 360) and 905 c. g. (Kuba XI, 47, X, 11). It consists of the anticipated repetition of the first syllable in a word: *Više se-, sela* (<*Više sela*); *Kiša pa-, pade* (<*Kiša pade*); *Udri kir, -kiša* (<*Udri kiša*);[80] although there the repeat is functionally a substitution for the exclamation Oj. It seems to be used for humorous effect. We mention it in spite of its rarity, since the Rumanian material contains some specimens, too: Bartók, *Rumanian Folk Music,* Vol. II, Nos. 428, 600. This either shows Serbo-Croatian influence on Rumanian material, or it indicates that the phenomenon is a characteristic trait of Balkan folk music. We have no data about its existence in the material of other peoples.

Syllabication[81] of consonants.—This is the result of an emphatic pronunciation of a single (mostly syllable closing) consonant, and is achieved by adding the sound *ə* (more-or-less similar to the Rumanian *ă* or the Bulgarian *ň*, or to the blurred vowel in unaccented English *-er*) to the consonant.[82] The so-called liquids *l*, *r*—sometimes also *j*, *m*, *n*—do not generally need this addition (for instance, music ex. No. 14, syllable 1: *Si-tə*; No. 21 a., measure 11: *po-də-*. For syllable *l*, *r*, see mus. ex. No. 21 a., St. 2, measure 3: *di-l-be-r*; No. 22, St. 2, next-to-last measure, *vi-ha-r*; in measure 2, 5, however, *vi-ha-rə*; etc.). The new syllable thus created must, of course, never be regarded and counted as an independent sylla-

[80] Cf. footnote 21 on p. 32.

[81] This word is used here in the sense of "making a syllable out of" a consonant.

[82] This is not to be mistaken for another well-known phenomenon in the Slavic languages, that is, the use of *r* (in Serbo-Croatian, for example, in *hrt*), or of *r* and *l* (in some other Slavic languages, for instance, Slovak *smrť, vlk*), as syllabic consonants.

ble. No trace of this peculiarity can be discovered in the printed collections, except in Kuhač No. 812, where he explains that "praviti" was sung as "piraviti" (more correctly, *pə-raviti*?).

A deviation from the official Serbo-Croatian syllabication rules must be mentioned in this connection. The singers seem to be inclined to divide words into syllables in a more natural way; for example, instead of *ka-kvo*, we have *kak-vo* in mus. ex. No. 28 a., St. 6, measure 5; instead of *la-dna*, we have *la-də-|-na* in our mus. ex. No. 39 b. measure before the last; *i-gə-|-re* in No. 33, St. 4, measure 3, instead of *i-gre*; and even *u-gə-|-le-|-da-|-o* in No. 8 b., St. 2, measures 2, 3, instead of *u-|-gle-|-da-|-o*. When a word begins with two or more consonants, it may happen that the first will become syllabified and will be thrown back to the end of the preceding note value, so that it will function as an upbeat to the following value; for example, mus. ex. No. 27 e., St. 3, bars 8–9; No. 6 a., St. 3, bar 4; No. 24, St. 5, bar 1; No. 23 b., St. 4, bar 1. As these examples show, the syllabified consonants receive an individual ornamental tone in the melody.

This usage is spread over all central-eastern Europe and probably over many other territories.

SOME OTHER PECULIARITIES OF PERFORMANCE

1. Structurally essential upbeats are unknown in Eastern European folk music (except in Great-Russian and Greek). The beginning of a section, especially after a rest, seems to need some short "preparation," however. This is provided by structurally unessential, usually very short upbeats, sung to syllables not belonging to the text proper. Such elements in Serbo-Croatian songs are: *ə* (see p. 79), *əj*, *həj*, *i*, *n*, *m*, *hn*, sometimes *ej*, *oj* (the latter not to be mistaken for ej, oj, used on downbeats: see p. 32), and so forth.

Anticipated repetition (doubling) of word-beginning "liquid" consonants may substitute for these syllables, or other syllable consonants taken from a word-beginning group of consonants. Examples in our melodies, Nos. 14, St. 1, 2, 5, 6, and 31 b., St. 2. These upbeats may appear even after line and syllable interruptions (for example, No. 14, St. 2–5).

This usage is very common in the folk-song performance also of other Eastern European peoples.

2. Hiatus-filling consonants are used in Serbo-Croatian folk songs rather rarely (at least, in our melodies, the other editors having neglected this phenomenon), except for the two final syllables of the participle perf. ending, *io*, which generally appears as *ijo*. *J* is used in other instances, too (for instance, mus. ex. No. 28 b., St. 4, measure 2). Hungarians, Slovaks, and Rumanians use *j* for the same purpose, Rumanians also *d;* Turks prefer *d;* these peoples, however, use hiatus-filling consonants much more frequently.

RELATION BETWEEN TEXT AND MELODY

When a great many melodies of identical structure exist in a body of folk-song material, it is very improbable that each of them will have its own text: texts and melodies will be more probably interchangeable.[83] Although this might have been the case in the Serbo-Croatian material, too, in the course of time some of the texts have become linked to some of the melodies. Examples: Among our variant groups, only Nos. 21, 23, 31, and 44 contain identical texts, for two variants in each of these groups. In the subgroup "Tab. of Mat." 111–201 (*8*, = *4* + *4*) there are 43 variant groups; among these 11 contain two (or, in a few cases, more than two) melodies with the same text. Examining the largest variant groups—"Tab. of Mat." 983 a.–ll. and our No. 27 a.–e.—we find not more than ten variants (out of 41) of which several have the same texts: five (g., l., bb., ee., ii.) with *U Omera više Sarajeva,* three (c., bb., our No. 27 b.) with *Beg Alibeg* (or other name) *na kuli* (or somewhere else) *sjedaše,* and two (p. t.) with the same lullaby text.

These data prove that in the majority of the songs text and melody have remained interchangeable, within the limits given by the differences in the metrical structure of the text lines (and excepting songs of urban origin).

Ceremonial songs and songs for special occasions.—The Parry Collection contains few songs designated by the singers as connected with the per-

[83] This is the actual situation in the Rumanian rural material, for instance, within the limits set by the differences in the subject matter of the various ceremonial categories, as well as of the nonceremonial songs (but not in songs of urban origin).

formance of ceremonies, or with special occasions, distinguishable from others by style or subject matter.[84] The printed collections, especially those of Đorđević and of Bušetić (Iz Levča), contain many ceremonial or other designations. An enumeration of these is given below, in various groups and subgroups.

Songs performed in connection with:

I. Outstanding events

1. *Svatovska*[85] (wedding song); 2. *Naricanje* (song of mourning)

II. Events of every-day life

1. *Uspavanka* (lullaby); 2. *Na ranilu* (morning song)

III. Work

a) Work in the fields

1. *Žetvarska* (harvest song); 2. *Kad se bere seno* (hay-gathering song); 3. *Na kopanju* (*kad se kopa loza; pri kopanju kukuruza*) (hoeing song [when hoeing vine; when hoeing maize]); 4. *Kad se ide u branje zdravca* (at "*zdravac*"[86] gathering); 5. *Pri radu* (when at work); 6. *Kad se vraća sa rada* (when returning from work [in the fields])

b) Work in or around the house

1. *Kad se vlači vuna* (when combing wool); 2. *Ćilimarska* (carpet-weaving song); 3. *Na prelu* (spinning song); 4. *Pri bučkanu* (butter-whipping song)

IV. Recreation

1. *Sedeljka* (evening gathering of girls for some kind of light work); 2. *Pripev*[87] (song to match a girl and a boy); 3. *Pozdrav devojaka na saboru* (girls' greeting song); 4. *Ljuljaška pesma na Đurđevdan* (swing song for St. George's day); 5. *Slavna* (drinking song)

V. Dance and play songs

1. *Kolo* (*žensko-*, *muško-* and so forth), round dance [for women, for men, and so forth]; 2. *Poskočnica* (jumping dance); 3. *Pljeskavica* (clapping dance); 4. *Čaružanke;* 5. *Balkanka;* 6. *Paraćinka* (4.–6. are designations of various dances); 7. *Vanjkušac* (pillow [or cushion?] dance); 8. *Oro* (round dance); 9. *Igra* (*Dečja igra*) (play or dance song [children's play song])

[84] See Part Two, p. 253.

[85] Various forms of the same designation are used by the various editors; only one form is given here.

[86] Crane's bill (geranium macrorhizum).

[87] This word means also "refrain."

VI. Songs connected with certain days of the year

1. *Lazarička* (Lazarus's day song); 2. *Kraljička* ([Song] of the "Queen" [on Trinity Sunday?]); 3. *Kralja na Spasovdan* ([Song] of the "King" on Ascension day); 4. *Na Svetog Nikolu* (St. Nicholas's day song); 5. *U oči Jeremijinog dana* (on the eve of Jeremy's day); 6. *U oči Đurđevdana* (on the eve of St. George's day); 7. "*Pevaju se prilikom maskarada o Beloj Nedelji*" (on Carnival Sunday); 8. *Krstonoška* (Rogation day song); 9. *Uskršnja* (Easter song); 10. *Na premlaz* (*bačija*) (At the milking festival); 11. *Koleda* (winter-solstice [or Christmas] song); 12. *U vreme mesopusta* (song for the Lenten season)

VII. Songs connected with rainfall

1. *Dodola* (rain-begging song); 2. "*Pevaju deca kad pada kiša*" (children's song when it is raining)

REMARKS

I. 2.: Represented, unfortunately, by only two melodies (Đorđević, Iz Levča); despite the fact that a scarcity of songs of mourning is scarcely conceivable.

IV. 1.: Almost every song not connected with some other ceremony or occasion bears the designation *sedeljka* in Đorđević and in "Iz Levča." The designation is apt to mean that they are generally sung at such gatherings as the most suitable occasion for community singing.

IV. 5.: Sung on name-day festivals.

V. 8.: Only in Kuhač (*Oro* seems to be the Bulgarian equivalent for *Kolo*).

VI. 11.: Represented by only two examples. Would this mean that the usage is dying out or that the collectors had neglected this category of songs?

VII. 1.: Represented by four examples, although rain-begging songs probably are known in every village.

Very frequently the designations apply only to the content of the text.

A text in the Parry Collection which contains conversations among singers concerning songs, has references, in addition, to "songs for lovemaking" (*pjesme za ašikovanje*), to different kinds of *kolo* dance songs (*pjesme za kolo*), to game-songs of children and adults, humorous songs (*smiješne pjesme*), songs of auto and bus drivers (*šoferske pjesme*), and, among Mohammedans, songs for the circumcision rite. According to this source, there are no special songs chosen for evening gatherings (*za sijelo*). Some songs are designated as shepherds' songs (*čobanske pjesme*). (A.B.L.)

Probably all these categories of songs exist also in the Bulgarian material. The Rumanians have wedding songs and songs of mourning (in every village, at least one kind); lullabies; harvesting and hay-gathering songs; winter-solstice or Christmas songs (their material is extremely rich in "Colinde," as they call the *Koleda*);[88] rain-begging songs (only in the southwestern areas); and many types of dance melodies (most of them only in instrumental form). The Hungarians have wedding songs and songs of mourning; harvest songs; name-day songs; songs to match a girl and a boy; a kind of winter-solstice or wassailing song (called *regösének*); and in addition a type of summer-solstice song which is apparently lacking in the Serbo-Croatian material. The Slovaks have the same categories as the Hungarians except the winter-solstice song, and in addition they have lullabies, "christening," and some other songs.[89]

As has been pointed out on p. 35, ceremonial songs in the Serbo-Croatian material have no specific group features in their melodies except that dance melodies are less ornamented, and the rather ancient looking melodies of certain categories (for various special days, such as Lazarus's day, St. Nicholas's day, and others) have a narrow range. These traits, however, do not justify placing them in independent classes.

Only one kind of Serbo-Croatian song, the heroic (or *gusle*) song bears special melodic characteristics, and it has to be treated apart; this category, however, does not belong to the subject-matter of this book.

A category quite apart and very well known in the Hungarian, Slovak, German, and French material is that of the "children's play songs." These melodies often have no symmetrical form, but seem to be a potpourri of shorter or longer fragments of a certain kind. The Turkish material has this kind of melody in its rain-begging songs; the Rumanians do not know it at all. It exists in the Serbo-Croatian material, too; their melodies, besides being real children's play songs, serve also as dance songs, name-day songs, festival songs, and (in one case) as wedding songs. Since they have an undeterminable structure, they are placed in a separate category ("Tab. of Mat.," p. 135).

[88] See *Rumanian Folk Music,* Vol. IV (Carols and Christmas Songs [*Colinde*]).
[89] It is not pretended that these enumerations are complete.

Morphology

CONCLUSIONS

After our intensive analysis of Serbo-Croatian folk-music we can state its main characteristics as follows:

In *melody:* Heterometric syllabic structures are characteristic; they result from the so-called splitting of text lines (see pp. 37ff.). The prevalent structures of melodic content may be expressed with the formulas $\mathrm{A\,A_{(v)}}$, $\mathrm{A\,A\,A_{(v)}}$ or $\mathrm{A\,A_{(v)}\,A}$, and $\mathrm{A\,B\,B_{(v)}}$ or $\mathrm{A\,A_{(v)}\,B}$ (pp. 47–50). The main caesura in the melodies, which consist of two or three sections or phrases, is prevalently on the first degree of the scale, or on the (major or minor) second above. The characteristic range is narrow, between a fourth and a sixth; very often from a second below the first degree of the scale to the fourth (or fifth) above, or from the first degree to the fourth above (p. 52). The characteristic scale is a pentachord formation, VII–4 or VII–5, with f^1, a^1 or a^1 flat, and c^2 as its main degrees and final stop on the second degree, g^1 (pp. 59–61).

As for *text structure,* there is no stanza structure. Ten-syllable lines are preponderant.

As for *mode of performance:* heavy ornamentation is frequent (pp. 73–74). Rests are used not so much for articulating as for decorative, expressive purposes (p. 74). The performance of many ornamental tones is emphatic (p. 78).

Melodies with these characteristics are spread mainly over the "autochthonous" territories of Serbia, Old-Serbia, Montenegro, Hercegovina, and Bosnia.

Foreign influences are found chiefly in the remaining territories, especially in Croatia, the Croatian seashore, Istria, and Dalmatia. Slavonia, Banat and Bačka are, perhaps, transitional territories in this regard. The very small area of Međumurje is almost completely saturated with foreign melodies (p. 24). Foreign influence is shown by the preponderance of four-section melody structures, wide-range melodies, $\mathrm{A^5\,B^5\,A\,B}$ or similar content structures, and text-stanza structures. It is not strong in the "autochthonous" territories. As for the few older melodies there which suggest foreign influence, it originates probably from Turkish sources, either directly or indirectly through Bulgarian mediation (pp. 54–56); as for the numerous more recent melodies in the western areas, it originates from central or western Europe. The very few recent[90] borrowings

[90] "Recent" means here, within the last sixty or seventy years.

in the "autochthonous" territories come from New Hungarian material (p. 56–59).

INFLUENCE OF THE SERBO-CROATIAN "AUTOCHTHONOUS" MATERIAL ON THE FOLK MUSIC OF OTHER PEOPLES

On Hungarian material there has been no Serbo-Croatian influence.

On Rumanian material some influence can be traced in the Banat area (including the counties of Torontal, Temeš, Arad, Karaš-Severin, and, perhaps, Hunedoara). This influence appears in the frequent use of the scale described above, with the final stop on the second degree. The very characteristic Serbo-Croatian heterometric structures, however, did not exert any influence. Some melodies of urban origin are common in Serbo-Croatian, Rumanian and Hungarian material. This fact, however, is irrelevant when it comes to the "autochthonous" material of either of these peoples. Instrumental Rumanian dance melodies have probably undergone some Serbo-Croatian influence. The scarcity of published Serbo-Croatian instrumental melodies unfortunately prevents satisfactory comparative investigation.

RELATION OF SERBO-CROATIAN AND BULGARIAN FOLK SONGS

The relation seems to be very close (p. 37). Since I have not yet been able thoroughly to study the great bulk of Bulgarian material which comprises almost 10,000 published melodies and in manuscript another 10,000, I must be content with the results of a superficial examination, which shows two main differences.

(*a*) Text lines of 10 syllables are in the majority in Serbo-Croatia, those of 8*b* syllables in Bulgaria.

(*b*) So-called "Bulgarian" rhythm formations are completely lacking in the Serbo-Croatian material.[91]

SIGNS POINTING TOWARD AN ANCIENT COMMON SLAVIC MUSICAL STYLE

The very meager data concerning this question allow only two tentative hypotheses:

[91] This opinion is based mainly on the Parry Collection; the published material cannot be regarded as quite reliable in this respect.

(*a*) a possibly ancient common style of narrow-range melodies (p. 54).

(*b*) a possibly ancient common trait of performance, described as "syllable-interruption" on pp. 75–76.

In handling many thousands of figures and symbols it is impossible to avoid slips and errors. Even mistakes of greater importance concerning details may have crept into this book. We shall be only too grateful if our readers who have the endurance to study the book thoroughly will call our attention to those which they discover. Nevertheless, we hope to have been right as to the main statements and to have given a firm basis for the continuation of research on Serbo-Croatian folk music.

REGIONS, VILLAGES, SINGERS, AND OTHER DATA

Place	Singer	Date of Recording	Song Number in Collection on Pages 95–230	Number of Melodies
Bosnia				
Bare	Mustafa Goro (male)	Oct. 10, 1934	35	1
Bihać	Zejnil Sinanović (male)	April 13, 1935	27e., 39b., 44b.	3
Kulen Vakuf	Ibrahim Mašinović (male, 65 years of age)	Sept. 24, 1934	7, 34	2
Dalmatia				
Kijevo	Girls	Sept. 22, 1934	1	1
Livno	Meho Jarić (male, 28)	Sept. 21, 1934	20, 28b., c., 36, 42	5
Hercegovina				
Gacko	Derviša Biberović (female, 50)	May 21, 1935	4, 6b., 21b.	3
	Džefa Grebović (female, 45)	April 26, 1935	18, 31	2
	Halida Habeš (female, 22)	April 24, 1935	6a., 8b.	2
	Ibrahim Hrustanović (male, 23)	April 20, May 21, 1935	33, 38	2
	Halima Hrvo (female, 60)	April 22, 23, 26, 27, 1935	5, 9, 12d., 14, 15, 23a., 27d., 30, 40, 54	10
	Fata Krajišnik (female, 65)	April 24, 1935	10a.,b., 25	3
	Ćerima Kurtović (female, 12)	April 24, May 21, 1935	17, 26, 27a., 29	4
	Fata Šaković (female, 60)	April 22, 1935	12b., 19	2
	Hajrija Šaković (female, 18)	April 22, 26, 27, May 20, 21, 1935	2, 6c., 12a., 16, 31a., 32, 37,[1] 44a., 45, 46, 49,[2] 52	12
	Almasa Zvizdić (female, 45)	April 22, 23, 24, 26, 27, May 19, 20, 21, 1935	3, 8a., 11, 22, 23b., 24, 27b., c., 31b., c., 39a., 41, 43, 47, 48, 50, 51, 53	18
	Raba Zvizdić (female, 32)	April 24, 1935	12e., 21a.	2
	Šerifa Zvizdić (female, 55)	April 22, 1935	12c.	1
Rotimja, district of Stolac	Naza Rokić (female, 26 or 27 years old)[3]	Dec. 15, 1934	13, 28a.	2
Total				75

Remark. For further information on the singers and on the circumstances of the recording, see pp. 249–252. [1] With Ibrahim Hrustanović. [2] With Almasa Zvizdić.
[3] She says this about her age in a recorded conversation.

Morphology

CHARACTERISTICS OF SOME OF THE SINGERS

Meho Jarić has a so-called "beautiful" voice. The voice of a singer is considered "beautiful" by rural people when he or she tries to imitate urban dramatized performance by putting much "sentiment" into his voice, using exaggerated *parlando* rhythm and too many ornamental notes. The reader may compare the nobly simple rural performance of Naza Rokić in No. 28a. with the performance of the same piece by Meho Jarić in No. 28b. in order to grasp the difference between the two styles.

In *Halima Hrvo*'s pieces the most remarkable feature is the almost unvarying pitch; eight out of ten have $e^1\flat$ or a somewhat high d^1 for the final tone. She has less sense for constancy in tempo; in almost all her performances there is a gradual and considerable *accelerando*.

Hajrija Šaković, on the contrary, tends to raise her voice gradually during the performance; the differences in pitch are rather conspicuous. She evidently always begins in a pitch too low and is compelled to raise her voice in order to reach a more comfortable level. Her tempo, however, shows more constancy; only slight *accelerandos* appear in her performances.

Almasa Zvizdić keeps the pitch constant in the single pieces, although it is different in each of her performances; she has no absolute sense of pitch. Her sense for constancy in tempo is rather marked: no changes occur in her pieces, except in one or two. Her performance has on the whole a rural character, except in some of the *8, 5, 8, 5,* melodies; there, especially in the pieces with sentimental urban texts, her style resembles somewhat that of Meho Jarić.

The performance of Halima Hrvo, Hajrija Šaković, and of the other singers—except Zejnil Sinanović—has an altogether rural character.

EXPLANATION OF THE SIGNS USED IN THE MUSIC NOTATIONS

Some melodies have one or more variants. These variants are given the same Arabic number, but are distinguished by a small letter following the number (1a., 1b., 1c., etc.).

Each section of a melody stanza occupies a separate staff, except in No. 1, in which a prolonged bar (-line) indicates the end of each melody stanza (each melody stanza having only one melody section). At the end of each section, generally in the first stanza, above the last tone, or the tone considered as structurally the last tone, appear the numbers designating these tones in] or □ or [. Above the first staff, at the right, appear the numbers indicating the syllable number of the melody sections and the range of the melody. For these symbols see pp. 27–28.

At least three (sometimes more) melody stanzas are written out in full; those portions of the remaining melody stanzas which show essential changes appear after the full forms as notes or variants. For example, "St. 6 (ref. to St. 4)" means: "Stanza 6 has essential changes; see numbers over the respective portions of Stanza 4."

After the piece follow the record number, the name of the place (village) where the recording was made or from which the singer came, the name of the district (in parentheses), the name of the singer, and the date of the recording.

Preceding the first measure of the piece stands the pitch indication: a black note without stem, in treble clef for women singers, in bass clef for men singers. This note always gives the pitch on which the singer sang the notes written as g^1 (see p. 13).

In order to facilitate a quick grasp of the melodic structure, the skeleton form of the melody (stripped of all ornamental tones) is added to almost all the pieces, placed generally underneath the first stanza.

In the melody stanzas that are written out in full, metronome figures are used in tempo designations. If there are any changes in the remaining melody stanzas, this is indicated in the Notes to the Melodies. If there is no general tempo indication, such as *rubato*, etc., this means *tempo giusto* (that is, more or less rigid rhythm), except when no time signatures are used (see below).

Time signatures in parentheses mean that, although the values indicated by the signature are originally intended in the respective measures, nevertheless, certain deviations appear in some or in all the measures (see p. 6). When no time signatures are used, the performance is *parlando-rubato*, without any systematic succession of note values.

Key signatures are used only when the respective degree is affected throughout the whole piece (excepting small-head notes). See p. 13.

The sign ⌒ above a note indicates a slight lengthening; ⌣ a slight shortening.

The wavy line connecting two notes means a glide (*portamento* or *glissando*) in which single pitches are not discernible; above or underneath a melismatic group of notes it indicates a blurring of the group by gliding. Above a note it indicates *vibrato*.

The arrow above a note, pointing upward, means slightly higher pitch than noted; pointing downward, slightly lower pitch. They are used above note heads and above flats and sharps; in the latter case they are valid as long as are the respective flats and sharps; if they are in parentheses, it means that their validity may sometimes be interrupted.

Brackets above the staff line mean that the respective portion of the melody is an interpolation from the structural point of view, and is disregarded when establishing the structure of the melody.

Melismatic groups always bear a slur or tie; each single note in groups without a slur is sung to a separate syllable. Broken slurs mean that the two (or more) syllables of the respective group are regarded as being structurally one syllable.

(No. 12 d., St. 4, measure 3) means that the quadruplet has a value of the current notation; (No. 23b., St. 2, measure 5) means that the quintuplet has a value; and so forth.

The values of small-head notes connected with a large-head note by a slur (but not by a beam), have to be subtracted from the value of the large-head note, for example:

equals ; equals ; equals .

When connected by a beam, no subtraction will be made: .

Single small-head notes have their own value (for example in No. 7, St. 2, first note). For the meaning of small-head notes see p. 17. In addition to the commonly known note values, the (4/2, the "breve") and the corresponding rest are also used in the transcriptions.

Small-head notes with heads in outline are used for "clucking" sounds (see p. 17): for definite pitch; for indefinite (approximate) pitch. The use of × instead of note heads means indefinite (approximate) pitch.

Letters in italics are used for syllables or sounds not belonging to the text proper (below the music also indicated by a wavy line), for example, *ə* (inverted e), *hn*, hiatus-filling *j*, *h* for emphatic coloring of vowels (dra-*h*a-ga stands for dra-ga). See pp. 78–80. Syllables or words marked with ⌐ represent interpolations not taken into consideration when establishing the syllable numbers.

Morphology

Dots are substituted for unprintable words, each dot standing for a letter.

A tie inderneath two vowels connected by a hyphen (*e-i*, *o-o*) means that they constitute only one syllable. In the first example (No. 20., measure 14) the different second vowel is an arbitrary addition and does not modify the sense of the word; the second example (No. 27e., measure 6) represents a syllable interruption.

Ụ is a bilabial *v*, added sometimes before a word beginning with *o* (No. 21b., St. 2, measure 11).

The signs * or **, etc., refer to the Notes to the Music.

Works Cited In Part One

For Serbo-Croatian publications see pp. 22–25.

Bartók, Béla. Five Village Scenes; for voice and piano. Vienna: Universal Edition, 1927.

—— 44 Duets for Two Violins. Vienna: Universal Edition, 1933. Reprint by Boosey & Hawkes, New York.

—— *Hungarian Folk Music* (352 melodies). London: Oxford University Press, 1931.

—— La Musique populaire des hongrois et des peuples voisins (about 100 melodies). *Archivum Europae Centro-Orientalis,* II (Budapest, 1936), 197–244.

—— *Rumanian Folk Music* (ed. Benjamin Suchoff). The Hague: Martinus Nijhoff, 1967, 1975, Vols. I–II (2,555 melodies), Vol. III (1,752 texts); Vol. IV (Carols and Christmas Songs [*Colinde*], 484 melodies); Vol. V (Maramureș County, 378 melodies).

—— *Turkish Folk Music from Asia Minor* (ed. Benjamin Suchoff). New Jersey: Princeton University Press, 1976 (87 melodies).

Bartoš, Fr. *Národní Písně Moravské* (about 1,000 melodies). Brno, 1889.

—— *Národní Písně Moravské* (about 2,000 melodies). Praha, 1899, 1901.

Černík, J. *Zpěvy Moravských Kopaničářů* (about 300 melodies), Praha, 1908.

Folklore musical. Paris: Institut International de Coöpération Intellectuelle, Vol. II., 1939.

Peck, E. *Valašské Národní Písně* (a few hundred melodies). Brno, 1860.

Slovenské Spevy, Vols. I–III (about 1,800 melodies). Turčiansky Svätý Martín, 1880, 1890, 1899.

Sušil, *Fr. Moravské Národní Písně* (about 1,600 melodies). Brno, 1859.

Szabolcsi, B., and A. Tóth. *Zenei Lexikon.* Budapest, 1931.

Music Examples

1

1 (continued)

♩ = ca. 118 (quasi rubato)

Hej hoj hə-hə-hə hoj hə-hə-hə hoj hə-hə-hə hoj

Hoj hoj hoj hoj

hə-hə-hə hoj hoj hoj.

hoj hoj hoj.

Var.

3)–4) ♩ = ca. 86 (quasi rubato)

– –. Hə-hə hoj hə-hə hoj hə-hə hoj hoj hoj hə-hə hoj.

– –. Hoj hoj hoj hoj.

R. 553, 554; Kijevo (Dalmatia), đevojke, Sept. 22, 1934

2

2 (continued)

Var. (ref. to St.1) St. 15 1)

R. 3572-3; Gacko (Hercegovina), Hajrija Šaković, May 21, 1935

3

8,VII-4

3 (continued)

R. 3557-9; Gacko (Hercegovina), Almasa Zvizdić, May 21, 1935

4

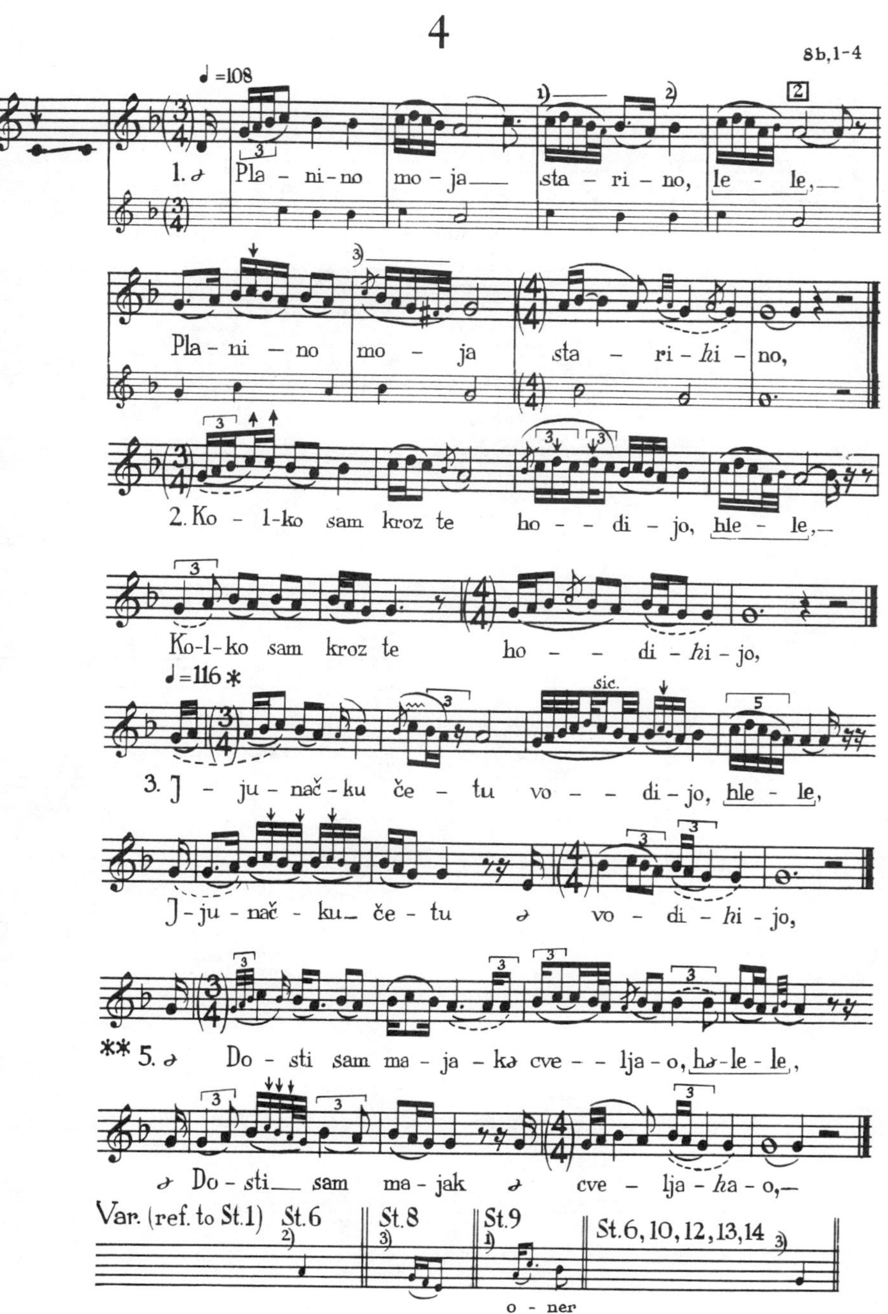

R. 3586; Gacko (Hercegovina), Derviša Biberović, May 21, 1935

5

8b, VII-4
♩ = 90*
1. Hn Puh - ni mi, puh- ni, la - da - ne,
Puh - ni mi-hi puh- ni, la - da - ne,
2. Hn Do - đi mi, do - đi, dra - ga - ne,
Do - đi mi, do-đi, dra - ga-ha-ha - ne,
3. U mo - je do - re bi - - je - - le,
U mo - je do - re bi - - je - he - le.
4. ∂ Do - ve - di đo - ga za so - ho - bo - - - m,
Do - ve - di đo - ga za so - ho - bom

5 (continued)

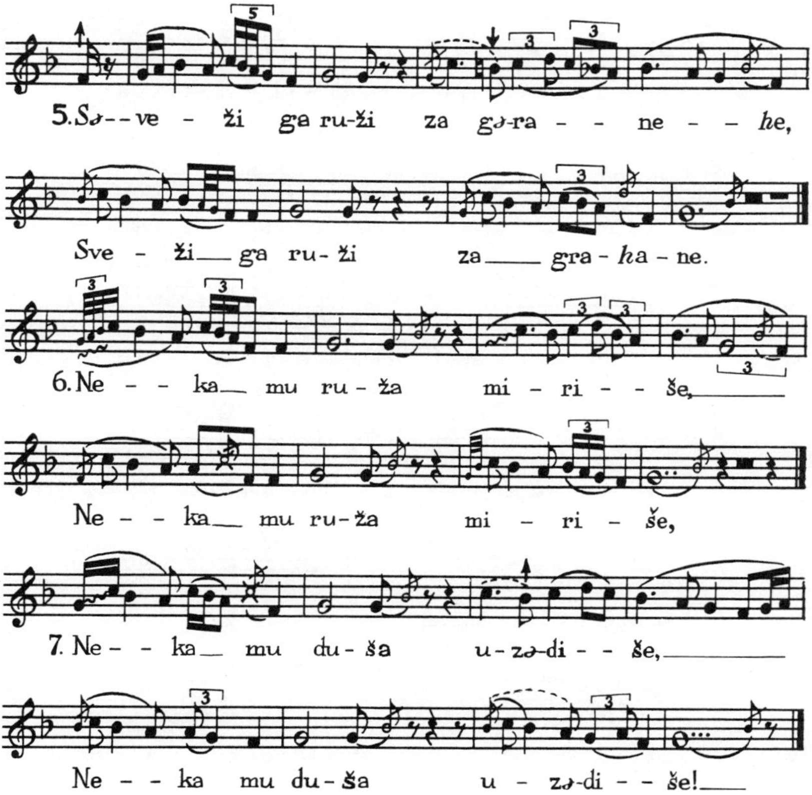
5. Sə-- ve - ži ga ru-ži za gə-ra - - ne - - he,
Sve - ži ga ru- ži za gra - ha - ne.
3 3 3 3 3
6. Ne - - ka mu ru - ža mi - ri - - še,
Ne - - ka mu ru- ža mi - ri - še,
7. Ne - - ka mu du - ša u - zə-di - - še,
Ne - - ka mu du - ša u - zə-di - - še!

R. 3074; Gacko (Hercegovina), Halima Hrvo, April 22, 1935

6a

10, VII - 4
♩= 112 *
VII
St.1 - St.12 - St.25
1. Raz-bo-lje se Đe - her - đe-lez A - li - - ja
U pla - ni-ni pod je - lom ze - le - nom.

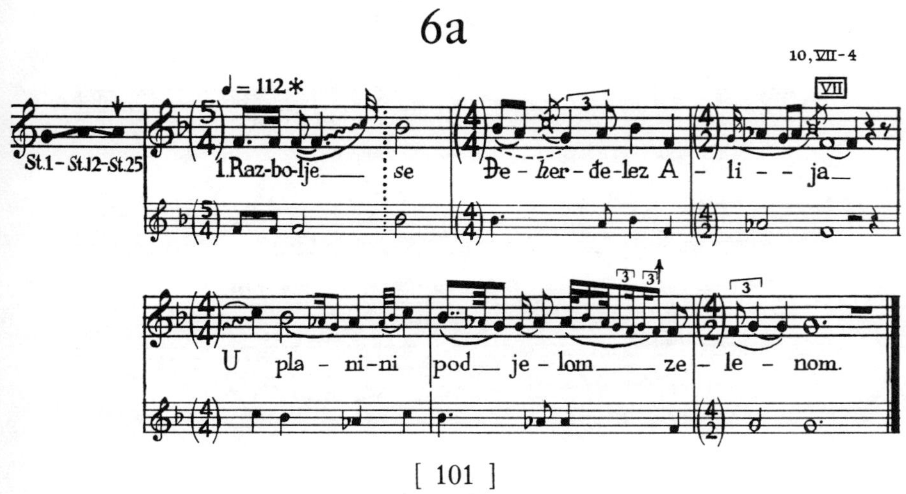

6a (continued)

Var. (ref. to St. 3)

St. 8 — da - ha

St. 9 — lo - - vo

St. 10 — Bi - - li

St. 11. — ə Da — od-le - ti - šə

St. 12 — po - u -

St. 13 (first half only!)

St. 14 — ma — aj

St. 15 — ma — aj

St. 16

St. 17

St. 18

St. 21.

St. 22

St. 23 — zdra-və-lje —

St. 24 — mo — ga A-la klju -

St. 25

St. 28 — Sa - bə-ljom

St. 29

St. 30 — A za zdra-və - lje — sic

St. 31

R. 3153-5. Gacko (Hercegovina), Halida Habeš, April 24, 1935

6b

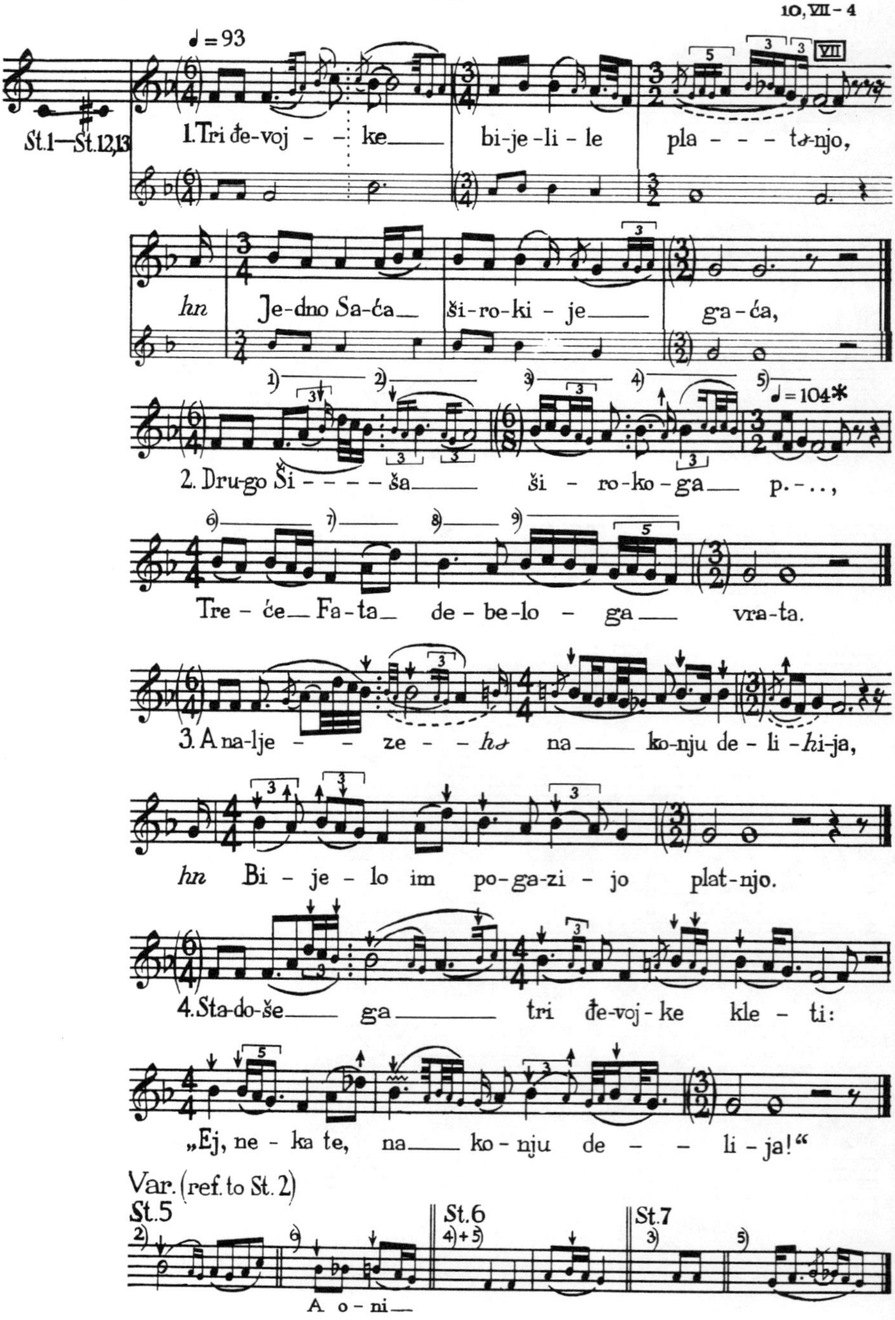

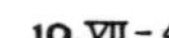

♩ = 93

St.1—St.12,13

1. Tri đe-voj - - ke bi-je-li-le pla - - - tə-njo, *hn*
Je-dno Sa-ća ši-ro-ki-je ga-ća,

♩ = 104*

2. Dru-go Ši - - - - ša ši - ro-ko-ga p.-. . .,
Tre - će Fa-ta de-be-lo-ga vra-ta.

3. A na-lje - - ze - - *hə* na ko-nju de - li - *hi*-ja,
hn Bi - je - lo im po-ga-zi - jo plat-njo.

4. Sta-do-še ga tri đe-voj - ke kle - ti:
„Ej, ne - ka te, na ko - nju de - - li - ja!“

Var. (ref. to St. 2)

St.5

A o - ni

St.6

St.7

6b (continued)
St.8
St.9
St.11
sic
R. 3574-5; Gacko (Hercegovina), Derviša Biberović, May 21, 1935
6c
10, VII-4
St. 1 beginning—end
St. 2 begin.–end
St. 3 begin.–end
St. 4 begin.–end
tempo: slower, not sure
♩=92
a) 1. Ve-zak ve - - zla u ve-dri-ni Aj- -ka,
hn Ve - zak ve - zla u - hu ve-dri - ni Aj - ka,
♩=88
2. N-na kri-lu jo - - - jə Da - lif-a - gić Mu - jo,
Na kri - lu joj Da - lif - a - gić Mu - jo.
3. Pro-go-va - ha - ra i - hiz o-dža - ka maj - ka,
hn Pro - go - va - ra i - hiz o-dža - ka maj - ka:

6c (continued)

R. 3071-3; Gacko (Hercegovina); Hajrija Šaković (ca. 25), April 22, 1935

7
10,VII-4
VII
Quasi parlando, ♩=116
1. Beg A - li - beg i - - kin - di - ju kla-nja,
Gusle *
Ej
Ej, — siv mu so - ko — na ser - dža - ku pa-da.
accel.
2. Ne-ma — ka - da da se-lam pri - da-de,
(accel.)
Ve - će — pi - ta siv ze - len so - ko - la:
(accel)
al
„Siv so-ko - le, — si - vo — pe - ro mo-je!

7 (continued)

♩ = 130
Je - si l' sko - ro bi - jo pod Lož - ni-com?

Je - li tur - ska po - d Lož - ni - com voj - ska?

Vi - ja - ju l' se ze - - le - ni ba-r - ja - ci,

Svi - ra l' zvir - ka - - - ž be-ga Fir - duž - be-ga?"

♩ = 144
3. Nje - mu so - ko po ji - sti - ni ka - že:
* * *
sic

7 (continued)

4. „Sko-ro je - sam pod___ Lož - ni - com bi-jo,
sic
3

E, Vi - di - jo sam si - lo - vi - tu___ voj - sku,___

♩=160
5
5. Vi - ja - ju se ze - le - ni o - bla-ci,

6. Ka - no zi - mi de - be - li o - bla - ci,

poco ritenuto
3
7. Sve pje-va-ju po ji- zbor ju - - na-ci,___

7 (continued)

R. 609; Kulen Vakuf (Bosnia); Ibrahim Mašinović (65), September 24, 1934

8a

8a (continued)

8a (continued)
Var. (ref. to St. 7)
St. 8.
St. 11
St. 12
Je-da-va
se - r
St. 18
St. 19
St. 20
St. 21
St. 27
St. 28
St. 30
St. 31
St. 35
St. 38
St. 40
R. 3125-7; Gacko (Hercegovina), Almasa Zvizdić, April 24, 1935
8b
♩ = 106
St. 1–St. 9
1. Hn Gla – vu — ve – že A – li – be – go – vi – ca,
Gla – vu — ve – že A – li – be – go – vi – ca,
2. I A – li – be-gə je be – že — u – gə-le – da – o,
A – li – be-gə je be – že — u – gə – le – da – o. —
3. I „Lje – pa ti — si, — vje – re – ni – ce lju – bo,
Lje – pa — ti — si, vje – re – hə-ni – ce lju – bo!

8b (continued)

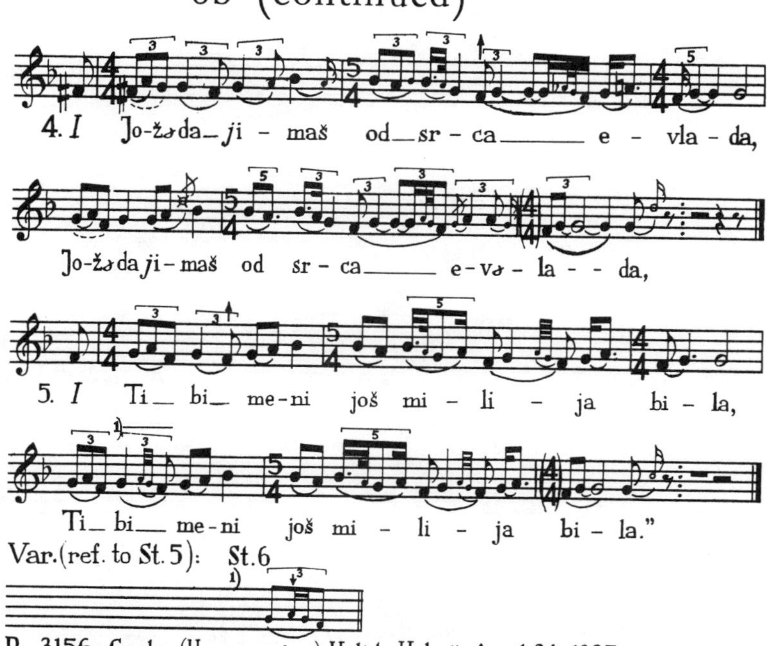

R. 3156; Gacko, (Hercegovina), Halida Habeš, April 24, 1935

9

9 (continued)

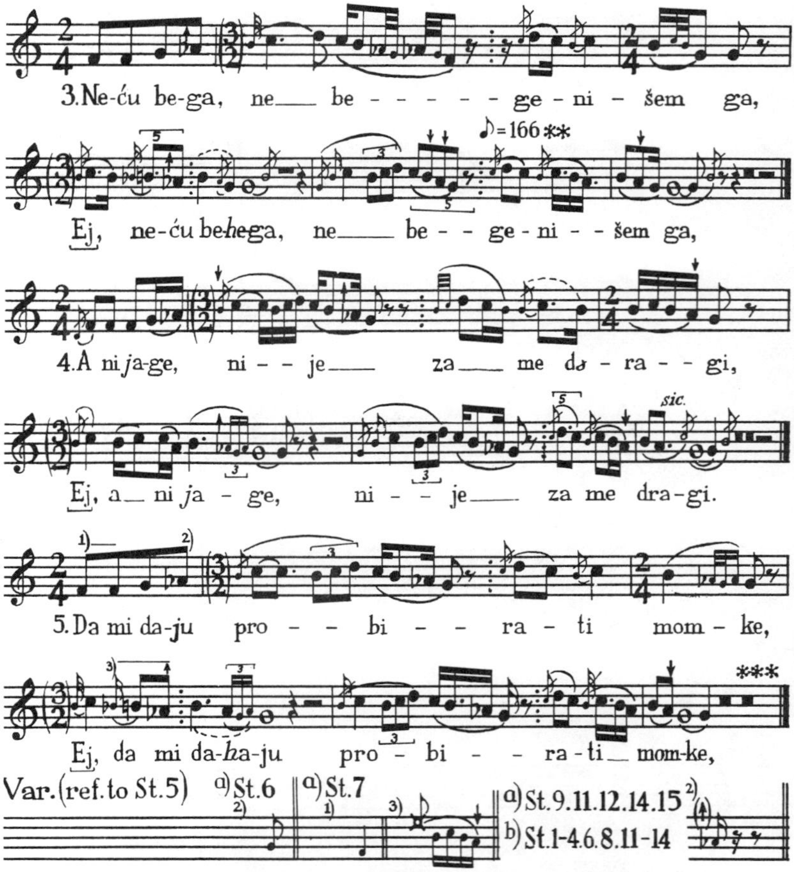

3. Ne-ću be-ga, ne___ be - - - - - - ge - ni - šem ga,

♪=166 **

Ej, ne-ću be-*h*e-ga, ne___ be - - ge - ni - - šem ga,

4. A ni *j*a-ge, ni - - je___ za___ me də - - ra - - gi,

sic.

Ej, a___ ni *j*a - ge, ni - - je___ za me dra-gi.

5. Da mi da-ju pro - - - bi - - - ra - ti mom - ke,

***

Ej, da mi da-*h*a-ju pro - bi - - - ra-ti___ mom-ke,

Var. (ref. to St. 5) a) St. 6 a) St. 7 a) St. 9.11.12.14.15 b) St. 1-4.6.8.11-14

R. 3197-3200; Gacko (Hercegovina), Halima Hrvo, April 26, 1935

10a

10a (continued)

R. 3137-3141; Gacko (Hercegovina), Fata Krajišnik, April 24, 1935

10b

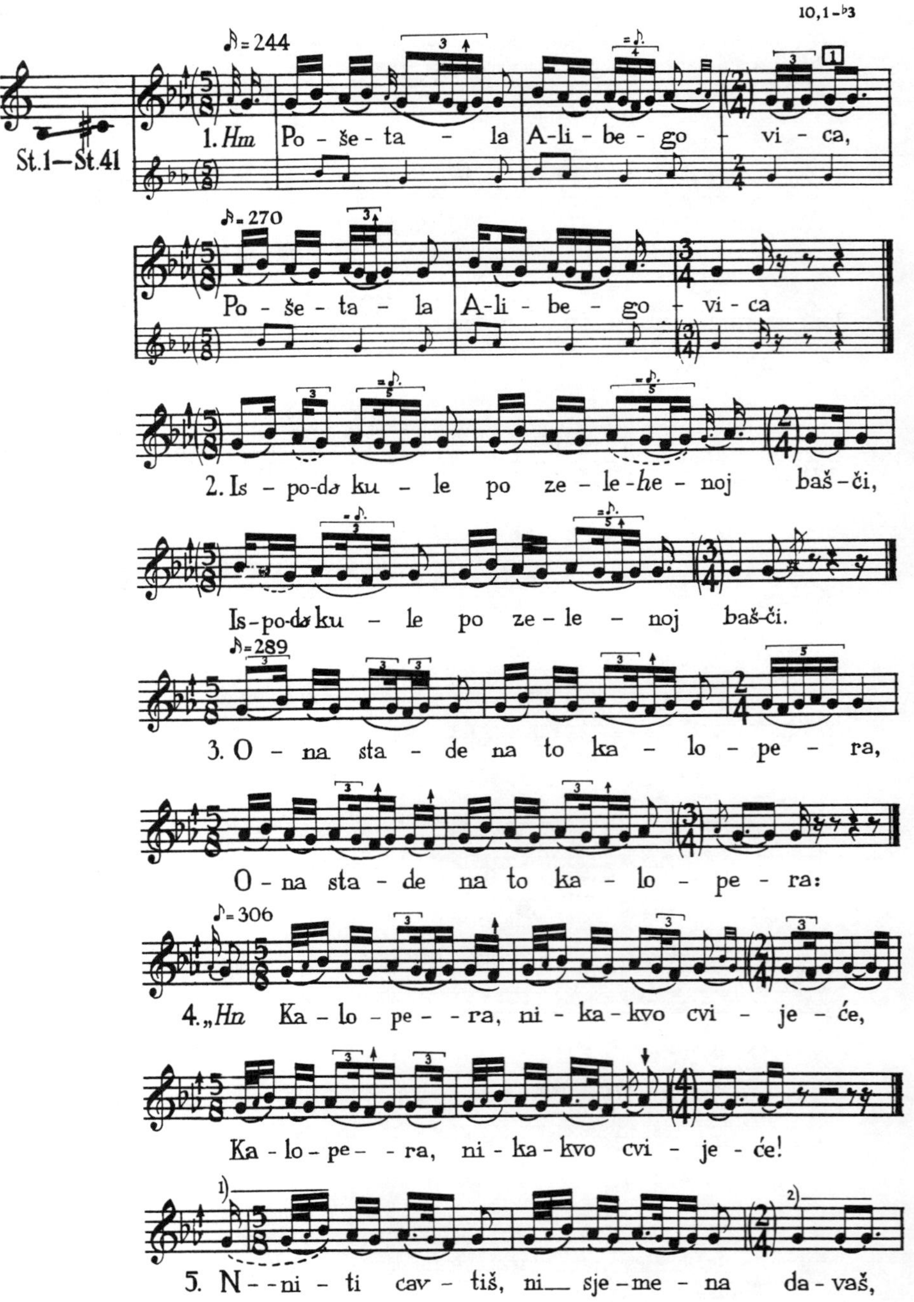
10,1-♭3
♪=244
St.1—St.41
1. Hm Po - še - ta - la A-li - be - go - vi - ca,
♪=270
Po - še - ta - la A-li - be - go - vi - ca
2. Is - po-də ku - le po ze - le-he - noj baš - či,
Is-po-də ku - le po ze - le - noj baš-či.
♪=289
3. O - na sta - de na to ka - lo - pe - ra,
O - na sta - de na to ka - lo - pe - ra:
♪=306
4. „Hn Ka - lo - pe - - ra, ni - ka - kvo cvi - je - će,
Ka - lo - pe - - ra, ni - ka - kvo cvi - je - će!
5. N - - ni - ti cav - tiš, ni sje - me - na da - vaš,

10b (continued)

11 (continued)

R. 3109-12; Gacko (Hercegovina), Almasa Zvizdić, April 23, 1935

12a

St.1 beginning—end
St.9
St.19—St.27
St.28—St.40—St.44
St.45 beginning—end
St.47
St.49
*
♩=94**
10,VII – 4
b3
*** 1. San u-sni-la Ha - - san - a - gi - ni - - - ca,
San u-sni-la, u snu se pə-re - nu-la.
2. O-na bu-di šćer-ku Me-leć - ha - - - nu:
„U - - staj si-ne, šće-ri Me-leć - ha - na!
3. E-vo ti se raz-bo-lje-la maj - - - ka,
I Bog zna-de da pre-bo-ljet ne-ću,
4. I Bog zna-de da pre-bo-ljet ne - - ću,
Jer - - bo sam ti ru-žan san u - - - sni-la,

12a (continued)

5. Jer-bo sam ti___ ru -žan__ san u - - sni - - - la,
ə Da s' na me - ni za - pa - li - la di - ba,
Var.(ref.to St.5) St.6 St.12 St.13 St.14, 15 St.16
St.21 St.35 St.51 St.62 St.64

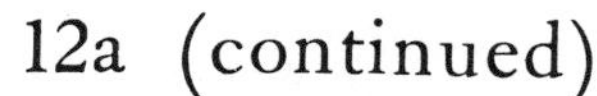

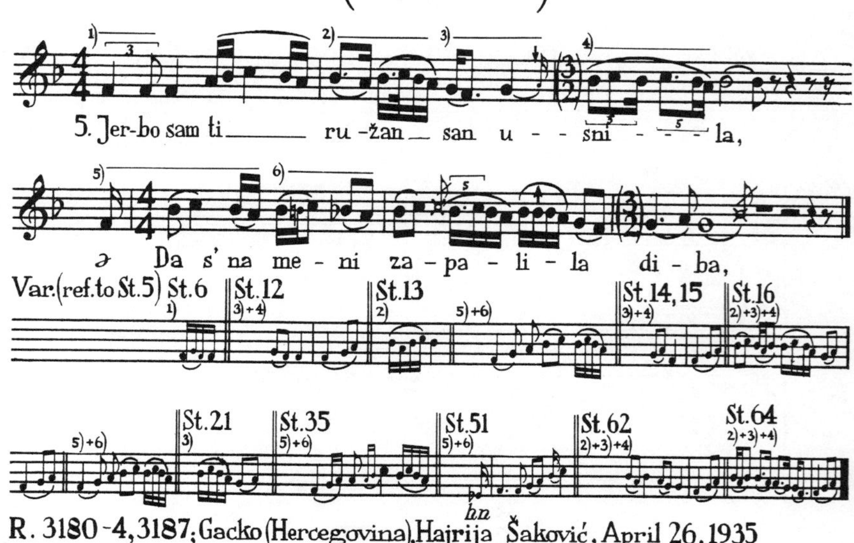

R. 3180-4, 3187; Gacko (Hercegovina), Hajrija Šaković, April 26, 1935

12b

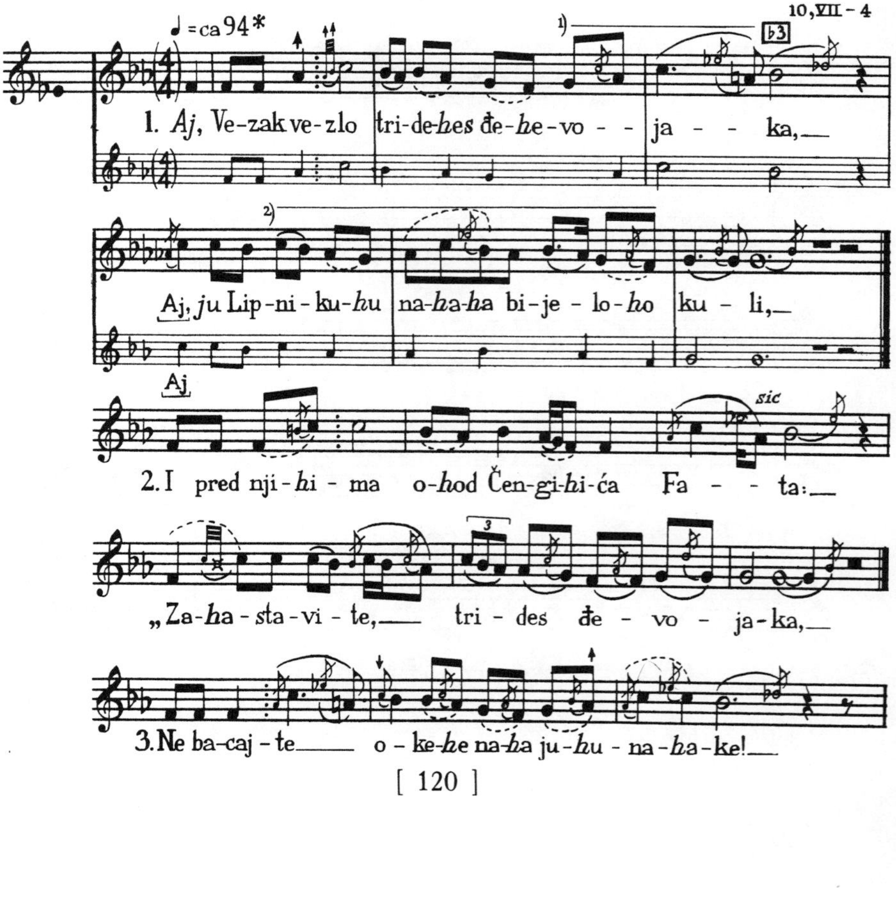

♩ = ca 94*
10, VII - 4
1. Aj, Ve-zak ve-zlo tri-de-hes đe-he-vo - - ja - - ka,__
Aj, ju Lip-ni - ku-hu na-ha-ha bi-je - lo-ho ku - li,__
Aj
2. I pred nji - hi - ma o-hod Čen-gi-hi-ća Fa - - ta:__
sic
„Za-ha - sta-vi - te,__ tri - des đe - vo - ja-ka,__
3. Ne ba-caj - te___ o - ke-he na-ha ju-hu - na - ha-ke!__

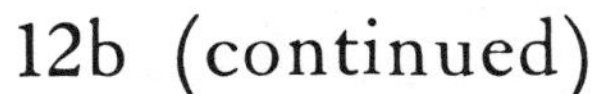

12b (continued)

A-*h*aj, ju-na-ci su-*h*u vje - ra-*h*a i - *h*i ne-*h*e-vje-*h*e-ra; —

4. Kad te lju - - bi: — „„U - ze-ću te-*h*e, du - - šo!"" —

A-*h*aj, kad te lju-bi: „„U - ze-*h*e-ću te - *h*e, du - šo!"" —

5. Kad ob-lju - bi: „„Če - kaj do - *h*o je - se - - ni!""

A-*h*aj, kad ob-lju - bi: „„Če - *h*e-ka-*h*aj do - *h*o je-*h*e-se-ni!""

6. Zi-ma do - đe, — ja ji - *h*i lje - to - *h*o pro - - đe,

A-*h*aj, zi-ma do-*h*o-đe-*h*e, ja - *h*a ji - *h*i lje - *h*e-to-*h*o pro - đe.

♩=108

9. Pre-va-ri me, — o - bə-lju-bi mi-*h*i li - - - ce, —

sic.

A-*h*aj, pre-va-ri me-*h*e, o-*h*ob-lju-*h*u-bi - *h*i mi - *h*i - li - ce. —

Var. (ref to St. 1) St. 7 2) St. 14 1)

se - stre-*h*e, ni-*h*i-je-*h*e da-vno-*h*o

R. 3052-3; Gacko (Hercegovina), Fata Šaković, April 22, 1935

12c

10, VII - 4
♩ = 100
b3
1. Te-lar vi - ka o - də ju - če do po - - də-ne,
Te - lar vi - ka o - də ju - če do po - dne:
♩ = 102
2. „Ko j'u ko - ga no - ća - sə na ko - na - - ku,
Ko j' u ko - ga no - ća - sə na ko - na - ku,
♩ = 104
3. N - nek ne i - de ra - no sa ko - na - ka,
Nek ne i - de ra - no sa ko - na - ka!
♩ = 106
4. U - te - kla je pa - ši - na ro - bi - - nja,
U - te - kla je pa - ši - na ro - bi - - nja,
♩ = 108
5. I od - ni - la dva pa - ši - na si - - - na,

12c (continued)

R.3079–3080; Gacko (Hercegovina), Šerifa Zvizdić, April 22, 1935

12d

10, VII – 4

12d (continued)

12d (continued)

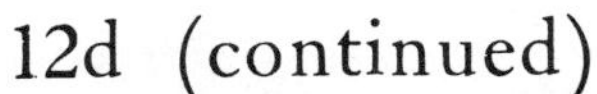

Ju - nak o - - že - ni - jo,
Sə-va tri pu - ta sum - bul u - do - vi - - com."
6. „U - - do - - vi - ce, u - - - do - vi - ce,
O-ba t'o - ka və - ra - - - na!
Aj, ko - li - ko se lju-bi - - la ja - ra - na!"
Tri pu - ta sam, gə - le - daj, ko - li - ko sam,
Sa - - mo je - dnom, sa - - - mo je - də-no - m
Li - je - po' ə đe - - - hə-vo - hoj - kom.

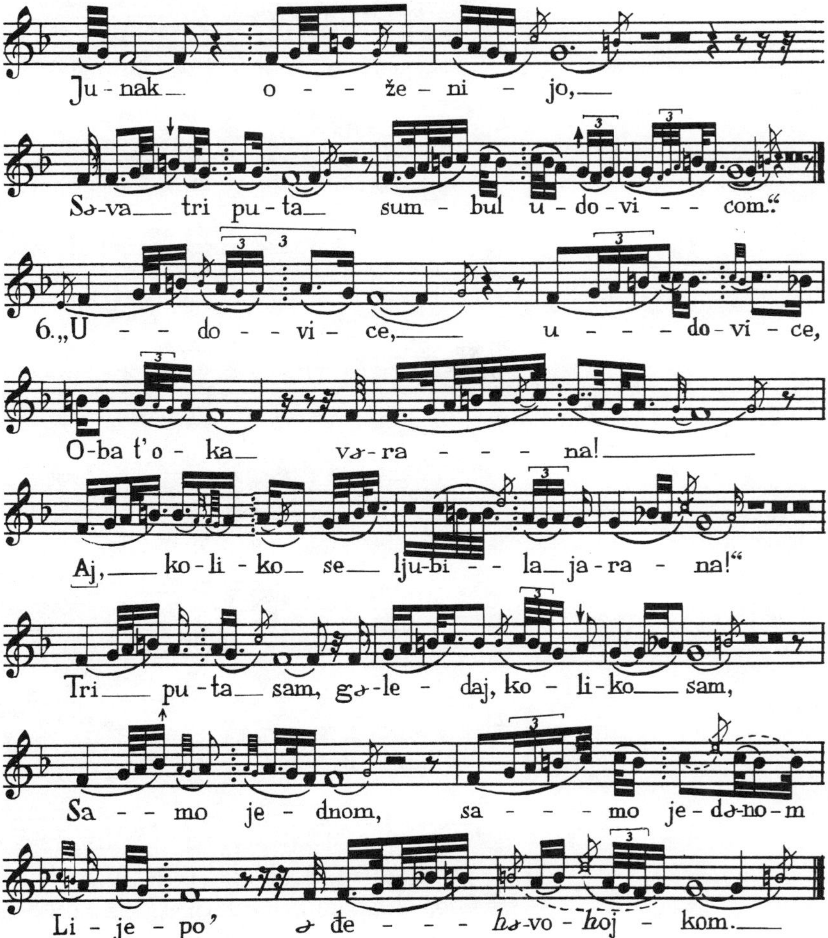

R. 3225-6; Gacko (Hercegovina), Halima Hrvo, April 27, 1935

12e

♩=106*
10,VII -5
St.1(beg.) St.1(end) St.13 St.24
1. Go-rom ja - še be - že A - li - be - - - - že,
E - j, go-rom ja - še, go - ru ku - ni - ja - še:
sic
Ej

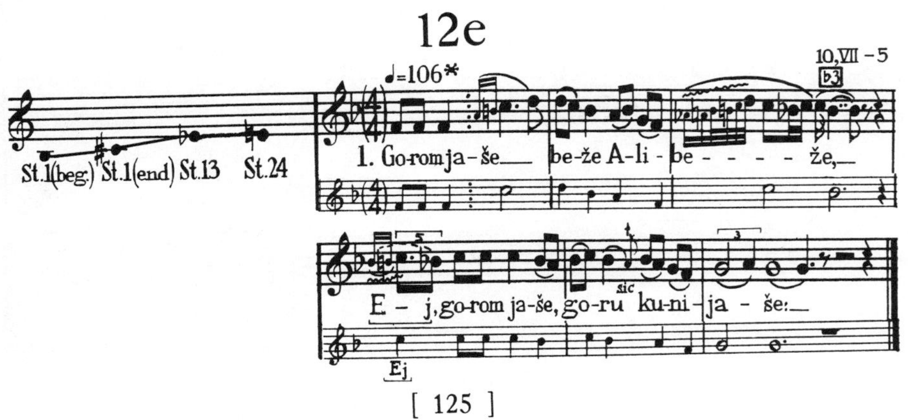

12e (continued)

R. 3163-4; Gacko (Hercegovina), Raba Zvizdić, April 24, 35

13

13 (continued)

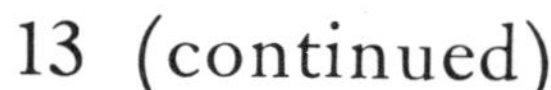

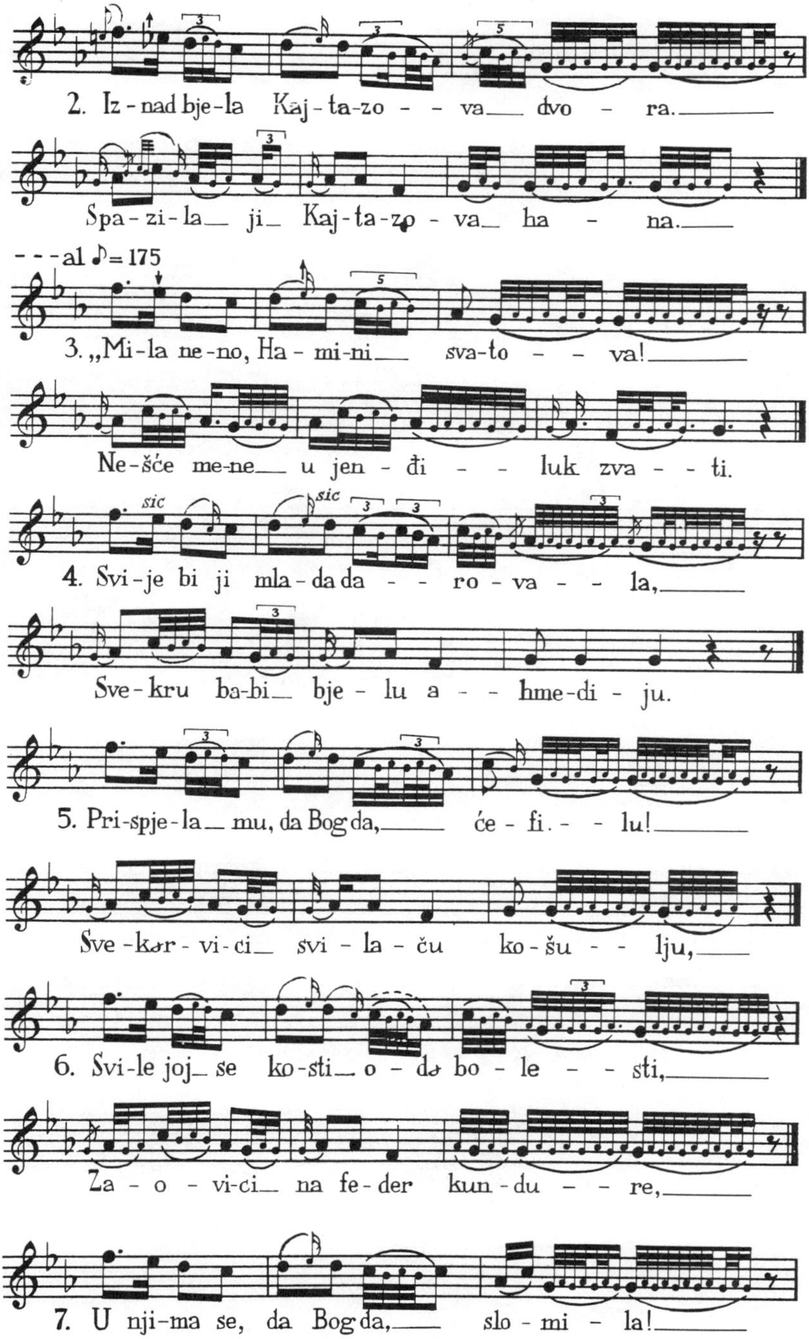
2. Iz - nad bje - la Kaj - ta - zo - - va dvo - ra.
Spa - zi - la ji Kaj - ta - zo - va ha - na.
- - - al ♪ = 175
3. „Mi - la ne - no, Ha - mi - ni sva - to - - - va!
Ne - šće me - ne u jen - đi - - luk zva - - ti.
sic
sic
4. Svi - je bi ji mla - da da - - ro - va - - la,
Sve - kru ba - bi bje - lu a - - hme - di - ju.
5. Pri - spje - la mu, da Bog da, će - fi. - - lu!
Sve - kər - vi - ci svi - la - ču ko - šu - - lju,
6. Svi - le joj se ko - sti - o - də bo - le - - sti,
Za - o - vi - ci na fe - der kun - du - - re,
7. U nji - ma se, da Bog da, slo - mi - la!

13 (continued)

R. 1547; Rotinja srez Stolac u Stocu (Hercegovina), Naza Rokić, Dec. 15, 1934

14

♩=92
(7)11,1-4
sic
1. ə Si - tə - na tra-vo-ho, si-tə-na tra - - vo — ze - le-na,
♩=100
Sit - na tra-vo, sit- na tra - - - vo ze - le-he - na
♩=112
2. N Do svi-le - na, do svi - le - - na — ča-do - ra, —
Do svi-le-na, do svi - l - le - - - na ča - do-ho - ra.
sic
3. Pod — ča-do - rom, Pod ča - ə - do - - ro-m đe-vo-hoj-ka,
Pod ča-do-rom, pod ča - - ə - do - - - rom đe - vo-hoj-ka
♩=118 sic
4. Ši - je, ve - ze, ši-je, ve - ə-ze — da - ro-ho-ve, —
Ši - je, ve-ze, ši-je n ve - - ze — da - ro-ho - ve,
5. Hn Da — da-ru-je, da da - ə-ru - - je — sva-to-ho-ve, —

14 (continued)

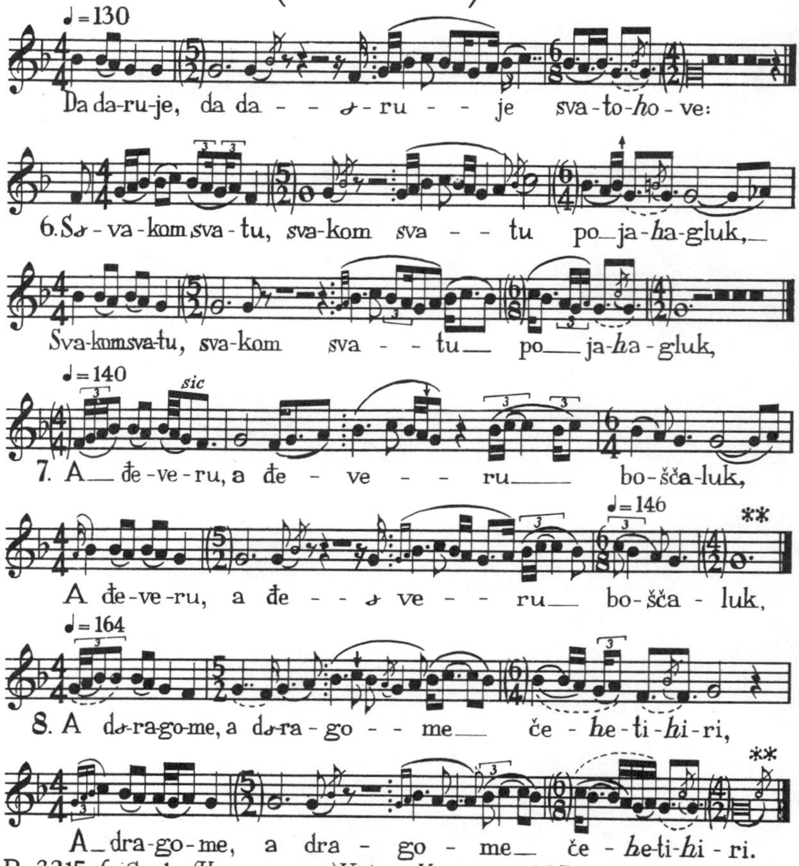
♩=130
Da da-ru-je, da da - - ə - ru - - je sva-to-ho-ve:
6. Sə - va - kom sva - tu, sva-kom sva - - - tu po_ja-ha-gluk,_
Sva-kom sva-tu, sva-kom sva - - - tu_ po_ ja-ha-gluk,
♩=140
sic
7. A_ đe-ve-ru, a đe - ve - - - ru___ bo-šča-luk,
♩=146
**
A đe-ve-ru, a đe - - ə ve - - - ru__ bo-šča - luk,
♩=164
8. A də-ra-go-me, a də-ra - go - - - me__ če - he-ti-hi-ri,
**
A_dra-go-me, a dra - go - me__ če - he-ti-hi - ri.

R. 3215-6; Gacko (Hercegovina), Halima Hrvo, April 27, 1935

15

11, 1 - 5
accel. - - - - -
♩=70
♩=74
b3
1. Fa-li-jo se ə žu - ti li-mun kraj mo-ra, a-man, a - man,
- - ♩=89
=𝅗𝅥
7
Fa-li-jo se ə žu-ti___ li - mun kraj mo - ra:

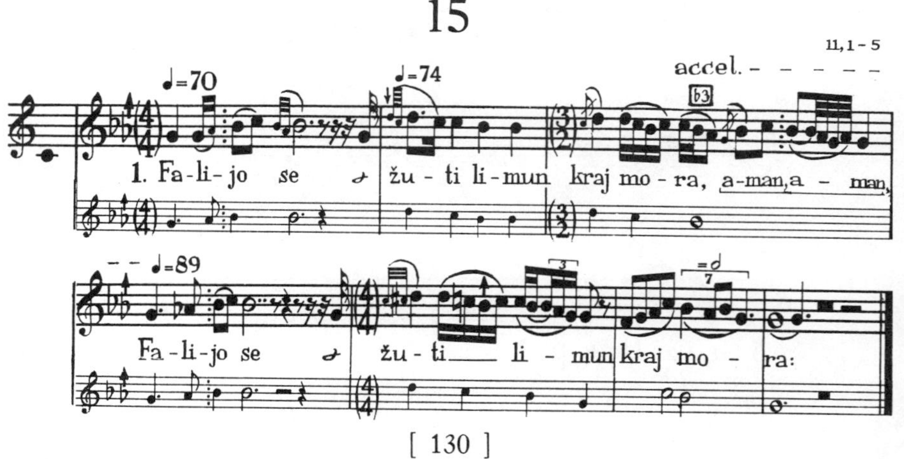

15 (continued)

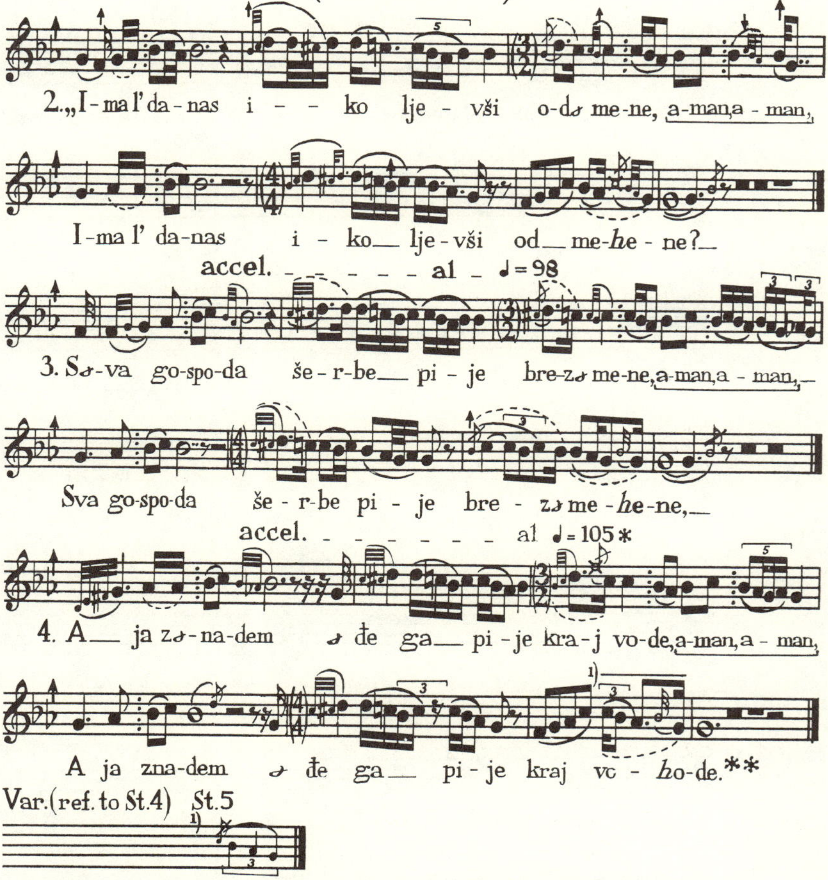
2. „I-ma l' da-nas i - - ko lje - vši o-də me-ne, a-man,a - man,
I-ma l' da-nas i - ko lje-vši od me-he - ne?
accel. - - - - - - al - ♩=98
3. Sə-va go-spo-da še-r-be pi-je bre-zə me-ne,a-man,a - man,
Sva go-spo-da še - r-be pi - je bre - zə me - he-ne,
accel. - - - - - - - al ♩=105*
4. A ja zə-na-dem ə đe ga pi-je kra-j vo-de,a-man,a - man,
A ja zna-dem ə đe ga pi-je kraj vo - ho-de.**
Var.(ref. to St.4) St.5
1)

R. 3213-4; Gacko (Hercegovina), Halima Hrvo, April 27, 1935

a.

16a

♩=92
(8)12,1-b3
1
1. Si - tə-na knji-ga, na ža-los je si-tə-na knji-ga,
Si-tə-na knji-ga, na ža - los je si-tə-na knji-ga,

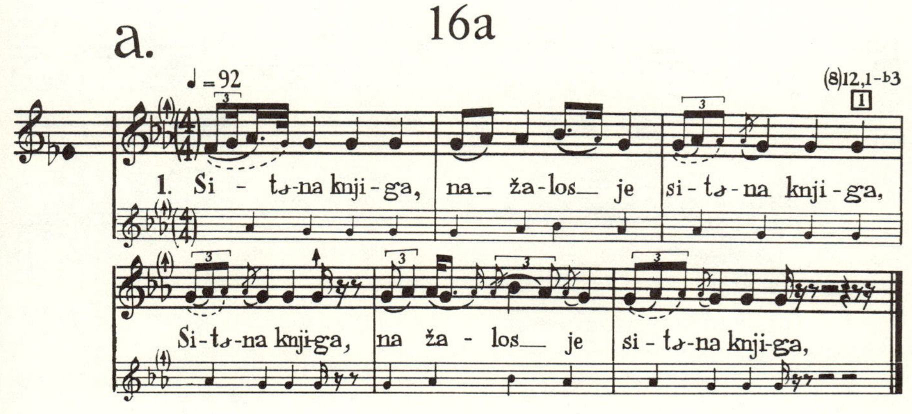

R. 3232–3; Gacko (Hercegovina), Hajrija Šaković, April 27, 1935

17

(8)12,1-4

St.1— last stanzas

♩=80

1

1. Raz-bo-lje se zo-r-na Zo-r-ka, zo-r-na Zo-r-ka,

Raz-bo-lje se zo-r-na Zo-r-ka, zo-r-na Zo-r-ka

♩=84

2. Na Ce-ti-nju Cə-r-no-go-r-ka, Cə-r-no-go-r-ka,

Na Ce-ti-nju Cə-r-no-go-r-ka, Cə-r-no-go-r-ka.

3. K njoj do-la-zi mi-jo_ta-ta, mi-jo ta-ta,

K njoj do-la-zi mi-jo ta-ta, mi-jo ta-ta,

♩=80*

4. Mi-jo_ta-ta, kra-lj Ni-ko-la, kra-lj Ni-ko-la,

Mi-jo_ta-ta, kra-lj Ni-ko-la, kra-lj Ni-ko-la.

5. „Što je_te-bi, šće-ri Zo-r-ka, šće-ri Zo-r-ka,

17 (continued)

Što je_ te-bi, šće - ri Zo-r-ka, šće - ri Zo-r-ka?
17. Ro-da_ mo-ga i_ po-no - sa, i_ po - no - sa,
Ro - da mo-ga i_ po-no-sa, i_ po - no - sa."

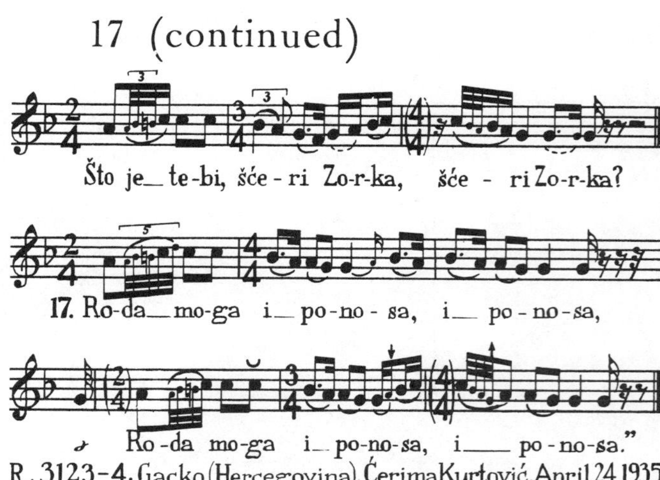

R. 3123-4, Gacko (Hercegovina), Ćerima Kurtović, April 24, 1935

18

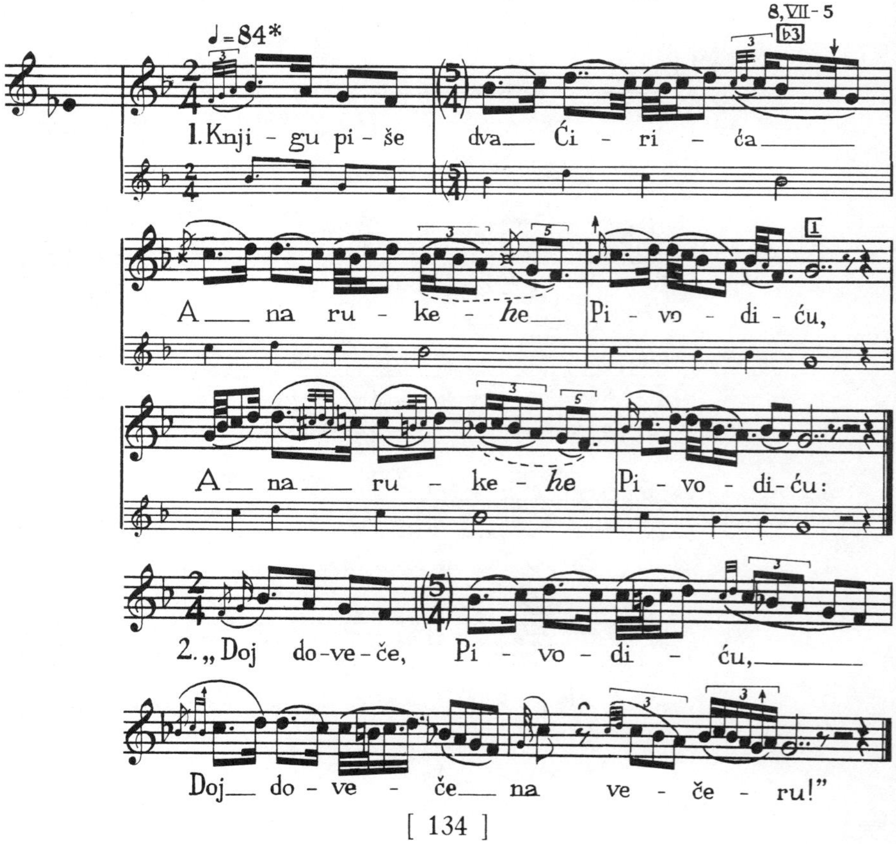
♩=84*
8, VII - 5
♭3
1. Knji - gu pi - še dva_ Ći - ri - ća_
A_ na ru - ke - he_ Pi - vo - di - ću,
1
A_ na_ ru - ke - he Pi - vo - di- ću:
2. „Doj do-ve - če, Pi - vo - di - ću,_
Doj_ do - ve - če_ na ve - če - ru!"

18 (continued)

Var. (ref. to St. 4) St. 12 1) St. 15., 16 2)

R. 3178 – 9; Gacko (Hercegovina), Džefa Grebović, April 26, 1935

19
10, 1 - 5
♪= 152
1. Vi - le - ni - ca bu - ko - vi - cu pi - *h*i - ta - *h*a:
„Bu - ko - vi - ce - *h*e, što si po - *h*o - ta - vi - *h*i - la,
Bu - ko - vi - ce, što si po - *h*o - ta - vi - la?
2. U so - bo - tu u se - da - m sa - ha - *h*a - ti - *h*i
Ma - *h*a - ši - na se - *h*e sa S-r - da - ća kre - *h*e - će,
Ma - ši - na - *h*a se - *h*e sa Se - r - da - ća kre - *h*e - će.
3. Iz ma - *h*a - ši - ne i - skra iz - le - ti - *h*i - la - *h*a,
Za - *h*a - pa - li - la - *h*a ku - će i du - ća - ne,
Za - pa - li - *h*i - la - *h*a ku - će i du - ća - ne,

19 (continued)

R. 3050-1; Gacko (Hercegovina), Fata Šaković, April 22, 1935

20

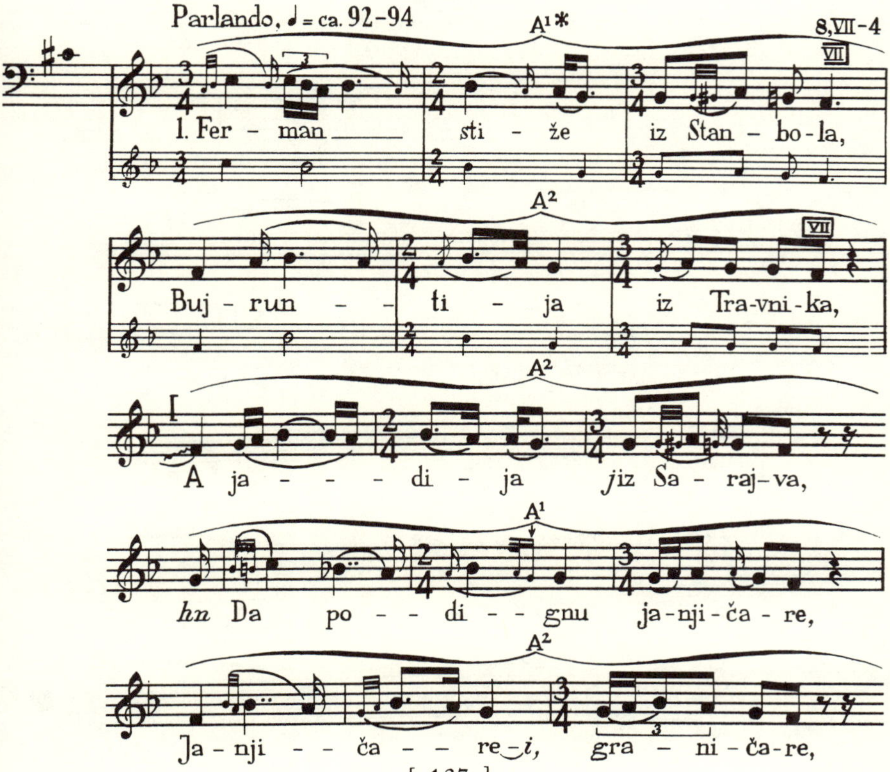

Parlando, ♩ = ca. 92–94

A¹* 8,VII-4

VII

1. Fer - man stí - že iz Stan - bo - la,

A²

VII

Buj - run - ti - ja iz Tra-vni - ka,

A²

A ja - - - - di - ja jiz Sa - raj - va,

A¹

hn Da po - - di - - gnu ja - nji - ča - re,

A²

Ja - nji - - ča - - re i, gra - ni - ča - re,

20 (continued)

20 (continued)

20 (continued)

R. 526 - 8, Livno (Dalmatia), Meho Jarić (28), September 21, 1934

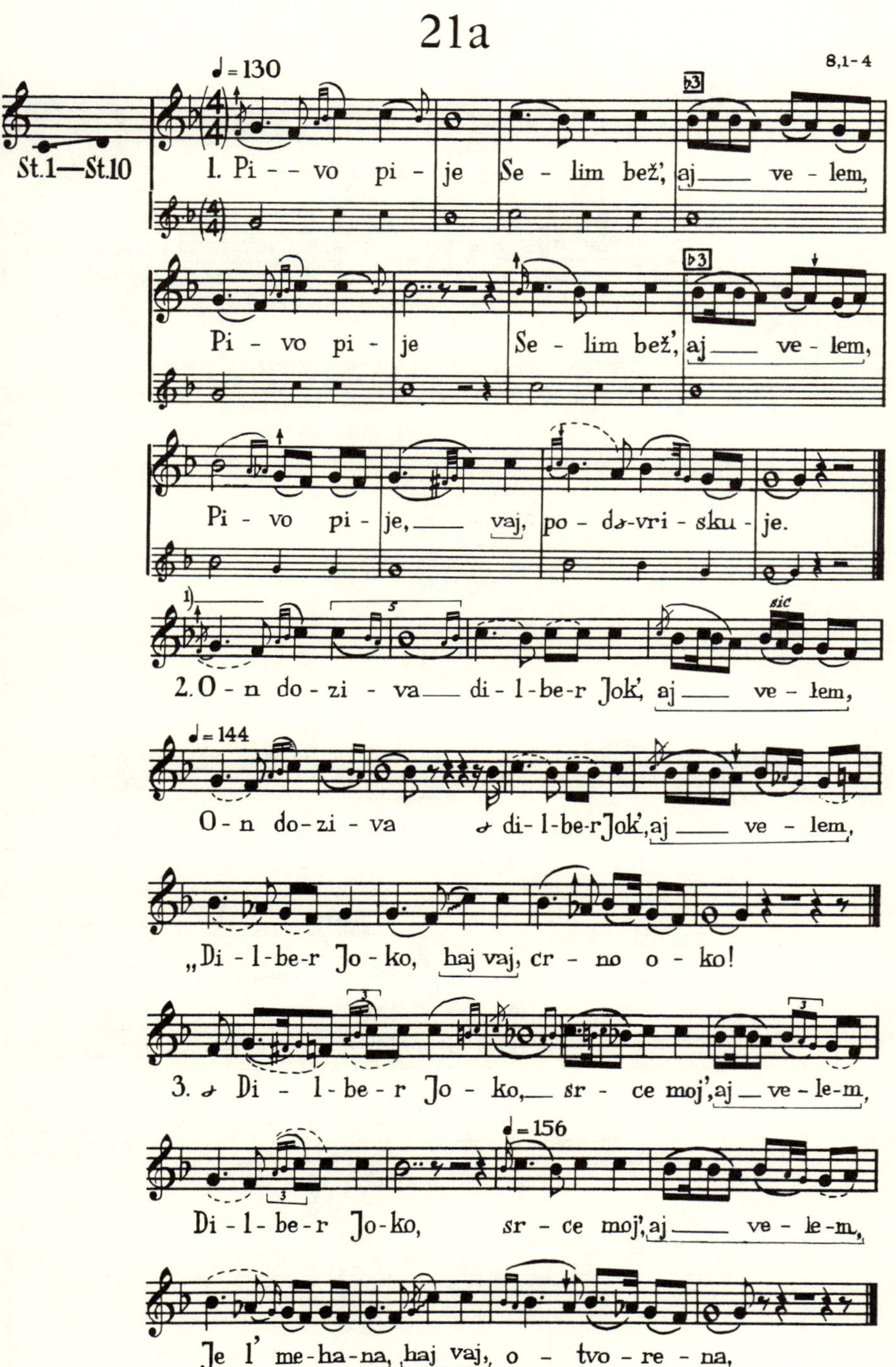
21a
♩= 130
8,1-4
St.1—St.10
1. Pi - - vo pi - je Se - lim bež', aj ve - lem,
Pi - vo pi - je Se - lim bež', aj ve - lem,
Pi - vo pi - je, vaj, po - dǝ-vri - sku - je.
sic
2. O - n do - zi - va di - l-be-r Jok', aj ve - lem,
♩= 144
O - n do - zi - va ǝ di - l-be-r Jok', aj ve - lem,
„Di - l-be-r Jo - ko, haj vaj, cr - no o - ko!
3. ǝ Di - l-be - r Jo - ko, sr - ce moj', aj ve - le-m,
♩= 156
Di - l - be - r Jo-ko, sr - ce moj', aj ve - le-m,
Je l' me-ha-na, haj vaj, o - tvo - re - na,

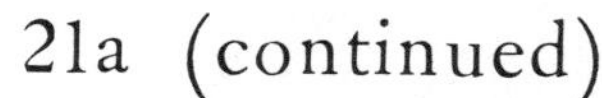

21a (continued)

R. 3161; Gacko (Hercegovina), Raba Zvizdić, April 24, 1935

21b

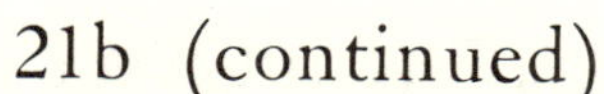

21b (continued)

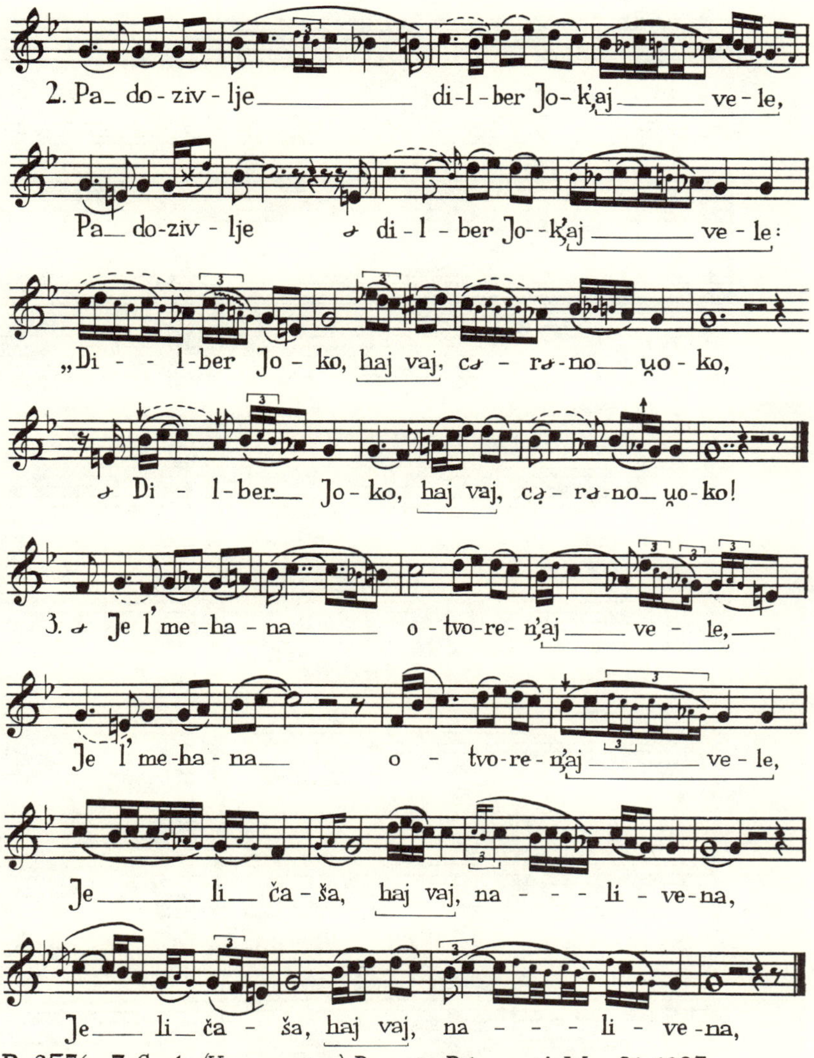

2. Pa_ do - ziv - lje_______ di - l - ber Jo - k'aj_______ ve - le,

Pa_ do-ziv - lje ə di - l - ber Jo - - k'aj_______ ve - le:

„Di - - l-ber Jo - ko, haj vaj, cə - rə-no_ uo - ko,

ə Di - l-ber_ Jo - ko, haj vaj, cạ - rə-no_ uo-ko!

3. ə Je l'me -ha - na_______ o - tvo-re- n'aj_______ ve - le,_____

Je l'me-ha - na_ o - tvo-re - n'aj_______ ve - le,

Je_______ li_ ča - ša, haj vaj, na - - - li - ve-na,

Je_ li_ ča - ša, haj vaj, na - - - - li - ve -na,

R. 3576–7; Gacko (Hercegovina), Derviša Biberović, May 21, 1935

22

22 (continued)

22 (continued)

R. 3121; Gacko (Hercegovina), Almasa Zvizdić, April 23, 1935

23a

23a (continued)

23a (continued)

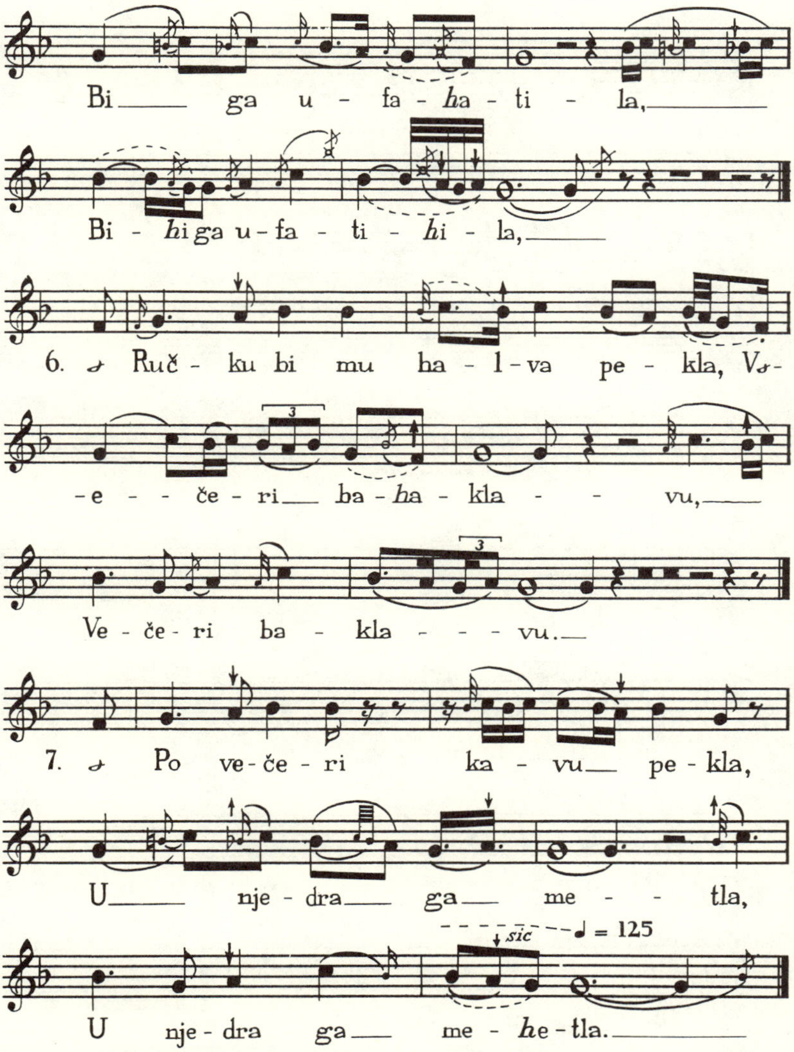

Bi — ga u - fa - *h*a - ti - la, —

Bi - *h*i ga u - fa - ti - *h*i - la, —

6. ♩ Ruč - ku bi mu ha - l - va pe - kla, V-

-e - - če - ri — ba - *h*a - kla - - vu, —

Ve - če - ri ba - kla - - - - vu. —

7. ♩ Po ve - če - ri ka - vu — pe - kla,

U — nje - dra — ga — me - - tla,

sic ♩ = 125

U nje - dra ga — me - *h*e - tla. —

R. 3081 – 82;*** Gacko (Hercegovina), Halima Hrvo, April 23, 1935

23b

23b (continued)

23b (continued)

Bi - se - ro - m ki - ti - - - la,
Bi - - - - - se - ro - m ki - - ti - - - - la,
Var. (ref. to St.3) b) St.1
St.6–11
b) St.6

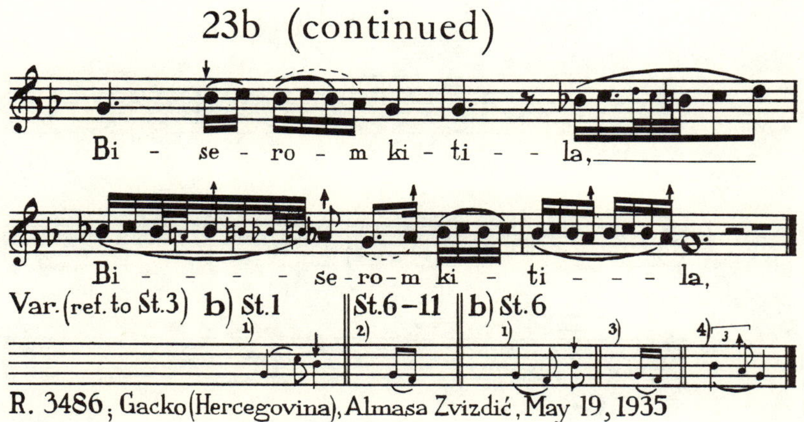

R. 3486; Gacko (Hercegovina), Almasa Zvizdić, May 19, 1935

24

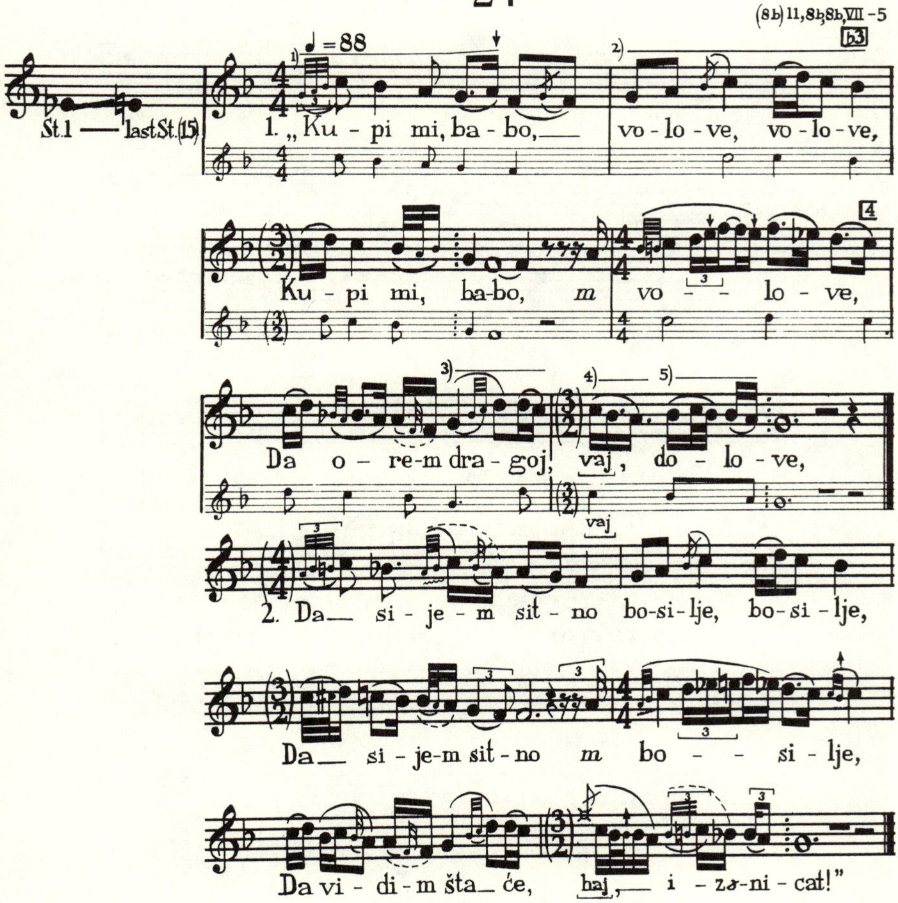

(8♭) 11, 8♭, 8♭, VII - 5
♩ = 88
St.1 — last St. (15)
1. „Ku - pi mi, ba - bo, vo - lo - ve, vo - lo - ve,
Ku - pi mi, ba-bo, m vo - - lo - ve,
Da o - re-m dra - goj, vaj, do - lo - ve,
vaj
2. Da si - je - m sit - no bo-si - lje, bo-si - lje,
Da si - je-m sit - no m bo - - - si - lje,
Da vi - di - m šta će, haj, i - zə - ni - cat!"

24 (continued)

3. Iz - ni - če tra - va ze-le-na, ze - le - na,

Iz - ni - če tra - va ze - le - na,

U tra - vi ru - ža, vaj, ru-me-na.

4. Tu - da mi dra - gi na-la-zi, na - la - zi,

Tu-da mi dra - gi na - la - zi,

Đo-ga - ta ko - nja, vaj, pro-vo - di.

5. Gə - le-dam ga ja-də-na spen-dže-ra, spen-dže - ra,

Gle-dam ga ja-də-na spen - dže - ra,

Gle-da-ham ga jad[sic] - na, vaj, spen-dže - ra.

Var. (ref. to St. 1) St. 10 3) 4) St. 11 3)+4)+5) St. 13 1) 3)+4)+5) St. 14 2) 3) 5) St. 15 3)+4)+5)

va-Bajina pors

R. 3547–8, Gacko (Hercegovina), Almasa Zvizdić, May 21, 1935

25

♩=100*
(10) 6,6,10,1 - 4
1. Vi - har be - har, a - - go,
Vi - har be - har, be - - go,
1.r.
2.r.
♩=106
Aj, vi-har be - - har niz po-lje no - sa - še,
2. Na Mu - jo - - ve, a - go,
1.r.
Na Mu - jo - ve, be - - go,
2.r.
♩=115
Aj, na Mu-jo - ve dvo-re na-no - sa - - še.
Aj
♩=104
3. U dvo - - ri - - ma, a - go,
1.r.
**
U dvo - - ri - ma, be - - go,
2.r.
Aj, u dvo-ri - - ma ni-ko ne bi - ja - - še,

25 (continued)

25 (continued)

Var. (ref. to St.6)
St.35
1)
St.26,34
1) similar to St. 35
2)–3)

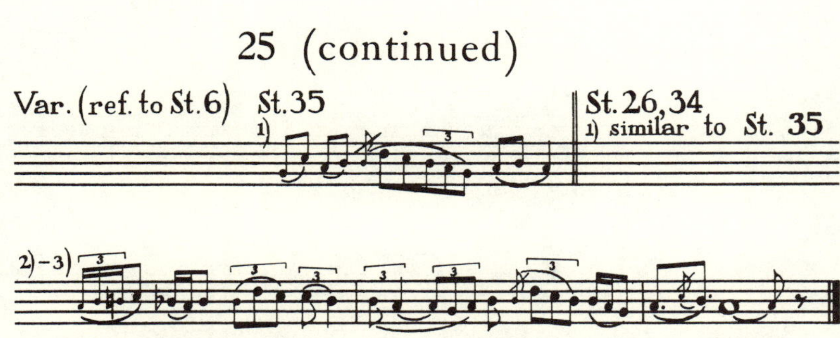

R. 3131–2, 3130; Gacko (Hercegovina), Fata Krajišnik, April 24, 1935

26

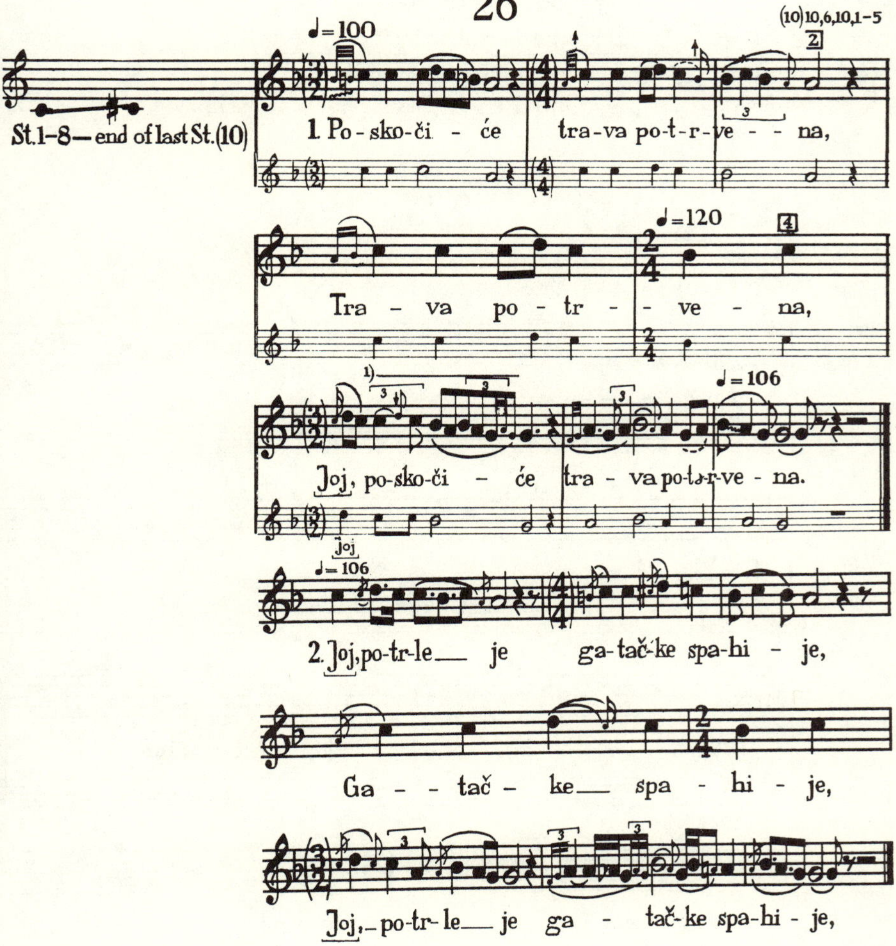

♩=100
(10)10,6,10,1–5
2
St.1–8—end of last St.(10)
1. Po - sko-či - će tra-va po-t-r-ve - - na,
♩=120
4
Tra - va po - tr - - ve - na,
1)
♩=106
Joj, po-sko-či - će tra - va po-tə-r-ve - na.
Joj
♩=106
2. Joj, po-tr-le___ je ga-tač-ke spa-hi - je,
Ga - - tač - ke___ spa - hi - je,
Joj, – po-tr- le___ je ga - tač-ke spa-hi - je,

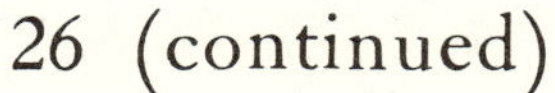

26 (continued)

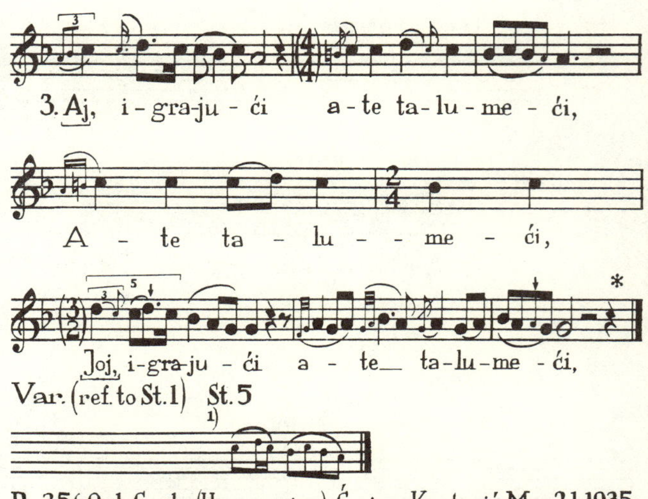

R. 3560-1; Gacko (Hercegovina), Ćerima Kurtović, May 21, 1935

27a

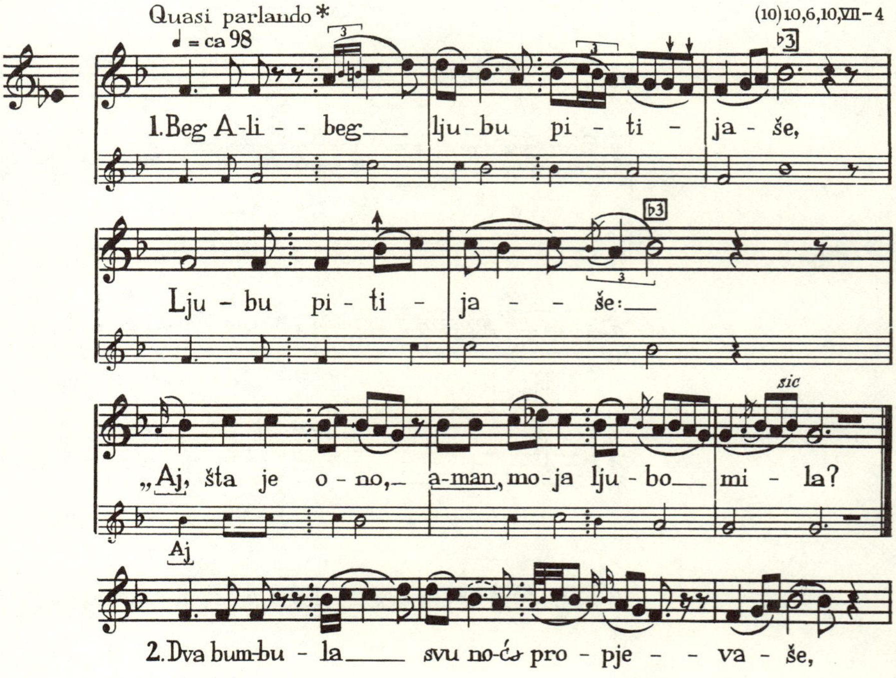

Quasi parlando * ♩ = ca 98

(10)10,6,10,VII-4

1. Beg A-li - - beg___ lju-bu pi - ti - ja - še,

Lju - bu pi - ti - ja - - še:___

„Aj, šta je o - no,_ a-man, mo-ja lju - bo___ mi - la?

Aj

2. Dva bum-bu - la___ svu no-ćə pro - pje - - va - še,

27a (continued)

R. 3553-6; Gacko (Hercegovina), Ćerima Kurtović, May 21, 1935

27b

(10) 10,6,10,VII-4
♩=80
sic
Aj, beg A-li-be - ga na ku-li sje - da - - še - he,
Aj,
Na ku - li sje - - da - - - - še,
♩=88
Aj, ve-r-nu lju - bu, a-man, na kri-lu d - r - ža - še,
Aj
2. Aj, pa o-va - - ko lju - bi go - vo - ra - še,
'Va - - ko go - vo - ra - - - še:
„Aj, ver - na lju - bo, a-man ve-ra te u - bi - la,
♩=76
♩=88
sic
Aj, ve-r-na lju - bo a-man ve-ra te u - bi - la!
♩=96
3. Što te pi - ta - m, ho - ćeš li mi ka - zat',
Ho - - ćeš li mi ka - - - - zat',
Aj, što te pi - tam, a-man, ho-ćeš li mi ka - zat'?"

27b (continued)

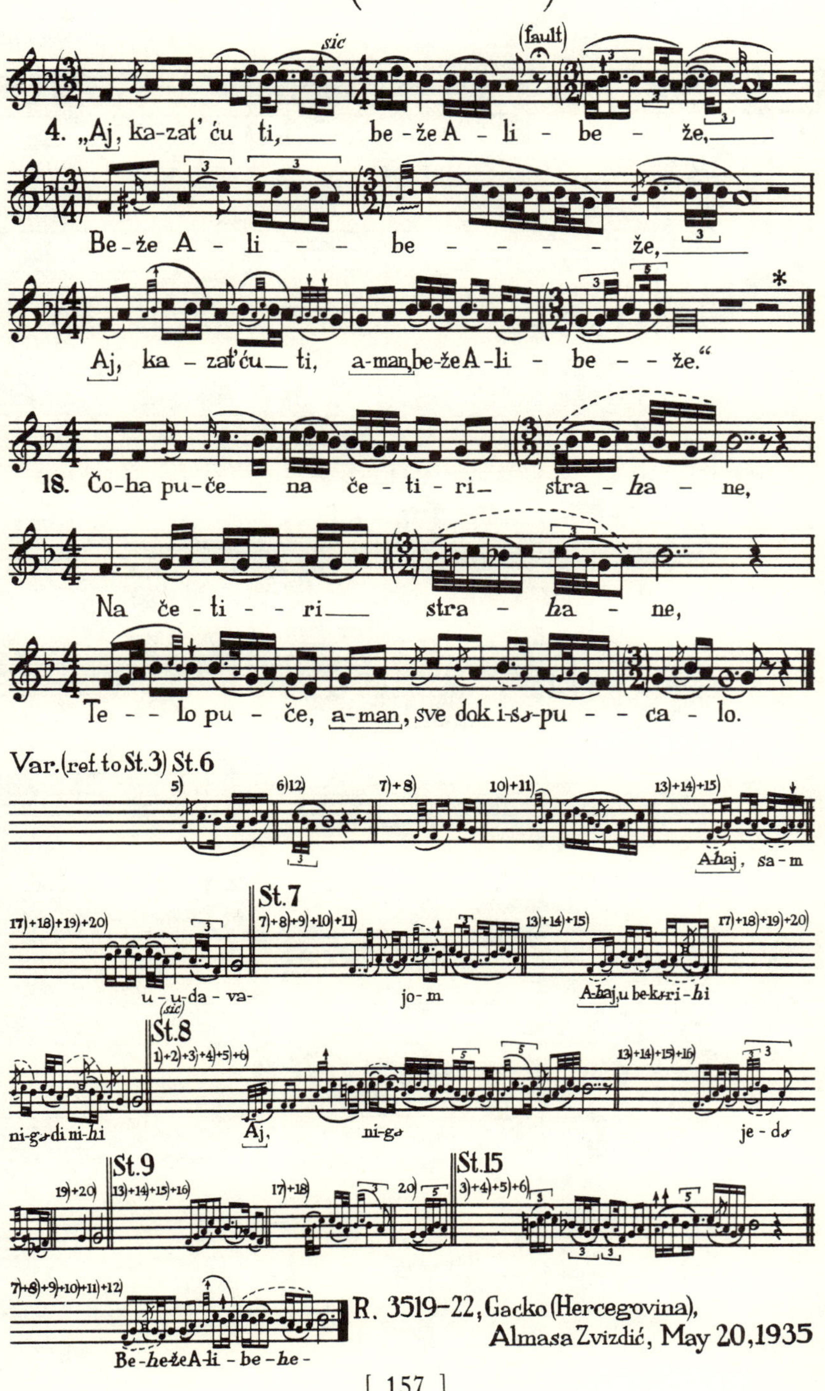

27c

♩ = ca 82
(10) 10,6,10,VII-4
St.1—St.12
1. Aj, po-le-će-la dva vra-na ga-vra - - - - na,
Dva vra-na ga - va - ra - - - - - na
O - - da Ni-ši - ća, a-man, pre-ko Koj-re-ni - - - ća,
O - - da Ni-ši - ća, a-man, preko Koj - re-ni - ća.
2. To ne bi-la dva vra-na ga-vra - - na,
Dva vra-na ga - - - vra - - - na,
Ve' to bi - la, a-man, dva mi-la ja - ra - - - na.
3. O-ni tra - žu mla - di' đe - vo - ja - - - ka,
Mla - - di' đe - vo - ja - - - - ka,
O - - ni tra - žu, a-man, mla-di' đe - vo - ja - ka,

27c (continued)

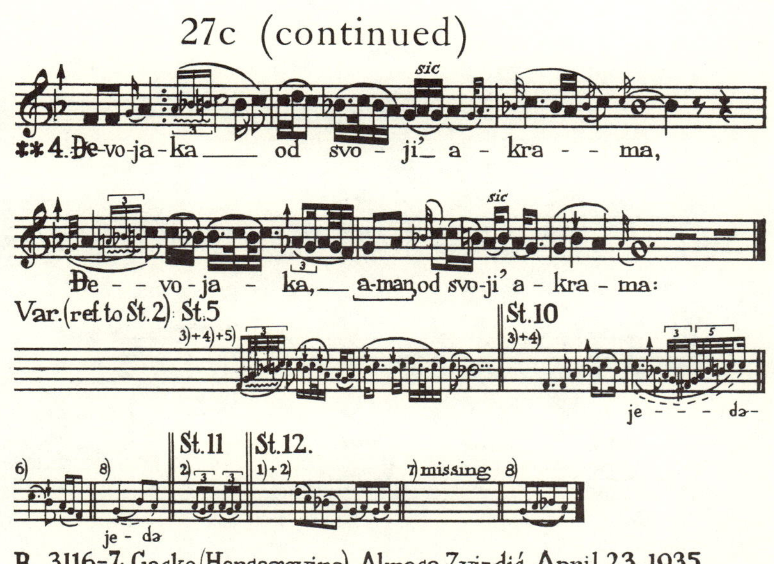

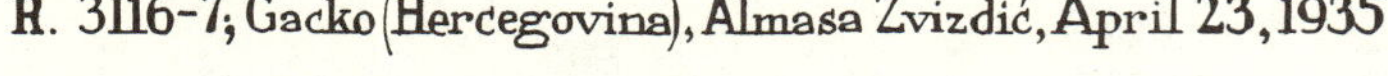
R. 3116-7; Gacko (Hercegovina), Almasa Zvizdić, April 23, 1935

27d

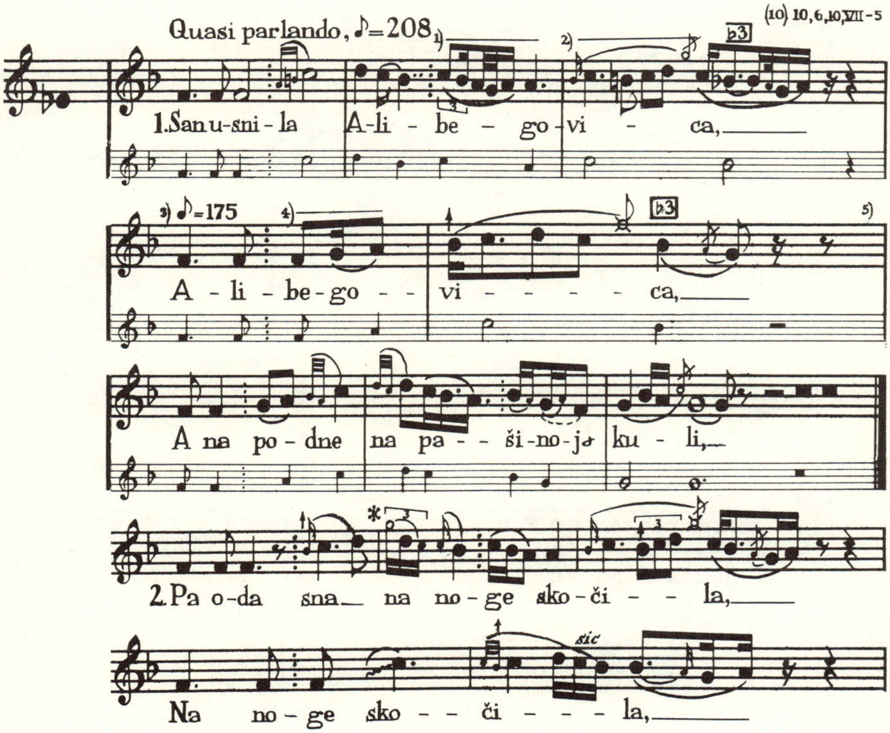

(10) 10, 6, 10, VII - 5

Quasi parlando, ♪ = 208 1) 2) ♭3

1. Sanu-sni-la A-li - be - go - vi - ca,

3) ♪ = 175 4) ♭3 5)

A - li - be-go - - vi - - - - - ca,

A na po - dne na pa - - ši-no-ja ku - li,

*

2. Pa o-da sna na no - ge sko-či - - - la,

sic

Na no - ge sko - - či - - - la,

27d (continued)

R. 3211-2; Gacko (Hercegovina), Halima Hrvo, April 26, 1935

27e

(10) 10, 6, 10, VII - 5
♪ = ca 406
Pl 2934
* 2. Aj, pod Za-gor - je, pod Čen-gi-ća d - vo - re, a-man, a-man,
Tambura
**
Aj, pod Čen-gi - ća dvo - o - re,
Đe bo-lu - je, a-man Čengić Sma-jil - a - ga?
Tambura sola
♩ = 125
***
♪ = ca 406
3. Aj, vi-še gla - ve dva mu sve-tla go - re, a-man, a-man,

27e (continued)

27e (continued)

27e (continued)

27e (continued)

R. 2934-5, Bihać (Bosnia), Zejnil Sinanović, April 1, 1935

28a

(10) 10, 6, 10, VII – 7

♭3

♩ = ca 110

1) 2)

1. Aj, u go-ri se zе-len baj-rak vi – – ja, što ću ja – dna,
**

*

♩ = ca 108

vi-*hi* – – ja,

♭3

Ze – *he* – len baj – rak vi – – – – ja, a – a,
**

Ze – – len

3) 4) 5)

Pod njim le-ži ra – njen baj – rak – ta – re.

5

4

2. Aj, na nje – mu se bi – je-li ko – šu-*hu* – lja,

3

28a (continued)

28a (continued)

28a (continued)

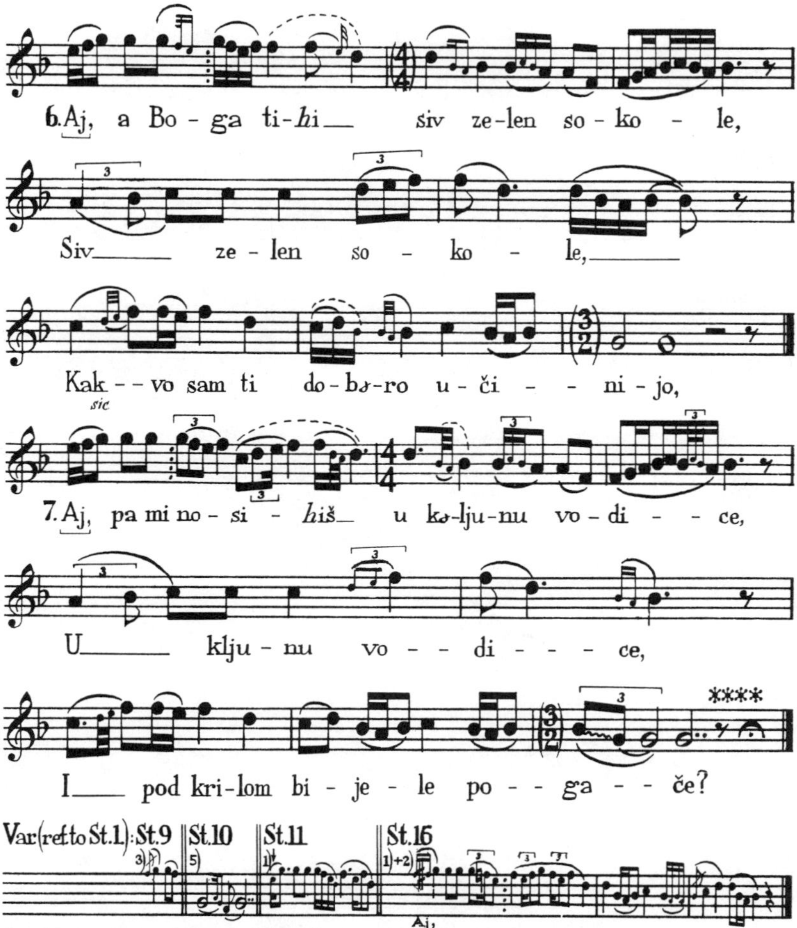

6. Aj, a Bo - ga ti - *h*i __ siv ze - len so - ko - le,

Siv __ ze - len so - ko - le, __

Kak - - vo sam ti do - bə - ro u - či - - - ni - jo,
sic

7. Aj, pa mi no - si - *h*iš __ u kə - lju - nu vo - di - - - ce,

U __ klju - nu vo - - di - - - ce,

I __ pod kri - lom bi - je - le po - - ga - - - če?

****

Var (ref to St. 1): St. 9 | St. 10 | St. 11 | St. 16

Aj,

R. 1538 a), 1539–1540; Rotinja, srez Stolac, u Stocu (Hercegovina),
Naza Rokić, Dec. 15, 1934

28b

28b (continued)

28b (continued)

Joj, i_pa - ri - pi,___ a-man, Še-sto-kri-lo - vi - ća?

(♪= ca 140) 1)

5. Joj, pu-ca - ju li ___ pu - ške Balj-ko-vi - - ća,___

2)

A - man, pu - ške Balj - ko - vi - - - ća?___

3) 4)

Jo - ji, sja - ji___ li se,___ a-man, ćor - da Lju-bo-vi-ća?

Var. (ref. to St. 5): St. 6 1) li___ se i___

St. 8 2) 3)+4)

bi - la.___

St. 9 2) Aj, 3)+4) Aj, a-man,

St. 10 2) A-man 3) Jo-j je li kod i___ Ma - re___

R. 524-5; Livno (Dalmatia), Meho Jarić (28), September 21, 1934

28c

28c (continued)

R. 532-3; Livno (Dalmatia), Meho Jarić (28), September 21, 1934.

R. 3122; Gacko (Hercegovina), Ćerima Kurtović, April 24, 1935

(11) 8,6,5, 1–5

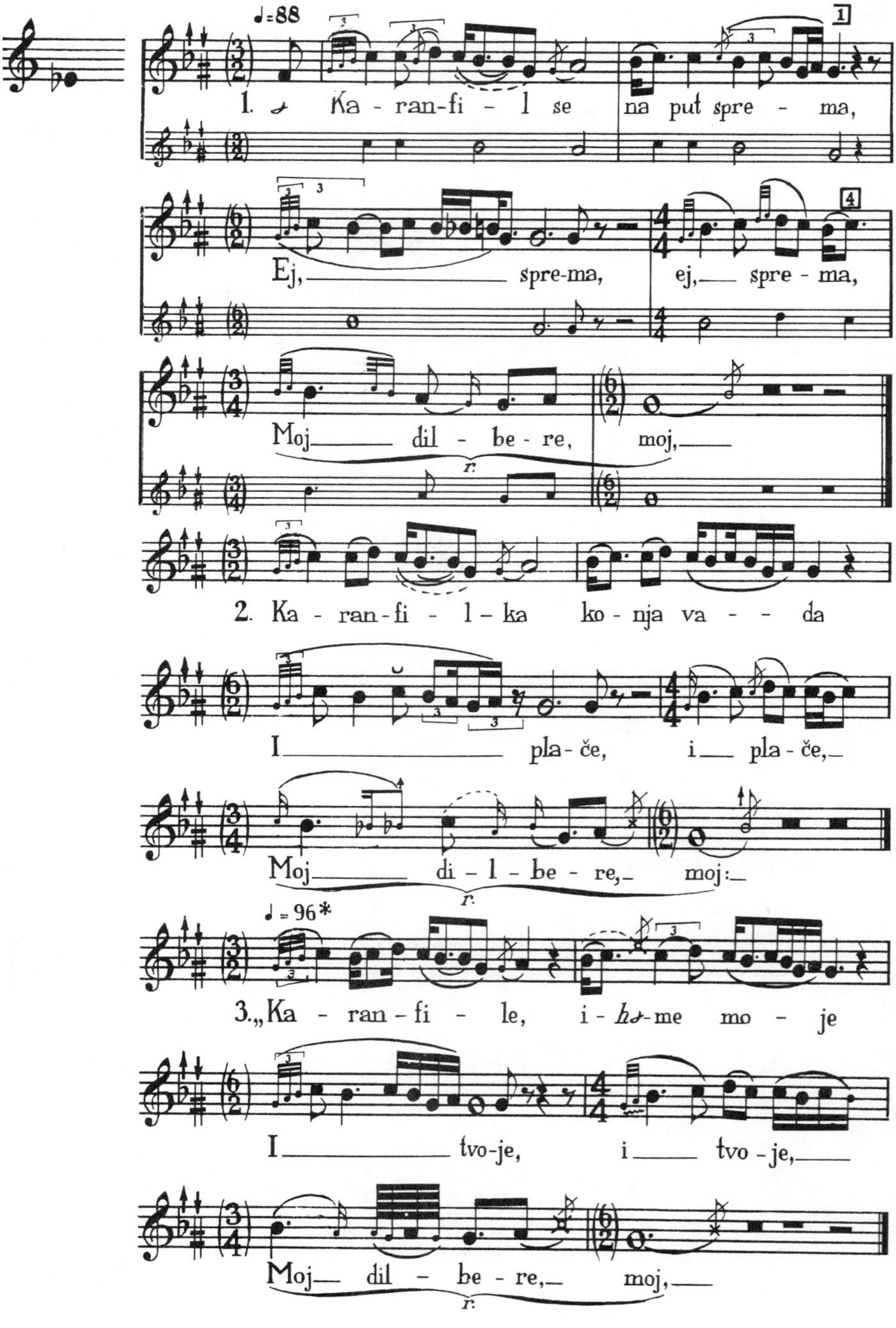

♩=88

1. Ka - ran - fi - l se na put spre - ma,
Ej, spre-ma, ej, spre - ma,
Moj dil - be - re, moj,
r.

2. Ka - ran - fi - l - ka ko - nja va - - - da
I pla - če, i pla - če,
Moj di - l - be - re, moj:
r.

♩ = 96*

3. „Ka - ran - fi - le, i - h-me mo - je
I tvo-je, i tvo - je,
Moj dil - be - re, moj,
r.

30 (continued)

R. 3206–7; Gacko (Hercegovina); Halima Hrvo, April 26, 1935

31a

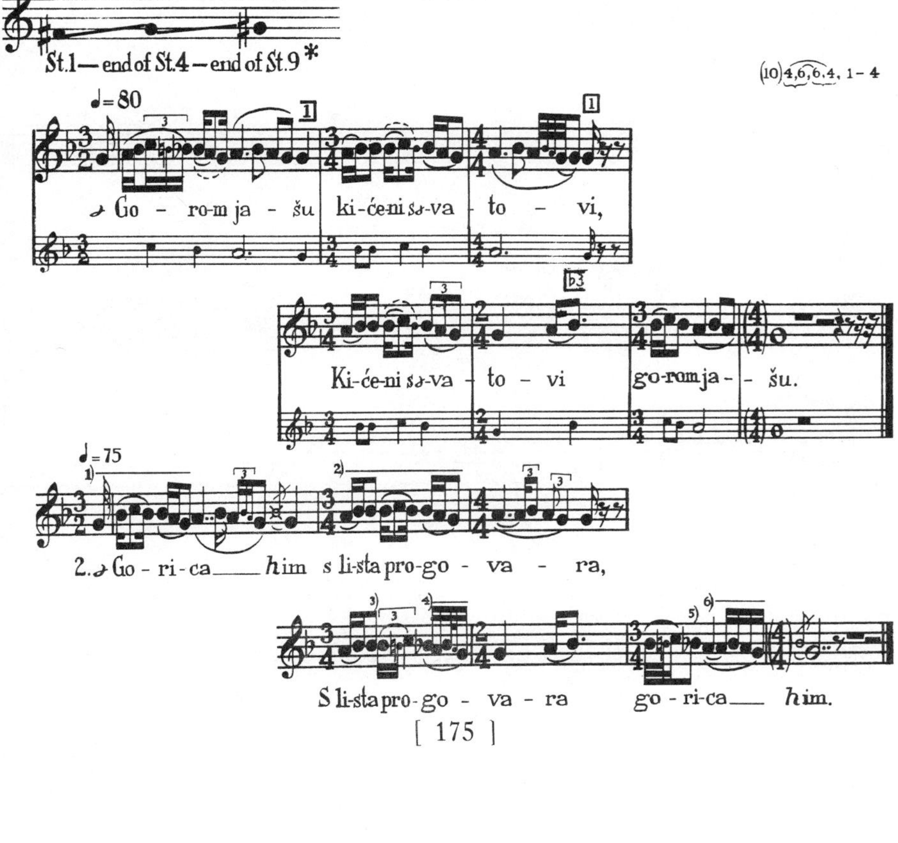

St. 1 — end of St. 4 — end of St. 9 *

(10) 4, 6, 6, 4, 1–4

♩= 80

Go - ro-m ja - šu ki-će-ni sə-va - to - vi,

Ki-će-ni sə-va - to - vi go-ro-m ja - - šu.

♩= 75

2. Go - ri - ca___ him s li-sta pro-go - va - ra,

S li-sta pro-go - va - ra go - ri-ca___ him.

31a (continued)

R. 3509-II; Gacko (Hercegovina), Hajrija Šaković, May 20, 1935

31b

(10) 4,6,6,4, 1 - 5
♩= ca 110
1. Go - rom ja - šu ki-će-ni sva-to - vi,
Ki - će-ni sva-to-vi go-rom ja - - - šu.
2. Go - ri - ca ___ him sli-sta pro-go-va - ra,
Sli-sta pro-go - va-ra go-ri-ca ___ him:
3. „Kud i - de - - te, ki - će-ni sva-to - - vi,
Ki - će-ni sva - to - vi kud i-de - - te,
sic sic
4. Kud i - de - - te, _ i _ ko-nje mo - ri - te,
I ___ ko-nje mo - ri - te, kud i-de - te?
5. U - mr - la ______ je mla-da is-pro-se - na,
Mla - - da is-pro-se-na u-mr-la _ - je.

R. 3086-9; Gacko (Hercegovina), Almasa Zvizdić, April 23, 1935

♩= 150

St.1–St.4

1. Ej, Fa-ti - - ma, gro-mom iz - goj - re - la,

Ej, Fa-ti-ma, g-ro-momiz - goj - re - la, Ej, Fa-ti-ma,

2. Što se pri - mi me - ki - je' ko - la - ča,

Što se pri-mi me - ki - je' ko - la - ča, Što se pri-mi,

3. Da hi pe - če-š, gro-mom iz - goj - re - la,

Da hi pe-češ, gro-mom iz - goj - re - la, Da hi pe-češ,

4. Što ćeš lu - ga na sać na - ba - či - la,

Što ćeš lu-ga na sać na - ba - či - la, Što ćeš lu-ga,

8. Ja sa-m do - šla Fa - ti - mu raz - - go - vo-ri - ti,

Ja sa-m do - šla Fa - ti - mu raz - - go - vo - ri - ti.

Var. (ref. to St.2): St.6 | St.7 | St.9

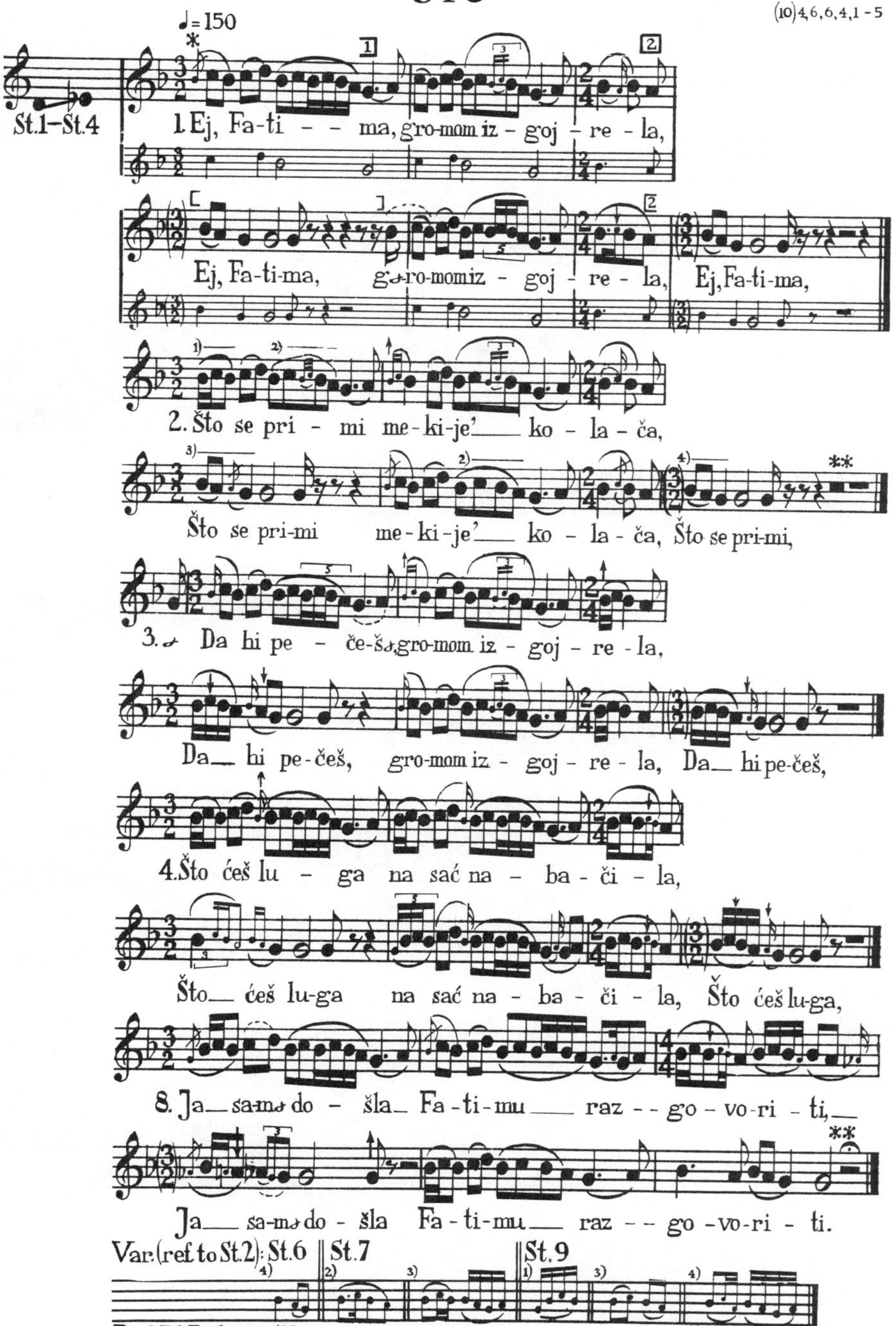

R. 3527; Gacko (Hercegovina), Almasa Zvizdić, May 20, 1935

31d
a)St.1– a)St.6–d)St.2
(10)4,6,6,4, 1 - 4
♩= 82
♩ =76
a) 1. Ruž-nu cu - ru du - ka-ti u-da - ju,
Du - ka-ti u-da - ju, Ru-, ruž-nu cu-ru;
2. Ja si-ro-ta, me - ne će lje - po - ta,
Me-ne će lje - po-ta, Ja, ja si-ro-ta.
♩= 74
3. Mi - sli ne-ko, đe sam ja si-ro - ta,
Đe sam ja si-ro - ta, Mi - hi-, mi-sli ne-ko,
♩=76
4. hn Da se ne-ću u-dad za ži-vo - ta,
U-dad za ži - vo - ta, Da, da se ne-ću.
♩=80
5. M – me-ne mo-ja sje-to-va-la maj - ka,

31d (continued)

Sje-to-va-la maj - ka,__ Me-,__me-ne mo-ja:
♩=78**
6.hn „Do-bro gle-daj, u ru-ke se ne__ daj,__
U ru-ke se ne__ daj,__ Do-,___ do-bro gle-daj!"
Var.(ref.to St.3): St. c)1.
1)

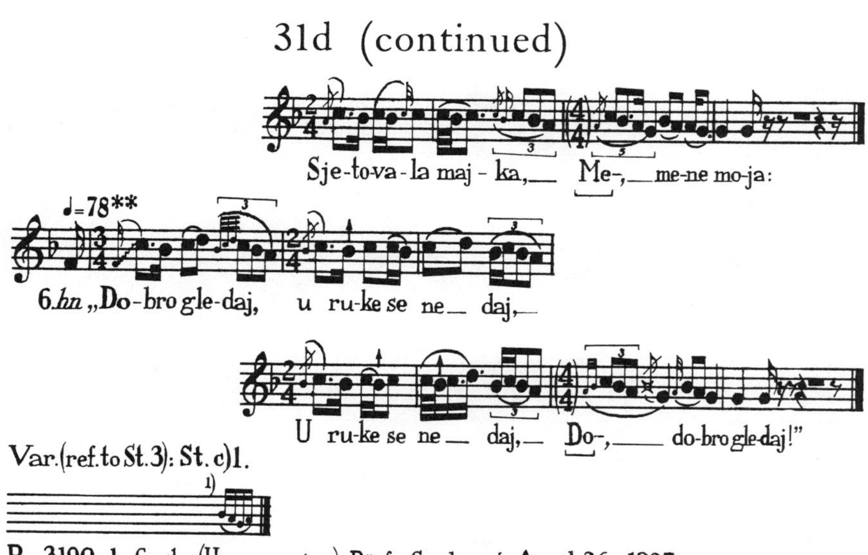

R. 3190-1; Gacko (Hercegovina), Džefa Grebović, April 26, 1935

32

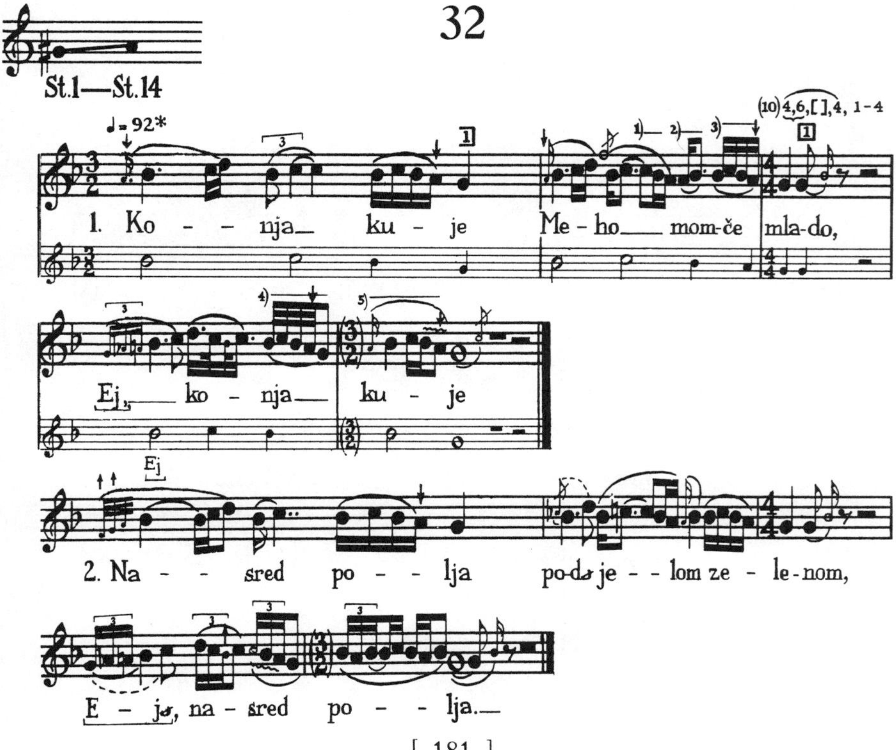
St.1—St.14
♩=92*
(10) 4,6,[ ],4, 1-4
1. Ko - - nja__ ku - je Me - ho__ mom-če mla-do,
Ej,__ ko - nja__ ku - je
Ej
2. Na - - sred po - - lja po-d je - - lom ze - le-nom,
E - j, na - sred po - - lja.__

32 (continued)

32 (continued)

Var.(ref.to St.1): St.5
St.7
St.8
St.9
St.10
bad tracking
St.10,11,12

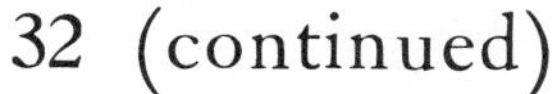

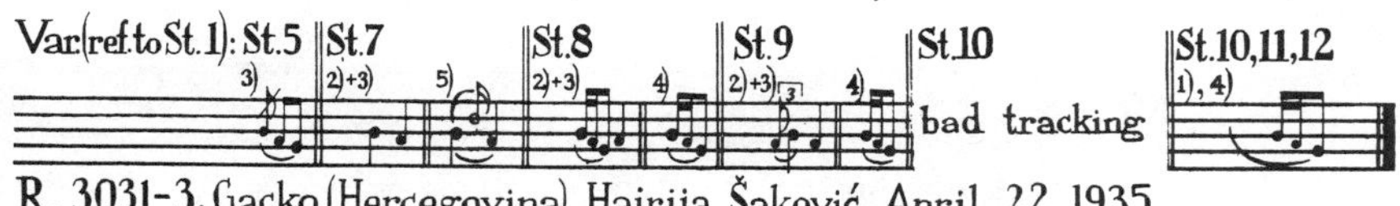

R. 3031-3; Gacko (Hercegovina), Hajrija Šaković, April 22, 1935

33

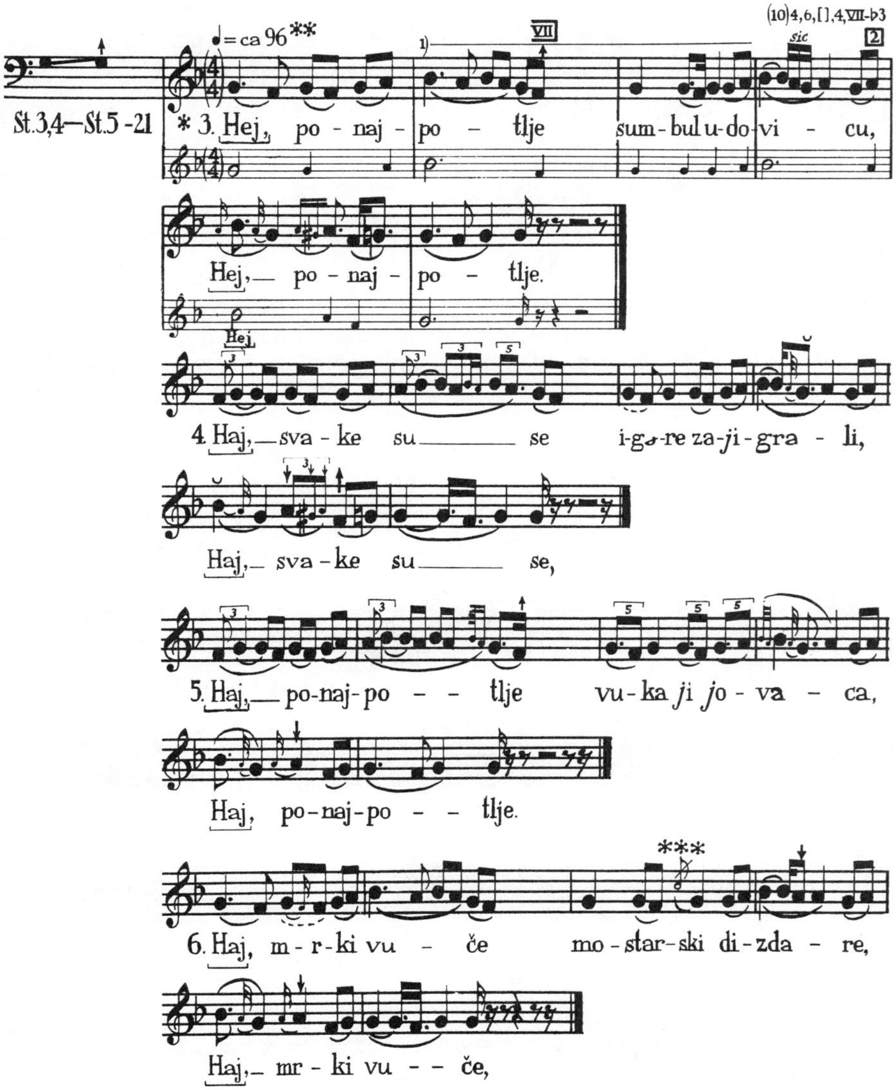
♩= ca 96 **
St.3,4—St.5-21
(10)4,6,[ ],4,VII-♭3
sic
* 3. Hej, po - naj - po - tlje sum-bul u-do-vi - cu,
Hej, — po - naj - po - tlje.
Hej
4. Haj, — sva - ke su — se i-g-re za-ji-gra - li,
Haj, — sva - ke su — se,
5. Haj, — po-naj-po - - tlje vu-ka ji jo - va - ca,
Haj, po-naj-po - - tlje.
***
6. Haj, m - r - ki vu - če mo - star-ski di - zda - re,
Haj, — mr - ki vu - - če,

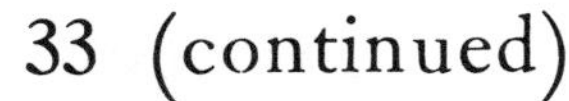

33 (continued)

R. 3019-20; Gacko (Hercegovina), Ibrahim Hrustanović, April 20, 1935

34

34 (continued)

34 (continued)

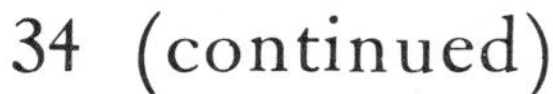

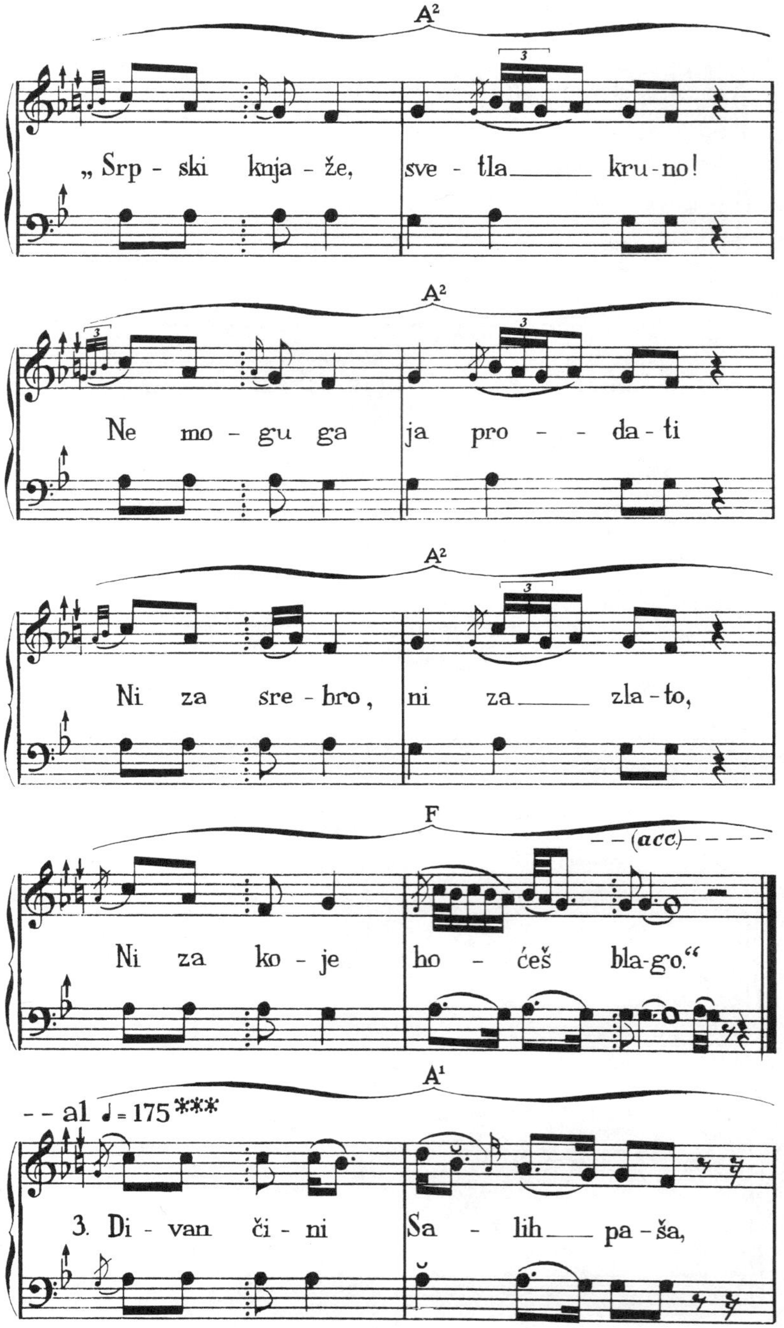
A²
„Srp - ski knja - že, sve - tla kru - no!
A²
Ne mo - gu ga ja pro - - da - ti
A²
Ni za sre - bro, ni za zla - to,
F
(acc.)
Ni za ko - je ho - ćeš bla - go."
A¹
al ♩= 175***
3. Di - van či - ni Sa - lih pa - ša,

34 (continued)

R. 606-8; Kulen Vakuf (Bosnia), Ibrahim Mašinović, September 24, 1934

35

♩= 132*
A**
8,VII-7
1. Knji - gu pi - še Knjaz Mi - la - ne,
F¹
Knjaz Mi - la - ne, ko - pi - lja - nej,
B
Na ko - lje - no Sa - lih pa - ši:
F¹
„Sa - lih pa - šo, maj - ko na - šo,
B
Daj nam pro - daj Him - zi - be - ga
F¹
Jal' za sre - bro, jal za zla - to,
F¹
Jal' za žu - te ma - dža - ri - je!"
B
2. Nje - mu pi - še Sa - lih pa - ša
F¹
Na ko - lje - no knjaz Mi - la - nu:
B
3. „Knjaz Mi - la - ne, srp - ski ca - re!

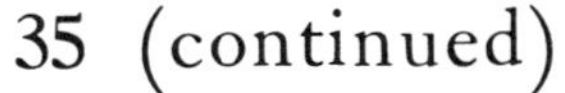

35 (continued)

F1

Ne— mo - gu ti— Him - za da - ti:

B

4. Him - zi - beg je— mu - ška gla - va,—

F1

Za Him - za— nam— i— car zna - dej,

F1

I— ca - re - vi— svi— ve - zi - ri.

B

18. Him - zo— ba - bi— du - kat da - de:—

F3

„Maj to te - bi,— sta - ra ba - ba!—

F4

Pa ti— haj - de— svo - me dvo - ru,

F4

A ja o - do— kud sam po - šo.

Var.: St. 14 line 3 — F2 — I sa ba-bom mla- do Srp-če.

St. 24 line 2 — F5 — I— taj bo-gaz pro - lo - mi-jo.—

St. 27 line 3 — F6 — O- smi Him-za po-go- di-jo

1), 2) later also

R. 855-7; Bare (Bosnia), Mustafa Goro, October 10, 1934

Parlando-rubato, ♪=230

A¹* 8,1-7

St. 1—St. 11

1. Knigu piše srpski knjaže,

A²

Aj, na ruke Salih paši:

„Salih pašo, la – la naša!

poco a poco acc.

A³

Daj nam, prodaj Himzi – bega

A¹

Jal' za srebro, i – l' za zlato,

A³

Jal' za koje pusto blago,

B¹

Oj, il' za pare, aman, carevine,

F

– – (acc.) – – al

Jal' za pare carevine."

– – ♪=260

2. Oj, otpisuje Salih paša:

36 (continued)

36 (continued)

„Bo-ro - za - ni, đe - co mo - ja!

Za - svi - raj - te, za - pi - - vaj - te,

sic

Him - zi - be - ga, a - man, do - zi - - vaj - te,

**

Him - zi - be - ga, do - zi - - vaj - te!"

4. Aj, bo - ro - za - ni za - svi - - ra - še,

Him - zi - be - ga za - - - vi - - ka - še:

C

„Haj - de, Him - zo, car - ski si - ne!

B3

Te - be zo - ve, a - man, Sa - lih pa - ša,

Te - be zo - ve Sa - - lih pa - ša.

Var.: St. 5

line 3 ♪=320***

D1

1) Var. later. or

line 4

A po-ja-ha be - log a - ta, Ko - ji

36 (continued)

R. 519-521; Livno (Dalmatia), Meho Jarić, September 21, 1934

37

R. 3562; Gacko (Hercegovina); *** Hajrija Šaković and Ibrahim Hrustanović, May 21, 1935

38

38 (continued)

38 (continued)

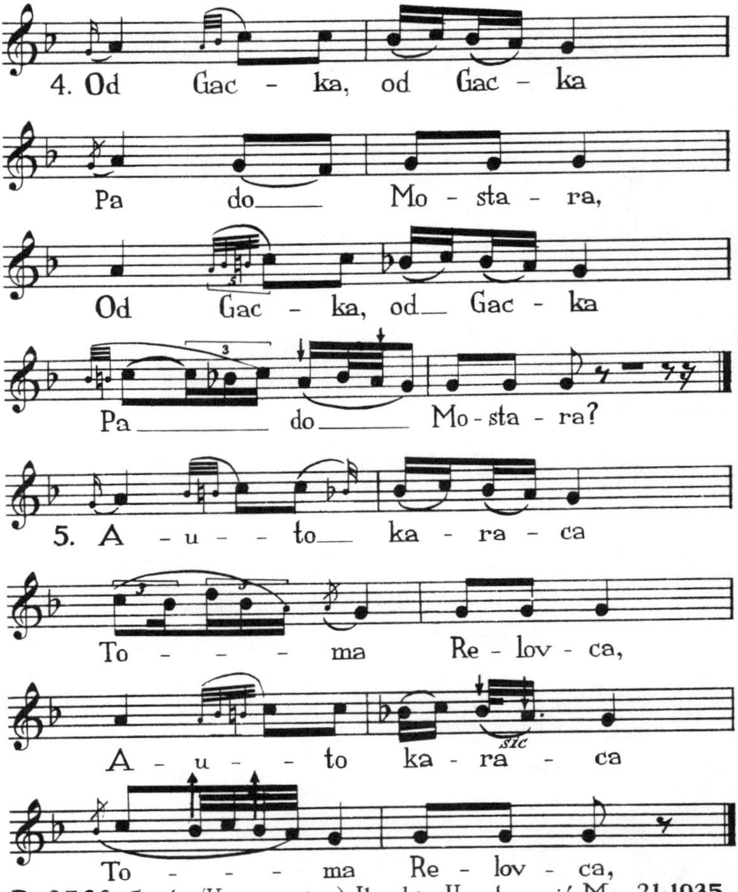

4. Od Gac - ka, od Gac - ka
Pa do Mo - sta - ra,
Od Gac - ka, od Gac - ka
Pa do Mo - sta - ra?
5. A - u - - to ka - ra - ca
To - - - ma Re - lov - ca,
A - u - - to ka - ra - ca
sic
To - - - ma Re - lov - ca,

R. 3566; Gacko (Hercegovina), Ibrahim Hrustanović, May 21, 1935

39a

8,5,8,5,VII-5

Parlando, ♪=290
VII
1. „O Al - ma - sa, du - šo raj - ska,
♪=266
1
Kra - san po - - gled tvoj!

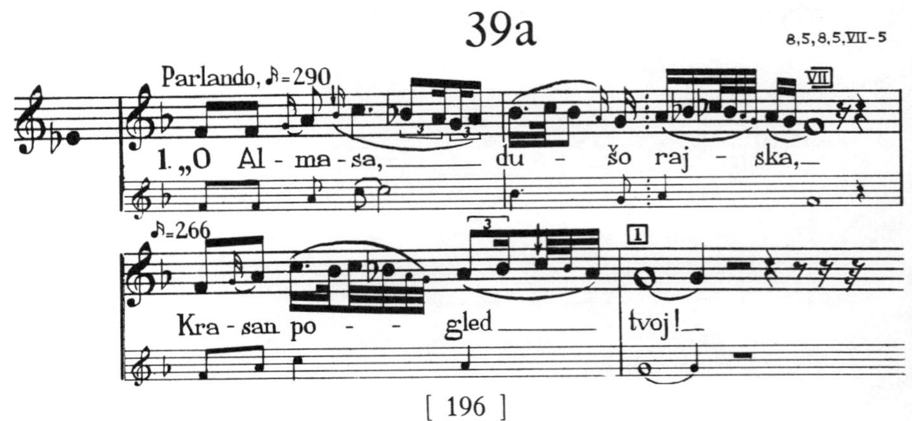

39a (continued)

R. 3157; Gacko (Hercegovina), Almasa Zvizdić, April 24, 1935

39b

Tambura *
Parlando-rubato
♪= 414
♪= 360
8,5,8,5,VII-5
♪= 414
♪= 327
♪= 414
♪= 310
♪= 265
♪= 226
(♪= 226)
VII
♪= 236
1. U ba-šči mi sum-bul cva-ti,
b2
Al ga ne be - - - rem,
U ba-šči mi sum-bul cva - ti,
VII

39b (continued)

39b (continued)

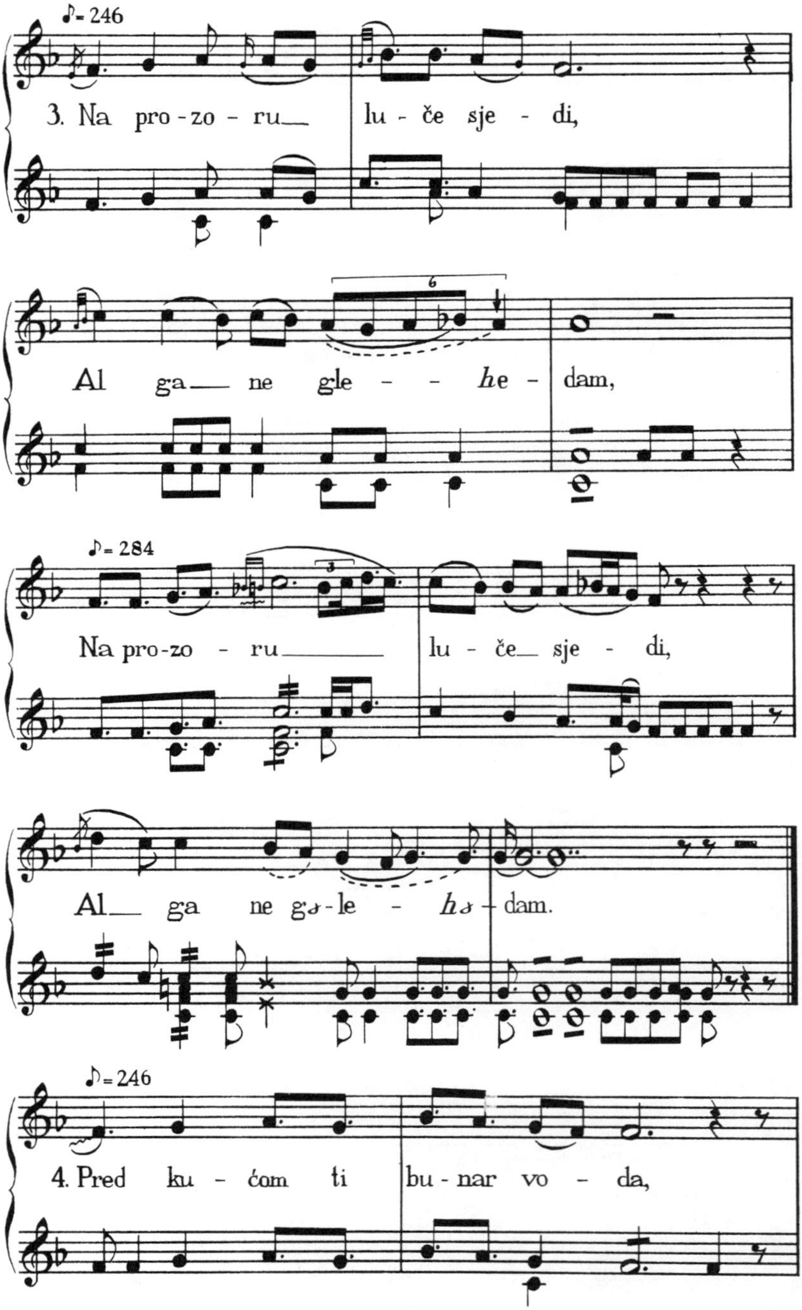
♪= 246
3. Na pro - zo - ru lu - če sje - di,
Al ga ne gle - - he - dam,
♪= 284
Na pro-zo - ru lu - če sje - di,
Al ga ne gə-le - hə - dam.
♪= 246
4. Pred ku - ćom ti bu - nar vo - da,

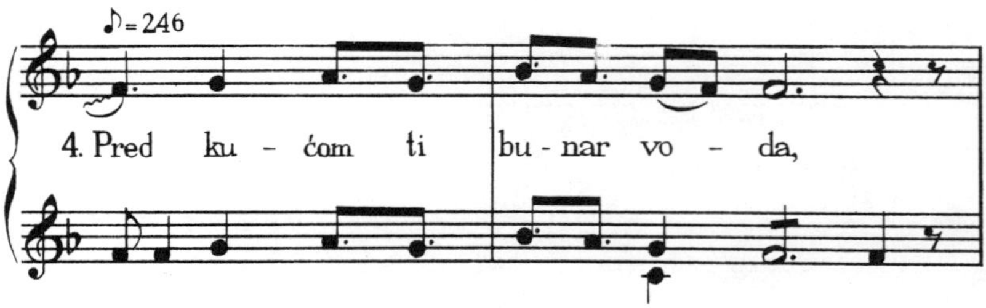

39b (continued)

R. 2938; Bihać (Bosnia), Zejnil Sinanović, April 13, 1935

40

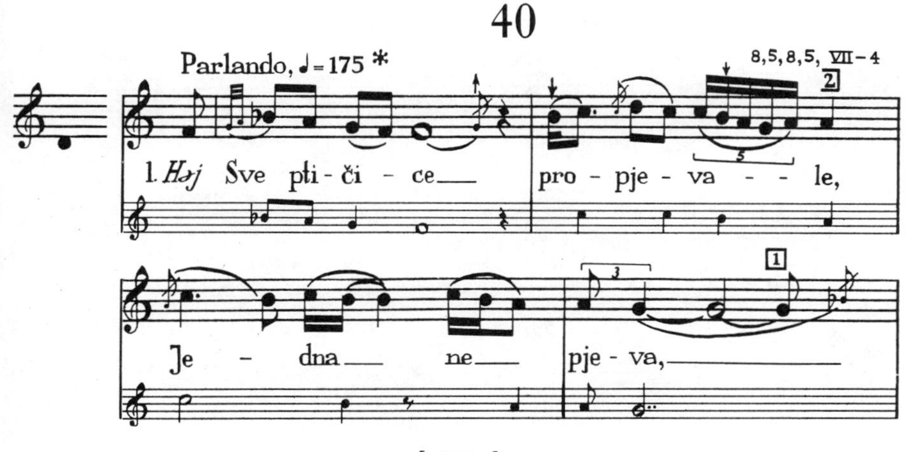

40 (continued)

40 (continued)

41

41 (continued)

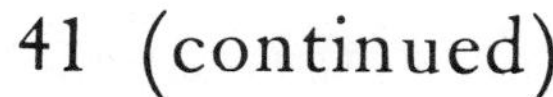

Pu - - na bi - - - se - ra,
2. O - vi na - ši be - - li dvo - ri
Pu - - ni ve - se - - lja,
Aj, o - vi na - ši be - li də-vo - ri
Pu - - ni ve - - - se - lja.
3. Kak - vo va-mə je to ve - - se - lje,
sic
Što se ve - se - - - - lje,
Aj, kak-vo na - mə je to ve - - se - lje,
Što se ve - - se - lje?
4. O - - va maj - ka si - na že - ni

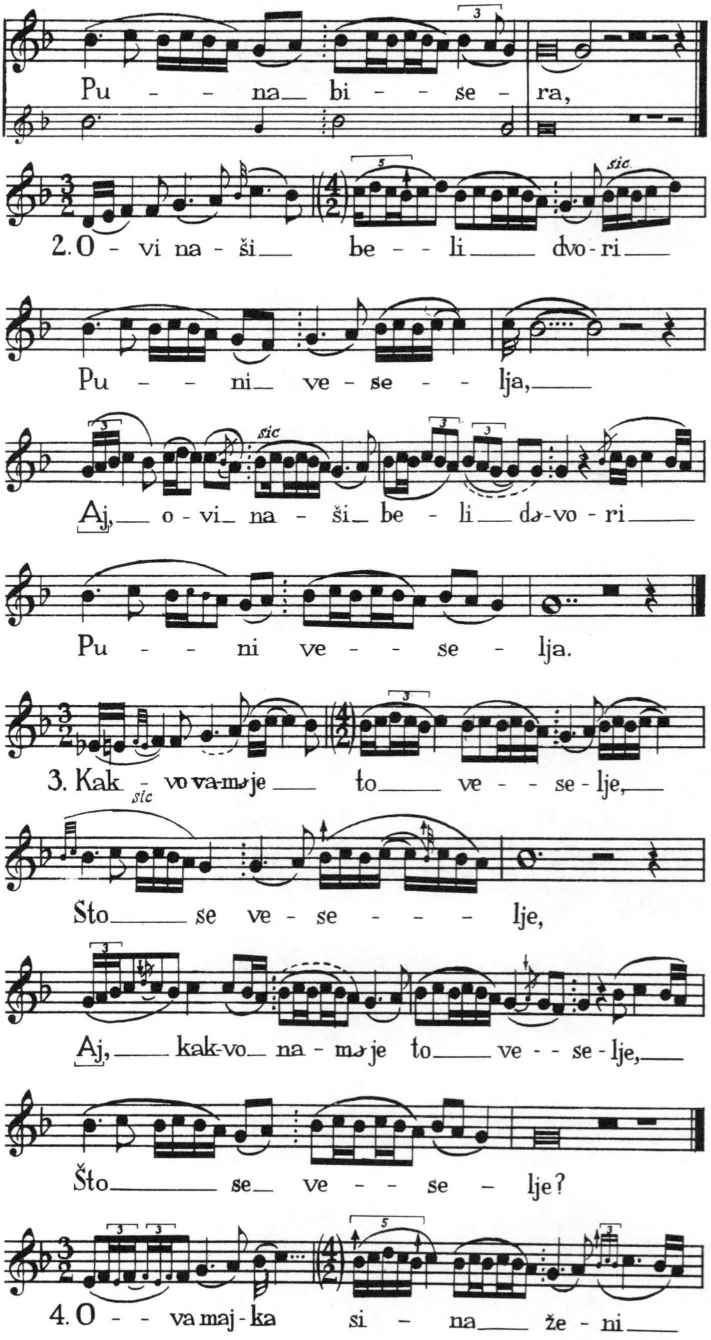

41 (continued)

41 (continued)

R. 3077-8; Gacko (Hercegovina), Almasa Zvizdić, April 22, 1935

42

42 (continued)

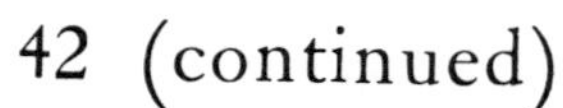

42 (continued)

R. 529–530; Livno (Dalmatia), Meho Jarić, September 21, 1934

43

43 (continued)

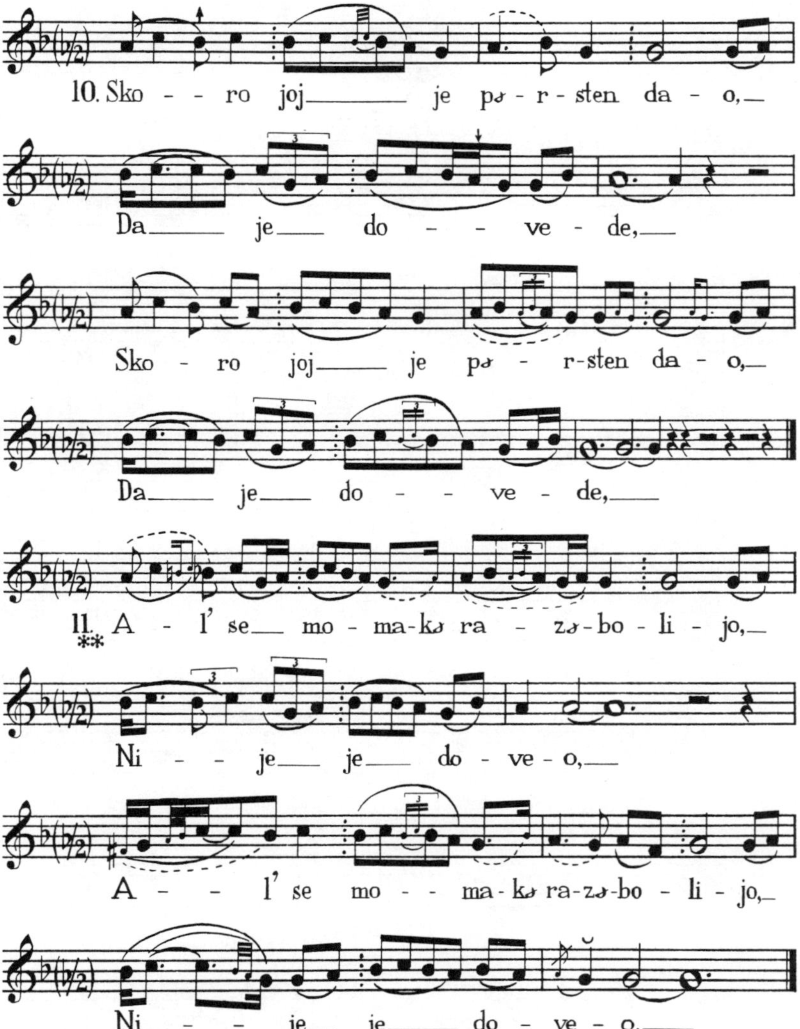
10. Sko - - ro joj je pə - r - sten da - o,
Da je do - - ve - de,
Sko - ro joj je pə - r-sten da - o,
Da je do - - ve - de,
11. ** A - l' se mo - ma-kə ra - zə-bo - li - jo,
Ni - - je je do - ve - o,
A - - l' se mo - - ma - kə ra-zə-bo - li - jo,
Ni - - je je do - ve - o.

R. 3174-5; Gacko (Hercegovina), Almasa Zvizdić, April 26, 1935

44a

♩=94*
8,5,8,5,VII-5
VII
St.1—St.11
1. ə Za - pla - ka - la sta - ra maj - ka

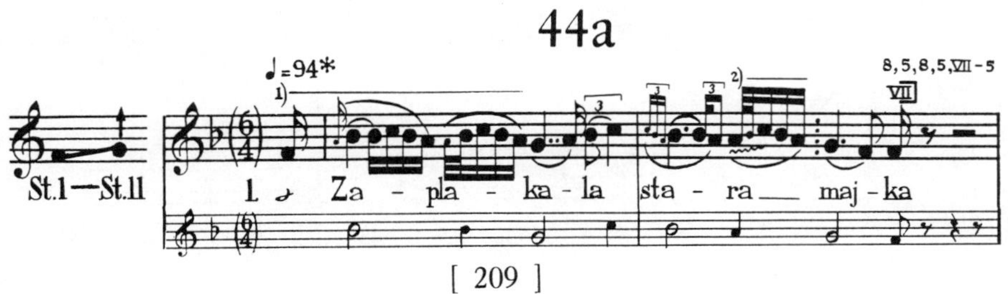

44a (continued)

44a (continued)

Ne - - će da_ ra - di,

4. ♪ Vet_ se_ be - li_ i_ ba - ka - mi,

♪ Da a - ši - - ku - je,___

♪ Vet se be - li_ i_ ba - ka - mi,

♪ Da_ a - ši - ku - - je."

Var. (ref. to St. 1): St. 5. 1) 4) St. 6 3) 5 4) St. 7 2) 3) 4) 5) 3 St. 8 2) 5) 3 St. 9 3) 5) 5 St. 10 3) 5) St. 11 faulty record

R. 3034-5; Gacko (Hercegovina), Hajrija Šaković, April 22, 1935

44b

44b (continued)

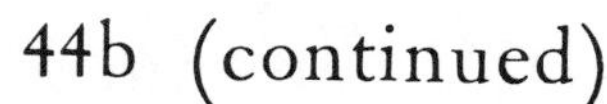

44b (continued)

6)

Dža - fer - be - - - go - va:

*   ?

7)

♩=120

2. „Dža - fer - be - - - že, lu - - - - do de - to, (sic)

*

Što nam do - ve - de,

Dža - fer - be - že, lu - do det’,

*   ?

rallent. - - al ♩=115

Što nam do - - ve - de?

?   ?

44b (continued)

R. 2936; Bihać (Bosnia), Zejnil Sinanović, April 13, 1935

45

Parlando, ♪=ca 154**
8,5,8,5, VII-4
St.1—St.8(last)
1. Ni - ti spa - vam, ni - ti dre - mam,
Ni - ti sna i - - mam,
Ni - ti spa - vam, ni - ti dre - mam,
Ni - ti sna i - - - mam,
sic
2. Vet to vaz- dan na tu- - hžna što
***
Su - ze pro - lje - - vam,
Vet to vaz- da-n a tu - - - huž-na što
Su - ze pro - hə-lje - vam.
3. Ka - ko ko - ja ti - ca le - ti,
Ja je o - pla - čem,

45 (continued)

Ka - ko ko - ja ti - ca le - ti,
Ja hə-je o - pə-la - čem,

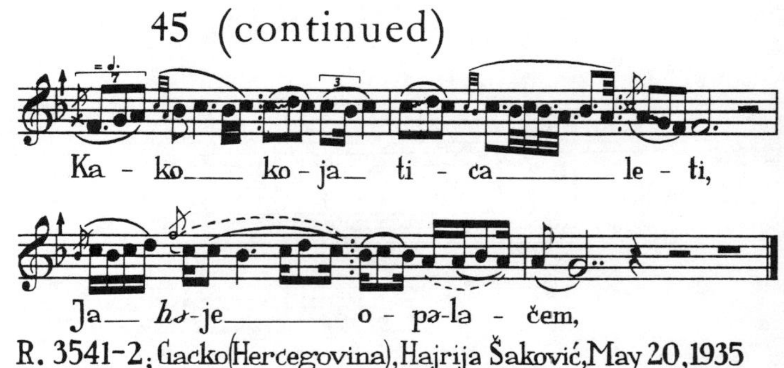

R. 3541-2; Gacko (Hercegovina), Hajrija Šaković, May 20, 1935

46

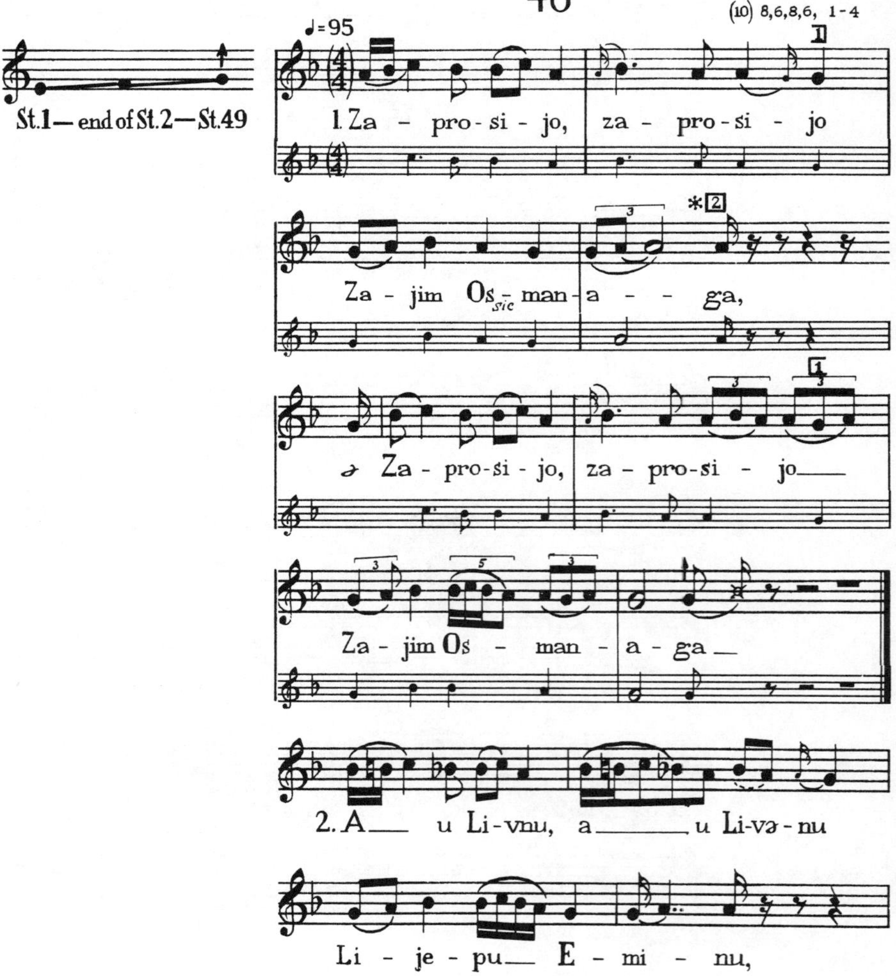

(10) 8,6,8,6, 1-4
♩=95
St.1— end of St.2—St.49
1. Za - pro-si - jo, za - pro-si - jo
Za - jim Os sic - man - a - - ga,
ə Za - pro-si - jo, za - pro-si - jo
Za - jim Os - man - a - ga
2. A u Li-vnu, a u Li-və-nu
Li - je - pu E - mi - nu,

46 (continued)

46 (continued)

Var.(ref. to St.4): St.7
6)+7)+8)
St.12
9)+10)
St.15
9)+10)
St.18
1)+2)+3)
St.19, 22, 23, 25 – 32, 35 – 49
5)
St.38
4) 9)+10)
St.39
9)+10)
St.44
9)+10)

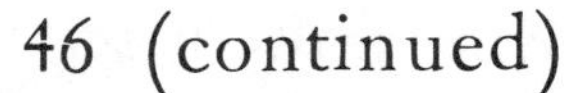

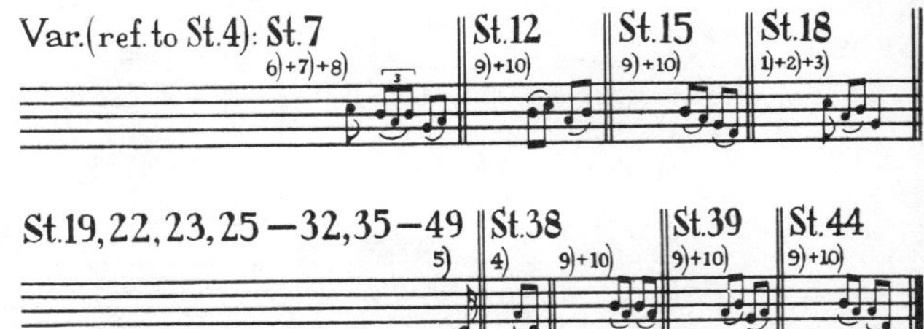

R. 3192-6; Gacko (Hercegovina), Hajrija Šaković, April 26, 1935

47

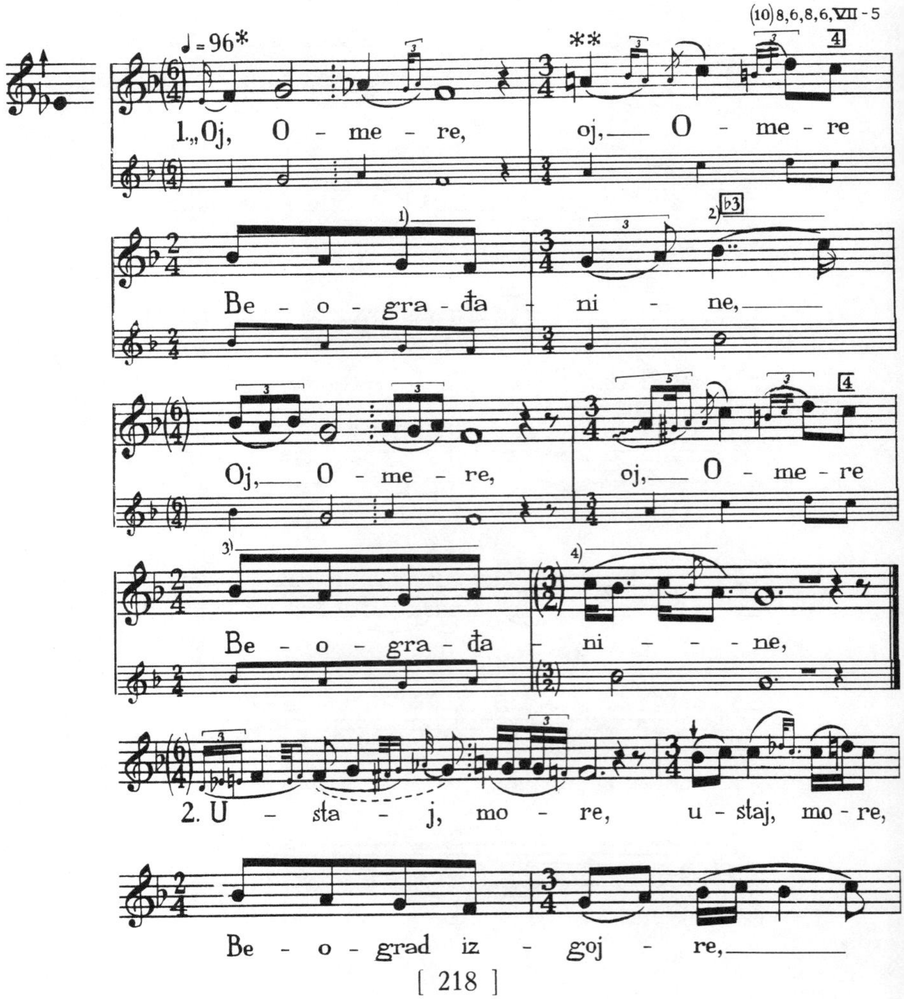

♩ = 96*
**
(10) 8, 6, 8, 6, VII - 5
1. „Oj, O - me - re, oj, O - me - re
Be - o - gra - đa - ni - ne,
Oj, O - me - re, oj, O - me - re
Be - o - gra - đa - ni - - - ne,
2. U - sta - j, mo - re, u - staj, mo - re,
Be - o - grad iz - goj - re,

47 (continued)

47 (continued)

Var. (ref. to St. 1): St. 8, 10
St. 13
St. 15
St. 16
St. 17
1)
3)+4)
2)
1)
3)+4)
4)

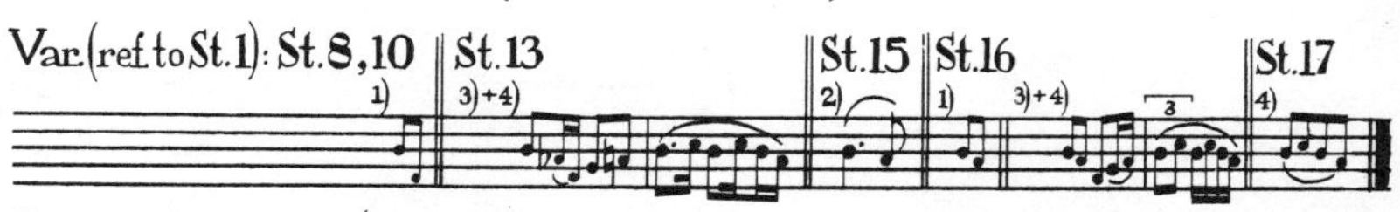

R. 3170-1; Gacko (Hercegovina), Almasa Zvizdić, April 24, 1935

48

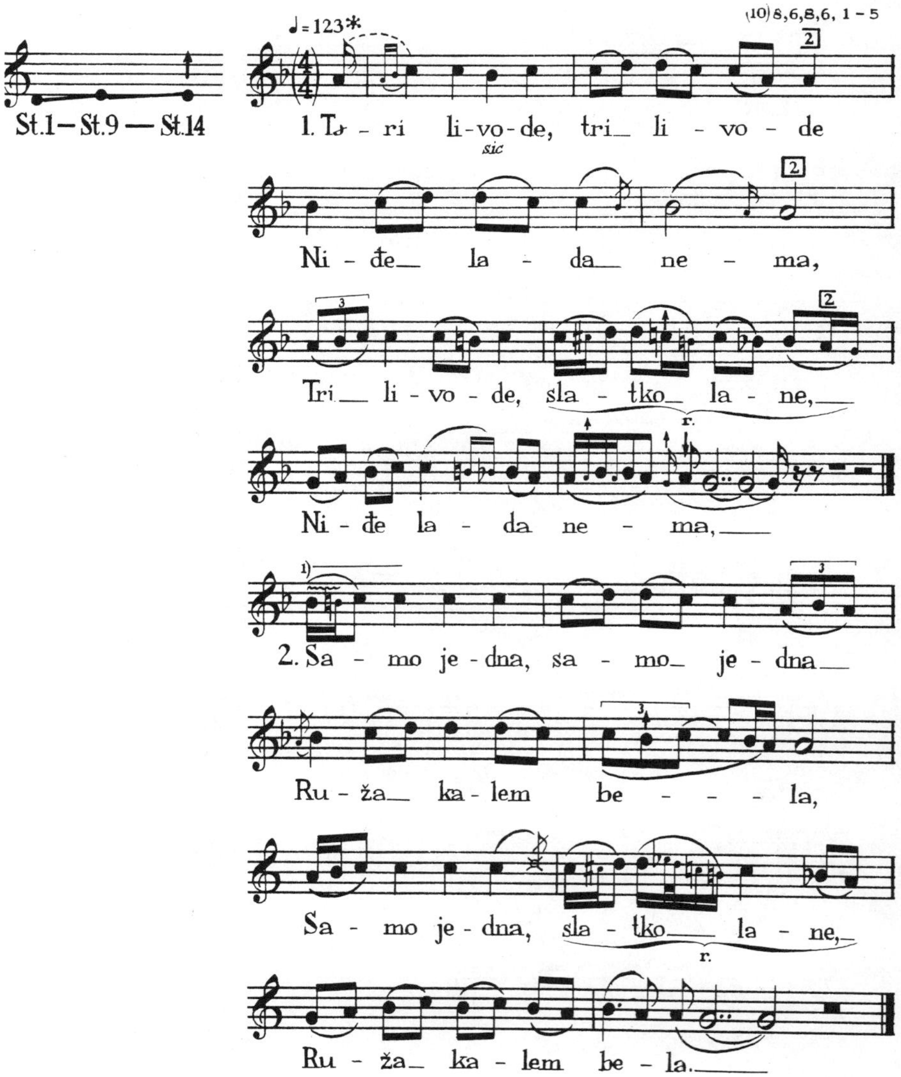
St.1 — St.9 — St.14
♩ = 123*
(10) 8,6,8,6, 1 – 5
1. Tə - ri li-vo-de, tri li - vo - de
sic
Ni - đe la - da ne - ma,
Tri li - vo - de, sla - tko la - ne,
r.
Ni - đe la - da ne - ma,
1)
2. Sa - mo je - dna, sa - mo je - dna
Ru - ža ka - lem be - - - - la,
Sa - mo je - dna, sla - tko la - ne,
r.
Ru - ža ka - lem be - la.

48 (continued)

R. 3568-9, 3567; Gacko (Hercegovina)
Hajrija Šaković, May 21, 1935

49

49 (continued)
2. U — toj ba - šči, u — toj ba - šči
Je - dno vre - lo — pro - - vre - lo, —
U toj — ba - šči, u — toj ba - šči
Je - dno vre - lo — pro - - vre - lo,
3. Kraj — tog vre - la, kraj — tog vre - la
Je - dna plo - ča — mer - - me - ra, —
Kraj tog vre - la, kraj — tog vre - la
Je - dna plo - ča — mer - me - ra, —
Var. (ref. to St. 2): St. 4
St. 5
St. 6
St. 8
N.B. 6) later in several stanzas
R. 3505,
Gacko (Hercegovina), Hajrija Šaković and Almasa Zvizdić, May 20, 1935

50

Parlando, ♪ = ca 160
8,7,8,7,VII-5
*1. Šta je u-zro - - ka, moj dra-ga-ne,
Što me mla-du ne vo - liš?
Šta je u-zro - ka, moj dra-ga-ne,
Što me mla-du ne vo - liš?
2. I - l' ti ni - sa - - - m ču - - sic sta sta-sa,
I - l' go-spo-ska ple - - - - - - me - na,
3. I - l' da mla-da maj - - ke ne-mam,
Te sam ja-dna si - - - - rot - na?
4. Ja si-ro-ta, maj - - ke nej-mam,
Taj-nu lju-bav ot - - - - - - kri - vam.

50 (continued)

Var.(ref. to St.4): St.10
St.11
Var.(ref. to St.1): St.12

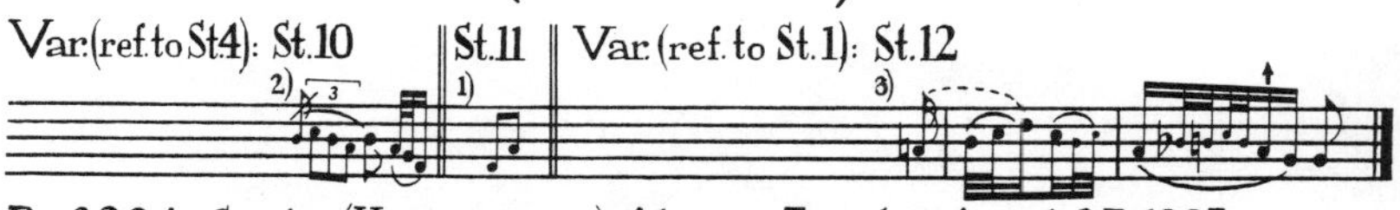

R. 3234; Gacko (Hercegovina), Almasa Zvizdić, April 27, 1935

51

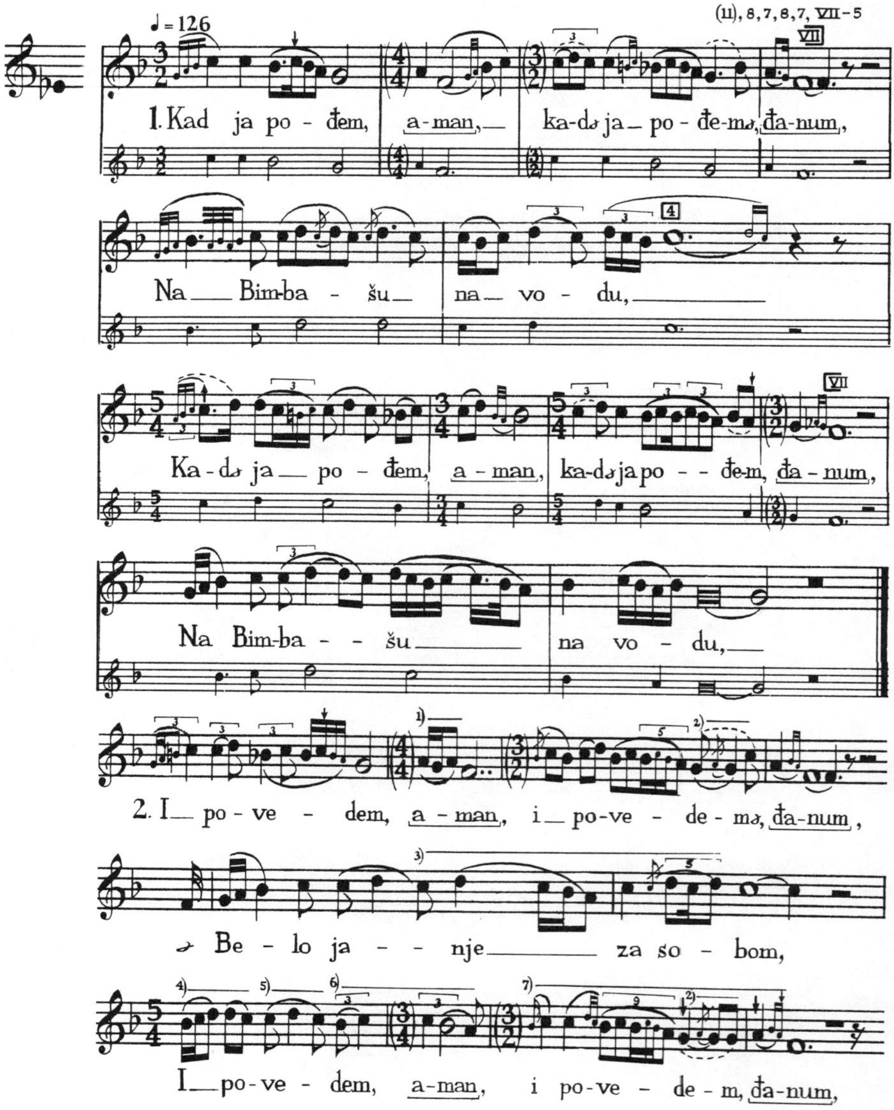

♩ = 126
(11), 8, 7, 8, 7, VII-5
1. Kad ja po - đem, a-man, ka-də ja po - đe-mə, đa-num,
Na Bim-ba - šu na vo - du,
Ka-də ja po - đem, a-man, ka-də ja po - - đe-m, đa-num,
Na Bim-ba - - šu na vo - du,
2. I po - ve - dem, a - man, i po-ve - de - mə, đa-num,
ə Be - lo ja - - nje za so - bom,
I po-ve - dem, a-man, i po-ve - de - m, đa-num,

51 (continued)

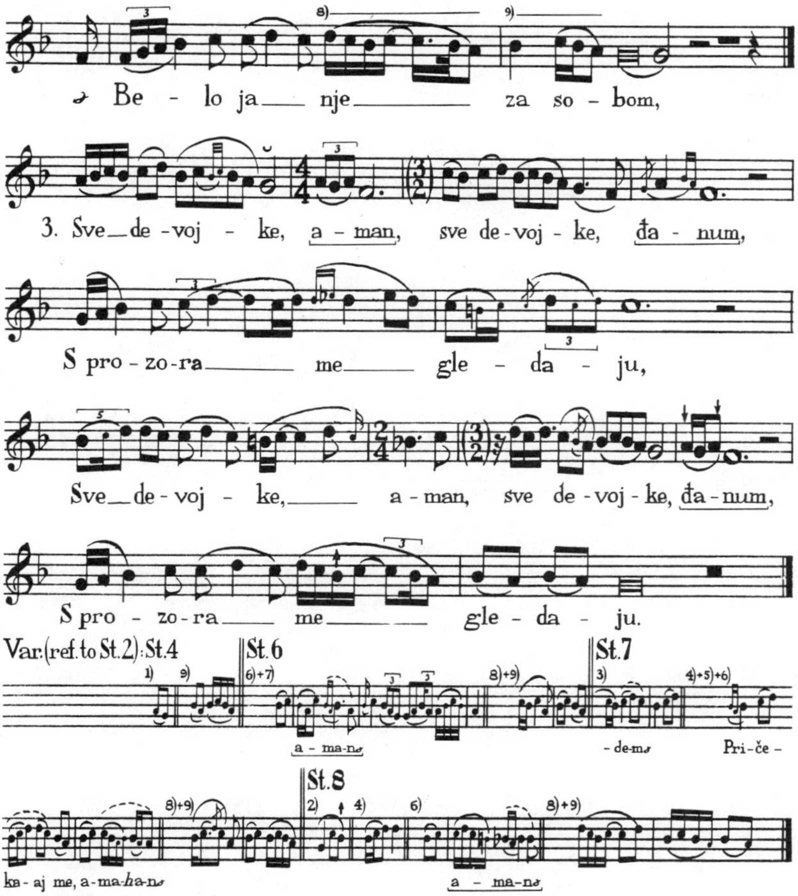

8) 9)

Be - lo ja___ nje___ za so - bom,

3. Sve__de - voj - ke, a - man, sve de - voj - ke, đa - num,

S pro - zo - ra___ me___ gle - da - ju,

Sve__de - voj - ke,___ a - man, sve de - voj - ke, đa - num,

S pro - zo - ra___ me___ gle - da - ju.

Var. (ref. to St. 2): St. 4 1) 9) | St. 6 6)+7) 8)+9) | St. 7 3) 4)+5)+6)

a - ma-n - dem Pri - če -

8)+9) | St. 8 2) 4) 6) 8)+9)

ka - aj me, a - ma-ha-n a - ma-n

R. 3487-8; Gacko (Hercegovina), Almasa Zvizdić, May 20, 1935

52

52 (continued)

52 (continued)
4. Ka - ko ko-me, na-ne, ka - ko ko-me, na - ne,
Ča - še_ do - da - va - še,
Ka - ko ko-me, na-ne, ka - ko ko-me, na-ne,
Ča-še do - da - va - še,_
7. Pə - ro - go - va - ra, na-ne, pro - go - va - ra, na-ne,
Sa-raj - ka_ də - je - voj - ka,
Pə - ro - go-va - ra, na-ne, pro-go - va-ra, na-ne,
Sa - raj - ka_ də-je - voj-ka:
Var. (ref. to St. 1): St. 8
St. 9
ti sə-va-ko - m
ve - r - na_
R. 3523-4, 3525-6; Gacko (Hercegovina)
Hajrija Šaković, May 20, 1935

53
5+5,5+5,5+6,5,VII-7
♩=90*
1. Hn „Gra-na o-do bo - ra cva-la kraj mo - ra,
Gra - na o - do bo - ra cva - la kraj mo - ra,
sic
Ej joj, Ma - ri - ce, di-vo-na krč-ma-ri - ce,
Do-đi, sje - di kraj me - ne!
2. Gra-na o-do je - le cva-la kraj me - ne, Go-
-ra - na o-do je - le cva-la kraj me - ne;
Ej joj, Ma - ri - ce, i sr - ce i du - šo,
Sje - di kraj me - - ne,
Ej joj, Ma - ri - ce, i sr-ce i du - šo,

Gacko (Hercegovina), Almasa Zvizdić, May 20, 1935

54

R. 3224; Gacko (Hercegovina), Halima Hrvo, April 27, 1935

Notes to the Music Examples

1. * This and the following fermatas are deliberate stops; the singers stopped because the respective texts came to an end. After the fermatas they continued the song with a different text.

** Five more repeats of the same two-measure motif follow; the deviations are given below under "Var. 1) 2)." The text of these additional repeats is not transcribed. After the first coda, the whole song is repeated again with different texts (not transcribed) and with different arrangement of the motifs. Then follows the second coda as given under "Var. 3)–4)."

This is the only two-part song among the melodies of the Parry Collection included in this book. Texts of 10-syllable and 8-syllable lines are equally used in this type of song, the peculiarity of which consists in the addition of a coda which uses the clucking sounds described on p. 77 and is sung to the syllable *"Oj;"* therefore, it is apparently called *"Ojkanje"* (see below). Kuba published two variants in his article N. g. u. D., Nos. 59 and 60 (No. 59 is quoted below); he says these songs are *Kolo* (dance songs).

L. Kuba, N. g. u. D. No. 59

Vrlika (probably girls)

Kuba B. H. 1018 ("Tab. of Mat." No. 303 f.) is another example for this type of song. See also Kuhač 1062 and A. Dobronić, *Ojkanje. Zbornik za narodni život i običaje južnih slavena.* Vol. XX, Zagreb, 1915, Pp. 1–25.

Variants: ("Tab. of Mat." 310) Kuba B. H. 2, 318, 319, 321, 398, 825; Đorđević 569 b., 578, 580 (with 10-syllable lines).

("Tab. of Mat." 146) Đorđević 168, 183, 211 (with 8-syllable lines).

2. Variants: ("Tab. of Mat." 130) Kuba B. H. 458, 461, 767, 1041, Kuhač 1045 a.
3. Variants: ("Tab. of Mat." 181) Đorđević 380.
4. * Later gradual *accelerando* leading to ♩ = 126 at St. 6, and to ♩ = 138 at St. 12–14 (last stanza).

   ** St. 4 is faulty at the beginning, and, therefore, was not transcribed.

   Variants: ("Tab. of Mat." 236) Đorđević 31.
5. * Gradual *accelerando* until the end of the seventh (last) stanza where ♩ = 150(!) is attained.

   Variants: ("Tab. of Mat." 243) Đorđević 20, 28, 44, 55, 175, 249, 311, 332, 379, 394, 556, 558; Kuba B. H. 786.

6 a. * Tempo from St. 13 on is gradually faster, reaching ♩ = 140 at the end of the song.

** These sixteenths are due to a mistake. The singer began here the words of St. 3 and sang three eighths on f^1 with "*Nit ga pe-*" syllables; then, perceiving the mistake, she continued without any stop, yet hurriedly, with the words of St. 2.

6 b. * From St. 5 on slight gradual increase of tempo, leading to ♩ = 116 in the last stanzas.

6 c. * From St. 5 on the pitch remains $b^1\flat$ with only a slight tendency toward rising.

** The raising of pitch occurs mainly on this tone. It is sung slightly higher than it should be and this higher pitch is maintained in the following measures.

The same singer sings other texts to the same melody on: (1) R. 3142–44, (2) R. 3217–20, (3) R. 3489–93; the last one is again recorded on R. 3498–3502 (with the same text).

Variants: ("Tab. of Mat." 265) Kuba B. H. 151, 174, 264, 730, 745, 746; Đorđević 16, 19, 72, 74, 424.

Cf. our Nos. 12 and 27; these three variant groups are very closely related. As a matter of fact, No. 27 is a three-section form of Nos. 6 and 12. Nevertheless, as an exception, we chose to place the three groups separately, in order to make more conspicuous what essential changes the structure of a melody may undergo.

7. * See first note to No. 34 on *gusle*, below.

   ** In this section, as well as in St. 7–8, the metrical articulation of the dekasyllable is, exceptionally, $4 + 3 + 3$, instead of $4 + 4 + 2$.

   *** From St. 3 on the melody stanza omits the first melody section.

Line 2 of St. 4 is an example of the vary rare case of an upbeat, for the syllable "E"; the treatment of "Ej" in line 2, St. 1, is quite different. There are no variants; the place of the melody would be between Nos. 268 and 269 in "Tab. of Mat."

8 a. * The tempo grows gradually faster: ♩ = 150 at St. 14, ♩ = 155 at St. 38.

8 b. Variants: ("Tab. of Mat." 284) Đorđević 79.

9. * From St. a) 15 on, there is a slight gradual lowering of pitch, leading to d^1 at St. b) 7. Then on the following disk face again $e^1\flat$, this gradually changing to a low $e^1\flat$ in b) 14 (last) stanza. Perhaps these changes are due to technical imperfections in the recording procedure (see remark on the singer p. 233).

** No further change.

*** The same singer sings this melody to a different text on R. 3235–38. The first melody stanza differs in some essential details from the following stanzas; the singer apparently did not yet hit on the real form of the melody. Therefore the symbols and the skeleton form are given for the second melody stanza.

Variants: ("Tab. of Mat." 298) Kuba B. H. 946.

10 a. * The tempo becomes gradually faster in the following stanzas, reaching ♪ = 150 at about St. 40, and ♪ = 175 toward the last stanza; the low $f^1\sharp$ approaches $f^1\natural$, the low a^1, however, remains neutral.

10 b. * The tempo becomes gradually faster, reaching 𝅘𝅥𝅯 = 360 in St. 41. The structure is changed into *(10) 8, 6, 8, 6*, in St. 36! See third note to No. 12 d.

Variants: ("Tab. of Mat." 303) Kuba B. H. 387, 391, 1018, X, 34; Kuhač 250, 251.

11. *This pause is due to the performer's momentary faltering.

Variants: ("Tab. of Mat." 365–66) Kuba B. H. 528, 529, 575, 711.

12 a. * This and the following similar sudden drops of pitch are probably due to a voluntary or involuntary rest in the performance. After St. 49 several other drops occur. The raising of pitch usually occurs on the long-drawn-out tones, especially on the last tone of the melody stanza; these are sung on a slightly higher pitch, which is maintained in the following parts.

** From about St. 20 on a slight gradual increase of tempo occurs, leading to ♩ = 108 at St. 54. At St. 55 there is a sudden drop to ♩ = 90 (at the same time a drop of pitch from a^1 to f^1), probably due to a new beginning after a rest. Then a gradual increase leads to ♩ = 102 at St. 61 and to ♩ = 108 at the last stanza.

*** The same singer performs this melody to a different text on R. 3550–52. The beginning of the latter is again recorded on R. 3549 with a different arrangement of the same text lines:

The text-line arrangement for the two-section melody is as follows.

Record 3550	*Record 3549*
1. Jeli rano, jel' sunce granulo, Ogrijalo Đerđeleza dvore?	1. Same
2. U tom dvoru niko ne bijaše, Sem četiri mlade jetrvice,	2. Same
3. Sem četiri mlade jetrvice, Među njima Ajka zaovica.	3. Same
4. U dvoru se redom voda nosi. Došla reda skorom dovedeno,	4. Same
5. Došla reda skorom dovedeno Ne dade joj Ajka zaovica	5. Ne dade joj Ajka zaovica Vet natače burme i prstenje
6. Vet natače burme i prstenje, Pripe peču, prigrnu feredžu.	6. Vet natače burme i prstenje, Pripe peču, prigrnu feredžu.
7. Ona ode za goru na vodu, Kad na vodi neznana delija,	7. Pripe peču, prigrnu feredžu. Ona ode za goru na vodu,
8. Kad na vodi neznana delija Zlatnim kopljem bistru vodu muti.	8. Ona ode za goru na vodu, Kad na vodi neznana delija,
9. Progovara Ajkuna devojka: „Odmakni se, neznana delijo,	9. Kad na vodi neznana delija Zlatnim kopljem bistru vodu muti.

These deviations—among other proofs—fully justify the statements given on pp. 46–47.

Translation of Records 3550–3549

1. Is it early? Has the sun shed its warmth?
   Has it warmed the dwelling of Đerđelez?
2. In his home there was no one,
   Except four young daughters-in-law,
3. Except four young daughters-in law,
   And with them his sister Ajka.
4. Each takes her turn in carrying water.
   When the new bride's turn came,
5. When the new bride's turn came,
   His sister Ajka would not let her go,
6. But she put on her rings and ringlets,
   Fastened her veil, and wrapped her cloak about her.
7. She went up the hill to the spring.
   At the spring was an unknown warrior,
8. At the spring was an unknown warrior,
   Muddying the clear water with his golden spear.
9. The maiden Ajkuna said to him:
   "Move away, unknown warrior!"

12 b. * The tempo becomes gradually faster, reaching ♩ = 108 at St. 9, and ♩ = 116 at St. 11. From there on no further changes.

12 c. * St. 7–8, 10–17: the record is faulty.

12 d. b^1♭ is frequently slightly higher, b^1♮ lower, throughout the whole piece; the deviations are so slight that the use of arrows would not be advisable.

** The performance is rather *rubato*, changing the basic rhythm which can be seen in the variants of this melody.

*** The following four measures represent an expansion of the stanza structure. In St. 5–6 the structure becomes *8*, *6*, *10*, followed by an additional expansion of six, respectively seven measures. This example shows to what extent the stanza structure may be subject to change.

The interruption after the eighth syllable of the first section does not belong in the category of "decorative" interruptions (see p. 74) because of its brevity.

12 e. * There is a slight gradual increase of tempo from about St. 12 on, leading to ♩ = 118 at St. 23–24.

** Involuntary break of voice on d^2.

Variants: ("Tab. of Mat." 384) Kuba B. H. 111, 821, 1013, 1108. See last note to No. 6 c.

13. * The same singer sings this melody to a different text (a ballad in 54 melody stanzas) on R. 1547 (end) and 1548–49. This melody seems to be a fragment of a four- (or three-?) section melody; it reminds us of certain Old-Hungarian types.

It has no variants; its place would be between Nos. 403 and 404 in "Tab. of Mat."

Text variants of 13 b): Kuhač, 1121; Bartók, *Rumanian Folk Music*, Vol. III, No. 940.

14. * The pitch becomes gradually slightly lower toward the end of the song; in St. 7: d^1; in St. 8 d^1 is again slightly sharp. Cf. first note to No. 9.

** The rest between stanzas 7 and 8 could not be measured because of the transition from one disk face to another.

The interruption in the first melody section appears either after the seventh or after the sixth syllable and is of lesser weight; later on it disappears entirely.

According to the content the text is that of a wedding-song.

Variants: ("Tab. of Mat." 418) Đorđević 181.

Cf. ("Tab. of Mat." 592) Kuba B. H. 457, 478, 799, 805; and "Tab. of Mat." 679; Kuba B. H. 262, 523–25.

Text variants: Kuba B. H. 457, 478.

15. * From St. 5 on a similar *accelerando* leads to ♩ = 138 at the end of St. 6.

** St. 7: the record is faulty; end of the text is missing.

Variants: ("Tab. of Mat." 432) Kuba B. H. 184, 315; Kuhač 508, 578.

16 a. b. * A slight *accelerando* in St. 8–10 leads to ♩ = 102 at St. 11.

** In St. 12 (on the following disk face), a^1♭ is not raised.

*** The inconsistency of the pronunciation of the word *devojka* may perhaps be explained as due to a conflict between the *ekavski* and *ijekavski* dialects. See also No. 52 (from the same singer), St. 3, measures 3–4 with *devojka,* St. 3, measures 3–4 and St. 7, measures 3–4 with *d + jevojka.*

This piece is a peculiar example of shifting from one of two related structures to the other: the singer uses, in fact, alternately two melodies for the same song (the second in St. 7, 8, 11)!

Variants of form a.: ("Tab. of Mat." 452) Đorđević 485, 486, 497; Kuhač 1042, 1245.

Variants of form b.: ("Tab. of Mat." 993) Kuba B. H. 454, X. 39, XI. 22; Kuhač 963, 1037, 1041. Cf. mus. ex. No. 29.

17. * This tempo is maintained until the end of the song, sometimes tending toward ♩ = 84.

Variants: ("Tab. of Mat." 34) Đorđević 8 (a one-section fragment).

18. * From St. 6 on, the tempo becomes gradually faster, reaching ♩ = 105 at St. 10; this speed is maintained until the end.

** This exceptionally short value (St. 3) and, later on, the break (St. 5) are due to the singer's getting out of breath.

*** Probably slip of the tongue for *pije, noći* and *Do-* respectively.

There are no variants; the melody's place would be between Nos. 639–40 and 641 in the "Tab. of Mat."

19. * The tempo is still getting gradually faster, it reaches ♪ = 180 at St. 13.

** St. 6–13 are in a two-section form similar to St. 4–5. The record of St. 14–18 was not available for this study.

There are no variants; the melody's place would be between Nos. 654 *bis* and 655 in "Tab. of Mat."

20. * For explanation on the use of capital letter symbols see first note to No. 36, below.

** At this point there is a slip of the tongue of the performer.

*** From St. 6 on ♩ = approximately 96–100.

This melody could as well be regarded as a four-section structure: VII VII VII. There are no variants; the melody's place (as a three-section melody) would be between Nos. 682 and 683 in "Tab. of Mat."

21 a. * The tempo is gradually rising from here on, reaching ♩ = 166 in St. 10. The elided vowels are: St. 1, bež*e;* St. 2, Jok*o;* St. 3, moj*e;* St. 4, otvoren*a.*

They are considered and counted, of course, as essential syllables, the following *aj* being merely substituted for them.

21 b. * For the elisions see note to variant a.

** These too-short values probably are due to some slip of the tongue.

There are no variants; the variant-group's place would be between Nos. 693 and 694 in "Tab. of Mat."

22. * Unfinished; the record breaks off in the middle of the second section of the last (seventh) stanza.

There are no variants; the melody's place would be between Nos. 727 and 728–29 in "Tab. of Mat."

23 a. * This tone is faulty, its pitch unclear on the record; probably it was intended to be c^2, as notated.

** Barely audible.

*** On R. 3082, St. 1, 2, 5–7 are recorded again by the same singer and Almasa Zvizdić; the latter seems to be uncertain of the melody. Halima Hrvo sings the degrees a^1 and b^1 with more deviations from the normal pitch on this record than previously. Otherwise, there are no essential changes.

23 b. * This 4/4 measure probably stands for a 3/4 (see all the other stanzas) and may have been caused by uncertainty of the singer at the beginning of the piece, which occurs sometimes.

** Later [♭2]!

*** The last two stanzas—b) 4, 5—again have ♩ = 112. From St. b) 1 on ten-syllable text lines are used: *(10) 8, 6, 6*.

Variants: ("Tab. of Mat." 786) Kuba B. H. 954.

24. * A similar stanza-beginning appears in St. 10–12, 14, 15.

The first *volove* (etc.) in the first melody section is considered a non-essential addition.

Variants: ("Tab. of Mat." 827) Đorđević Nar. Pev., p. 106 (first melody); Kačerovski 54; Kuba XII, 20.

25 * No change in tempo. However, the *parlando-rubato* character of the performance, appearing as early as St. 5–6, becomes more accentuated in the following stanzas.

** This stop is due to the performer's faltering.

*** From St. 6 on, the first half of the melody stanza does not appear again; instead, the second half is repeated as shown in St. 6.

Variants: ("Tab. of Mat." 956) Kuhač 346.

Cf. ("Tab. of Mat." 1778) Kuba XI, 9; Đorđević Nar. Pev., p. 14 (first melody); Kačerovski 1.

26. * A slight *accelerando* leads to ♩ = 120 within St. 4–8; this tempo is kept until the last (tenth) stanza.

As a matter of fact, [4] should be [2]: the second section is virtually a repeat of measures 2 and 3 of the first section. The quoted Kuba has [2], also.

Variants: ("Tab. of Mat." 980) Kuba B. H. 700.

27 a. * As the variants show, this melody seems originally to have had a *tempo giusto* rhythm. Considering the rhythmically rather free performance of variant a., we preferred to omit time signatures even in parentheses.

** No further change in tempo.

27 b. * From St. 5 on, a slight gradual *accelerando* leads to ♩ = 110 at St. 24, which is the last one.

In St. 5, b^1 is kept for the final tone of the second section (that is, no lowering to a^1 occurs); this has happened already in St. 3; from St. 6 on, the final tone of both first and second sections is b^1.

St. 8, 9, 19–21, 23–24 omit the second section and become, therefore, similar to the two-section form of this melody, as seen in No. 6.

27 c. * Unusual prolongation of this tone, caused probably by some embarrassment or hesitation on the part of the singer.

** In this stanza and in St. 12 the second section is omitted, which again shows the malleability of the structure.

27 d. * This break of voice (marked g^2) seems to be unintentional.

** There is an error on the part of the singer here, followed by faulty repeats of some tones that are not transcribed.

*** The sixteenth (that is last) stanza has ♪ = 280, reached by a gradual accelerando.

The first note to variant a. applies to this piece as well.

27 e. * The same piece was recorded twice: first on R. 2934, and then on R. 2935; 2934 has no instrumental introduction, and St. 1 is faulty. We thought it better not to begin with a faulty stanza and placed, therefore, St. 2 of this record at the head of the piece. Of the second recording only St. 1 has been transcribed; this is placed at the end of the piece with the faulty first stanza of the first recording in order to make comparison between the two performances of the same stanza easier. In St. 2–7 of the second recording there are no essential changes except the following: there is one more melody stanza because of some variations in the text; St. 4, 6, 7 have pure 6/8 rhythm; St. 5 has at the end of the melody sections one or two measures of the 2/4 instrumental interlude. The raising of the melody line which appears in bar 7 of R. 2935 never occurs again.

** The question marks indicate that the *tambura* part is barely audible in these portions because the sound of the singer's voice drowned it out on the record.

The *tambura* is a string instrument with frets, about the size of a viola, played with a plectrum. It has four pairs of strings, both strings of a pair are tuned to the same pitch, the pairs themselves are tuned differently. Further data concerning the tuning are missing.

*** A gradual transition from ♩ ♫ to ♪. ♫, at the same time *ritardando* leading to tempo I.

**** Slip of memory: he began with "*jes sva*[*nulo*]," and perceiving his error, skipped to "*rano*" in the middle of the wrong word.

This piece shows a peculiar wavering between a so-called "Bulgarian" rhythm and a 6/8 rhythm; the latter wins out in the end.

It did not seem necessary to add a skeleton-form of the melody to this piece.

Variants: ("Tab. of Mat." 983) Kuba B. H. 126, 214, 289, 340, 408, 537, 623, 783, 880, 956, 1097–1107, 1109, XI, 46; Kuhač 108, 241, 703, 830, 1467, 1508–11; Đorđević Nar. Pev. pp. 132 (first melody), 138 (first melody); Bosiljevac 1, 46.

See last note to No. 6 c.

28 a. * The first stanzas of this song were recorded twice: first on R. 1538 a) and then on 1539. The lower staff shows the first version.

** These additional syllables appear rather seldom: in St. 5 (*e-e*), St. 8 (both), St. 11 and 17 ([*h*]*a-a*). The same singer sings three other texts to this melody on R. 1541–46, where *ha-a* appears in four instances and no *što ću jadna* occurs. These additions seem to be traditional (not individual) features; they are found in one of the published variants as well: Đorđević Nar. Pev. p. 161 (second tune), as *a-a*.

*** The first record comes to an end here.

**** Rest caused by the performer's faltering.

The same singer sings this melody to a different text on R. 1541–42 (13 melody stanzas), to another on R. 1543–44 (13 melody stanzas), and still another on R. 1544–46 (25 melody stanzas). She seems to belong to those singers who virtually know only two or three melodies and sing all their texts to these. Cf. note to No. 13.

28 b. c. Variants: ("Tab. of Mat." 984) Kuba B. H. 234, 245, 1110–1112, 1114, 1115; Kuhač 361, 1522; Đorđević Nar. Pev. pp. 147 (first melody), 161 (second melody).

29. * St. 16–18 have ♩ = 85.

This melody seems to be a fragmentary two-section form, when compared with the variant Kuba XI, 22.

Variants: ("Tab. of Mat." 993) Kuba XI, 22, X, 39; B. H. 454; Kuhač 963, 1037, 1041. All these variants, except the first, are fragmentary 12-syllable two-section structures.

30. * St. 7 has ♩ = 92.

Variants: ("Tab. of Mat." 1014) Đorđević Nar. Pev. p. 188 (first tune).

Text variants: Kuba 735, 736; Đorđević Nar. Pev. p. 188, first song.

31 a. * There is no further change in pitch.

31 b. * The final tone (of the first and second melody sections), a^1, seen at 5) and 10), is later more and more frequently changed to g^1, and is finally, from about St. 20 on, stabilized to g^1. Final tones generally are not subject to such changes. The same singer sings this melody to a different text on R. 3158–60 where again a wavering between a^1 and g^1 as final tone is seen: St. 1–5 has a^1, St. 6–8  ; from St. 9 on g^1 appears as the stabilized final tone.

31 c. * The first four measures of St. 1 are rather off pitch, the singer evidently did not catch the right pitch when she started.

** This extremely long rest seems to be an involuntary stop.

31 d. * This song has the designation *čobanske pjesme* (herdsmen's songs); no explanation has been given regarding this title.

** The last stanza, f) 3, has again ♩ = 75.

Variants: ("Tab. of Mat." 1033) Kuba XI, 30; B. H. 193, 208, 406; Kuhač 736, 892, 1208; Đorđević Nar. Pev. p. 186 (second melody); Bosiljevac 16.

32. * The tempo is gradually getting faster, reaching ♩ = 98–100 at St. 9.

There are no variants; the melody's place would be between Nos. 1040–41 and 1042 in "Tab. of Mat.," before our No. 33.

33. * St. 1, 2, 11, 13, 15–21: the recording is faulty.

** Gradually faster; St. 14 has ♩ = 100.

*** This "clucking" tone seems to be accidental.

There are no variants; the melody's place would be between Nos. 1040–41 and 1042 in "Tab. of Mat.," after our No. 32.

34 * The *gusle* is a one-stringed instrument played with a bow. It has a long neck; the total length is about that of a viola. The string is made of horsehair; the bow has horsehair as well. It is played in the oriental manner, that is, like a cello, held upright and resting on the thigh of the seated singer. The tuning varies according to the voice range of the various singers (mostly around *a*). Generally the first, second, and fourth fingers of the left hand are used (the third seldom). The singer of No. 34

and No. 7 used only the first finger and produced, accordingly, only one tone (a raised *a*♭) beside the open-string tone (*g*). The latter has, quite obviously, the function of the "final tone"; this seems to be an established rule with *gusle* playing, corroborated by hundreds of examples. Therefore, if the sung melody turns below the final tone (for example, to VII), some other tone must be substituted for this tone on the accompanying *gusle* (on which, by the way, the melody is always played with more or less deviation from the sung form), although an agreement between the melody range and *gusle* range could easily have been attained by a change of pitch. That this was not done is by no means a sign of awkwardness or accident; the procedure must be regarded as intentional.

** For explanation of the use of the capital letter symbols, see first note to No. 36, below.

*** From St. 7 on, ♩ = 200; preceding this is a gradual *accelerando*.

Variants: ("Tab. of Mat." 1208) Kuhač 801.

35. * Gradual slowing down (!) to ♩ = 116 which is reached in St. 38.

** For explanation of the use of the capital letter symbols, see first note to No. 36.

There are no variants, the melody's place would be between Nos. 1224 and 1225 in "Tab. of Mat."

36. * The various motifs or motif-groups are marked with different capital letters. These letters are added to each text line in the corresponding number of Part II, in order to indicate which type of motif was sung to the respective line.

** Rest caused by performer's faltering.

*** A gradual *accelerando* follows, leading to ♪ = 370 at St. 11.

Variants: ("Tab. of Mat." 1247) Kuba B. H. 1010, 1014; Đorđević Nar. Pev. p. 10 (first melody); *Hungarian Folk Music*, No. 14 (with *d*♮). Cf. ("Tab. of Mat." 1268) Đorđević 113.

37. * From St. 4 on, slight *accelerando*, leading to ♩ = 90 at the end of the eighth (last) stanza.

** Variant 2) does not occur again in St. 4–8.

*** I. Hrustanović sings, of course, an octave lower, mostly in the same way as H. Šaković. There may be slight deviations between the two voices; they cannot be very well distinguished on the record.

There are no variants; the melody's place would be between Nos. 1339 and 1340 in "Tab. of Mat."

38. Variants: ("Tab. of Mat." 1469) Đorđević 41; Kuba B. H. 400, 492, XI, 37.

This melody seems to be a fragmentary form of an unknown (urban?) melody, although Đorđević 41 is somewhat more "elaborate": it has

[2] as main caesura, and thus a differentiation between the two halves of the melody.

39 a. * Melody section 4 of St. 4 and 5 is similar to that of St. 1 and 3.

The performance is in an exaggerated sentimental manner, approaching the urban style. The text is, in fact, urban, with a text stanza structure and rhymes. See remarks on *8, 5, 8, 5,* structures, p. 51.

39 b. * See second note to No. 27 e., above.

** This rest between St. 4 and St. 5 is unusually long and filled out by the instrumental accompaniment because of the singer's coughing.

Variants: ("Tab. of Mat." 1495) Kuba B. H. 695.

Variant of the text: our No. 50; see note on the text there.

40. * Gradual *accelerando*, leading to ♩ = 195 at St. 4; this tempo is maintained until the end.

** The second half of St. 7 is missing.

There are no variants; the melody's place would be between Nos. 1498 and 1499 in "Tab. of Mat."

41. * Probably an interruption in the performance (perhaps a new beginning) accounts for this sudden drop of pitch to the original degree; St. 9–10 are recorded on another disk face.

** Involuntary prolongation of the rest caused by coughing.

Variants: ("Tab. of Mat." 1502) Kuba B. H. 522, 535, 598, 621.

42. * St. 1–3, 5 could not be transcribed, the corresponding parts of the record being faulty; the text is semirural, probably of urban origin. See remarks on *8, 5, 8, 5,* structures, p. 51.

Variants: ("Tab. of Mat." 1505) Kuba B. H. 576, 698; Đorđević Nar. Pev. p. 131 (first tune); Bosiljevac 49.

Cf. ("Tab. of Mat." 1557) Đorđević Nar. Pev. p. 146 (first melody); Kačerovski 18.

43. * R. 3174, which contains St. 1–8, was not available for this study; therefore, only St. 9–11 are transcribed.

St. 11 has a *8, 6, 8, 6,* structure!

There are no variants; the melody's place would be between Nos. 1506 and 1507 in "Tab. of Mat."

44 a. * The tempo becomes gradually faster, reaching ♩ = approximately 104 in St. 7; from there on, no further changes.

** Evidently instead of f^1 (see the following stanzas).

*** Not quite clear, because of coughing.

44 b. * From here on until the next notation of 16th-pairs, it is not clear on the record whether there are any 16th-pairs instead of single eighths in the upper voice of the *tambura* part.

** See second note to No. 27 e., above.

*** The singer stopped in the middle of the melody stanza; apparently he did not know the rest of the words.

Variants: ("Tab. of Mat." 1514) Kuba 213, 1054, 1056, 1057, 1059.

45. * Frequently almost b^1♮! In later stanzas the b^1 of measure 4 has no lowering of the pitch.

** Slight gradual *accelerando*, reaching ♪ = 200 in the last (8th) stanza.

*** "*Što*" is an addition which has no specific sense here. It is added as a complementary syllable to make an 8-syllable line out of a 7-syllable.

There are no variants; the melody's place would be between Nos. 1521 and 1522 in "Tab. of Mat."

46. * Some stanzas after St. 18 have VII!

** The tempo becomes gradually faster, reaching ♩ = 115 at St. 10, and ♩ = 126 at the last (46th) stanza.

Variants: ("Tab. of Mat." 1561) Iz Levča 19, 27, 29; Đorđević 259.

47. * The tempo becomes gradually faster, reaching ♩ = 104 in St. 17.

** In the first few bars, a^1 sometimes is slightly lower.

There are no variants; the melody's place would be between Nos. 1572 and 1573 in "Tab. of Mat."

48. * There is a slight *accelerando* between St. 10 and St. 14, leading to ♩ = 132.

** St. 1–9 are recorded once more on R. 3567; this record has a tempo beginning with ♩ = 135, then an *accelerando* leading to ♩ = 140 at St. 6; this tempo is maintained until the end.

Variants: ("Tab. of Mat." 1580) Kuhač 1433.

49. * H. Šaković, one of the two women who sang for this recording, seems to know the melody better and to be leading.

** After St. 5 or 6, there is a slight gradual *accelerando* leading to ♩ = 104 in the last (11th) stanza. There is no change in pitch; this is probably due to the participation of the other singer, A. Zvizdić.

The piece is probably a fragment of a melody of recent origin, or, at any rate, of a not very old one. The rhythm of the single sections, especially of the compressed 2/4 measure, reminds us of the rhythm in certain New-Hungarian melody types.

There are no variants; the melody's place would be between Nos. 1610 and 1611 in "Tab. of Mat."

50. * The complete four-section form of the melody appears in St. 1 and St.12 only; the others were sung to the second half of the melody. The per-

formance is rather *rubato;* its supposed original rhythm can be seen in the skeleton form.

The text seems to be of urban origin; it has a *8*, *5*, *8*, *5*, variant in our No. 39 b.!

There are no variants; the melody's place would be between Nos. 1615 and 1616 in "Tab. of Mat."

51. Variants: ("Tab. of Mat." 1622) Juž. Srb. 414.

Cf. ("Tab. of Mat." 915) Kuba B. H. 237; ("Tab. of Mat." 1619) Kuba B. H. 116, 117, 231, 642, 646–48, 697.

Text variant: Kuba B. H. 101, 627, 935.

52. * Later also 4] and [4.

** See third note to No. 16 a. b.

*** The same song is recorded by the same singer again on R. 3525. In that version the pitch level is a somewhat low e^1 at the beginning, e^1 at the end. The tempo is ♩ = 95–108. There are a few slight changes in the text.

The melody seems to be of more or less recent origin (a borrowing from some urban or foreign material?).

There are no variants; its place would be between Nos. 1637 and 1638 in "Tab. of Mat."

Cf. ("Tab. of Mat." 1724) Kačerovski 20.

53. * An *accelerando* leads to ♩ = 130 which is reached at St. 5.

** St. 4 is similar to St. 3. The recording is faulty throughout St. 6. The same song is recorded by the same singer on R. 1514–15 again. Deviations: pitch level c^1; tempo constantly ca. ♩ = 100.

Variants: ("Tab. of Mat." 1679) Kuba B. H. 963, 1091; Đorđević Nar. Pev. p. 136 (first tune). Slovak variants: *Slovenské Spevy* I, 45, 483, 585, III, 135. Moravian variants: Bartoš II (*Národní Písně Moravské,* Brno, 1889), 443, III (*Národní Písně Moravské,* Praha, 1899, 1901), 605, 1521, 1745; Černík 74; Peck 243; Sušil, p. 798.

54. * See remarks about the text on p. 425.

Cf. ("Tab. of Mat." 869) Kuba B. H. 3.

The melody has no definite structure; no place, therefore, could be assigned to it among those with definite structure.

Part Two

by ALBERT B. LORD

Introduction to Part Two

THE SEVENTY-FIVE SONGS presented in this book are from the collection of Southslavic folk songs made by Professor Milman Parry, of Harvard University, in the years 1934 and 1935 in Yugoslavia, where I had the privilege to assist him. Of the 12,554 texts in that collection, 758 were recorded on aluminum phonograph disks. Most of these recorded texts are of "men's songs"; long narrative heroic poems sung or, more properly, chanted to the accompaniment of the primitive one-stringed gusle. There are, however, more than 205 "women's songs" on the disks of the collection, and it is from these that the following were taken. In addition, the collection contains approximately 11,000 texts of women's songs and approximately 800 men's songs, taken down from dictation.

By far the largest number of the women's songs were recorded at Gacko, on the old border between Hercegovina and Montenegro. But two texts of this present group (Nos. 13 and 28a) are from Stolac in central Hercegovina; one (No. 35) is from Bare, high on the road between Sarajevo and Goražde, in Bosnia; three (Nos. 27a, 44b, and 39b) are from Bihać, in northern Bosnia; two (Nos. 7 and 34) are from Livno, and five (Nos. 36, 28b, 20, 42, and 28c) are from Kulen Vakuf, both in Bosnia. Finally, there is one song, the first in this book, sung by a group of girls from Kijevo-by-Dinara in Dalmatia.

Most of the songs were sung by women, but those from Bihać, Bare, Livno, and Kulen Vakuf were sung by men. One young man, Ibrahim Hrustanović, sang for us at Gacko, and he is represented in this book by three songs (Nos. 33, 37, and 38), one of which (No. 37) was performed in unison with one of the girls.

The songs which we collected from these singers are called women's songs, in order to distinguish them from the "men's" or heroic songs. This does not mean that they are the exclusive property of the women or that they are sung only by women. The men's songs are peculiar to the social life of the men, they always have a narrative text, and the cases on record in which women have practiced this type of singing are exceptional and only prove the rule. If we define the men's songs as narrative poems of ten syllable lines sung or chanted to the accompaniment of the gusle or tambura by men for the entertainment of the men, then we must define women's songs as lyric or narrative poems, having lines of various lengths, sung with or without accompaniment (usually without) by women or young men for their own amusement.

Vuk Karadžić was among the first, if not the first, to use the term "women's songs," and he describes them in the 1824 introduction to his famous collection as follows: "All our folk songs are divided into *heroic songs*, which men sing to the *gusle*, and *women's*, which not only women and girls, but also men, especially young men, sing, and that in unison. One or two people sing women's songs *for others to listen to*, and for that reason in singing women's songs more attention is given to the *singing* than to the *song*."[1] Further on, however, Vuk makes reference to a third type of song, which was "recited" rather than sung; that is, similar in performance, apparently, to "men's songs," but recited by women: "There are some songs that are on the border between women's and men's songs, so that one does not know where to place them. . . . Such songs are more like heroic songs than like women's, but one never hears them sung by men to the gusle (even to women) and because of their length they are not sung as women's songs either, but are only recited."[2]

In the introduction to the fifth volume of the collection of Croatian folk-songs published by the Matica Hrvatska Society, in Zagreb, Dr. Nikola Andrić elaborates a bit more on the subject of these "recited" women's songs:

"As to which songs the young girls sing and which the middle-aged and older women recite, I have found a classic bit of evidence of this slight difference in the manuscript collection of a certain Slavic collector. In one of the books of Luka Ilić Oriovčanin there is a note of sixteen pages in which Antun Rodić, the last editor of the greater Slavic Franciscan writers, has written down thirty-two women's songs from Nurkovac, his birthplace, in the year 1846. Most of the songs were dictated by Margita Ilijašević and the old mother of the collector himself.

Margita sang for him *only the shorter* love songs, 'which are sung for dancing or at get-togethers in the evening in front of the house,' but his mother *recited* the longer songs. The young girls—says Rodić—praise *their own* songs and

[1] Vuk Stefanović Karadžić, *Srpske Narodne Pjesme,* I, p. vi.
[2] Karadžić, *op. cit.*, p. vii.

maintain that they are finer than 'those old ones which the women recite,' but on the other hand the women like their own better, because 'the old ones are better.' This document is particularly important because it classifies the popular songs by the age of the singers and reciters, and shows in which category each belongs."[3]

By 1935 this distinction seems to have disappeared. We did not come across this practice of "reciting" women's songs. The longer narrative "women's" songs were *sung*, with a few exceptions,[4] in stanzas, even as the ballads of the English traditional narrative poetry are rendered. Moreover, these are no more the exclusive property of the older women, but are sung by old and young alike.

The women's songs in the Parry Collection were at first recorded somewhat incidentally, most of the attention being given to the heroic songs. But in Gacko the circumstances for collecting women's songs turned out to be so favorable that Mr. Parry seized eagerly the opportunity offered for a systematic canvassing of the musical lore of that district. I would estimate that at least two thirds of the traditional music of this region was recorded, and the large proportion of songs from Gacko in this collection reflects the richness of the provinces of Bosnia and Hercegovina. The work started with the commissioning of two young Moslems, Ibrahim Hrustanović and Hamdija Šaković, to supervise the collecting of songs from the Moslem women in Gacko and the surrounding villages. All the children and young people, encouraged by the monetary reward, were pressed into service; they began to record in notebooks the texts known to their mothers and grandmothers. In this district only the young could write. At first many notebooks were received which were so badly written they could not be read; some were merely copied from printed songbooks (*pjesmarice*). It was found necessary to have Ibrahim and Hamdija, both very honest and intelligent young men, control this amorphous mass. The texts submitted under their supervision were much better. Coming from good and highly esteemed Moslem families, these youths were accepted everywhere and treated with the utmost respect. The reputation of Mr. Parry, the American professor, was enhanced by Ibrahim and Hamdija. We visited Ibrahim's family and took many pictures in the seclusion of the courtyard of his house. It was possible in this friendly setting to meet

[3] Matica Hrvatska, *Hrvatske Narodne Pjesme*, V, p. xii, xiii.
[4] See pp. 21, 65–66.

the women of his family and others who would come as visitors and later give their songs to be recorded. Normally, because of the rules of the Koran, this would not have been possible.

After a while Mr. Parry asked Ibrahim and Hamdija if they knew of any Moslem home in Gacko to which the women would come and where we would be allowed to set up our apparatus and make records. The written texts already obtained would be worth much more if sung versions of the same songs could be recorded and if first-hand accounts of the lives and opinions of the singers could be caught on the records. The technique which in the previous months had been developed for collecting men's songs could thus be employed for the women's songs. In response to the appeal for a headquarters in which to work, Salih Zvizdić offered us the hospitality of his home. Salih was *muezzin* of the local mosque, and a stanch Moslem, whose faith nobody could possibly question. As he himself said in conversation before the microphone, he knew more about Islam than all the others.

Two rooms on the second story of the old stone house were turned over to us. The smaller of the two was the "studio." Rugs were hung on the walls to reduce echo. Squatting Turkish fashion on the floor, the women, unveiled and completely at their ease, gathered around Mr. Parry and Nikola Vujnović, our faithful and wise Hercegovinian interlocutor. Nikola, prompted by Mr. Parry, managed the whole proceedings. In the other room, seated cross-legged on the floor, I presided over the recording apparatus. In this room was also the stove on which coffee, strong, black Turkish coffee, was constantly being brewed. These were by far the most comfortable surroundings in which we worked during our entire stay in Yugoslavia. Besides Mr. Parry, Nikola, and myself, Salih and Ibrahim were in constant attendance.

Five women formed the nucleus of the otherwise ever-changing group of singers. First came Almasa Zvizdić, Salih's wife and our gracious hostess. She was at that time, I believe, in her late thirties. She had been born in the village of Medanići, not far from Gacko, but had spent much time visiting relatives in the town. Thus, she prided herself on being a townswoman (*građanka*), not a peasant, and she was well aware of her position in the community. Hers had always been a sheltered life. She had never worked in the fields or tended the sheep and goats on the mountains. There were no children from her marriage with Salih, who was comfortably situated, though by no means well-to-do, and Almasa had only her housework and embroidery to occupy her. She had learned songs from her mother in Medanići and the other women in Gacko who came frequently to visit her. She was our best singer. Eighteen of the songs in this book are from her.

In picturesque contrast to Almasa was Halima Hrvo from Borče, which is nearer to Foča, in Bosnia, than it is to Gacko. She was a real peasant (*seljanka*). Hers had been a hard and unhappy life. She was about sixty when we were in Gacko. When she was young she had been married to a man much older than herself—the connection was financially profitable for her father. Her respect, as a peasant, for Almasa and the way of life of the town was deep. She felt inferior and was inordinately shy, always giving way to Almasa. Her songs were almost purely from her own village, with infiltrations from Foča, her nearest market and cultural center. To me her deep-throated tones and simpler melodies were more pleasing than Almasa's shriller, more ornate singing. From Halima come ten songs in this book.

Hajrija Šaković represented the younger generation. She was in her early twenties, a dark-haired, chubby-faced girl with long braids, which indicated her unmarried state. Like Almasa she sang in a shrill voice. She knew many old songs and nearly all the new ones. Thirteen of the songs in this book were sung by Hajrija.

The other two women, who complete the nucleus of the group, are not represented in the following songs—and for a good reason. Fatima Biberović knew only Turkish and Albanian songs—her Serbian was not very good. Đula Dizdarević was seventy-five and somewhat deaf. She had lost her voice and all idea of pitch. Mr. Bartók found that her melodies could be transcribed only approximately; therefore they were not suitable for musical study and are not represented here. Her age, however, and the dignity of her family won her a place in this gathering. She remembered the old days very well and was always ready to talk about them. Moreover, the texts of her songs were good, even though her singing was not what it had once been. The Dizdarevići had been rich landowners in Korite, a small place on the road between Bileća and Gacko, during the Turkish occupation. Her stories of historical events at the end of the last century and the early part of the twentieth will be well worth publication when they are translated.

Old Đula, as we affectionately called her, used to roll a large copper pan, a *tevsija*, about eighteen inches in diameter, on a short wooden table, while young Hajrija sang across it. The rumble of the *tevsija* furnished a weird and crude accompaniment to Hajrija's tight-voiced song. Đula was the only singer in the region who employed this accompaniment, which is mentioned by some authorities. I owe to Mr. Bartók the information that this type of accompaniment is used also for Turkish melodies performed by women and that its use by Serbo-Croatian women is probably the result of Turkish influence.[5]

Fatima, the last of our women, is in a class by herself. Although none of the songs in this book is from her, she is the subject, or object if you will, of one of them (see note to No. 31c). She was born and brought up in and around Prizren in Macedonia where more Turkish and Albanian is spoken than Serbian, and those were her mother tongues. I believe that Turkish was more natural to her than Albanian. Probably she was in her thirties. She had been married four times, and her husbands had been a motley crew. One was a highway robber; he had been caught and hanged. Another was a baker, and respectable. Biberović, the incumbent in 1935, was a gypsy, a worthless individual who was languishing in jail in Dubrovnik for having knifed one of his fellows. Fatima was glad that he was in jail, because when he was free he would beat her. She knew no Serbian songs, but she did know some of the common ones in Turkish and Albanian, and we recorded a few of them, as well as a long conversation with her about her life.

Of the other singers from Gacko we have no further information except their names and ages. I was not present at Kijevo at the recording of the first text in this book, nor did I know Ibrahim Mašinović and Meho Jarić. Particulars of the life of Zejnil Sinanović of Bihać are lacking, though I remember him vaguely and have a picture of him.

I do recall vividly, however, the day on which we recorded Mustafa Goro's version of "Himzi Beg." It was October 9, 1934, a day famous in Yugoslav history as the tragic day on which King Alexander the First was assassinated at Marseilles. We had left Sarajevo early that morning in the rain and crossed Mt. Romanija. The village of Bare is on the road along the level top of this mountain. There was a coffee house (*kafana*) on that road run by a Turkish *hodža*. On a previous visit he had furnished Mr. Parry with a number of songs, so we stopped at his *kafana* in mid-afternoon, set up our apparatus, and began to make records. Hajdar Đozo, the hodža, started a version of "Himzi Beg," but had to stop part

[5] Bartók, *Turkish Folk Music from Asia Minor,* melody No. 40 and note.

way through because he had forgotten it. Mustafa Goro volunteered from the small group which had gathered and sang it through. Shortly after that the recording apparatus broke down, and we went on in the rain to Goražde, but not without having photographed the hodža, his wife, and his pretty little daughter.

The seventy-five songs in this book were chosen for publication chiefly on musical grounds. For this reason it seemed best not to rearrange them in some other order. Besides, the classification of these texts is difficult, and no one system would be completely satisfactory. The singers themselves—at least in the regions covered by our work—do not seem to recognize any categories other than a few rough and indeterminate ones.[6] There are songs that are sung at weddings, and there are lullabies; there are songs for dancing, and there are a few children's game songs. When questioned about songs sung on any given occasion or under particular circumstances, as, for example, songs for dancing or reaping or weddings, the singers are likely to think of songs about weddings or reaping rather than songs sung at those times. Most of the songs are general love songs and can be sung on any occasion.

Choosing the songs for publication primarily for their musical interest offers an advantage for the student of the texts. Since they represent an impartial cross-section of the tradition, they do not suffer from "literary" bias. Many of them are not the "best" version of the song in the Parry Collection or elsewhere. Some of the texts are incomplete, and corrupted, yet they are excellent laboratory specimens and they furnish a rare opportunity to investigate the traditional style. We can observe in them the tradition actually at work.

The Serbo-Croatian texts in this book were transcribed from the original disks by Nikola Vujnović, partly in the field and partly during a prolonged visit of his to the United States in 1938–40. They are exactly as recorded; they have not been altered in editing except for minor emendations, but many points were checked with the records. For the punctuation I am responsible. Footnotes refer to some minor differences between Vujnović's and Mr. Bartók's transcriptions, which are given with the music. Otherwise the two sets of texts agree. The text transcriptions follow the conventional Serbo-Croatian spelling, which is phonetic, except for a few minor additions called for by phonetic accuracy. For instance, in a few cases *dj* and *tj* were written for variants of the common

[6] For a detailed list of Serbo-Croatian song categories see pp. 81–84.

đ and *ć* sounds, which had a more pronounced glide than these sounds usually possess (e.g., *sitjan* in No. 8a).

In conformity with the musical patterns, most of our songs contain many repetitions. It might have been preferable to write them all out here, but in order to save space, only the essential text line is printed and the repetitions are indicated in the notes to each song. Meaningless, ornamental syllables which do not form part of the meter are in italics and given either in the texts or in footnotes. The numbers in the left-hand margin of the texts are melody stanza numbers; those on the right are verse numbers. Where the stanza consists of one printed line only, with its repetition, no stanza number appears on the left. As for the division of the texts into stanzas, aside from a few exceptions there is no purely textual feature on which such a division could be based, only musical features and the repetitions which show up in the actual performance of the song. In some cases the stanza structure is irregular (for instance, Nos. 7, 12d, 18, 20, etc.), because the musical structure itself lacks regularity. Each side of every disk in the Parry Collection has a number, and that is given in the right-hand margin opposite the line which begins that side. The number of the text in the collection is given in parentheses, following the name of the singer and the place and date of the recording.

Text and melody do not always form an inseparable unit in Serbo-Croatian folksong. On the one hand, some of our text variants are sung to entirely different melodies (Nos. 7 and 28b). On the other hand, different texts are sung, sometimes to the same melody or to close variants of a melody, as may be seen in some of our examples which were numbered as variants merely for the sake of uniformity with the musical grouping (Nos. 12a, b, c, d, and e). Also, in some cases different and apparently unrelated texts are sung in succession to the same melody, as if they formed a single song (No. 23b). These texts are designated by capital letters on the left, but the numbering of their lines is consecutive where uniformity with the numbering of the musical lines called for it.

The translations are not intended to be polished literary productions. It is hoped that they do, however, present the meaning of each line of text in idiomatic English. Wherever the exact meaning was uncertain, this fact has been noted. It was my desire to make the translations at once literal and readable. The notes to the translations are intended to clarify, wherever possible, obscure portions of the texts. For this purpose all the versions of each song which were available in the Parry Collection were read. This task was possible thanks to the excellent series of indices made by John Hastings in 1938–39. References to versions in other collections are not exhaustive, but they point to useful comparisons.

I am indebted to many people for aid in the preparation of my section of this book. The Parry Collection was made under the auspices of Harvard University, the American Council of Learned Societies, and the Milton Fund and the Clark Bequest at Harvard University, with the co-operation of Yugoslav government authorities. My own research has been sponsored by the Society of Fellows at Harvard University, the American Council of Learned Societies, and the Milton Fund. The committee for the Parry Collection at Harvard, consisting of Professor Robert P. Blake, the late Professor Samuel H. Cross, and Professor John H. Finley, Jr., has always been helpful and co-operative. They and Mr. Metcalf, director of the Harvard University Library, made it possible to combine some of the results of my work on the texts with the fruits of the musical scholarship of Dr. Béla Bartók. The library co-operated by sending the required materials to Columbia University for his use. Dr. Bartók himself has aided me much with suggestions and guidance in the editing. I have followed his advice in almost all instances. Professor George Herzog, then of Columbia University, has been helpful in every way. To him fell some of the burden of correlating the two parts of this book, especially after Dr. Bartók's death. Mr. Samuel P. Bayard, of State College, Pennsylvania, who, with Professor Herzog, was one of the first to show an interest in the music of the Parry Collection and has himself made a number of musical transcriptions, has read the manuscript and has made many valuable recommendations.

My indebtedness, and that of the Parry Collection, is due in the greatest measure, however, to Nikola Vujnović, our indefatigable guide, assistant, and enthusiastic coworker, who took a great personal interest in every detail of our work in Yugoslavia and to all the singers who contributed the beautiful products of their old rural culture of which the melodies and poems in this book represent a sample. Placing it before the reader seems a fitting memorial to the man who thought of the importance of preserving these songs on records and with whom I had the great privilege to work, the late Milman Parry.

Texts and Translations

I

A

Nona Una vode udovice,[1] R. 553
Nego tebe molja drugarice.[2]

B

1. "Mene, majko, kotom posla."
"Nemoj, ćeri, ni s kim posla;
Nemoj, lipo,[3] nemoj ružno,
Je' je moje srce tužno!"
2. "Mene, majko, kotom zove.
Diko mora kuća zove,
Diko mora do Todora.
3. Moj dragane, da te nađu
Kućo gdi je momo zadžu.
Nosi kuću, nosi voljo,
Pa me hodi ko' te voljo!"

Sung by girls from Kijevo, Dalmatia (Text 511), Sept. 22, 1934.

[1] The words of this song were not transcribed by Nikola Vujnović. The text begins on record 552 and ends on 554, but only 553 has been transcribed. A begins with six lines on 552, but B is complete on 553. The transcription given here, with the exception of lines 8–10, was made at the request of Mr. Bartók by Yasha Herzog, a Yugoslav musician; lines 8–10 have been tentatively transcribed by A. B. L. The music of these three lines was not transcribed by Mr. Bartók. The meaning of this text as it stands is obscure and it defies translation. B appears to be a conversation between a mother and her daughter. Lines 4–6 seem to mean, "My daughter, you mustn't have anything to do with anyone, either good or bad, for my heart is filled with sorrow."

[2] Lines 2–4, 7–11, and 13 are repeated.

[3] Note the "ikavski" dialect form of this word and of "gdi" in line 11.

2

"Sad moj dragi kulu gradi,[1] R. 3572
Oko[2] kule lozu sadi.
Hoće mene da prevari.
Neka gradi, neka sadi!
Neće mene prevariti.
Sedam sam hi prevarila,
Sve begova Tanovića,
I *j*osmoga Fazlagića.
Vego hoću Muhameda,
Pa govorim Muhamedu:
'Čuješ li me, Muhamede!
Davno si me isprosijo. R. 3573
Kupi svate, Muhamede!' "
Kupi svate Muhamede.
Odvede je svome dvoru.

Hajrija Šakovič, Gacko (Text 6488)
May 21, 1935[3]

[1] Each line is repeated.
[2] "*J*oko" in the repeat.
[3] In the notes to all the songs the name of the singer is mentioned first, followed by the name of the place in which the song was collected, the number of the text in the Parry Collection, and the date of recording.

2[1]

"My beloved is now building a tower
And planting a vineyard around it.
He wants to ensnare me.
Let him build and let him plant!
He will not ensnare me.
There are seven I have ensnared,
All of the lordly house of Tanović,
And the eighth a Fazlagić.
But it is Muhamed whom I want.
So I say to Muhamed:
'Listen to me, Muhamed!
It's a long time since we were betrothed.
Gather the wedding-guests, Muhamed!' "
Muhamed gathers the wedding-guests,
And takes her home to his house.

[1] There is only one other text of this song in the Parry Collection, No. 5395, dictated by Najla Šaković (age 35) and written down by Ćamila Šaković (age 20). It is like the published version except for the use of "premamiti" instead of "prevariti."

3

A

Oj, mlađano mlado mom(če),[1] R. 3557
Ne šeći se kraj Nere(tve)!
Neretva je voda pla(ha).
Sinoć momka zanijel(a),
A jutros ga na vrh ba(ci).
Da j' u momka svoja ma(jka),
Za dan bi mu glase ču(la),
A za drugi razuzna(la),
A za treći na grob do(šla).
Vet j' u momka tuđa majka,
Za godinu glase čul(a),
A za drugu razumil(a),
A za treću na grob do(šla).
Po grobu mu rasla tra(va),

B

Rasla trava đetelin(a). R. 3558
Tu je pasu dva paun(a),
I četvero paunčadi.
Čuvala hi devojči(ca);
Na njoj tanka košulji(ca),
Ni vezena, ni plete(na),
Ni u niti uveden(a),
Već od zlata saliven(a).
Tud nalaze tri derviš(a);
Prvi derviš progova(ra):
"Voljo bi je poljubi(ti),
Vet sa carom večera(ti)!"
Drugi derviš progovar(a):
"Voljo bi je poljubit(i),
Veg muhtija postanuti!"
Treći derviš progova(ra): R. 3559
"Voljo bi je poljubiti,
Vego vezir postanu(ti)!"

Almasa Zvizdić, Gacko (Text 6479)
May 21, 1935

[1] Each line is repeated. The last letter or letters (in parentheses) are dropped in the repeat.

3[1]

A

Oh young man,
Walk not by the Neretva.
The Neretva is an evil river.
Last night it carried away a youth,
And this morning it threw him onto the shore.
Had the youth a mother of his own,
She would have heard his cry the first day,
On the second she would have understood his need,
And on the third she would have come to his grave.
But the youth had only a stepmother.
In a year she heard his cry,
In the second she understood his need,
And in the third she came to his grave.
On his grave grass had grown,

B

Clover and grass had grown.
Two peacocks were grazing there,
And four young peacocks.
A little girl was watching them.
She wore a thin blouse.
It was neither woven nor embroidered,
Nor was it worked with needles,
But it was of 'fined gold.
Three dervishes came passing by.
The first dervish said:
"I would rather kiss her
Than dine with the sultan!"
The second dervish said:
"I would rather kiss her
Than become a judge!"
The third dervish said:
"I would rather kiss her
Than become vezir!"

[1] There are thirty-four other texts of A and one other of B (No. 4880) in the Parry Collection, beside five other texts of A and B combined (Nos. 3424, 5932, 9360, 9781, and 788). As an example of the way in which songs are made and remade, this text is most instructive. Unlike many instances in which the folk singer merely adds one song to another, the version given here shows no definite line of demarcation. One song modulates neatly into the other; line 14 is common to both and forms the connecting link. Mr. Bayard has called my attention to the theme of the rapacious river in Child, *Ballads*, IV, Nos. 215 and 216 (pp. 178–91). For A cf. Odobašić, II, 137; Vuk, Vol. I, No. 598, p. 393; Matica, Vol. V, No. 20, p. 25; Stanoyevich, p. 307. For B cf. Vuk, Vol. V, Nos. 429–32, pp. 292–94.

4

Planino, moja starino,[1] R. 3586
Kolko sam kroz te hodijo,
Junačku četu vodijo,
Junački bajrak nosijo![2]
Dosti sam majak' cveljao,
Najviše majku Mujovu!
Sina joj Muja zaklao,
Njegova baba naćero,
Te sina svoga ispeko[3];
Njegovu majku naćero,
Od sina mesa pojela;
Njegove seke naćero,
Te su mu kolo hitale,
I pjesme Muju pjevale!

Dervиša Biberović, Gacko (Text 6496)
May 21, 1935

5

Puhni mi, puhni, ladane,[4] R. 3074
Dođi mi, dođi, dragane,
U moje dvore[5] bijele!
Dovedi đoga za sobom!
Sveži ga ruži za grane!
Neka mu ruža miriše!
Neka mu duša uzdiše!

Halima Hrvo, Gacko (Text 6341)
April 22, 1935

[1] "Lele" (ll. 1, 13, 14) or "hlele" (ll. 2–12) is suffixed to each line, after which the line is repeated.
[2] Line begins "do—"; slip of tongue, due to anticipating the following line.
[3] The singer sang "Oner" for the syllable "is" the first time. This is probably a slip of the tongue; "Omer" occurs as the name of the son in a variant text.
[4] Each line is repeated.
[5] This is "dore" on the record.

4[1]

O mountain, my ancestral home,
How many times have I crossed you,
And led a band of heroes,
And carried the heroes' standard!
Many a mother have I made to mourn,
But especially Mujo's mother.
I slew her son Mujo,
And forced his father
To roast his own son,
And I forced his mother
To eat her own son's flesh,
And I forced his sisters
To dance for him,
And to sing songs for Mujo!

5[2]

Blow, blow cold wind!
Come to me, beloved,
Into my white dwelling!
Bring your white horse with you,
And tie him to a branch of the rose tree.
Let the rose envelope him in its fragrance,
And let his spirit be filled with longing.

[1] There are two other versions of this gruesome poem in the Parry Collection: No. 2483 from Halima Hrvo, and No. 6204 from Arifa Zvizdić. The unfortunate son in both these texts is named Jovan instead of Mujo. Compare also Odobašić, IV, 31.

[2] There are forty-four other texts of this song in the Parry Collection; thirty of them have the same simple pattern as our text. Cf. Odobašić, IV, 65; Vuk, Vol. V, No. 298, p. 204.

6a

1. Razbolje se Đerđelez Alija R. 3153
U planini pod jelom zelenom.
2. Na njemu se bijeli košulja,
Kajno gruda u planini snjega.
3. Nit ga pere majka ni sestrica,
Ni vjerena skoro dovedena.
4. Siv mu soko vode donosaše,
Đerđelezu rane ispiraše.
5. Govori mu Đerđelez Alija:
"Aj, Boga ti, siv sokole beli!
6. Kakvo sam ti dobro učinijo,
Te me pojiš tihom vodom ladnom?"
7. "Velko si mi dobro učinijo.
Jako moji tići polećeli,
8. U zelenu travu popadali,
A ti sjaha sa konja vilena,
9. Pokupijo moje tiće lude,
Bacijo hi *j*u jelovo granje."
10. "O Boga ti, siv sokole beli!
Bi li mene nešto poslušao,
11. Da odletiš mom bijelu dvoru,
Pa da vidiš je l' mi uzgor kula,
12. Je l' mi stara u životu majka,
Jesu li se seje poudale, R. 3154
13. Je li mi se ljuba preudala?"[1]
14. Kad mu majka po avliji hoda.
"Ovuda je moj Ale hodijo,
15. Ovuda je moj Ale hodijo,
Staru majku za ruku vodijo!"
16. Kad mu seke ljube basamake.
"Ovudi je naš brat povodijo,
17. Mile seke za ruku vodijo!"
Kad mu ljuba po odaji hoda.

[1] This is a partial stanza, of one line only.

6a[1]

1. Đerđelez Alija was lying ill
On the mountain, beneath a green pine tree.
2. His white shirt glistened,
White as a ball of snow upon the mountain.
3. Neither his mother nor his little sister washed him,
Nor his newly wed wife.
4. A gray falcon brought him water,[2]
And washed Đerđelez's wounds.
5. Đerđelez Alija spoke to it:
"By God, my fine gray falcon,
6. What good thing have I done for you,
That you should bring me cool water?"
7. "You have done me great service.
My fledglings were in flight,
8. And they fell to the green earth,
And you dismounted from your wondrous horse,
9. Gathered my helpless young,
And placed them on a pine branch."
10. "By God, my fine gray falcon,
Would you do something for me?
11. Would you fly to my white house,
To see whether my tower still stands,
12. Whether my aged mother is still alive,
My sisters married,
13. And my wife betrothed again?"[3]
14. Alija's mother was walking in the courtyard.
"This is where my Ale used to walk,
15. This is where my Ale used to walk,
And lead his old mother by the hand!"
16. His sisters were kissing the steps.
"This is where our brother used to walk,
17. And lead his dear sisters by the hand!"
His wife was walking in the room.

[1] There are twenty-five other texts of this song in the Parry Collection, of which twelve are defective. The remaining texts vary considerably in the narration of the events after the return of the falcon with news of what he had seen.

[2] For the theme of the falcon caring for the wounded hero compare "Marko Kraljević i Soko," see Vuk, Vol. II, Nos. 53 and 54. Compare also the note to the translation of our text No. 28a.

[3] There are obviously one or more lines missing after this, telling of the flight of the falcon to Alija's house.

6a (continued)

18. "*J*eto moji kićeni svatova,
Iz daleka Jasić Hasanage!"
19. To sve sluša siv sokole beli,
Pa se vrati Đerđelez Aliji.
20. Sve mu kaže šta je i kako je.
Podiže se Đerđelez Alija,
21. Pa on ode svojoj beloj kuli.
U odaju majci ulazijo.
22. "Udijeli, Alagina majko,
Za nezdravlje age Alibega,
23. A za zdravlje Jasić Hasanage!"
"Ajd' otole, crna prosjakinjo!
24. Da su meni moga Ala ključi,
Sabljom bi' ti otkinula glavu."
25. Pa on ode Alagini seki:
"Udijeli, Alagina seko, 49
26. Za nezdravlje Đerđelez Alije, R. 3155
A za zdravlje Jasić Hasanage!"
27. "Ajd' otole, crna prosjakinjo!
Da su meni moga brata ključi,
28. Sabljom bi' ti otkinula glavu!"
Pa on ode Alahinoj ljubi:
29. "Udijeli, Alagina ljubo,
Za nezdravlje Đerđeleza tvoga,
30. A za zdravlje Jasić Hasanage!"
Izvadi mu tri žuta dukata.
31. "Evo tebi, crna prosjakinjo!
Kup' opanke, i napi se vina!"

Halida Habeš, Gacko (Text 6376)
April 24, 1935

6a (continued)

18. "There are my well-dight wedding guests,
From Jasić Hasanaga[4], from a far country!"
19. The gray falcon heard all this,
And then he returned to Đerđelez Alija.
20. He told him just how things were.
Đerđelez Alija arose,
21. And he went to his white tower.
He went to his mother's chamber.
22. "Give alms, Aliaga's mother!
Misfortune to Alibeg!
23. But long life to Jasić Hasanaga!"
"Off with you, black beggar!
24. Had I my Ali's keys,
I would cut off your head with his sword!"
25. Then he went to Aliaga's sister.
"Give alms, sister of Aliaga!
26. Misfortune to Đerđelez Alija!
Long life to Jasić Hasanaga!"
27. "Off with you, black beggar!
Had I my brother's keys,
28. I would cut off your head with his sword!"
Then he went to Aliaga's wife.
29. "Give alms, wife of Aliaga!
Misfortune to your Đerđelez!
30. Long life to Jasić Hasanaga!"
She took out three golden ducats for him.
31. "Take these, black beggar!
Buy yourself sandals and drink your fill of wine!"

[4] The Turkish titles "aga," "beg," "pasha," "vezir," and so forth, have been kept in the translation. As used in the poetry, they are rather vague, particularly the first two, and it is believed that they are well enough known to cause no confusion.

6b

1. Tri đevojke bijelile platnjo, R. 3574
   Jedno Saća širokije gaća,
2. Drugo Šiša širokoga . . . ,
   Treće Fata debeloga vrata.
3. A naljeze na konju delija,
   Bijelo im pogazijo platnjo.
4. Stadoše ga tri đevojke kleti:
   "Ej, neka te, na konju delija!"
5. Otpučaju puca niz njedarca,
   A oni vade prebijele dojke.
6. "Ej, neka te, na konju delija!
   Vaka tebi udarila krupa,
7. Sve to tvoje žito pomlatila!"
   Kad to začu na konju delija,
8. On se fača za . . . . doru.
   "Vako meni jako žito bilo.
9. Ne mogla mu krupa nahuditi."
   Kad to čuše tri dobre đevojke,
10. Odriješe učkur od dimija,
    Oni zbore na konju junaku:
11. "Vaka tebi udarila čavka,
    Sve to tvoje žito pozobala!"
12. Kad to začu na konju delija, R. 3575
    Odriješi učkur od čakšira:
13. "A[1] neka vas, tri dobre đevojke!
    Vakijem se udavile zrncom!"

Derviša Biberović, Gacko (Text 6489)
May 21, 1935

[1] Sings "vakijem," slip of tongue.

6b[1]

1. Three girls were washing clothes.
One was Saća of the broad pants,
2. The second was Šiša of the broad . . . ,
The third was Fata of the thick neck.
3. A warrior came by on his horse,
And trampled on their clean clothes.
4. The three girls began to curse him:
"Out upon you, mounted warrior!"
5. They unbuttoned their waists,
And took out their white breasts.
6. "Out upon you, mounted warrior!
May hail as large as these strike you,
7. And destroy all your grain!"
When the mounted warrior heard this,
8. He seized his horse's . . . .
"May my grain be as strong as this,
9. And the hail will not be able to harm it!"
When the three good girls heard this,
10. They undid the buckle on their pants,
And they said to the mounted hero:
11. "May a jackdaw . . .
Eat up all your grain!"
12. When the mounted warrior heard this,
He undid the buckle on his trousers.
13. "Out upon you, three good girls!
May you be throttled with an ear of corn . . .!"

[1] The singer heard this song from her father. There are no other texts of it in the Parry Collection.

6c

A

1. Vezak vezla u Vedrini Ajka,[1] R. 3071
2. Na krilu joj Dalifagić Mujo.
3. Progovara iz odžaka majka:
4. "Zlo ti jutro, Dalifagić Mujo!
5. Eto Ajki iz čaršije[2] babe!" 5
6. Ne šće Mujo da okrene glave.
7. Knjigu piše u Vedrini Hajki:
8. "Srce, dušo, u Vedrini Ajko!
9. Šalji meni sahat i oružlje.[3]" 9
10. Odgovara iz Vedrine Ajka: R. 3072
11. "Srce, dušo, Dalifagić Mujo!
12. . . .[4]
13. A oružlje u sanduk složila.
14. Meni sahat na prsima kuca.
Sahat kuca, Ajki srce puca." 15

B

Hasanaga ikindiju klanja.
Siv mu soko na serdžadu pada.
Hiškala ga Hasanaginica:
"Hiš' otale, siv zelen sokole!"
Ode soko od jele do jele, 5
Pa on traži hana neležana, R. 3073
Pa on traži hana . . .[5]

Hajrija Saković, Gacko (Text 6340)
April 22, 1935

[1] Each line is repeated in both A and B, except stanza A 14.

[2] Mr. Bartók hears "ćatije" ("writing-room") which would make sense too, in this context. However, other versions have "čaršije."

[3] Sung as "*j*oružlje" the first time.

[4] This line is indistinct on the record.

[5] The last four syllables of this line are indistinct.

6c[1]

A

1. Ajka was embroidering in Vedrina.
2. Dalifagić Mujo was lying on her lap.
3. Her mother spoke from the kitchen:
4. "This is a bad morning for you, Dalifagić Mujo!
5. Here comes Ajka's father from the square."
6. Mujo did not stop to look back.
7. He wrote a letter to Hajka in Vedrina.
8. "My heart, my soul, Ajka of Vedrina,
9. Send me my watch and my arms!"
10. Ajka of Vedrina replied:
11. "My heart, my soul, Dalifagić Mujo,
12. . . .
13. And I have put your arms into a chest,
14. Your watch ticks upon my breast,
Your watch ticks on, but Ajka's heart has burst!"

B

Hasanaga is saying his evening prayers.
A gray falcon lights upon his prayer rug.
Hasanaga's wife shooed him away.
"Fly away, light-gray falcon!"
The falcon flew from pine to pine,
And he sought an uninhabited inn,
And he sought an inn . . .

[1] Of the fourteen other texts of this song in the Parry Collection, twelve are short and vary little from the published text. For A cf. Vuk, Vol. V, Nos. 401–402, pp. 267–268.

For the opening theme of B compare our Nos. 7 and 10. There is only one other version in the Parry Collection (No. 11489). The last four lines of this —the first five are substantially the same as the published text—are as follows:

Pa on traži hlada nepijana,	Then he sought untasted coolness,
Pa on traži hladna neležanja.	Then he sought virgin shade.
Ruke su mu hladne neležana,	His loved one's arms are virgin shade for him,
Usta su me ladna nepijana.	His loved one's lips are his untasted coolness.

7

1. Beg Alibeg ikindiju klanja. R. 609
Ej, siv mu soko na serdžadu[1] pada.
2. Nema kada da selam pridade,
Veće pita siv zelen sokola:
"Siv sokole, sivo pero moje!
Jesi l' skoro bijo pod Ložnicom?
Je li turska pod Ložnicom vojska?
Vijaju l' se zeleni barjaci?
Svira l' zvirka[2] bega Firdužbega[3]?"
3. Njemu soko po *j*istini kaže:
4. "Skoro jesam pod Ložnicom bijo,
E vidijo sam silovitu vojsku.
5. Vijaju se zeleni oblaci,[4]
6. Kano zimi debeli oblaci.
7. Sve pjevaju po *j*izbor junaci.
8. *E* tuče bubanj bega Kuljenbega,
9. I talambas bega Firdusbega.
10. Zdravo jeste poboljela vojska."

Ibrahim Mašinović, Kulen Vakuf (Text 522)
September 24, 1934

[1] Mr. Bartók hears "serdžaku."
[2] = svirka (he adds a ž and thus sings "zvirkaž," probably by false analogy with "Firdužbega.")
[3] = Firdusbega.
[4] Mistake for "barjaci." After "ob" the singer pauses, and then completes with something like "raci."

7[1]

1. Beg Alibeg is saying his evening prayers.
   A gray falcon lights upon his prayer rug.
2. There is no time for formal greeting,
   But he asks the light-gray falcon:
   "Gray falcon, my gray feathered one,
   Were you lately at Ložnica?
   Is the Turkish army at Ložnica?
   Are the green banners waving?
   Are the trumpets of Firdušbeg sounding?"
3. The falcon tells him truly:
4. "I was lately at Ložnica.
   I saw a mighty army.
5. The green banners are waving,
6. Like thick clouds in winter.
7. Chosen heroes are singing.
8. The drums of Kulenbeg are rolling,
9. And the cymbals of Firdušbeg are clashing.
10. The army is in fine fettle."

[1] There are three different songs in the Parry Collection introduced by this same first line. No. 6684 from Emina Hrla, of Ljubinje, tells how a falcon brings news that Ali's betrothed is being besieged by suitors and Ali sends a message that he will come for her. Another song is represented by our No. 6cB. Nos. 7 and 28b in this book belong to the third group, and there are ten other texts of it in the collection. Compare also Odobašić, IV, 28; Ristić, No. 39, p. 53.

8a

Biser niže Biserbegovica,[1] R. 3125
Biser niže, o grlu ga veže.
"Niži mi se, moj sitan[2] bisere!
Ja tę nižem kao nevjestica,
A[3] nosim te baš ko djevojčica."
Midinjaše[4] niko ne čujaše.
To j' začula Biserbega majka.
To je majci vrlo mučno bilo.
Kod doma joj Biser ne bijaše,
Veg u lovu otišo da lovi.
Jedva čeka ostajrela majka,
Kad će doći sine Biserbeže,
Da ga pita za snahinu riječ,
Je l' istina što mu ljuba kaže.
Kada kucnu halka na vratima,
Brže skoči Biserbega majka.
Otvora mu od avlije vrata.
"Mijo sine, jesi l' s' umorijo?"
Pristupi joj, poljubi joj ruku. R. 3126
"Mila majko, dobro sam umoran,
Dok nijesam dobro zadovoljan."
Zapita ga opet[5] mila majka:
"A što ti je, moj milostan sine?"
"Ne pitaj me, moja mila majko!
Ti ne pitaš, a ja ne kazujem.
Kad si mene oženila mlada,
Moja mlados i truhne i vehne.
Kad je bilo na prvom konaku,
Ja joj dižem purli duvak z glave.
Ona mene bratom pobratila:
" 'Ne, Biserbeg, moj po Bogu brate!' "
Raspučam joj puca niz njedarca.
Opet mene bratom pobratila:
" 'Ne, Biserbeg, ja te bratom kumim!' "
Pa ja uze' kuran hamajliju,
Da ja vidim što mi kuran kaže.

[1] Each line is repeated.
[2] Mr. Bartók hears "sitjan."
[3] "A" omitted in the repeat, unless it merged with the final "a" of "djevojčica."
[4] For the more common "mlidijaše."
[5] Sung as "*j*opet" the first time.

8a[1]

Biserbeg's wife is stringing pearls,
Stringing pearls and hanging them about her neck.
"Be thou strung, my little pearl!
I string thee as a bride,
But I wear thee as a maiden."
She thought that no one heard,
But Biserbeg's mother heard,
And she was greatly disturbed.
Biserbeg was not at home,
But had gone hunting.
The old mother could scarcely wait
Until her son Biserbeg should come,
That she might ask him about what her
daughter-in-law had said;
Whether it was true what his bride had said.
When the knocker struck upon the door,
Biserbeg's mother arose quickly.
She opened the courtyard door for him.
"My dear son, are you tired?"
He took her hand and kissed it.
"Mother dear, I am very tired,
And I am not well satisfied."
Again his mother asked him:
"What is wrong, my dear son?"
"Do not ask, mother dear,
Do not ask, and I shall not have to tell you.
When I was married I was young.
My youth fades and spoils.
When we were together that first night,
I raised the marriage veil from her face,
And she implored me in the name of brother:
'Don't, Biserbeg, my brother in God!'
I unbuttoned the buttons on her blouse,
And again she called me brother:
'Don't, Biserbeg, I pray thee as my brother!'
Then I took the blessed Koran,
To see what the Koran said.

[1] There are thirty-four other texts of this song in the Parry Collection, and they show considerable variation. Our text is the only one including the Koran theme. For another version of this song, cf. Matica, Vol. V, No. 22, p. 27.

8a (continued)

Prvi kaže, i hoćeš i nećeš.
Drugi kaže, ko i seka ti je. R. 3127
Odma sam se okanijo, majko.
Stid mi bilo, nisam nikom kazo."

Almasa Zvizdić, Gacko (Text 6365)
April 24, 1935

8b

Glavu veže Alibegovica.[1] R. 3156
Alibeg je beže ugledao.[2]
"Ljepa ti si, vjerenice ljubo!
Jož[3] da *j*imaš od srca evlada,
Ti bi meni još milija bila."
Boga moli Alibegovica:
"Daj mi, Bože, od srca evlada!
Ne daj, Bože, kućni sahibija,
Vet đevojku kućneg dušmanina!"
Što molila, Boga umolila.
Bog joj dade od srca *j*evlada.
Ona[4] rodi lijepu đevojku,
Da raskući *j*Alibega dvore.

Halida Habeš, Gacko (Text 6377)
April 24, 1935

[1] Each line is repeated.
[2] In lines 2–5, possibly also in some of the subsequent lines, an "I" is sung at the beginning the first time.
[3] Sung thus for "još."
[4] Sung as "*J*ona" the first time.

8a (continued)

First it said: 'You may if you wish.'
Second it said: 'She is as a sister to you.'
Then immediately, mother, I abandoned her.
I was ashamed and told no one."

8b[1]

Alibeg's wife was putting on her kerchief.
Alibeg was watching her.
"My true love, you are beautiful.
If you only had a child,
You would be even dearer to me."
Alibeg's wife prayed:
"Oh God, give me a child.
Do not give me, God, a master for this house,
But give me a girl, the enemy of a house."
God granted what she asked.
God gave her a child.
She bore a beautiful baby girl
To bring discord to Alibeg's house.

[1] This song belongs to a large group of songs which begin with a similar theme of domestic life. In some instances the wife is arranging her hair, while her husband holds a mirror (*ogledalo*) for her. ("Ogledalo" might be a corruption of "ugledao," or vice versa.) Another combination of lines frequently used to introduce this theme is "Beg Alibeg na kuli sjedaše, Vjernu ljubu na krilu držaše." (Beg Alibeg was sitting in his house, holding his true love on his lap.) Among the songs which begin with this picture are "The Pale Wife" ("Blijedna Đevojka"), "Separation" ("Rastanak bega i begovice—Hasanaginica se preudaje i rodi sina"), and "The Tenth Girl-Baby" ("Deseta Đevojka"). The first of these shows the young wife as pale because of the mistreatment she is receiving from her in-laws. In the second, the *Hasanaginica,* hurt by the rebuke, marries again and bears a son. And finally, in the song of "The Tenth Girl-Baby," the husband threatens to kill his wife if the next baby is a girl, as she has already borne him nine girls. When the tenth girl is born, the wife drowns herself and it. (See footnote 1 to the translation of No. 27e in this book.) No. 9828 from Derviša Biberović of Gacko is an excellent example of a combination of the theme of Text 8b with that of "The Tenth Girl-Baby." One song is simply tacked on at the end of the other.

9

A

Mila majko, goji me u hladu,[1] R. 3197
Pa me podaj jednom begu mladu!
Neću bega, ne begenišem ga,
A ni *j*age, nije za me dragi.
Da mi daju probirati momke,
Ja bi znala oklen bi probrala,
Iz Gacka do dva Fazlagića,[2] R. 3198
Iz Trebinja Resulbegovića.
Jadna što ću, rekla sam da hoću?
Što ću sada, kad svatovi dojdu?
Majka veli: "Udaji[3] se, šćeri!"
Babo veli: "Hajirli[4] ti bilo!"
Seka veli: "Ispratit ću tebe."
Bratac veli: "Požalit ću tebe![5] R. 3199
Hajde,[6] seko, i ja ću z' ženiti!"

B

Selom idem, selo na me viče,
Đe ja gledam u majke jedinče.
Crkni selo, ja ću na sijelo.
Sijeliću i kako mi drago!
Nećem selo crknuti od jada,
Đe ja gledam Eminu đevojku.
Nit se belim, niti se rumenim.[7] R. 3200
Ja kaka je, vesela joj majka!
Dva obraza, dva đula rumena,
A dva oka, dva vrela studena,
Obrvice, morske pijavice,
Trepavice, krilo lastavice,
Crven đerdan o grlu bijelu!
To devojku vrlo[8] ponijelo!

Halima Hrvo, Gacko (Text 6395)
April 26, 1935

[1] Each line is repeated, with "ej" prefixed, except line 1, which has "aj."
[2] A nine-syllable line. Record 3198 begins with the last four syllables of line 7.
[3] Sung as "Uda' " the second time
[4] Syllable division is "ha-ji-rli" in the musical rendering, according to Mr. Bartók.
[5] Record 3199 begins with the last four syllables of line A 14.
[6] "Ajde" the first time.
[7] Record 3200 begins with the last four syallables of line B 7.
[8] "Lepo" is substituted in the repeat.

9[1]

A

"Mother dear, bring me up in the shade,
And then give me to some young Beg.
I do not want the Beg; I do not love him;
Nor the Aga; he's not my beloved.
Were I to choose a man,
I know whence I would choose him—
The two Fazlagići from Gacko,
Or Resulbegović from Trebinje.
Alas, what shall I do? I have agreed.
What shall I do now when the wedding guests come?
My mother says: 'Get married, daughter.'
My father says: 'You have my blessing.'
My sister says: 'I'll accompany you.'
My little brother says: 'I will mourn for you.
Go ahead, sister, I'll get married too.' "

B

I walk through the village and they mock me,
Because I am wooing an only daughter.
Let the village be hanged! I shall go to the feast.
I shall celebrate as I wish.
Let the village burst with sorrow,
Because I have my eye on Emina.
I do not grow pale, nor do I blush.
How lovely she is! A joy to her mother!
Her cheeks are two red roses,
Her eyes, two cooling pools,
Her eyebrows are like sea leeches,
Her lashes, like a swallow's wing.
She wears a red necklace on her white throat,
And it well becomes the maid!

[1] These are shepherds' songs and melodies. There are no texts of either A or B listed under their first lines in the Parry Collection, but Nos. 2261 and 4641 from Đula Dizdarević and Đula Čampara, respectively, of Gacko, have some elements in common with A.

10a

Uranijo bego Omerbego,[1] R. 3137
Uranijo u lov u planinu.
Tri godine po planini bijo,
A nikakva lova ne lovijo,
A on nađe lijepu đevojku:
"Al si vila, al si *j*utvornjica?
Al si danas lijepa đevojka?"
"Bogom brate, tuđa ja baž[2] bijo.
Evo ima tri godine dana,
Zir zobala, s lista vodu pila.
Sotom[3] sam ti živa mlada bila."
"Što si ođe, lijepa đevojko?"
"Mene brate preko mora dava,
Preko mora hiljadu dugana,[4]
Mene dava za morskoga kralja,
A ja mlada gori sam pobjegla."
"Ču li mene, lijepa đevojko!
Evo mene tri godine dana,
A nikakva lova ulovijo, R. 3138
Vego tebe u planini mladu.
Hoćemo li mom bijelu dvoru?"
Progovara lijepa đevojka:
"Dela', momče, i kako ti drago!"
Pa pođoše nis[5] planinu mladi,
Pa odoše nis planinu mladi.
Susreta je bego Hasanaga.
"Kud li ideš, lijepa đevojko?"
"Evo idem[6] mom bijelu dvoru."
"Đe su dvori, a đe li su kule?"
"Povede me aga Hasanaga."
Kad su bili pred bijele dvore,
Progovara lijepa đevojka:
"Srce, dušo, bego Alibego,
Đe je tvoja prebijela[7] kula?"

[1] Each line is repeated.
[2] Slip of the tongue for "baš," or assimilation in singing to the following voiced sound.
[3] "Sotem" the first time.
[4] The second time, "konaka."
[5] Assimilation in singing of "niz" to the following voiceless sound.
[6] "odo" in the repeat.
[7] The first time "prembijela"; both forms are common.

10a[1]

Omerbeg rose early;
He rose early to go hunting in the mountains.
For three years he was in the mountains,
And shot no game,
But he found a beautiful maiden.
"Are you a vila, or a spirit,
Or are you really a beautiful maiden?"
"Brother in God, I have been a wanderer
For three years now.
I have eaten acorns and drunk water from the leaves.
Thus I have kept alive."
"What are you doing here, beautiful maiden?"
"My brother gave me in marriage across the sea,
Across the sea a thousand days journey.
He gave me to the King of the Sea,[2]
But I fled to the mountains."
"Harken to me, beautiful maiden.
I've been here for three years
And I have caught nothing
In the mountains except you.
Shall we go to my white house?"
The beautiful maiden answered:
"Young man, do as you wish."
Then they went down from the mountain.
Then they went down from the mountain.
Hasanaga met her.[3]
"Where are you going, beautiful maiden?"
"I am going to my white house."
"Where is your house; where is your tower?"
"Hasanaga is taking me with him."
When they approached the white houses,
The beautiful maiden said:
"Alibeg, my heart, my soul,
Where is your white tower?"

[1] There are no other texts of this song in the Parry Collection.

[2] Could this be a corruption of "moskovska kralja," the King of Moscow?

[3] There is some confusion between this and line 30. Who is Hasanaga, and what is his connection with the story? It is possible that, having made an error in line 26 by harking back to the meeting of the beg with the maiden, the singer attempts in the following lines to correct the mistake. The change in names from Omerbeg to Hasanaga, and then later to Alibeg, heightens the confusion.

10a (continued)

"Ču li mene, lijepa đevojko!
A još ima tri bijela dana."
Njoj se čini do tri godinice.
Pa odoše poljem zelenijem,
Kad et' otud kite i svatova. R. 3139
"Či su, beže, kita i svatovi?"
"Jabandije[8], lijepa đevojko."
Kad su bili kroz goru zelenu,
Progovara lijepa đevojka:
"Daleko je, beže Alibeže."
"Ali nije, lijepa đevojko."
Oni prošli i gore zelene.
Kad u jutru jutro osvanulo,
A da vidiš lijepe đevojke!
"Daleko je, beže Alibeže."
"A ču li me, lijepa đevojko,
Još je, dušo, tri, četiri dana."
Kad su bili poljem[9] zelenijem,
Progovara lijepa đevojka:
"Nešto mene zaboljela glava."
Progovara bego Alibego:
"Ako si se umorila mlada,
Još nam nema četiri sahata."
To je milo vrlo curi bilo.
Kad su bili zelenoj planini, R. 3140
Progovara lijepa đevojka:
"Da su bili konji za jahanja,
I oni se umorili mladi."
"Aj, ne zbori, lijepa đevojko!
A sad ćemo našem bjelu dvoru."
Kad su bili gojre us planine,
Đevojka se Bogu zamolila:
"Bože mijo, na svemu ti fala!
Daj mi, puhni vihar sa planina,
Da mi malo da preboli glava.
Nije lasno putovati mladoj,
I konji se, beže, umorili,
A nekmo li mladi i zeleni[10]!"
Kad su bili poljem[9] zelenijem,

[8] Slip for "jabandžije."

[9] Pronounced in singing as "poljʒem" here.

[10] The singer sang "lirisu" the first time for "zeleni," probably an error; the word is not known to me.

10a (continued)

"Listen to me, beautiful maiden,
We have three white days more."
It seemed like three years to her.
As they were crossing the green plain,
They met a wedding procession.
"Oh beg, whose wedding guests are these?"
"They are strangers, beautiful maiden."
When they had crossed the green mountain,
The beautiful maiden said:
"It is far, Alibeg."
"No it isn't, beautiful maiden."
They crossed the green mountains,
And when morning dawned,
Then you should have seen the beautiful maiden.
"It is far, Alibeg."
"Listen to me, beautiful maiden.
We have three or four days more, my soul."
When they were on the green plain,
The beautiful maiden said:
"My head aches a little."
Alibeg said:
"If you are tired,
We have only less than four hours more."
The girl was very glad to hear that.
When they were on the green mountain,
The beautiful maiden said:
"If we had horses to ride,
They would be tired out."
"Be quiet, beautiful maiden.
In a moment we shall be at our white house."
When they were high in the mountains,
The maiden prayed to God.
"Dear God, thanks be to Thee for everything!
Grant that the wind blow from the mountain,
That my head may feel better.
It's not easy for a young girl to travel.
Even horses get tired,
Even though they be young and untried!"
When they were on the green plain,

10a (continued)

I četiri polja pregrabili,
I planine nogam pregazili,
Promoliše prembijele kule.
Progovara lijepa đevojka:
"Alibego,[11] ja ne mogu više."
"A sad ćemo svom bijelu dvoru." R. 3141
Kad su bili prembijelu kulu,
Susreta ga ostajrela majka:
"A moj sine, moje dobro teško!
Đe si evo četiri godine?"
"Ne pitaj me, moja stara majko!
Sve lovijo, ništa ulovijo,
Ulovijo lijepu đevojku."
"Ajde, sine, hajirli ti bilo!"
Tu su mladi[12] svadbu učinili,
I uze je za vjerenu ljubu.

Fata Krajišnik, Gacko (Text 6369)
April 24, 1935

10b

Pošetala Alibegovica,[1] R. 3128
Ispod kule po zelenoj bašči.
Ona stade na to kalopera:
"Kalopere,[2] nikakvo cvijeće!
Niti cavtiš, ni sjemena davaš,
Kolik' ni ja Alibegovica,
Nit se ljubim, ni poroda rađam,
Niti znadem đe mi bego spava,
Đe mi spava, đe mi večerava.
Zimi spava s momcim' na ahare,
Ljeti spava s momcim' na podrume."
Midijaše niko ne čujaše,
A to čula Alibega majka,
Pa doziva sina Muhameda:
"A moj sine, mijo Muhamede!
Čuješ li[3] nam naše snahe mile,

[11] "Alibeže" in the repeat.
[12] "mladu" the second time, a slip of the tongue.
[1] Each line is repeated.
[2] Mr. Bartók heard "kalopera"; perhaps misheard, or error of the singer.
[3] Actually something else was sung for "Čuješ li"; some slip of the tongue.

10a (continued)

And had traversed four plains
And crossed the mountains on foot,
The white towers came into sight
The beautiful maiden said:
"Alibeg, I can go no farther."
"But in a moment we will be home."
When they reached the white tower,
His old mother met him.
"My son, I have been worried.
Where have you been these four years?"
"Do not ask me, old mother.
I hunted all the time and caught nothing,
Except a beautiful maiden."
"Good, my son, my blessing on you."
And there the young people held their wedding,
And he took her to be his true love.

10b

Alibeg's wife was taking a walk
In the green garden by the tower
She stopped by the flowering balsam.
"O balsam, you are no flower!
You have no fragrance, and you bear no seed.
No more do I, Alibeg's wife.
I do not love, and I bear no offspring,
Nor do I know where my beg sleeps,
Where he sleeps and where he takes his sup.
In the winter he sleeps with the young men in the stable,
And in the summer he sleeps with the men in the cellar."
She thought that no one heard her,
But Alibeg's mother heard,
And she called her son Muhamed.
"My son, dear Muhamed!
Do you hear our dear daughter-in-law,

10b (continued)

Šta nam zbori u zelenoj bašči?"
"Ču li mene,[4] moja snaho draga?"
"Istina je, đever Muhamede." R. 3129
"Ve'[5] ti hajde u gornje bojeve,
Pa ti kuhaj gosposku večeru,
Da zovemo bega na večeru."
Donesoše rakije svakake,
I donese begu tu večeru,[6]
I[7] on zaspa ka i janje ludo.
Kad je bilo noći polovinu,
Đela zlato na bijelu ruku.
Ona dođe begu Alibegu,
. . . [8] na bijeloj ruci.
"Evo ima tri godine dana,
Od kako si tamo na aharu.
Zimi spavaš s momcim' na podrume,
A ni lice kona prevarila."[9]
Kad je bilo noći polovinu,
A da vidiš lijepe đevojke!
Stade škripa, stade zveka lipije dukata.
Ufati je đever Muhamede:
"Kujo, kučko, lijepa đevojko!
To je diba brata Alibega, R. 3133
To dukati brata Alibega!"
I spremi je svom bijelu dvoru.

Fata Krajišnik, Gacko (Text 6366)
April 24, 1935

[4] "Je l' istina" in the repeat.
[5] Before "Ve' " the singer sang an obscure word, perhaps "čule"; a slip of the tongue. "A" is sung for "Ve' " in the repeat.
[6] In the repeat the line is: "Pa donese tu večeru begu."
[7] "Pa" in the repeat.
[8] First four syllables are not clear on the record.
[9] Transcription of this line in doubt.

10b (continued)

What she says in the green garden?"
"Is it true, my dear daughter-in-law?"
"It is true, brother Muhamed."
"Go to the upper rooms,
And prepare a lordly supper,
That we may invite the beg to supper."
They brought several kinds of brandy,
And they brought the supper to the beg.
And he fell asleep like an innocent lamb.
When the night was half through,[1]
She put a gold bracelet on her white arm,[2]
And she came to Alibeg.
. . . on his white arm.
"It is now three years
Since you have been there in the stables.
In the winter you sleep with the young men in the cellar,
And no woman has touched your face."
When the night was half through,
Then you should see the beautiful maiden.[3]
There arose the sound of fine ducats.
Brother Muhamed caught her.
"You dog, you cur, beautiful maiden!
That silk is Alibeg's, my brother's.
Those ducats are Alibeg's, my brother's."
And he sent her to his own white house.

[1] From here to line 34 confusion reigns. The translation of line 27 is uncertain, the first half of line 29 is not clear on the records, and the text of line 33 is not definite. Nikola neglected to transcribe it, as he was not sure of it. As transcribed by Mr. Bartók it makes sense only if it is agreed that there is a reference to the practice of pederasty (common enough in the heroic society of the Balkans) in the mention of the Alibeg's sleeping with the young men in the stables and in the cellar. This, however, is not borne out by the conclusion of the poem (lines 34 to 41). It is interesting to note also that all other texts of this song which are available (there are sixteen in the Parry Collection, all from Gacko, although eight of them are so much alike that they are probably copied from the same original, and one text (No. 10384) is incomplete, ending at line six), are clear cases of the Alibeg having a mistress, of whom the wife knows. In many of them, she even mentions her name and says she can never be happy as long as the girl is around. A number of the other texts actually end with this girl's violent death. I believe that the singer is simply confused here, and does not return to the real theme until line 34. It is possible that the confusion has been caused by the crossing of two themes, one about the young men, the other about the mistress, but it is not likely. For a published version of this song see Dr. Vinko Vitezica's *Antologija Narodne Poezije,* Beograd, 1937, pp. 14–15.

[2] No. 1545 in the collection purports to be a dictated text from our singer, and it attests to the correctness of this line, as does also No. 4455 from Džemila Pošković, of Gacko; both omit the following lines and proceed immediately to the equivalent of our line 36.

[3] The mistress.

I I

Je l' ti žao, žalosna ti majka,[1] R. 3109
Je l' ti žao našega rastanka,
Rastajanja, al' ne sastavljanja?
Ja sam mlada juče[2] preprošena,
Isprošena, amanet uzela,[3]
Amaneta trides sufurina,
Zlatan prsten na desnicu ruku,
Zlatan eždep od suhoga zlata,
I na glavu od almasa granu. R. 3110
Ako mi se tome ne vjeruješ,
Dođi, dragi, pa ćeš mi viđeti.
Ja bi poći, a drugi ne poći.
Ja ću poći, pa da neću doći.
Sjutra ću ti ispred dvora proći
Sa svatima, među jenđijama,
Z đeverima, s mladim zaovama. R. 3111
Na dvor ću ti bajrak prisloniti.
Iskaću ti što u dvoru nejmaš,
Rujna vina od sedam godina,
I rakije sa nove kapije,
Đul baklavu na suncu pečenu.
Moj dragane, ako ne pripraviš,
Sokolovi moji đeverovi
Kulu će ti[4] novu salomiti, R. 3112
Glavu će to tvoju otkinuti.
Žalostan ti *j*i otac i majka!
Vego bježi u krajinu, dragi!
Sakriće te mladi krajišnici.

Almasa Zvizdić, Gacko (Text 6358)
April 23, 1935

[1] Each line is repeated, with "aj" prefixed.
[2] Sung as "jučen."
[3] Sung as "uzena"; a slip of the tongue.
[4] The first time, "tu," a slip of the tongue.

II[1]

"Are you sad, my luckless swain,
Are you sad that we must part,
Part never to meet again?
Yester eve another won me,
Won me, and a token gave;
Gave as token thirty shillings
And a gold ring for my right hand,
A golden circlet of 'fined gold,
With a diamond set in it.
But if you don't believe me,
Come, beloved, and you'll see.
I don't know whether to go or not.
I shall set out, even if I don't arrive.
Tomorrow I shall pass before your house
With wedding guests and bridesmaids,
With my brothers- and sisters-in-law.
I shall lean my standard against your house,
And I shall demand of you what you do not
  have in the house:
Ruddy wine seven years old,
And brandy from the new jar;
Sweet baklava[2] baked in the sun.
Beloved, if you do not prepare these for me,
My valiant brothers-in-law
Will destroy your new house
And cut off your head.
Sad will it be for your father and mother!
But flee to the borderland, beloved.
The young men of the border will hide you!"

[1] This song is sung at weddings, as Almasa herself tells us in recorded text No. 6519, record No. 3668. Other dictated texts which purport to be from Almasa (Nos. 1517, 4527, and 4685) vary considerably in detail. There are ten more dictated texts of this song in the collection, and they are all from Gacko. For another version cf. Vuk, Vol. V, No. 384, p. 254.

[2] A sweet cake, with honey and walnuts.

I 2a

1. San usnila Hasanaginica, R. 3180
San usnila, u snu se prenula.
2. Ona budi šćerku Melećhanu:
"Ustaj, sine, šćeri Melećhana!
3. Evo ti se razboljela majka,
I Bog znade da preboljet neću,
4. I Bog znade da preboljet neću,
Jerbo sam ti ružan san usnila,
5. Jerbo sam ti ružan san usnila,
Da s' na meni zapalila diba,
6. Da s' na meni zapalila diba.
Svi mi desni izgojreli skuti.
7. Što s' na meni zapalila diba,
To će tvoja umrijeti majka.
8. Što su desni izgojreli skuti,
To će ti se babo oženiti,
9. To će ti se babo oženiti
Prvom konom Kasum pašinicom,
10. Prvom konom Kasum pašinicom.
Dovešće mu njenu šćerku Ajku,
11. Dovešće mu njejnu šćerku Ajku. R. 3181
Pod pojasom muško čedo nosi.
12. Čuvaj, šćeri, tvoje ruho belo!
Eno ti ga u gornjem čardaku,
13. Što na njemu devet katanaca,
I deseta brava dubrovačka!"
14. I umrije Hasanaginica.
Skupiše se hodže i hadžije,
15. Skupiše se hodže i hadžije,
Skupiše se i nju zakopaše.
16. Kad se ljudi sa mezara vrate,
Ponajzadnji aga Hasanaga.
17. Gledala ga Kasum pašinica,
Gledala ga, pa mu govorila:
18. "Jesi li se, aga, umorijo,
Ili si se, aga, okahrijo?
19. Ako si se, aga, umorijo,
Evo taze kahve u ibriku;

I 2a[1]

1. Hasanaga's wife dreamt a dream.
   She dreamt a dream, and from her dream awoke.
2. She awakened her daughter Melećhana:
   "Arise, daughter Melećhana,
3. Your mother has fallen ill,
   And God knows that I shall not recover.
4. God knows that I shall not recover,
   For I have had a bad dream.
5. I have had a bad dream,
   That my brocade caught fire.
6. My brocade caught fire,
   And the right hem of my skirt was burned.
7. That my brocade caught fire
   Means that your mother will die.
8. That the right hem of my skirt was burned
   Means that your father will marry again.
9. That means that your father will marry again
   With our next-door neighbor, Kasum pasha's wife,
10. With our next-door neighbor, Kasum pasha's wife.
    She will bring with her her daughter Ajka.
11. She will bring with her her daughter Ajka,
    Who is carrying a boy child.
12. My daughter, guard well your possessions.
    They are in the upper room,
13. Which has nine locks,
    And the tenth the lock of Dubrovnik."
14. The wife of Hasanaga died.
    The priests and the pilgrims came.
15. The priests and the pilgrims came;
    They came, and they buried her.
16. When the men returned from the grave,
    The last to come was Hasanaga.
17. Kasum pasha's wife saw him,
    Saw him, and said to him:
18. "Are you tired, Hasanaga,
    Or are you lonely?
19. If you are tired, Hasanaga,
    There is a cup of coffee in the urn.

[1] There are thirty other texts listed under this first line in the Parry Collection, all from Gacko and all dictated.

12a (continued)

20. Ako si se, aga, okahrijo,
Evo mene Kasum pašinice!"
21. Pođe aga uz bijelu kulu,
Pa je uze za bijelu ruku,
22. Pa je uze za bijelu ruku, R. 3182
Odvede je svom bijelu dvoru.
23. Tuj dolaze sve redom kadune.
Neke idu agi na veselje,
24. Neke idu agi na veselje,
Neke idu Melki na žalošće.
25. Pored vrata dilber Melećhana,
U crnu se futu zamotala,
26. U crnu se futu zamotala.
Sve kadunma prifaća feredža.
27. Ponajzadnja njena mila teta.
Govori joj njena mila teta:
28. "Šćeri moja, dilber Melećhana,
Kad je tvoja preumila majka,
29. Kad je tvoja preumila majka,
Je l' ti išta ruha ostavila?"
30. Dočekala Kasum pašinica:
"Nije kučka ništa ostavila,
31. Nije kučka ništa ostavila,
Nije, bogme, ni bele mahrame!"
32. A to Melki milo ne bijaše.
Uze tetku za bijelu ruku,
33. Uze tetku za bijelu ruku, R. 3183
Odvede je u gornje čardake.
34. Otvora joj devet katanaca,
I desetu bravu dubrovačku.
35. Otvora joj sve devet sanduka,
Meka ruha i bakrena suda.
36. Govori joj njena mila teta:
"Šćeri moja, dilber Melećhana,
37. Mehmedbeg te u majke prosijo,
On te prosi, majka te ne daje."
38. Knjigu piše begu Mehmedbegu:
"Čuješ li me, bego Mehmedbego!
39. Ti si mene u majke prosijo,
Ti prosijo, majka me ne dala.

12a (continued)

20. If you are lonely,
Here am I, Kasum pasha's wife."
21. Hasanaga went into the white[2] house.
He took her by her white hand.
22. He took her by her white hand
And led her into his own white house.
23. All the ladies came there.
Some came to rejoice with Hasanaga.
24. Some came to rejoice with Hasanaga,
And some came to mourn with Melka.
25. By the door stood lovely Melećhana,
Enveloped in black mourning,
26. Enveloped in black mourning.
She took the ladies' cloaks.
27. Last of all came her dear aunt.
Her dear aunt said to her:
28. "My daughter, lovely Melećhana,
When your mother died,
29. When your mother died,
Did she leave you anything?"
30. Kasum pasha's wife heard this and said:
"The woman didn't leave a thing;
31. The woman didn't leave a thing,
Not even a single handkerchief."
32. This was displeasing to Melka.
She took her aunt by the white hand,
33. She took her aunt by the white hand,
And led her to the upper rooms.
34. She unlocked the nine locks,
And the tenth, the lock of Dubrovnik.
35. She opened all nine chests
Of soft silks and copper kettles.
36. Her dear aunt said to her:
"My daughter, lovely Melećhana,
37. Mehmedbeg sought you from your mother.
He sought you, but your mother would not give you away."
38. She wrote a letter to Mehmedbeg.
"Hear me, Mehmedbeg,
39. You sought me from my mother,
You sought me, my mother would not give me away.

[2] The use of "white" as a formulaic epithet is well illustrated in this poem: "white day," "white house," "white throat," "white hand." Probably it is the most common epithet in Yugoslav traditional poetry.

12a (continued)

40. Sad je moja preminula majka.
Kupi svate, hajde po devojku,
41. Kupi svate, hajde po devojku,
I to svadba do desetak dana!"
42. Sigura se dilber Melećhana,
Sigurala devet seisana,
43. I dođoše kićeni svatovi.
Tuj su bili tri bijela dana,
44. Tuj su bili tri bijela dana. R. 3184
Kad četvrto jutro osvanulo,
45. A da vidiš Kasum pašinice!
Uze Melku za bijelu ruku,
46. Uze Melku za bijelu ruku,
Odvede je uz bijelu kulu.
47. Udri na nju devet katanaca,
I desetu bravu dubrovačku.
48. Povrati se Kasum pašinica,
Pa obuče svoju šćerku Ajku.
49. Progovara beže Mehmedbeže:
"Hazur, svati, hazur je đevojka!"
50. I pođoše kićeni svatovi.
Povrati se beže Mehmedbeže,
51. Povrati se beže Mehmedbeže,
Da dariva svasti i punice.
52. Kad to čula dilber Melećhana,
Rukama je u džam udarala,
53. Rukama je u džam udarala,
Sve je džame na testu sasula,
54. Pa prekida đerdan sa grlaca,
Pa ga baci na sokaku pjevu.
55. "Pjevni, pjevo, moj po Bogu brate,[1] R. 3187
Ne bi l' čuo beže Mehmedbeže!
56. Zlo ti jutro, beže Mehmedbeže!
Ti ne vodiš dilber Melećhanu,
57. Ti ne vodiš dilber Melećhanu,
Neg ti vodiš Kasumovu Ajku."
58. Od svatova niko ne čujaše,
Već to čuo beže Mehmedbeže.
59. Pa poleće uz bijelu kulu,
Pa odvali devet katanaca,

[1] The section on record 3187 was recorded also on records 3185 and 3186; there lines 110 and 125 to 130 are omitted, line 114 has "veg" (an error for "vet" or "ve' ") instead of "neg," and the first four syllables of line 123 read "pa on viče."

12a (continued)

40. Now my mother has died.
Gather the wedding guests, and come for your bride;
41. Gather the wedding guests, and come for your bride.
The wedding will be in ten days."
42. Lovely Melećhana prepared herself.
She prepared nine beasts of burden,
43. And the wedding guests came.
They were there for three white days;
44. They were there for three white days.
When the fourth morning dawned,
45. Then you should have seen Kasum pasha's wife!
She took Melka by the white hand;
46. She took Melka by the white hand
And led her upstairs in the white house.
47. She locked her behind the nine locks,
And the tenth, the lock of Dubrovnik.
48. Then Kasum pasha's wife returned
And dressed her own daughter Hajka.
49. Mehmedbeg said:
"The wedding guests are ready, the bride is ready."
50. And the wedding guests set out.
Mehmedbeg returned;
51. Mehmedbeg returned
To give gifts to his sisters-in-law and his
mother-in-law.
52. When lovely Melećhana heard him,
She struck the window with her hands;
53. She struck the window with her hands,
And the glass fell to the pavement.
54. Then she plucked the necklace from her throat,
And threw it to the streetsinger:
55. "Sing, oh singer, my brother,
Perhaps Mehmedbeg will hear you.
56. Woe to you, Mehmedbeg!
You are not carrying away lovely Melećhana;
57. You are not carrying away lovely Melećhana,
But Kasum pasha's daughter Ajka."
58. None of the wedding guests heard this,
But Mehmedbeg heard,
59. And he flew upstairs in the white house
And unlocked the nine locks,

12a (continued)

60. Pa odvali devet katanaca,
I desetu bravu dubrovačku.
61. Povede je niz bijelu kulu.
Izvede je pred mermer avliju.
62. Pa zavika iz bijela grla:
"Stan'te malo, kićeni svatovi!"
63. Dovede je do svoga dorina.
Baci Ajku u zelenu travu,
64. Baci Ajku u zelenu travu,
Pa uzjaha dilber Melećhana.
65. Odvede je svom bijelu dvoru,
I uze je za vjerenu ljubu.

Hajrija Šaković, Gacko (Text 6391a)
April 26, 1935[2]

[2] For another text, sung by the same singer to the same melody, and its translation see p. 234.

12a (continued)

60. And unlocked the nine locks,
And the tenth, the lock of Dubrovnik,
61. And he led her down through the white house
And out into the marble courtyard.
62. He cried out from his white throat:
"Wait, my wedding guests!"
63. He led her to his horse.
He cast Ajka down onto the green grass;
64. He cast Ajka down onto the green grass,
And lovely Melećhana mounted.
65. He led her to his own white house
And took her for his true love.

12b

1. Vezak vezlo trides đevojaka, R. 3052
   *J*u Lipniku na bijeloj[1] kuli,
2. I pred njima od Čengića Fata:
   "Zastavite, trides đevojaka,
3. Ne bacajte oke na junake!
   Junaci su vjera i nevjera.
4. Kad te ljubi: 'Uzeću te, dušo.'[2]
5. Kad obljubi: 'Čekaj do jeseni!' "
6. Zima dođe, *j*a *j*i ljeto prođe.
7. Znate l', sestre, nije davno bilo,
8. Kad Ljubović s Nevesinja dođe.
9. Prevari me, obljubi mi lice.
10. 'Čekaj mene do jeseni, dušo.'
11. Pa on ode stolu i Stambolu.
12. Iz Stambola sitna knjiga dođe. R. 3053
13. 'Vraćaj meni burme i prstenje!
14. I vraćaj mi nebrojeno blago!
15. I vraćaj mi dibu i kadifu!'
16. O kurviću, beže Ljuboviću,
17. Vraćaj lice ko što j' prije bilo,
    Daću tebi nebrojeno blago!

Fata Šaković, Gacko (Text 6331)
April 22, 1935

[1] Mr. Bartók heard "bijelo"; perhaps the singer's mistake.
[2] From here on through stanza 16 the line is repeated, with an added "Aj" at the beginning. "Aj" is found also before lines 1, 2, 6, 21.

12b[1]

1. Thirty maids sat embroidering
In a white tower in Lipnik.
2. At their head was Fata Čengić.
"Swear to me, my thirty maids!
3. Cast not a glance upon heroic men,
For they are changeable and unfaithful.
4. When one kisses you, he says: 'I shall marry you, my sweet.'
5. But when he has embraced you, it is: 'Wait until autumn!'
6. Winter comes, and summer passes.
7. You know, sisters, it was not long ago
8. That Ljubović came from Nevesinje.
9. He tricked me and kissed my lips.
10. 'Wait for me until autumn, my sweet!'
11. Then he went off to Stambol.
12. A brief note came from Stambol:
13. 'Return to me the ring I gave you!
14. Return to me my countless treasures!
15. Return to me my silk and satin!'
16. Beg Ljubović, you lowly cur!
17. Return their former loveliness to my lips,
And I shall give to you your countless treasures."

[1] There is only one other text of this song in the Parry Collection (No. 1178 from Pemba Džubur of Gacko), and it does not vary significantly from ours. For other versions cf. Vuk, Vol. V, Nos. 404–5, pp. 270–71.

I 2 C

Telar vika od juče do podne:[1] R. 3079
"Ko j' u koga noćas na konaku,
Nek ne ide rano sa konaka!
Utekla je[2] pašina robinja,
I odnila dva pašina sina,
I odvela Muja haznadara,
I odvela debela dorina,
I odnila sahat iz njedara!"
Prvu noćcu nju su susretili, 9
Susretili, natrag povrnuli. R. 3080
Pa je paša njojzi govorijo:
"Šta uradi, moja robinjice?
Kud odvede debela dorina?
Kud odnese sahat iz njedara?
Kud odvede Muja haznadara?"
"Sahat nosim,[3] da đe ne pridosnim.
Doru jašem, ne mogu brez dora."

Šerifa Zvizdić, Gacko (Text 6344)
April 22, 1935

[1] Each line is repeated.
[2] First sings "otišla je"; slip of tongue.
[3] "Sahat nosim" sung twice; slip of tongue.

I 2C[1]

From morning until noon the town crier cried:
"Let him who spends tonight at another's house
Not leave that house too early!
A slave girl of the pasha has run away,
And abducted the pasha's two sons,
And taken away Mujo, the keeper of the treasures,
And led away the pasha's well-fed steed,
And taken his watch from the pasha's belt!"
They came upon her that first night;
They came upon her and brought her back.
Then the pasha said to her:
"My slave, what have you done?
Where did you take my well-fed steed?
Where did you put the watch from my belt?
Where did you take Mujo, the keeper of the treasures?"
"I am carrying the watch that I may not be late,
And I am riding the horse, for without the horse
I could not ride!"

[1] This is a characteristic folksong in an incomplete and corrupt version. The answers given by the captured fugitive to the pasha are not as full as they should be. She should tell him that she took the pasha's sons to keep her company, and Mujo that she might not sleep alone. Other texts, of which there are twenty-eight in the collection, go on to narrate her fate. In some she is released, but in others she is executed. All these differ considerably in the details of the items stolen and in the reasons for stealing them. Compare also Odobašić, IV, 79.

12d

1. Tekla Sava nis kamenje sama,[1] R. 3225
2. Na njoj Naza bele none prala,
3. Bele none *j*i[2] bijele ruke.
4. Tura none u šikli nalune,
Bele ruke[3] u zlatne džepove.
5. "Ljuboviću, žalosna ti majka! R. 3226
Kad se ženiš, što se ne oženiš?"
"Tri put sam se junak oženijo,
Sva tri puta sumbul udovicom!
6. Udovice, oba t' oka vrana!
Koliko si ljubila jarana!
Tri puta sam, gledaj koliko sam,
Samo jednom lijepom đevojkom!"

Halima Hrvo, Gacko (Text 6408)
April 27, 1935

[1] Lines 1–4 are repeated. The repeat of lines 1 and 3 is preceded by "Aj," of line 2 by "Ej," of line 4 by "A." "Ej" also precedes line 7, and "Aj" precedes line 11.
[2] The "*j*" omitted in the repeat.
[3] The first four syllables of lines 5, 6, 8, 10, and 13 are repeated; in line 5 this repetition is preceded by "Aj."

12d[1]

1. The Sava was flowing along over the rocks.
2. By it Naza was washing her white feet,
3. Her white feet and her white arms.
4. She put her feet into carved sandals
   And her white arms into golden sleeves.
5. "Oh, Ljubović, woe to your mother!
   When you marry, why does your marriage not last?"
   "I married three times,
   All three times with a beautiful widow.
6. Oh widow, by both your black eyes,
   How many lovers have you kissed?
   Three times I married, just look at me;
   But only once with a pretty young girl!"

[1] This text is made up of two quite separate songs. Lines one to five present a vignette of small town life. There is only one other text of this part in the Parry Collection, a dictated text from the same singer, Halima Hrvo (No. 2482). Lines six to thirteen are a very much confused version of another song. The basic form of this second song, of which there are at least eleven texts in the Parry Collection, is as follows:

"Ljuboviću, žalosna ti majka!
Kad se ženiš, što se ne oženiš?
Tvoj se babo tri put oženio,
Sva tri puta lijepom đevojkom,
A ti jednom, i to udovicom!"

"Ljubović, woe to your mother!
When you marry, why does your marriage not last?
Your father married three times,
All three times with a pretty young girl,
But you married only once, and with a widow!"

(No. 3953 from Džefa Džubur of Gacko)

I 2e

1. Gorom jaše beže Alibeže, R. 3163
Gorom jaše, goru kunijaše:[1]
2. "Ej, gorice, ne ozelenjela![2]
3. Ej, travice, ne orumenjela!
4. Što u tebi niđe vode nejma,
5. Te je meni mladu dodijalo,
Da zakoljem debela dorina,
6. Dorove se krvi napojiti!"
7. A nešto ga iz[3] oblaka vika:
8. "Ne kun' goru, beže Alibeže,
Ne kun' goru, ne kolji dorina,
9. Već okreni z desna na lijevo!
10. Tu ćeš naći zeleno jezero,
11. Kraj jezera prembijela vila.
12. Radi, beže, vilu ufatiti!"
13. Ufati je beže Alibeže,
Ufatijo prembijelu vilu,
14. Pa je nosi caru čestitome, R. 3164
15. I cara je s vilom oženijo.
16. Tuj su bili porod izrodili,
Dvije šćeri i četiri sina.
17. Molila se prebijela[4] vila:
18. "Sultan, care, od istoka sunce!
19. Više vakat đecu sunetiti."
20. Zametnuše u dvoru veselje.
21. Do podne je kolom okretala,
22. O podne se dade izvijati.
23. "Sultan, care, od istoka sunce!
Ja sam davno majku ostavila."
24. Kupi krila, pa poleće sinja.

Raba Zvizdić, Gacko (Text No. 6381)
April 24, 1935

[1] The line is preceded by "*Ej*."
[2] The following lines are repeated: 2–4, 6, 7, 9–12, 14, 15, 17–22, 24.
[3] The first time sung as "*j*iz."
[4] The second time sung as "premijela" (slip of the tongue).

I 2e[1]

1. Alibeg was riding along the mountain.
As he rode along the mountain, he cursed it.
2. "Mountain, may you never turn green!
3. Grass, may you never ripen!
4. For there is not a drop of water anywhere upon you,
5. And I am sore distressed
To kill my well-fed steed
6. And drink its blood."
7. Then something spoke to him from the clouds:
8. "Do not curse the mountain, Alibeg,
Do not curse the mountain, do not kill your horse,
9. But turn to the left.
10. There you will find a green lake,
11. And beside the lake, a snow-white vila.
12. Try to catch the vila."
13. Alibeg caught her,
He caught the snow-white vila,
14. And he took her to the glorious emperor,
15. And married her to the emperor.
16. They had offspring,
Two daughters and four sons.
17. The snow-white vila asked the sultan:
18. "Sultan, emperor, eastern sun,
19. It is time to circumcise our children."
20. They held a feast in the castle.
21. All morning she danced.
22. In the afternoon she began to fly.
23. "Sultan, emperor, eastern sun,
It is long ago that I left my mother."
24. She spread her wings and flew away.

[1] This is a somewhat abbreviated version of a very popular folksong, of which there are seventeen other texts in the Parry Collection. The only other sung text (No. 6499, from Hatidža Tosun, of Gacko) varies somewhat from ours. Hasanaga keeps the vila as his own wife, and after she has borne him children, she escapes by requesting permission to dance with the girls and by then flying away. The longer versions devote more time to the details of capturing the vila. The voice from the clouds warns the hero to proceed carefully to the lake so as not to awaken the sleeping vila. But the vila hears him and jumps into the lake, leaving her wings on the shore. Ali takes the wings and gallops up the mountain. The vila pursues him, begging him to give her back her wings. He stops and takes her up behind him and flees with her to Stambol. Mr. Bayard rightly considers this song a Balkan version of the common tale of the man who traps a mermaid by stealing her scaly fish-skin. After bearing him children, she finds the fish-skin and returns to the sea forever. Compare also Matica, Vol. V, No. 30, p. 41. An interesting parallel is also found in the *Nibelungenlied*, Adventure XXV, Strophes 1533 ff.

13

A

R. 1547

1. Vi' te čuda, prije ne viđeste,
   Đe proleće jato golubova
2. Iznad bjela Kajtazova dvora.
   Spazila ji Kajtazova hana.
3. "Mila neno, Hamini svatova!
   Nešće mene u jenđiluk zvati.
4. Svije bi ji mlada darovala,
   Svekru babi bjelu ahmediju;
5. Prispjela mu, da Bog da, ćefilu!
   Svekrvici svilaču košulju;
6. Svile joj se kosti od bolesti!
   Zaovici na feder kundure;
7. U njima se, da Bog da, slomila!
   Mome Hami vezenu mahramu;
8. Koliko je u mahrami grana,
   Toliko ga dopanulo rana!"

B

1. Vi' te čuda, prije ne viđesmo!
   Viđoste li gusku osedlanu?
2. Viđoste li patku potkovanu?
   Viđoste li zeca u gaćama?
3. Ni se čudim patki potkovanoj,
   Ni se čudim guski osedlanoj,
4. Ve se čudim zecu u gaćama:
   Kada piši, ko mu gaće driši?

Naza Rokić, Stolac (Text 888)
Dec. 15, 1934

I 3[1]

A

1. Listen to a wonder never heard before!
   How a flock of doves flew
2. Over the white castle of Kajtaz.
   Lady Kajtaz saw them.
3. "Dear grandmother, those are Hamin's wedding guests.
   They will not invite me to be matron of honor.
4. I would give gifts to them all.
   A shining talisman to the father-in-law.
5. May it suit him to his satisfaction!
   To the mother-in-law a silk blouse.
6. May it bring disease to her bones!
   To the groom's sister a pair of boots.
7. May she fall and break her neck in them!
   To Hama an embroidered handkerchief.
8. As many as there are leaves in the embroidery,
   So many wounds may he receive!"

B

1. Listen to a wonder never heard before!
   Have you ever seen a goose in saddle?
2. Have you ever seen a shoed duck?
   Have you ever seen a rabbit in pants?
3. I do not wonder at a shoed duck,
   Nor do I wonder at a goose in saddle;
4. But I do wonder at a rabbit in pants.
   When he makes water, who undoes his pants?

[1] See the note to the translation of Text No. 23a in this book. A and B are related only by the first line, a very common one in the heroic poetry. B is a humorous "pripjev," or "foresong"; usually sung as an introduction to the singing of a longer epic. Its purpose is to attract the attention of the audience and quiet them before the real story begins. For another version of A see Vuk, Vol. V, No. 411, p. 274.

14

Sitna travo zelena[1] R. 3215
Do svilena čadora.
Pod čadorom đevojka
Šije veze, darove,
Da daruje svatove:
Svakom svatu po jagluk,
A đeveru, boščaluk,
A dragome, četiri. R. 3216

Halima Hrvo, Gacko (Text 6403)
April 27, 1935

15

Falijo se žuti limun kraj mora:[2] R. 3213
"Ima l' danas iko ljevši od mene?
Sva gospoda šerbe pije brez mene,
A ja znadem đe ga pije kraj vode.
Ima danas, Fato, zlato u majke."
Progovara šarenika jabuka:
"Ja sam danas više ljevše od tebe." R. 3214

Halima Hrvo, Gacko (Text 6402)
April 27, 1935

[1] The first four syllables in each line are repeated; and syllables five, six, and seven are added. This extended line is then repeated.
[2] To each line is added "aman, aman," and then the line is repeated without this addition.

14[1]

Oh, short green grass
Round about the silken tent!
Beneath the tent a maid
Sits sewing and embroidering gifts
To present to wedding guests;
A pillow cover for each guest,
An embroidered suit for the best man,
And four for her beloved.

15[2]

The yellow lemon tree beside the sea boasted:
"Is there anyone today more beautiful than I?
All the gentlemen drink sherbet without me,
But I know where they drink it beside water.
Is there, Fata, darling of your mother?"[3]
The mottled apple tree answered:
"Today I am more beautiful than you."

[1] Judging from the text, this is a wedding song. Of the ten other texts in the collection beginning with this line, three (Nos. 11300, 11710, and 11844) are different songs from ours. Two others (Nos. 2262 and 4642) vary from our text beyond line five, but the remainder are all similar to it.

[2] There are twenty-six other texts listed under this first line in the Parry Collection. Our text is not a good version of this "Contest of Flowers" song. In line three some texts read "od mene" ("made from me") which seems to make better sense, although this is not the only variant in which "brez mene," occurs. Lines four and five are likewise puzzling. This song is used in several texts as an introductory theme to another song, or songs, and line four is a transitional line in some cases. The reference in line five is not clear, but it may also be transitional. Cf. Odobašic, III, 97, and Clapier, p. 177.

[3] Dr. Rastko Petrović has pointed out to me that "zlato u majke" is a common expression, meaning "you who are dear to your mother." He would emend the line to "Ima l' danas," etc., as in line 2.

16a,b

Na žalos je sitna knjiga[1] R. 3232
Ljubovića dvoru stigla.
Ljubović je čita, gleda,
Pa je majci na sto baci.
"Da viš, majko, da viš, mila,
A od bega Lakišića,
Što nam piše beg Lakišić,[2]
Da j' Hajkuna nevjernica.
Ne zove se više moja,
Nego bega Lakišića.
Još mi ište moga doru
U svatove po đevojku!" R. 3233

Hajrija Šaković, Gacko (Text 6411)
April 27, 1935

17

Razbolje se Zorna Zorka[3] R. 3123
Na Cetinju Crnogorka.
K njoj dolazi mijo tata,
Mijo tata, kralj Nikola.
"Što je tebi, šćeri Zorka?
Il su rane od prebola,
Il su rane od umora?"
"Mijo tata, kralj Nikola,
Tri su bola od prebola,
A četiri od umora,
Već te molim, mijo tata,
Da mi đecu preporučiš,
Aleksandra u Francusku,
A Đorđiju u Rusiju,
Šćer Milenu Crnoj Gori.
To je dika roda moga,
Roda moga i ponosa!" R. 3124

Ćerima Kurtović, Gacko (Text 6364)
April 24, 1935

[1] The last four syllables of the line are prefixed to the beginning of the line, and each line is repeated with this prefix. Exceptions are lines 7, 8, 11, which are repeated three times; the first and second rendition without prefix, the third with prefix.

[2] Between line 7 and line 8 the following is inserted: "Više moja, ne da," which is a mistake.

[3] The last four syllables of each line are repeated, and then the whole line is repeated.

16a,b[1]

A brief, sad letter
Came to Ljubović's house.
Ljubović looked at it and read it.
Then he threw it on the table for his mother.
"See, dear mother,
It is from beg Lakišić.
See what beg Lakišić writes us;
That Hajkuna is untrue,
And is no longer mine,
But beg Lakišić's.
Besides, he asks for my brown horse
For the girl to ride in the wedding procession!"

17[2]

Zorna Zorka fell ill,
A Montenegrin lady in Cetinje.
Her dear father came to her,
Her dear father, King Nikola.
"What is wrong, Zorka, my daughter?
Can your wounds be healed,
Or are they mortal?"
"My dear father, King Nikola,
Three of my wounds can be healed,
But four are mortal.
I pray you, my dear father,
To send my children away—
Alexander to France,
George to Russia,
My daughter Milena to Montenegro.
They are the staff of my clan,
And the pride of my family!"

[1] There are thirty-one other texts of this song in the Parry Collection, all dictated. Cf. Odobašić, II, 100.

[2] There are thirteen other texts of this song in the collection, all dictated and all from Gacko. The material of this and of the preceding text (No. 16) is fairly constant.

18

1. Knjigu piše dva Ćirića[1] R. 3178
A na ruke Pivodiću:[2]
2. "Doj[3] doveče, Pivodiću,
Doj doveče na večeru!
3. Dovešćemo đevojaka,
I pred njima slatku Savu,
4. Slatku Savu, seju[4] našu."
Do ponoći[5] pivo piše,
Od ponoća[5] sjajne nože.
5. Jomamiše dva Ćirića,
Domamiše Pivodića,
I on dođe na večeru.
6. Do[6] ponoći pivo piše,
Od ponoća sjajne nože,
Sjajne nože povadiše,
7. U harar ga sasjekoše,
U Neretvu ga turiše.
8. To j' začulo ludo dite,[7]
Ludo dite na sokaku.
9. Trkom trči Osman paši,
Osman paša na borije,
A borije na nizame.
10. Dovedoše staru majku,
Staru majku Pivodića. R. 3179

[1] The singer begins with the two lines:

"Doj doveče, Pivodiću,	"Come this evening, Pivodić,
Doj doveče na večeru!"[2]	Come this evening for supper!"

This is a faulty beginning and has been omitted.

[2] The second line of stanzas 1, 7, 8, 10, 11, 13–16 is repeated.

[3] "Doj" is a dialectic form for "dođi."

[4] "Seja" a dialectic form for "seka."

[5] Mr. Bartók hears "da donoći" or "ta donoći" in line 8, and "A donoća" or "A tonoća" in line 9; perhaps errors of the singer.

[6] Pronounced "jo."[2]

[7] Note the "ikavski" dialect again. This singer's language is not wholly that of Gacko.

18[1]

1. The two Ćirići wrote a letter
To the hand of Pivodić:
2. "Come this evening, Pivodić,
Come to supper this evening;
3. We shall bring girls,
And at their head, sweet Sava,
4. Sweet Sava, our sister."
Up till midnight they drank;[2]
After midnight knives flashed.
5. The two Ćirići tempted him;
They tempted Pivodić,
And he came to supper.
6. Up till midnight they drank;
After midnight knives flashed.
They drew their shining knives.
7. They stabbed him and put him in a sack
And threw him into the Neretva.
8. A little child heard them,[3]
A little child on the street.
9. He ran to Osman pasha.
Osman pasha announced it to the trumpeters,
And the trumpeters to the judges.
10. They brought in the old mother,
The old mother of Pivodić.

[1] This is a rather confused version of a very bloody and dramatic poem. It would be well to sketch the story as told in other more nearly complete and less confused variants. The two Ćirići invite their sister's lover Pivodić for supper with malicious intent. After supper they fight, and in spite of their sister's entreaties, the brothers stab Pivodić to death, cut off his right hand and give it to their sister, and then throw the body into the river. The next morning Sava tells the authorities, and her brothers are arrested. The pasha calls in Pivodić's mother, and asks her what he should do with the Ćirići. But the mother has gone crazy, and she tells him to release them. He then asks Sava, and she decrees that they be impaled on a spear and carried through the town.

This is a reconstructed sketch. Not all these elements appear in exactly the same form in all versions, but this is the basic story. There are three other texts in the collection (8006, 4102, and 1646). No. 1646 calls the two brothers the two Morići, and it is the only text in which Sava pleads for Pivodić's life. The cutting off of the right hand does not appear in this version, although it is found in the other two. No. 1646 is also unique in its ending: Sava wants the brothers burned alive, and she carries out the sentence herself, after which she goes to Pivodić's house to live with his old mother.

[2] Lines 8 and 9 are in error here and are correctly repeated in lines 13 and 14.

[3] In all the other versions it is Sava who reports the murder.

18 (continued)

11. "Stara majko Pivodića,
Mi šta ćemo od Ćirića?"
12. "Bojno koplje donesite,
Donesite bojno koplje!
Objesite dva Ćirića!"
13. Stara majka podluđela,
Stara majka Pivodića.
14. "Vi pušćite dva Ćirića!
Ne griješ'te Pivodića!"
15. Progovara slatka Sava,
Slatka Sava, seja naša:
16. "Stara majka podluđela,
Stara majka Pivodića."

Džefa Grebović, Gacko (Text 6391)
April 26, 1935

18 (continued)

11. "Old mother of Pivodić,
What shall we do with the Ćirići?"
12. "Bring a war spear![4]
Bring a war spear!
Impale the two Ćirići!"
13. The old mother had gone mad,
The old mother of Pivodić.
14. "Let the two Ćirići go.
Do not bring sin to the Pivodići!"[5]
15. Said sweet Sava,
Sweet Sava, our sister:
16. "The old mother has gone mad,
The old mother of Pivodić."

[4] From this point on confusion again reigns. Lines 27–29 make better sense after line 37.

[5] I find this line difficult to understand, but I believe the translation is correct. It is common to all the texts.

19

1. Vilenica bukovicu pita: R. 3050
"Bukovice, što si potavila?"[1]
2. "U subotu u sedam sahati,
Mašina se sa Serdaća[2] kreće.
3. Iz mašine iskra izletila,
Zapalila kuće i dućane,
4. I džamije do Sulejmanije,[3]
5. Po varoši varoške dućane,
6. Do konaka bega Fadilbega.
7. . . . iz kuće u bašču[4]
8. Majka sina za ruku vođaše,
9. A sin majku za bijelu ruku,
10. A sve pita: 'Jeda moju majku?'
11. Majka pita: 'Jeda moga sina?'
12. A da vidiš bega Fadilbega!
13. Pa se fati ata vilenoga,
14. A on uze sjajna livervora, R. 3051
15. Pa uđaha ata golemoga,
16. Pa on ubi mlada konduktera.
17. Kondukter se napijo se vina,
18. Pa ne pazi ni kad pije vina."

Fata Šaković, Gacko (Text 6330)
April 22, 1935

[1] The second line of the first three stanzas is repeated.
[2] There is some doubt about this word. I have taken it as a place name.
[3] From here on, each line is repeated.
[4] The first four syllables of this line are not clear on the record.

19[1]

1. The pine tree asked the boxwood tree:[2]
"Boxwood, why are you all black?"
2. "At seven on Saturday,
A train left Serdač.
3. A spark flew from the train
And set fire to houses and shops,
4. As far as the Mosque of Sulejman
5. And to the shops in the town,
6. As far as the home of Fadilbeg.
7. . . . from the house to the garden,
8. The mother was leading her son by the hand,
9. And the son held his mother's white hand
10. And kept asking: 'Does it burn my mother?'
11. The mother asked: 'Does it burn my son?'
12. Then you should see Fadilbeg.
13. He seized his wondrous steed,
14. And he took his shining revolver,
15. And then he mounted his mighty horse,
16. And he killed the young engineer.
17. The engineer had become drunk on wine,
18. And he was careless when he drank."

[1] There are eight other texts of this poem in the Parry Collection. Four of them (Nos. 4060, 11615, 11684, and 12160) end with the cries of the women and children in the conflagration and the statement that the engineer was drunk. Three others, including the present text (Nos. 1196, 6330, and 8465) proceed to tell of the death of the engineer, and two others (Nos. 2418 and 4576) add to this a curse made by the engineer's sister on his slayer.

[2] All the versions in the Parry Collection except the published one and Text No. 1196 begin with "jelovica," "bukovica," "bukovina," or "borovica," all different kinds of trees. "Vilenica" does not make sense here. I have translated it as if it were "jelovica."

20

1. Ferman stiže iz Stanbola, A_1 R. 526
Bujruntija iz Travnika, A_2
A jadija *j*iz Sarajva, A_2
Da podignu janjičare, A_1
Janjičare-i[1] graničare, A_2
Da ufate dva Morića, A_1
Dva Morića, dva pašića.[2] F
2. Podigoše janjičare, A_1
Janjičare, graničare, A_2
Pofataše dva Morića, A_1
Dva Morića, dva pašića, A_2
Morić[3] Ibru i Aliju, A_2
Pofataše, zavezaše, A_1
Niz Sarajvo-i natiraše.[4] F
3. Kroz Sarače-i i Kovače, A_1
Progovara Morić Ale: A_2
"Oj, Boga ti, Dizdaraga! A_1
Popusti nam bele ruke! A_2
Nek moremo zapivati, A_1
Staru majku spominjati!" F
4. Zapjevaše dva Morića: A_1
"Oj, Sarajvo, dugo li si! A_2
Baš čaršijo, široka si! A_1
Krdžəmarice,[5] fina li si! A_2
Dosta si nam piva dala! A_1
Naša majko, mila li si! A_2
Dobro ti nas odhranila, A_1
Od dužmana učuvala, A_2
Do danas nas pričuvala." F

[1] The added "i" is pronounced as a semivowel, that is, with the preceding vowel as a diphthong. This applies also to lines 14, 15, 37, 66, 70, 74, 80.

[2] The last line of each stanza is repeated. Line 7 has "aman" and line 59 has "*j*aman" after the fourth syllable which does not appear in the repeat; line 7 has "dva Morića-i" in the repeat.

[3] The singer first sings "Alu i Ali" and then corrects himself.

[4] The repeat has an added *i* after the eighth syllable, not after the fourth.

[5] That is, "krčmarice." The singer sang, however, "krdžəmarice."

20[1]

1. A firman came from Stambol,
A decree from Travnik,
An order from Sarajevo,
To call out the Jannissaries,
Jannissaries and men of the border,
To seize the two Morić's,
The two Morić's, two sons of the pasha.[2]
2. They called out the Jannissaries,
Jannissaries, men of the border.
They seized the two Morić's[3]
The two Morić's, two sons of the pasha,
Morić Ibro and Alija.
They seized them and bound them.
They drove them through Sarajevo,
3. Through the saddlers' and blacksmiths' districts
Morić Ale spoke:
"By God, captain,
Free our white arms!
Allow us to strike up a song,
In memory of our old mother!"
4. The two Morić's began to sing:[4]
"O Sarajevo, your streets are long!
How broad your market is!
How fine is the wife of the tavern keeper!
You have given us much to drink.
Mother, you are dear to us.
You brought us up well
And defended us from our enemies.
Until today you have preserved us."

[1] There are twelve texts of this song in the Parry Collection. The published text is a good one, but some of the variations in the others are worth mentioning. For another published version see Odobašić, IV, 6.

[2] The crimes of the Morić brothers are spoken of in two of the texts. No. 11613a says that the imperial funds have been stolen, and No. 3037 tells that the two Morić's have terrorized the people and seduced unmarried maidens and newly-wed wives.

[3] Most of the texts say that they were seized while praying. One, however, begins with the common formula, "The two Morić's were drinking wine in the middle of Sarajevo."

[4] The song within a song is found in all the variants. No. 5975 tells that, as they were led through the blacksmiths' district, they sang to Mara the barmaid. She begged the guards to release them for two hours. They spent two hours at the tavern and then went on to the saddlers' district, where they sang to their mother.

20 (continued)

5. Pitu kuha stara majka, A_1
Stara majka dva Morića; A_2
U ruci joj oklagija, A
A u drugoj zlatan[6] ibrik. A_2
*J*a kad čula oba sina, A_1
Oklagiju salomila, A_2
Zlatan ibrik ulupila, A_1
Pa poleti niz Sarače-i A_2 R. 527
Bosonoga, bes papuča, A_1
Gologlava, bes fesića, A_2
A raspasa, bes pojasa. A_2
Kad je bila kros Sarače, A_2
Krozə Sarače, kros Kovače, A_2
Progovara stara majka: A_1
"Jazuk vama, svi Sarači, A_2
Svi Sarači, svi Kovači, A_1
Što pušćaste dva Morića, A_2
Da *j*i gone savezani!" F
6. Kad su čuli svi Saraći, A_1
Svi Sarači, svi Kovači, A_2
Svi ćefenke pritvoriše, A_1
Pa za majkom poletiše. A_2
Kad su bili na vratniku, A_1
Tuj stigoše Dizdaragu. A_2
Progovara stara majka: A_1
"Oj, Boga ti, Dizdaraga! A_2
Daj mi pusti jednog sina, A_1
Jali *j*Ibru, jali *j*Alu! A_2
Na poklon ti svi Sarači, A_2
Svi Sarači i Kovači!" F
7. Progovara Dizdaraga: A_1
"Aj, ne luduj, stara majko! A_2
Pustiću ti oba sina, A_1
Do kad sutra petak[6] svane." A_2

[6] The word is sung in the rhythm of a fourth and an eighth note in a triplet.

20 (continued)

5. The old mother was baking a pie,
The old mother of the two Morić's.
In one hand was a rolling pin,
And in the other, a golden pitcher.
When she heard her two sons,
She broke the rolling pin
And let fall the golden pitcher.
Then she sped through the saddlers' district[5]
Barefoot, without her slippers,
Bare-headed, without her fez,
With loose garments, without a sash.
When she had passed through the saddlers' district,
The saddlers' and the blacksmiths',
The old mother said:
"Shame on you, all saddlers,
All saddlers, all blacksmiths!
You have abandoned the two Morić's
And let them be bound and driven away."
6. When all the saddlers heard,
All the saddlers, all the blacksmiths,
They closed their shops,
And sped after the mother.
When they arrived at the gateway,
They came upon the captain of the guard.
The old mother said:
"By God, captain!
Free one of my sons,
Either Ibro or Ali.
Here are all the saddlers for you,
All the saddlers and blacksmiths."[6]
7. The captain of the guard said:
"Don't be foolish, old mother.
I will free your two sons,
Tomorrow, when Friday dawns."

[5] Although blacksmiths and saddlers are fixed elements in the song, this gathering of them in force is not found in any other text I have seen. No. 5505 shows the old mother rushing out to see her sons passing, a theme which persists in most of the versions. It goes on uniquely, however, as Ibro turns to his mother and tells her to return to his wife. "If she bears a son, give him my name, and tell him about Morić Ibro."

[6] In some of the texts the captain says that he will release one of the brothers, but not both. In No. 11613a the mother simply tells him to let Ibro go and to take Meho. But in No. 3037 each is ready to give up his life for his brother. So she tells the captain that they are both dear to her.

20 (continued)

Ode majka dvoru svomu. A_1
Otiraše dva Morića, A_2
U hapsanu-i zatvoriše-i. A_1
Da kad sutra petak[6] svanu, A_2
Istom sabah zaučijo, A_1
Izvedose[7] dva Morića, A_2
Dva Morića-i, dva pašića, A_1
Izvedose,[7] obisiše, A_2
Do dva topa opališe. F
8. Kad je majka tope[8] čula, A_2 R. 528
Poletila-i Dizdaragi. A_1
Kad ugleda dva Morića, A_2
Na rukam' *j*im lisičine, A_2
Na nogama bukagije, A_1
A o vratu zlatan[6] gajtan, A_2
Odma u njoj srce puče. F
Grdna rano-i dva Morića! F[9]

Meho Jarić, Livno, Dalmatia (Text 505)
Sept. 21, 1934

[7] "–doše" is sung in the rhythm of an eighth and a dotted fourth note.

[8] The word is sung in the rhythm of a fourth and an eighth note in a triplet, although both syllables are short (compare with footnote 6, where the first syllable is long).

[9] These letters indicate the distribution of three musical motifs over the text; A_1 and A_2 are related motifs; F is the final motif, different in musical content.

20 (continued)

The mother went home.
They drove on the two Morić's
And locked them in the dungeon.
The next day, when Friday dawned,
Just as the call for the first prayer was heard,
They led out the two Morić's,
The two Morić's, two pasha's sons,
They led them out and hanged them
And fired two cannon.
8. When the mother heard the cannon,
She sped to the captain of the guard.
When she saw the two Morić's,
With chains on their arms
And shackles on their feet
And a golden cord about their necks,
Her heart burst straightway.
Terrible wound, the two Morić's![7]

[7] No. 11613a ends with the arrival of a decree from Stambol pardoning the two Morić's. "But they replied that the two sons of the pasha had been hanged." No. 3037 ends with a common theme. The old mother goes home and fetches her son's sword. She then goes to the captain and offers it to him. When he holds out his hand for it, she kills him, thus avenging her children.

21a

1. Pivo pije Selimbeže,[1] R. 3161
Pivo pije, podvriskuje.
2. On doziva dilber Joku:
"Dilber Joko, crno oko!
3. Dilber Joko, srce moje,
Je l' mehana otvorena,
4. Je l' mehana otvorena,
Je li čaša natočena?"
5. Progovara dilber Joka:
"Selimbeže, srce moje!
6. Jes[2] ti čaša natočena,
Mehana je otvorena."
7. "Ko je grlo ogrlijo,
Ko je lice obljubijo,
8. Ko je oči pomutijo?"
"Selimbeže, oko moje,
9. Nije grlo ogrljeno,
Nije lice obljubljeno.
10. Mehana je otvorena, R. 3162
Čaša ti je natočena."

Raba Zvizdić, Gacko (Text 6380)
April 24, 1935

[1] The last vowel of the first line of each stanza is elided; "aj velem" is added, and with this addition the whole line is repeated. After the fourth syllable of the second line are added "haj vaj" (stanzas 2–4) or "vaj"' (stanza 1), and "hej vaj" (stanzas 5–10).

[2] This line is repeated; the first time "Nije" is sung instead of "Jes"; this must be an error, and the repetition of the line no doubt is for correcting it.

21a[1]

1. Selimbeg is drinking beer.
He is drinking beer, and he calls out
2. He calls lovely Joka:
"Lovely Joka, black eyes!
3. Lovely Joka, my heart!
Is the tavern open?
4. Is the tavern open?
Is the glass brimming?"
5. Lovely Joka answered:
"Selimbeg, my heart!
6. Yes, your glass is brimming,
The tavern is open."
7. "Who has embraced you?
Who has kissed your cheeks?
8. Who has clouded your eyes?"
"Selimbeg, my eyes!
9. No one has embraced me.
No one has kissed my cheeks.
10. The tavern is open.
Your glass is brimming."

[1]In addition to Nos. 21a and 21b, there are thirty-two others in the collection. Most of them are basically the same as the published versions. Many of them are shorter and have only the questions: "Is the tavern open? Is the glass brimming?" Nos. 8903 and 11970 are conflicting. Joka replies to the questions by saying that her eyes are clouded, her hair ruffled, her cheeks kissed, and so forth. Five texts (4323, 8570, 10361, 10937, and 12336) say that Joka has been waiting for Selimbeg to return that he might ruffle her locks, cloud her eyes, and kiss her cheeks.

21b

1. Vino pije Selimbeže,[1] R. 3576
Vino pije, podvriskuje,[2]
2. Pa dozivlje dilber Joku:
"Dilber Joko, crno u̯oko![3]
3. Je l' mehana otvorena,
Je li čaša nalivena,
4. Jesu l' oči pomućene,
Jesu l' kose pomršene,
5. Je li lice obljubljeno, R. 3577
Je li grlo ogrljeno?"
6. "Selimbeže, srce, dušo!
Jes, mehana otvorena,
7. Čaša ti je natočena.
Nisu oči pomućene,
8. Nit je lice obljubljeno,
Nit su kose pomršene,
9. Nije grlo ogrljeno,
Selimbeže, srce moje!"

Derviša Biberović, Gacko (Text 6490)
May 21, 1935

[1] The last vowel of the first line of each stanza is elided, "aj vele" is added, and with this addition the whole line is repeated.

[2] Between the fourth and the fifth syllables of the second line of each stanza "haj vaj" is inserted, and the whole line is repeated with this insertion.

[3] Sung in this form for "oko." Compare "majku̯o" for "majko" in the music notation, stanza 4, of No. 20.

21b[1]

1. Selimbeg is drinking wine.
He is drinking wine, and he calls out,
2. And he calls lovely Joka:
"Lovely Joka, black eyes!
3. Is the tavern open?
Is the glass filled?
4. Are your eyes clouded?
Is your hair ruffled?
5. Have your cheeks been kissed?
Have you been embraced?"
6. "Selimbeg, heart and soul!
Yes, the tavern is open.
7. Your glass is brimming.
My eyes are not clouded,
8. Nor have my cheeks been kissed,
Nor has my hair been ruffled,
9. Nor have I been embraced,
Selimbeg, my heart!"

[1] See footnote 1 to the translation of Text 21a.

22

Kraj mora Džeha zaspala.[1] R. 3121
Puhnu joj vihar sa mora,
Probudi Džehu đevojku.
Kune ga Džeha đevojka:
"Neka te, vihar sa mora!
Više ga nikad ne puhno!
Lepo ti bijah zaspala."[2]

Almasa Zvizdić, Gacko (Text 6362)
April 23, 1935

[1] This line and each following line is repeated, after which the last five syllables are again repeated.

[2] The singing of this stanza is incomplete. The record breaks off after the repetition of "lepo ti."

22[1]

Džeha fell asleep beside the sea.
The wind blew from the sea
And awakened the maiden Džeha.
The maiden Džeha cursed it.
"Leave me alone, wind from the sea!
May you never blow again!
I had just fallen beautifully asleep."

[1] There is not sufficient space to do this interesting text justice. What appears on the surface to be merely a charming vignette becomes on closer scrutiny a sinister and tragic poem with overtones of magic. Our text is only the beginning of the song. Beside the text presented here there are thirty-six others in the collection. (For another published version see Mirković, No. 116, p. 82. Compare also footnote 1 to the translation of No. 27d in this book.) Most of them are short, but they continue beyond the point at which our text, which is the shortest and most incomplete of all, ends, to tell that Džeha was dreaming of her wedding. A few texts say that she simply dreamed of the arrival of wedding guests to take her to Osman pasha or to Mehmed pasha. But twenty-four texts say that the guests were pilgrims, her father-in-law a "mufti," or doctor, her brother-in-law a judge, and her bridegroom a judge. No. 4674 adds that they had put on her veil, and the girl curses the wind for blowing it away. In No. 6919 we see the first note of tragedy, when Džeha says that her bridegroom is the black earth. It was not a wedding of which she was dreaming, but a funeral. Four texts then proceed to interpret the dream and to narrate its fulfillment. In No. 12008 a vila from the mountains calls to her and says that the arrival of the wedding-guests means that she will die; that her father-in-law is a pilgrim means that he will be the "efendi" at the funeral; and so on. This version and the next do not tell the consequences of the dream. No. 12134 says that it was the wind which interpreted the dream to her. But Nos. 2669 and 12334 continue beyond the interpretation. In the first it is a vila that interprets the dream, after which Džeha goes home and tells her mother to prepare her bed as she is going to die. Her mother says that she will care for her daughter, but Džeha assures her that no medicine can cure her; she had had a bad dream which a vila had interpreted to her. Finally, No. 12334 is the longest and best form of this poem in the collection. In this the dream is interpreted along the usual lines by "something from the sea." Džeha goes home, has her mother prepare her bed quickly, and lies down and dies immediately.

23a

Polećela dva goluba ispred dvora moga.[1] R. 3081
Jedan pade u đulbašču, drugi na moj pendžer.
Koji pade na moj pendžer, oni gleda mene,
Koji pade u đulbašču, oni bere ružu.
Da sam, Bog do, doma bila, bi ga ufatila,
Ručku bi mu halvu[2] pekla, večeri baklavu,
Po večeri kahvu pekla, u njedra ga metla.

Halima Hrvo, Gacko (Text 6345)
April 23, 1935

23b

A

Polećela dva goluba iznad[3] moga dvora,[4] R. 3486
Polećela, prelećela, ja hi ne viđela.
Da sam mlada doma bila, bi hi ufatila,
Zlatan bi him kafez plela, biserom kitila,
Ručku bi him halvu pekla, večeri baklavu.

B

Da se hoće dragi oženiti,[5]
Mene mladu na svadbu pozvati,
Odnila bi, što bi kader bila,
Svekru babu belu ahmediju,
A svekrvi svilaču košulju,
A zaovi mrku jameniju.

Almasa Zvizdić, Gacko (Text 6448)
May 19, 1935

[1] The last six syllables of each line are repeated. The ornamental syllable "*Ej*" precedes line 1, "*I*" precedes line 2, and "*ə*" precedes lines 6 and 7.
[2] Mr. Bartók heard "halva"; perhaps the singer's mistake.
[3] Sung as "izna'."
[4] In A the last six syllables of each line are repeated.
[5] In B the first four syllables of each line are repeated immediately, followed by the last six syllables, which are repeated in turn.

23a[1]

Two doves flew over my house.
One lighted in the rose garden, the other at my window.
The one that lighted at my window looked at me.
The one that lighted in the rose garden picked roses.
Had I been at home, I would have caught him
And cooked *halva* for his dinner and *baklava* for his supper.
After supper I would have brewed coffee for him and
cuddled him in my lap.

23b[2]

A

Two doves flew over my house.
They flew over and flew past, but I did not see them.
Had I been at home, I would have caught them.
I would have woven them a golden cage and decorated
it with pearls.
I would have cooked *halva* for their dinner, and *baklava*
for their supper.

B

If my love wanted to get married,
And to invite me to the wedding,
I would take whatever I could:
A white talisman for his father-in-law,
A silk blouse for his mother-in-law,
And a dark kerchief for his sister-in-law.

[1] In addition to the two published texts (23a and 23b), there are fifty others in the Parry Collection. Twenty-seven of them are like No. 23a, varying only in details, whereas twenty-one of them, like No. 23b, go on to tell that her lover overheard her and married someone else. Were he to invite her to the wedding she would bring a bad-luck charm for his father-in-law, a silk waist for his mother-in-law to bring illness upon her, and so forth. Compare also our No. 13A. For another published version see Ristić, No. 14, p. 31. No. 7806 is not like the others. The girl addresses the doves and asks if they have come to woo her, to look at her, or to take her away. They reply that they have come to take her away, and she tells them that they must ask her father. But if her mother will not give her away, she will escape by the window. The use of a dove as the symbol for a suitor and a falcon or a raven for a hero is widespread. Many poems begin: "Two ravens flew from . . . to . . . . They were not two ravens, but the brothers . . ."

[2] See footnote 1 to the translation of Text 23a.

24

1. "Kupi mi, babo, volove,[1] R. 3547
Da orem dragoj dolove,[2]
2. Da sijem sitno bosilje,
Da vidim šta će iznicat!"
3. Izniče trava zelena,
U travi ruža rumena.
4. Tuda mi dragi nalazi,
Đogata konja provodi.
5. Gledam ga jadna s pendžera.[3]
6. "Dođi mi, dragi, pod pendžer!
7. Mnogo ja brinim i mislim,
8. Ja mislim, dragi, za tobom.
9. Kad ideš, dušo, svom domu, R. 3548
10. Ja mislim da ćeš poginut,
Ja mislim jadna za tobom.
11. Dođi mi, dušo, pod pendžer.
12. Sadigni prsten sa ruke,
13. Natakni, dušo, na prs moj.
14. Neka se, dušo, poznaje,
15. Da su nam srca ljubezna!"

Almasa Zvizdić, Gacko (Text 6474)
May 21, 1935

[1] In stanzas 1–4 and 10 the last three syllables of the first line are repeated, then in stanzas 1–4 the line is repeated in its original form. In stanza 10 the second line is repeated.

[2] In the second line of stanzas 1, 3, and 4 and in the repeat of the second line of stanza 10 "*vaj*" is interpolated between the fifth and the sixth syllables; "*haj*" in the second line of stanza 2.

[3] The line of stanzas 5–9 and 11–15 is repeated three times; first, the last three syllables are repeated, and the third time, "*vaj*" is interpolated between the fifth and the sixth syllables.

24[1]

1. "Daddy, buy me some oxen
To plow my beloved's pastures,
2. To sow sweet basil,
To see what will spring forth."
3. Green grass sprang up,
And in the grass a red rose.
4. Thither my beloved comes
And leads his white horse.
5. I look at him in sorrow from my window.
6. "Come to my window, beloved.
7. I am much disturbed and I ponder,
8. I ponder on you, beloved.
9. My soul, when you go to your house,
10. I think that you will die.
I think of you in sorrow.
11. Come to my window, my soul.
12. Take the ring from your finger
13. And put it upon mine, my soul.
14. Let all the world know, my soul,
15. That our hearts are given to each other."

[1] There are six other texts of this song in the collection. Of these, only one is as long; four are much shorter. They differ only in details. No. 11221 becomes a different poem after the first few lines. Roses grew where the lover plowed, and a girl came and picked one. She sent it to her beloved with a letter. He answered and told her to wait for him until he had finished his military service.

25

Vihar behar niz polje nosaše,[1] R. 3131
Na Mujove dvore nanosaše.
U dvorima niko ne bijaše,
Vet sam Mujo i Mujova ljuba.
Mujo ljubu na krilu držaše.[2]
"Vjerna ljubo, za mila ti si me![3]
Da ti imaš od srca *j*evlada,[4]
Jož bi mene ti milija bila!"
"Ču li mene, beže Alibeže!
Sebe ženi, a mene udaji!"
Progovara bego Alibeže:
"Kupi ruho što si donijela!" R. 3132
Ona ode materinu dvoru.
Prošla jedna godinica dana,
Zaprosi je bego Alibego,[5]
Zaprosi je aga Hasanaga.
Udade se Alibegovica,
I ne prođe dvi godine dana,
Rodi sina Hasanaginica,
I drugoga u drugoj godini.
Rodi trećeg u trećoj godini.
Knjigu piše Hasanaginica:
"Ču li mene, bego Alibego!
Spremiću ti đecu u pohode."
Kad je bijo vakat godinice,
Kad su bili od sedam godina,
Posla na *j*i Hasanaginica,
I odoše begu Alibegu.
Beg je njenu đecu dočekao,
Lijepijem darom darivao. R. 3133
Jednom dava čohu nederanu,
Drugom dava ate nejahate,
Trećem dava svijetlo oružje.

[1] The first four syllables in lines 1–5 are sung three times, the first time followed by "ago," the second by "bego," and the third time preceded by "*aj*."

[2] This line is repeated once more.

[3] Lines 6, 10, 12, 13, 17, and 24 are preceded by "*aj*" and repeated. In line 6 Mr. Bartók hears "Zanila" for "Za mila."

[4] Lines 7–9, 11, 14–16, 18–23, 25, 27–33, 36 are preceded by "*aj*" or "*ej*" (8, 9).

[5] Actually sung as "Alibe-aga"; a slip of the tongue due to the singer's anticipating "aga" from "Hasanaga" in the next line.

25[1]

The wind carried a blossom across the plain.
It carried it to Mujo's house.
There was no one in the house
Except Mujo and his true love.
Mujo was holding his true love on his lap.
"My true love, dear you are to me, indeed,
But if you had children,
You would be still dearer to me."
"Harken to me, Alibeg.[2]
You get married and give me away in marriage."
Alibeg answered:
"Gather together the belongings which you brought with you."
She went to her mother's house.
A year passed.
Alibeg sought her in marriage.[3]
Hasanaga sought her in marriage.
Alibeg's wife married him.
Not two years passed
Before Hasanaga's wife bore a son,
And a second in the second year.
She bore a third in the third year.
Hasanaga's wife wrote a letter:
"Harken to me, Alibeg.
I shall send the children to you for a visit."
When the time had come
And they were seven years old,
Hasanaga's wife sent them,
And they went to Alibeg.
He received her children
And gave them lovely gifts.
To one he gave strong cloth,
To another he gave unridden stallions,
To the third he gave shining weapons.

[1] There are a number of songs in the Parry Collection which begin with the same theme, but the songs themselves are not the same as this. However, under the first line title "Hasanaga na kuli sjedaše" other versions of the published song are to be found.

[2] Note that Mujo has become Alibeg.

[3] This line is in error, but it is corrected by the following line.

25 (continued)

Aj, odoše svojoj miloj majci,
Aj, ostade ago Bećirbego,
I ostade na bijeloj kuli.

Fata Krajišnik, Gacko (Text 6367)
April 24, 1935

26

Poskočiće trava potrvena.[1] R. 3560
Potrle je gatačke spahije
Igrajući ate talumeći,
Ponajviše Dervišbega doro.
Da mu[2] beže uzdu ne priteže,
Skočijo bi gradu na bedemu,
Sa bedema dragoj na prozore,
Sa prozora dragoj na đerđefe, R. 3561
A je budi, među oći ljubi:
"Ustaj, srce, granulo je sunce!"

Ćerima Kurtović, Gacko (Text 6480)
May 21, 1935

[1] Line 2 is preceded by "*Joj,*" lines 3–9 by "*Aj,*" line 10 by "*Oj.*" The last six syllables of each line are repeated, then the line is repeated, preceded by "*Joj.*"
[2] Upon repetition of the line, the singer sings "Da j' " for "Da mu."

25 (continued)

They went home to their dear mother,
And Bećirbeg[4] remained,
Remained in his white tower.

26[1]

The grass that's trodden down will spring again.
The spahis of Gacko trampled it,
When exercising their spirited steeds,
And most of all the brown horse of Dervišbeg.
Had the beg not pulled tight the reins,
He would have leapt to the city walls,
From them to his loved one's window,
From the window to his loved one's sewing table.
He woke her and kissed her between the eyes.
"Arise, my heart, the sun has risen!"

[4] Bećirbeg is obviously wrong; it should be Alibeg.
[1] Compare also Odobašić, IV, 57, and Mirković, No. 84, p. 63.

27a

1. Beg Alibeg ljubu pitijaše:[1] R. 3553
“Šta je ono, moja ljubo mila?[2]
2. Dva bumbula svu noć propjevaše,
Meni mladom zaspat ne dadoše!”
3. Al govori Alibegovica:
“Ono nisu dve ptice bumbula,
4. Ve ašici Dženetića Ume.
A kakva je Dževetića[3] Uma,
5. Da ja *j*imam brata jal bratića,
Bratu mladu isprosila bi’ je,
6. A bratiću i dovela bi’ je!”
Sad govori beže Alibeže:
7. “Imaš, ljubo,[4] mene, dušo moja.
Dovedi mi Dženetića Ume.
8. Na poklon ti mline i dućane,
I na poklon kuće *j*i timare.”
9. Prevari se, ujede je guja! R. 3554
Pripe peču, prigrnu feredžu.
10. Ona ode Uminome dvoru.
Daleko je Uma ugledala,
11. Daleko je Uma ugledala,
Još suviše pred nju istrčala.
12. Al govori Alibegovica:
“Nemam kade sjesti ni besjesti,
13. Jer sam došla da te nešto molim.
U platna sam urnek započela,
14. U platna sam urnek započela,
Pa sam došla da mi urnek kažeš.”

[1] The last six syllables of the first line of each stanza (except stanzas 11 and 14) are repeated.

[2] The second line of each stanza, except stanzas 2, 11, 14, and 20, is preceded by “*Aj*.” In stanzas 2 and 20 it is preceded by “Aman.” “Aman” is interpolated between the fourth and the fifth syllables of line 2 in stanza 1.

[3] Sung as “Dževetića” this time.

[4] Actually sung as “lubo.”

27a[1]

1. Alibeg asked his true love:
"What does this mean, my true love?
2. Two nightingales sang all night,
And they would not let me sleep."
3. Alibeg's wife said:
"Those were not two nightingales.
4. Those were the suitors of Uma Dženetić.
What a woman is Uma Dženetić!
5. Had I a brother or a nephew,
I would seek her for my brother,
6. Or bring her home for my nephew."
Now Alibeg said:
7. "You have me, my love, my soul.
Bring me Uma Dženetić.
8. I will give you my mills and stores.
I will give you my houses and stables."
9. She was deceived, the serpent stung her!
She put on her veil and threw on her cloak.
10. She went to Uma's house.
Uma saw her from afar.
11. Uma saw her from afar,
And ran out to meet her.
12. Alibeg's wife said:
"I have no time to sit and talk,
13. For I have come to ask you something.
I have begun a pattern.
14. I have begun a pattern,
And I have come for you to explain the pattern to me."

[1] This song is listed in the index to the Parry Collection under the first line title "Dva bumbula svu noć propjevaše." There are two variants, the fifteen versions in the collection being divided almost equally between them: A: Nos. 2424, 3591, 4584, 6477 (published here), 8741, 8761, 8915, 8968, 9949, B: Nos. 4485, 5616, 5978, 7099, 9206, 10159, and 11158. Variant B is best represented by No. 7099. The birds keep Alibeg awake singing of Uma Dženetić, and his wife tells him that if he knew Uma, saw her, kissed her, and slept with her, he would feel better. So he asks his wife to arrange it for one night, promising her silks and satins, pearls and ducats. She goes to Uma's house and asks her mother to let the girl go home with her to help on some embroidery. Alibeg, she says, isn't home. He has gone hunting and won't be back for three or four days. Uma goes to Alibeg's house and spends the night there. But when Alibeg's wife calls her the next morning to take her home, Uma refuses, saying that she thinks she will spend the rest of her life where she spent last night. Then Alibeg's wife weeps and curses the silks and satins, the pearls and ducats.

27a (continued)

15. A u Ume prigovora nejma.
Pripe peču, prigrnu feredžu,
16. I odoše Alibega dvoru.[5]
17. Kad je bilo vakat od đerdeka,
Ulazi joj beže Alibeže.
18. Kad u jutru jutro osvanulo,
Biser meće prema ogledalu,
19. Biser meće, dukati joj zveče. R. 3555
Starija se iznad vrata vija:
20. "Vrzi, kučko, moje ogledalo,
Meni ga je aga nabavijo!"
21. Beg Alibeg Umu svjetovaše:
"Reci, Umo, draga dušo moja:
22. 'Sinoć ga je tebi nabavijo,
Jutros ga je meni poklonijo!' "
23. Kad to čula Alibegovica,
Ona uze svilene gajtane,
24. I povede sina Abdulaha,
Pa odšeta u bostan u bašču,
25. Pa objesi sina Abdulaha,
*J*i sebe je mlada obesila.
26. Dok zavika[6] Umija đevojka:
"Alibeže, žalosna ti majka!
27. Obesi se starija kaduna,
I obesi sina Abdulaha!"
28. "Nek se veša,[7] nek je mlađa ljevša!"[5] R. 3556

Ćerima Kurtović, Gacko (Text 6477)
May 21, 1935

[5] This line is repeated after the repeat of the last six syllables.
[6] The singer sings "dok zavika," stops, and then begins the line again, from the beginning (slip).
[7] Sung as "vješa" in the second line of the stanza.

27a (continued)

15. Uma did not object.
She put on her veil and threw on her cloak,
16. And she went to Alibeg's house.
17. When it was time for the marriage bed,
Alibeg went in to her.
18. In the morning, when morning dawned,
She put her pearls by the mirror.
19. She put down her pearls and the ducats clinked.
The older one cried from behind the door:
20. "You dog, get away from my mirror!
The aga bought it for me!"
21. Alibeg said to Uma:
"Tell her, Uma, my dear soul:
22. 'He got it for you last night,
But he gave it to me this morning!' "
23. When Alibeg's wife heard this,
She took silken cords,
24. And she led out her son Abdullah,
And she went out into the garden.
25. There she hanged her son Abdullah,
And she hanged herself.
26. Then the maid Umija cried out:
"Alibeg, woe to your mother!
27. Your older wife has hanged herself,
And she has hanged her son Abdullah!"
28. "Let her hang, the younger one is more beautiful!"

27b

1. Beg Alibeg na kuli sjedaše,[1] R. 3519
Vernu ljubu na krilu držaše,
2. Pa ovako ljubi govoraše:
"Verna ljubo, vera te ubila![2]
3. Što te pitam, hoćeš li mi kazat'?"
4. "Kazat' ću ti, beže Alibeže."
5. "Kolko si se puta udavala?"
6. "Tri put sam se mlada udavala. R. 3520
7. Prvi put sam za bekrijom bila.
U bekrije nigdi ništa nejma,
8. U bekrije nigdi ništa nejma,
Samo jedna sedefli tambura.
9. Bekrija me muški milovaše.
10. Drugi put sam za pašićem bila.
U pašića pusta blaga ima,
11. Al me pašić ženski milovaše.
12. Kad me ljubi, popali mu zubi.
13. Sad za tobom, beže Alibeže, R. 3521
Za tobom sam tri sina rodila.
14. Sva tri bi' hi na telala dala,
Bekriji bi' za akšamlug dala!"
15. Udari je beže Alibeže.
Kako je on lako udarijo,
16. Svaki njojzi zub je poletijo.
17. Udari se rukom po koljenu.
Još je sebe lakše udarijo,
18. Čoha puče na četiri strane,
Telo puče sve dok ispucalo.
19. "Jadna moja i žalosna majko!
20. Šta mi reče nevjernica ljuba! R. 3522
21. Prvi danak eždrom[3] je pašem,
22. Udarim joj dževahir na grlo.
23. Sve je ljuba dobro potomila,
24. Od Boga je sramota ubila!"

Almasa Zvizdić, Gacko (Text 6461) May 20, 1935

[1] The first line of stanzas 1, 2, 4, 6–12, 15, 21, 22 and the second line of stanzas 1–7, 10–17 are preceded by "*aj*." After the fourth syllable of the second line of each stanza (except stanzas 6 and 23) "aman" is inserted. In stanzas 1, 3–7, 10–18, 22 the last six syllables of the first line are repeated; in stanza 2 the third, fourth, and seventh through tenth syllables are repeated instead.

[2] Lines 4–8, 13, 16–17, 23–24, 29–34 including the "aman" after the fourth syllable (see above), are repeated; in stanzas 6 and 23 this "aman" does not occur.

[3] Sung as "*j*eždrom" in the first line.

27b[1]

1. Alibeg was sitting in his tower
And holding his true love on his lap.
2. And thus he spoke to his love:
"My true love, may your faith destroy you!
3. Will you tell me what I ask you?"
4. "Yes, Alibeg, I'll tell you."
5. "How many times were you married?"
6. "I was married three times.
7. The first time was to a young ne'er-do-well.
He didn't have anything.
8. He didn't have anything,
Except a mother-of-pearl tambura,
9. But he made love to me like a man.
10. The second time was to the son of a pasha,
And he had all the money I wanted,
11. But he didn't make love to me like a man.
12. When he kissed me, his teeth fell out.
13. Now I'm married to you, Alibeg,
And I have borne you three sons.
14. I'd sell all three at auction
For one night with the ne'er-do-well."
15. Alibeg struck her.
He hit her so lightly,
16. That all her teeth were knocked out.
17. He struck his hand on his knee,
And he hit himself so much more lightly,
18. That the cloth was ripped on all sides
And his skin was broken.
19. "Alas, alack, woe to my mother!
20. What has my unfaithful wife said!
21. The first day, I girded her with silver
22. And I put a jewel at her throat.
23. All this my love has hidden well.
24. May heaven-sent shame destroy her!"

[1] Compare also Odobašić, IV, 21.

27c

1. Polećela dva vrana gavrana[1] R. 3116
   Od Nišića preko Kojrenića.[2]
2. To ne bila dva vrana gavrana,
   Ve' to bila dva mila jarana.[3]
3. Oni tražu mladi' đevojaka,[4]
4. Đevojaka od svoji' akrama:[5]
5. Beg Lakišić od Mostara grada,
6. Beg Ljubović iz Odžaka grada.
7. Toj pročule trebinjske đevojke. R. 3117
8. Među se se dogovaraju se:
9. "Lepa grada od Mostara grada!
10. Od Odžaka to je selo jedno!
11. I *j*ako je selo pomaleno,
12. U njemu su bezi i *j*agalar."[6]

Almasa Zvizdić, Gacko (Text 6360)
April 23, 1935

[1] The last six syllables of the first line of this and of each succeeding stanza, with the exception of stanzas 4 and 12, are repeated. In stanza 1 this line is introduced by "*aj*."

[2] "Aman" is interpolated after the fourth syllable, and then the line is repeated.

[3] "Aman" is interpolated after the fourth syllable.

[4] In this and in all succeeding stanzas except 4 and 12 the first line is repeated (after the repetition of the last six syllables, cf. note 1), with the interpolation of "aman" after the fourth syllable.

[5] This line is simply repeated with the interpolation of "aman."

[6] This line is simply repeated as it is.

27c[1]

1. Two black ravens flew
From Nikšić to Kojrenić.
2. They were not two black ravens,
But two dear comrades.
3. They were seeking young maidens,
4. Maidens of their own age.
5. They were Beg Lakišić of Mostar,
6. And Beg Ljubović of Odžak.
7. The girls of Trebinje heard of it
8. And agreed among themselves:
9. "Mostar is a fine town,
10. But compared to Odžak it is a village.
11. Yet even if it is a very little village,
12. There are begs and agas in it."

[1] Three other texts of this song in the Parry Collection diverge after line eight. Two of them (Nos. 2499 and 4528) follow closely the published version up to this point, but then they become different songs; they tell how the friends Meho and Alija seek an aga's daughter in Travnik, find and woo her. The third (No. 2900) relates the wooing of Uma Dženetića by Osman and Salih. This is another good example of the migration of themes.

27d

1. San usnila Alibegovica,[1] R. 3211
A na podne na pašinoj kuli,
2. Pa oda sna na noge skočila,[2]
3. Đe se vedro nebo prolomilo,[3]
4. Sjajan[4] mjesec pano u Neretvu,
5. Đe šarena opasala guja
Oko svega Ali paše dvora,
6. Na kapiju donijela glavu.
7. "Svekrvice, božja nesretnice,
Kakav sam ti sanak borovila,
8. Đe se vedro nebo prolomilo, R. 3212
Sjajan mjesec pano u Neretvu,
9. Sve zvijezde kraju pribjegnule."
10. "Čuješ li me, moja snaho draga,
Je, da Bog da, i Bog naredijo,
11. Taj[5] se sanak ovđe ne kolijo,
12. Već u tvome domu rođenome!"
13. "Svekrvice, božja nesretnice,
Šta su tebi moja braća kriva?
14. Je, da Bog da, *j*i Bog naredijo,
Đe se snijo, onđe se kolijo!"
15. Ali pašu u vojsku spremiše,
16. I pogibe, žalosna mu majka.

Halima Hrvo, Gacko (Text 6401)
April 26, 1935

[1] The last six syllables of the first line of each stanza except stanza 6 are repeated.

[2] In stanzas 2–4, 6, 9, 11, 12, 15, 16 the first line is repeated after the repetition of the last six syllables; cf. note 1.

[3] There is faulty repetition in this stanza; between the end of the first line and the regular repetition of the last six syllables the singer inserted by error "nebo prolomilo, vedro nebo, đe se vedro nebo prolomilo."

[4] Sung as "Zjajan" the first time.

[5] Sung as "Ta" the first time.

27d[1]

1. Alibeg's wife dreamed a dream
At noon in the pasha's house.
2. She arose from her dream.
3. She dreamed that the clear sky was rent,
4. The shining moon fell into the Neretva,
5. And a poisonous serpent encircled
Ali pasha's house
6. And rested its head over the door.
7. "Mother-in-law, unhappy one,
What a dream I have had!
8. I dreamed that the clear sky was rent,
The shining moon fell into the Neretva,
9. And all the stars fled from the sky!"
10. "Hear me, my dear daughter-in-law!
May God grant and ordain,
11. That that dream be not consummated here,
12. But in the place of your birth!"
13. "Mother-in-law, unhappy one,
Why do you dislike my brothers?
14. May God grant and ordain,
That where it was dreamed, there it shall
come to pass!"
15. They sent Ali pasha into the army,
16. And he died. Woe to his mother!

[1] There are many songs in Yugoslav folklore of dreams and their interpretations. One of the commonest dreams is that with which this song opens. Yet the only version of the published song which I have found in the Parry Collection is No. 8480 from Čelebija Krvavac, 60 years old, of Gacko. Even this version varies considerably. Hasanaga's wife dreamed that the wind blew from the sea and carried away her kerchief. In its stead it brought her a black veil. She told the dream to her mother-in-law, who said that she hoped the dream would not be consummated in that place, but that it should happen to her daughter-in-law's brothers, the Atlagići. A week later Hasanaga was killed by lightning, and his mother was left alone in his house to mourn for her son. See footnote 1 to the translation of No. 22 in this book.

27e

A

1. [1]Je li rano, je l' svanulo davno,[2] R. 2934
   Mogu l' stići kud sam naumijo?[3]
2. Pod Zagorje, pod Čengića dvore,
   Đe boluje Čengić Smajilaga?
3. Više glave dva mu svetla gore,
   Niže nogu dvi' ga ljube dvore.
4. Mlađa plače, starija se smije.[4]
5. "Što se smiješ, moja verna ljubo?
   Što se smiješ? Umrijeću sada."
6. "Umri, umri, da se udam mlada!
   Ostaće mi češalj i pomada."

B

Stanzas one to five inclusive are the
same as above.[5] R. 2935

6. "Ostaće mi češalj i pomada."
   "Češalj podaj tvojoj drugarici!
7. Češalj podaj tvojoj drugarici,
   A pomadu tvom draganu mladu!"

Zejnil Sinanović, Bihać (Text 1979)
April 1, 1935

[1] The singer begins with "*Aj*, jes sva–," realizes that this is wrong, and begins again.

[2] The first line of each stanza except B6 begins with "*a*" (A1, A5, B1, B2, B7) "*aj*" (stanzas A2, A3, A4, B3) or "*ah*" (stanzas A6, B4, B5). The last six syllables of the first line of each stanza, preceded by "*a*" (stanzas A1, A6, B2), "*aj*" (stanzas A2, A5, B4, B7), "*oj*" (stanza B1), or "*ah*" (stanzas B3, B5, B6) are repeated. In A2, A5, B1, B3 and B5 this repetition is preceded also by "aman, aman."

[3] The second line of the stanza is preceded by "*aj*" (A3, B7), or "*oj*" (B1, B3), and always has "aman" interpolated between the fourth and fifth syllables.

[4] This line is repeated, with "aman," as the second line of the stanza; "zmije" is sung the last time for "smije."

[5] However, for minor differences see the music notation and the notes to the music examples, 27e.

27e[1]

A

1. Is it early, did dawn break long ago?
Can I arrive where I want to go?
2. To Zagorje, to the castle of Čengić,
Where Smajilaga Čengić lies ill?
3. At his head two candles are burning,
And at his feet his two wives attend him.
4. The younger is weeping, and the elder is smiling.
5. "Why do you smile, my true love?
Why do you smile? I am dying now."
6. "Die, die, that I may marry while I'm young.
My comb and powder will still be mine."

B

Stanzas one to five inclusive are the
same as above.

6. "My comb and powder will still be mine."
"Give the comb to your friend,
7. Give the comb to your friend,
And the powder to your young lover!"

[1] There are 52 other texts of this song in the Parry Collection; none mentions the comb and powder of the last few lines of the published text. The commonest variant relates how the elder wife tells Smailaga that if she knew he were going to recover, she would put on mourning, but that if she knew he were going to die, she would sing and dance and make plans to marry again. Other variants disclose the reasons for the elder wife's hatred of Smailaga, and here we find themes which have migrated from other songs. In one variant she claims that he had given all her dowry and possessions to the younger wife. In another, she reveals that she had borne him eight daughters, and, when the ninth daughter was born, in disappointment and anger he killed it (see footnote 1 to the translation of No. 8b in this book). Finally, in yet another variant, sometimes linked with the preceding, his wife accuses Smailaga of sending her back to her brothers because his mother had thought she was with child at the time of their marriage. Her brothers would not take her back, so Smailaga kept her secluded in a tent in the courtyard for a year, but no child appeared. Cf. also Odobašić, IV, 24.

28a

1. U gori se zelen bajrak vija,[1] R. 1539
Pod njim leži ranjen bajraktare.
2. Na njemu se bijeli košulja,
Baš ko gruda u planini snjega.
3. Nit' ga pere majka ni sestrica,
Ni jubovca[2] skoro dovedena.
4. Kiša pere, žarko sunce suši.
Njem dolazi siv zelen sokole,
5. Pa mu nosi u kljunu vodice,
I pod krilom bijele pogače.
6. "A Boga ti, siv zelen sokole,
Kakvo sam ti dobro učinijo,
7. Pa mi nosiš u kljunu vodice,
I pod krilom bijele pogače?
8. Blago meni o' sad do vijeka,
Ka' sam takog steko prijateja,[3]
9. Da odleti mome pustu dvoru,
Je li moja u životu majka,
10. Je li mi se juba[4] preudala.
Da j' odveće, još dalje doleće!"
11. "Majka ti je svijet preminula,
Tvoje seke basamake jube.[4]
12. 'Ovud nam je Ale odhodijo!' R. 1540
Ljuba ti se mamom pomamila,
13. Prodala ti doru iz ahara
Za belilo i za bakamilo.
14. Na ljubu ti svati navalili,
Ljuba tvoja hoće da se vodi."
15. Kad se Ale u nevoji[5] nađe,
Ode Ale gorom i planinom.

[1] The first line of each stanza is preceded by the interjection "*aj*" (in stanza 6, of the duplicate recording, R 1538, "*ej*"). The last six syllables of the first line of each stanza are repeated, with the following variations: in stanzas 1 and 8 "što ću jadna" is inserted between the end of the line and the repetition of the last six syllables; in stanzas 1 and 17 "*a,a*" is added after the repetition, "*ha,a*" in stanzas 2 and 11, "*a,ha*" in stanza 8, "*e,e*" in stanza 5.

[2] Sung thus for "ljubovca."

[3] Sung thus for "prijatelja."

[4] Sung thus for "ljuba" and "ljube," respectively.

[5] Sung thus for "nevolji."

28a[1]

1. On the mountain a green banner waves.
Beneath it lies a wounded warrior.
2. His shirt is gleaming white,
Even as a ball of snow on the mountainside.
3. Neither his mother nor his sister tend him,
Nor his newly-wed bride.
4. The rain washes him; the warm sun dries him.
A light-gray falcon visits him
5. And brings him water in its beak
And white cakes under its wings.
6. "By heaven, light-gray falcon,
What kind deed did I do for you,
7. That you bring me water in your beak
And cakes under your wing?
8. Blessed am I for all time,
To have gained such a friend!
9. Let him fly to my deserted castle,
To see whether my mother is still alive,
10. Whether my true love has married another.
If he is an even better friend, he will fly still farther."
11. "Your mother has departed from this world,
And your sisters kiss the steps, saying:
12. 'This is where Ale trod when he went away',
And your true love has lost her reason.
13. She has sold your horse from the stable
For powder and rouge.
14. The wedding guests have come for your true love.
Your true love wants to be led away."
15. When Ale found himself in trouble,
He fled to the mountains.

[1] Lines 1 to 30 are a somewhat broken down version of No. 6a in this book (q.v.). Line 40 begins another song, but only the opening theme is presented. It is probably the heroic ballad of the contest between Marko Kraljević and Đerđelez Alija.

28a (continued)

16. Kad je bijo kroz Šargan planinu,
Susrete ga Vlašće momče mlado
17. Na konjćiću dorcu od mejdana.
Sitno pjeva, jasno pokuciva.
18. Njemu veli Vlašće momče mlado:
"Turče momče, ukloni se s puta!"
19. Neće mu se da ukloni s puta,
A on jami krivu ćemerliju,
20. Sasječe mu sa dva rama glavu.
Pita majka Kraljevića Marka:
21. "A Boga ti, Kraljeviću Marko,
Jesi li se ikad prepanuo?"
22. "Ciglom jednom u vijeku, majko,
Ud Kunaru Raminu bunaru."

Naza Rokić, Stolac (Text 886)
December 15, 1934

28a (continued)

16. As he was crossing Šargan plateau,
He met a young Vlah
17. Riding a brown war horse.
He was singing softly and playing loudly.
18. The young Vlah said to him:
"Young Turk, get out of my path!"
19. He would not get out of his path,
But he drew his curved saber
20. And cut his head from his shoulders.
Kraljević Marko's mother asked him:
21. "By heaven, Kraljević Marko,
Have you ever been afraid?"
22. "Only once in my life, mother,
On Kunar, at Ramin's well."

28b

1. Beg Alibeg ikindiju klanja,[1] R. 524
   Siv mu soko na ziliju pada.[2]
2. Nejma kada pridati selama,
   Već on pita siv zelen sokola:
3. "Moj sokole, sivo perje moje,
   Je li sada pod Loznicom vojska?
4. Igraju li ati *j*Atlagića,
   I paripi Šestokrilovića?
5. Pucaju li puške Baljkovića?
   Sjaji li se ćorda Ljubovića?
6. Čuje li se‿i[3] grlo Badnjevića?
   Je li sada Tuzla kapetane?
7. Viđe l' viju paše Tukulije
   Na bedenim' Beograda stojna?
8. Je l' mehana kraj Bosnića hana? R. 525
   Ima l' sada piva iz obila?
9. Je li pivo pošto j' prija bilo?
   Je li u njoj krčmarica Mara?
10. Je li u njoj krčmarica Mara?
    Je li kod i[4] Mare Imamović Ibro?"

Meho Jarić, Livno (Text 504)
Sept. 21, 1934

[1] Line 1 in each stanza is preceded by "*aj*" (stanzas 1, 2, 4, 6, 7, 8), or "*joj*" (stanzas 3, 5, 9, 10), and the last six syllables of the line are repeated, the repetition being preceded by "aman" (stanzas 1, 3, 4, 5, 6, 7, 8, 10), "*joj*" (stanza 2), and "*aj*" (stanza 9).

[2] Line 2 is preceded by "*aj*" (stanzas 3, 8, 9), "aman" (stanza 2), and "*joj*" (stanzas 1, 4, 5, 6, 7, 10), and in stanzas 1, 3, 4, 5, 7, 9, 10 "aman" is inserted after the fourth syllable.

[3] "se i," sung as two syllables. See p. 318.

[4] Insertion of "i" due to slip of the tongue on the part of the singer.

28b[1]

1. Alibeg is saying his evening prayers,
When a gray falcon lights upon his prayer-rug.
2. There is no time for formal greeting,
But he asks the light-gray falcon:
3. "Falcon mine, my gray feathered one,
Is the army at Loznica now?
4. Do the steeds of the Atlagići prance,
And the horses of the Šestokrilovići?
5. Are the rifles of the Baljkovići firing?
Does the sword of Ljubović flash?
6. Can one hear the shout of Badnjević?
Is the Captain of Tuzla there now?
7. Are the standards of Pasha Tukulija to be seen
On the ramparts of mighty Belgrade?
8. Is there still a tavern at Bosnić Inn?
Do they still draw drinks from the casks?
9. Do the drinks cost what they used to,
And is Mara the host's wife still there?
10. Is Mara the host's wife still there,
And with her Imamović Ibro?"

[1] For another version of this song see our Text No. 7. Compare also Odobašić, IV, 28; Ristić, No. 39, p. 53; Matica, Vol. V, Nos. 64–65, pp. 96–97.

28c

1. Pod Tuzlom se zeleni meraja,[1] R. 532
Na meraji prostrta[2] serdžada,
2. Na serdžadi Čelebiću Mujo.
Što na cure đumruk uzimaše,[3]
3. Svaka cura žuti dukat daje,[4]
Lepa Fata ogru ispod[5] vrata.
4. Tud se šeće Zlata Atlagića.
Vriska stade Muja Čelebića.
5. Kriska stade Zlate Atlagića:
"Nemoj, Mujo, obadva ti svjeta!
6. Nemoj, Mujo, obadva ti svjeta,
Ugrisćeš me, karaće me majka!"
7. Kako ju je slatko poljubijo, R. 533
Četiri joj dagme napravijo,
8. Dvije dagme na bijelu vratu,
A dvi' dagme na rumenom licu!

Meho Jarić, Livno (Text 508)
Sept. 21, 1934

[1] The last six syllables of the first line of each stanza are repeated.
[2] Sung as "prostarta."
[3] The second line of each stanza is preceded by "*joj*," and "aman" is inserted after the fourth syllable. (The second line of stanza 1 is preceded by "aman," and the insertion is "*joj*".)
[4] "Aman" is inserted between line one and the repetition of its last six syllables.
[5] Sung as "izpod".

28c[1]

1. The meadow was green by Tuzla,
And on it was spread a prayer-rug;
2. On the prayer-rug was Mujo Čelebić,
And he was taking forfeits from the girls.
3. Each girl gave a golden ducat,
But lovely Fata gave him her necklace.
4. Zlata Atlagić came walking by.
Mujo Čelebić cried out.
5. Zlata Atlagić screamed:
"Don't, Mujo, on your life!
6. Don't, Mujo, on your life!
You will bite me, and mother will scold."
7. How sweetly he kissed her!
He left four scars on her—
8. Two scars on her white neck
And two on her rosy cheeks.

[1] The five other texts of this song in the Parry Collection are all variants of the published text. Compare also Odobašić, IV, 84, and *Omladinka*, p. 21.

29

Pošetala cura mlada,[1] R. 3122
Sestra mila popa Luke,
Popa Luke s Orje Luke.
Sretila je dva džandara:
"Kuda ideš, curo mlada?
Koga na dom imaš, curo?"
"Imala sam devet braće.
Četiri su u tamnice,
A četiri u glavice,
A kod kuće sam pop Luka."
"Kuda ideš, curo mlada?"
"Nosim pismo u Nikšiće
Radojici Nikčeviću,
Crnogorskom odmetniku.
Kolika je Pandurica,
Naš je viši Radojica.
Viša mu je kabanica,
Vet sve brdo Pandurica."

Ćerima Kurtović, Gacko (Text 6363)
April 24, 1935

[1] Each line is repeated.

29[1]

A young maid went walking,
The dear sister of Father Luka,
Of Father Luka from Orja Luka.
Two gendarmes met her.
"Whither are you going, young maiden?
Whom have you at home, young maid?"
"I once had nine brothers;
Four are now in prison,
And four are on the mountain tops.
Father Luka is the only one at home."
"Whither are you going, young maiden?"
"I am carrying a letter to Nikšić,
To Radojica of Nikšić,
To the Montenegrin rebel.
As high as is Pandurica,
Our Radojica is taller.
His cloak is greater
Than all Mount Pandurica!"

[1] There is one other text of this song in the Parry Collection, No. 8937, from Melća Kurtović, of Gacko. It follows ours very closely.

30

Karanfil se na put sprema, ej sprema.[1] R. 3206
Karanfilka konja vada i plače.
"Karanfile, ime moje i tvoje,
S kim ti mene ludu mladu ostavljaš?"
"Ostavljam te s tvojom majkom i s mojom."
"Što će meni tvoja majka i moja,
Kad mi nema tebe bega kraj mene?
Kad ja pođem u ložnicu da spavam, R. 3207
Men' se čini ta ložnica tamnica."

Halima Hrvo, Gacko (Text 6398)
April 26, 1935

[1] The last three syllables of each line are repeated and followed by "moj dilbere moj."

30[1]

Karamfil[2] prepares for a journey.[3]
Karamfilka brings his horse and weeps.
"Oh Karamfil, by our troth,
With whom will you leave young, innocent me?"
"I shall leave you with your mother and mine."
"What are your mother and mine to me,
When I have not you, my beg, beside me?
When I go to my room to sleep,
My room seems to me a prison."

[1] This is a very well-known song. The first line is frequently "Moj se dragi na put sprema" (My beloved prepares for a journey). Of the 31 texts of this song in the Parry Collection, not including the published one, 26 are variants of the published text, all very close to it. The remaining five texts use this as a point of departure and add to the basic text a dozen or so lines to complete the story. The lover promises to return in three years, there is an exchange of letters, and in some texts the lover dies. For another version see Mirković, No. 41, p. 37.

[2] "Karamfil" means "carnation," but I have treated it as a proper name. "Karamfilka" is a feminine form of the same name.

[3] Line 1 should read "Karamfil se na put sprema i pjeva" (Karamfil prepares for a journey and sings). The repetition of "sprema" is a slip.

31a

Gorom jašu kićeni svatovi.[1] R. 3509
Gorica him s lista progovara:
"Kud idete, kićeni svatovi,
Kud idete kud konje morite?
Umrla je prošena devojka,
Na umoru majci govorila:
'Dobro, majko, svate dočekajte!
Izved'te[2] hi u gornje bojove,
Moga dragog u moju odaju!
Častite hi slatkom limunatom, R. 3510
Moga dragog grkom čemerikom!
Neka mu je grko i čemerno!
Svakom svatu po boščaluk dajte,
Mom draganu devet boščaluka!
Nek oblači na devet Bajrama!
Neka dere, neka me spomene!
Neka nosi, neka se ponosi!
I ja ću se ponositi mlada
Crnom zemljom i zelenom travom.' " R. 3511

Hajrija Šaković, Gacko (Text 6457)
May 20, 1935

[1] The last six syllables of each line are repeated, followed by the repetition of the first four syllables.
[2] Pronounced "izvette" in singing.

31a[1]

The wedding guests are riding along the mountainside,
And the leaves on the mountain speak to them:
"Whither are you going, wedding guests?
Whither are you going? Whither urge you your horses?
The bride has died.
On her deathbed she said to her mother:
'Mother, entertain the wedding guests well.
Take them to the upper rooms.
But take my beloved to my room.
Give the wedding guests sweet lemonade to drink,
But give it to my beloved bitter and unsweetened.
Let it be bitter and sorrowful for him.
Give a gold embroidered suit to each guest,
And nine to my beloved.
Let him wear them for nine Bajrams![2]
Let him rend them and think of me!
Let him wear them and be proud in them!
I too shall be proud of my covering
Of black earth and green grass.' "

[1] In addition to Nos. 31a and 31b in this book there are sixty-one other texts of this song in the Parry Collection. Sixty of these are variants of 31a. One of them, No. 2137, is much longer and fuller. When Hamdija Šaković wrote it down from seventy-year-old Hamida Tanović, he added the note: "This song is different from the others which begin with the same lines." After the usual opening, the bride directs that the horses should be let out onto the meadow and the guests seated in groups of five. But her lover should be taken to her room to see where she had died. There follows then the theme of the suits. Afterwards the bride says: "Give him the pillow embroidered with silver which I myself decorated. Let him gaze upon the branches and sing: 'O orphaned pillow, where are the hands which worked you, the sweet lips which counted the stitches, and the dark eyes which looked on?' " No. 780 from Ziba Rizvanbegović of Stolac belongs to a different version from either 31a or 31b. The gifts are not the same: a mirror for the beloved, silk waists for the bridesmaids, silk shirts for the bride's in-laws, etc. The dying bride also gives instructions for her own funeral, and breathes her last. Her mother weeps and prepares the girl for burial. No. 31b is unique from line 22 to its close. Cf. also Odobašić, II, 69.

[2] The Mohammedan feast of Bajram.

31b

Gorom jašu kićeni svatovi.[1] R. 3086
Gorica him s lista progovara:
"Kud idete, kićeni svatovi,
Kud idete i konje morite?
Umrla je mlada isprošena.[2]
Kad je bila na umoru mlada,
Svojoj majci vako govorila:
'Mila majko, kad mi svati dojdu,
Dobro moje svate dočekajte!
Sve him konje u podrume svež'te,
A svatove u gornje ahare,
Dragog moga u šikli odaju, R. 3087
Đe no mu je zlato bolovalo,
I đe no je dušu ispustila!
Svakom svatu podaj limunatu,
Mome dragom grku limunatu,
Ko[3] kad mu je grko i čemerno!
Svate ćeš mi, mati, nadariti.
Svakom svatu po boščaluk podaj,
Mome dragom dvanes boščaluka!
Nek s' opravlja dvanes godin' dana,
Nek s' opravlja, nek mene spominje!
Ako bi ga smrca prevarila, R. 3088
Kopajte mu kabur krajem moga!
Viž' glave mu ružu posadite,
Meni malu, a njemu golemu!
Ja sam žensko, pa je žalos mala,
On je junak, golema je žalos.
On je junak u majke jedinjak.
Njega majka u želju rodila,
A u njegi boljoj odgojila.
Ja sam mlada deveta u majke.
Istina je tu žalosti nema. R. 3089
Ipak će me ožaliti majka.
Dosta sam joj ja hajirli bila.
Kako me je porodila majka,
Moj je babo kulu napravijo,
A prozore srmom okovao.' "

Almasa Zvizdić, Gacko (Text 6348) April 23, 1935

[1] The last six syllables of each line are repeated, followed by the repetition of the first four syllables. [2] Mr. Bartók heard "isprosena." [3] Sung as "Jo."

31b[1]

The wedding guests are riding along the mountainside,
And the leaves on the mountain speak to them:
"Whither are you going, wedding guests?
Whither are you going? Whither urge you your horses?
The young bride has died.
When she was on her deathbed,
She spoke thus to her mother:
'Mother, dear, when my wedding guests come,
Entertain them well.
Tie their horses in the stable,
And lead the guests to the upper chambers,
But take my beloved to the richly dight room,
Where his treasure lay dying,
And where she breathed her last.
Give each guest sweet lemonade,
But give my beloved unsweetened lemonade,
As his lot is bitter and sorrowful.
You will give gifts to the wedding guests,
To each guest a gold-embroidered suit,
But twelve to my beloved.
Let him bedeck himself for twelve years,
Let him bedeck himself and think of me.
And if death should quietly overtake him,
Dig his grave next to mine.
Plant a rosebush above his head,[2]
A small one for me and a large one for him,
For I am a woman, and the sorrow is less;
But he is a hero, and the sorrow is mighty.
He is a hero and the only son of his mother.
His mother bore him with rejoicing,
And brought him up with tenderness.
But I am young and the ninth daughter of my mother.
Truly there is not such sorrow here.
Yet my mother will mourn for me,
For I have brought her much happiness.
When my mother bore me,
My father built a house
And gilded the windows with silver.' "

[1] See No. 31a.
[2] A hint of the "true-lovers knot" theme so common in English balladry.

31c

"Ej, Fatima, gromom izgojrela,[1] R. 3527
Što se primi mekije' kolača
Da hi pečeš, gromom izgojrela!
Što ćeš luga na sač nabačila,
Da te fata iz svog srca tuga!"
Kad Fatima sače podignula,
Sama sobom o tli udarila.
Ja sam došla Fatimu razgovoriti,
Kada Fata u mutvaku sjedi.
Što bi medom kolače polila?
To hi Fata suzam' natopila!

Almasa Zvizdić, Gacko (Text 6464)
May 20, 1935

[1] After the repetition of each line the first four syllables of the line are sung again, except in stanza 8.

31c[1]

"O Fatima, may the thunder strike you,
For you tried to make sweet pastry,
To bake it, may the thunder strike you!
What was the use of putting wood in the stove,
That sorrow might seize your heart!"
When Fatima took out the pan,
She threw it to the ground.
I came to talk with Fatima,
And Fatima was sitting in the kitchen.
What need to put honey on the pastry?
Fata has drowned it with her tears!

[1] While we were recording at Salih Zvizdić's house, Professor Parry asked Fatima Biberović to make us some Turkish cakes. The pastry was prepared with fond care, as his request was felt to be a great honor, a compliment to Fatima's ability as a cook. But after the cakes had been placed in the oven, Fatima became absorbed in the singing and recording, and forgot her cooking until it was too late. The cakes were burned to a crisp. Fata burst into tears of bitter humiliation. Our hostess, Almasa, deftly turned this tragic situation into an amusing incident by making up a song about it. Text number 31c is her impromptu composition. Fatima retaliated later the same day with a song of her own in Albanian, which has not yet been transcribed (No. 6467).

31d[1]

A Ružnu curu dukati udaju,[2] R. 3190
Ja sirota, mene će ljepota.
Misli neko, đe sam ja sirota,
Da se neću udat[3] za života.
Mene moja sjetovala majka:
"Dobro gledaj, u ruke se ne daj!"

B Ogrija me sunce s Rogatice.
Neka grije, meni brige nije!
Da me hoće ogrijat od Foče,
To bi meni vrlo milo bilo.

C Mijo Bože, svakom pravo nećeš.[4]

D Alaj imam oči migavice.
Kad namignem, sedmericu dignem.

E Ide lola i novi i stari. R. 3191
Starog volim, s mlađijem govorim.

F "Moj kosbaša, more li ti kosa?"
"More kosa, dok je trava rosa."
"Oj kosbaša, diže sunce rosu."

Džefa Grebović, Gacko (Text 6393)
April 26, 1935

[1] The songs of this text are called "Čobanske Pjesme" (Shepherd's Songs).

[2] The last six syllables of each line are repeated and then followed by a repetition of the first four syllables of the line, the first of these being sung twice. For example, line 1, "Dukati udaju, ru-, ružnu curu."

[3] Sung as "udad."

[4] C consists of two lines, but the second was omitted in Vujnović's transcription of the text. I also find it unintelligible.

31d[1]

A It's money that marries off a homely girl.
I am poor, and my beauty will marry me off.
Some think that since I am poor
I shall never in my life get married,
But my mother advised me:
"See to it that you don't give yourself into anyone's arms."

B The sun warms me from Rogatica.
Let it! I don't care.
Were it to warm me from Foča,
I should like it very much.

C Dear God, you are not just to all.

D By Allah, I have winking eyes!
When I wink, I make seven rise.

E The young and the old fellows are coming.
I love the older, but I talk with the younger.

F "My reaper, can your scythe cut?"
"The scythe can cut when the grass is dewy."
"O reaper, the sun will dry the dew."

[1] This text is a conglomerate of fragments, bits of traditional themes torn from context. Separately these fragments make some sort of sense, but together they do not form a unified song. In perusing the Parry Collection I have come across five texts which contain the same fragments present in 31d, though sometimes in different groupings.

1. No. 5769 from Zada Agović of Stolac begins with B (word for word the same) and adds lines 1 and 2 of A.
2. No. 2096, from Halida Dizdarević, of Gacko, also begins with the first two lines of B, and then goes on: "My mother enclosed me in glass. May the glass break and the youth kiss me! Her dear mother said to her: 'My daughter, may ill luck follow you! How will the young man kiss you? He will kiss you and then leave you!' "
3. No. 1733 from Almasa Zvizdić has two lines (the first and the last) in common with 31d and shows a connection between A and F: "The sun warms me in Rogatica. O moon, shine on Saturday evening! Let my boy walk in my sight, that I may not lose the sound of his footsteps! My beloved from Ostrvica, sharpen your scythe! The sun will dry the dew." This seems to be the same sort of conglomerate text.
4. No. 2794 from Zulka Tanović (written by Ibrahim Hrustanović) seems to be another version of a nonsense poem, or possibly a collection of proverbs and witty sayings, strung together. At any rate it shows a relationship between E and F. It begins with the first two lines of F and then continues: "Sharpen your scythe! The sun will dry the dew. O maiden of Ostrvica, send me a letter [one word obscure—A.B.L.]. The young fellows and the old have come. I like the old, but I talk with the young." And so forth for twenty-one lines more.
5. No. 3300, written by Mejra Zvizdić at Almasa Zvizdić's dictation, belongs in the same category as the preceding. It begins with the same three lines as No. 2794 and then continues: "The young fellows and the old have come. I like the old, but I talk with the younger. By Allah, I have winking eyes! When I wink, I make seven rise. O maiden of Ostrvica, send me a letter [again a word is obscure—A.B.L.]." There are twenty-nine more lines.

32

Konja kuje Meho momče mlado[1] R. 3031
Nasred polja pod jelom zelenom.
Gledala ga vila iz oblaka,
Gledala ga, pa mu govorila:
"Ne kuj konja, Meho momče mlado,
Ne kuj konja, a ne s' rosi, mlado,
Jerbo ti se Zlato preudalo."
Kad to čuo Meho momče mlado,
Pusti konja u zelenu travu,
Pa on ide svom bijelu dvoru. R. 3032
S rafa skida sedefli tamburu,
I oblači gosposko odelo,
Pa on ide Zlati pod prozore.
Tanko kuca, jasno popijeva,
I u svaku Zlatu pripijeva:
"Moje Zlato, kome si mi dato?
Moja vilo, uz kog si se knila?
Moje srebro, uz kog si mi leglo?" R. 3033
Kad to čula u odaji Zlata,
Rukama je u džam udarila,
Vas je prozor na testu[2] sasula.

Hajrija Šaković, Gacko (Text 6321)
April 22, 1935

[1] The first four syllables of each line are repeated at the end of the line, preceded by "*ej*."
[2] Sung as "testo."

32[1]

Young Meho was shoeing his horse
Under a green pine tree in the field.
A vila watched him from a cloud.
She watched him and then said to him:
"Do not shoe your horse, young Meho!
Do not shoe your horse; do not perspire from labor,
  young man,
For your Zlata has married another."
When young Meho heard that,
He let his horse go into the green field,
And he went to his white house.
From its peg he took his mother-of-pearl tambura,
And put on his best suit.
Then he went to Zlata's window.
Lightly he strummed and loudly he sang,
And ever he sang of Zlata:
"O Zlata mine, to whom are you given?
My vila, with whom have you . . .
Silver treasure mine, with whom have you lain?"
When Zlata heard that from her room,
She struck the window with her hands
And hurled it to the street.

[1] This is a song with numerous relatives, some very close and others more distant. There are sixty-five texts beside the published one under this first line title in the Parry Collection. Seventeen of these are direct variants of No. 32: thirty belong to another stock ("Mujo kuje konja po mesecu"—"Mujo is shoeing his horse in the moonlight"), which is also rich in versions and variants. The remaining eighteen are mongrels, versions, or different songs. The published text belongs to the main group of variants and is somewhat incomplete. In the fuller versions the girl jumps into Meho's arms and is carried away to his house.

33

Prelo kupi dizdaraginica.[1] R. 3019
Sav je Mostar na prelo sazvala,
Ponajpotlje sumbul udovicu.
Svake su se igre zaigrali,
Ponajpotlje vuka *j*i *j*ovaca.
Mrki vuče, mostarski dizdare,
Bela ovca, sumbul udovica.
Uhvati je mostarski dizdare,
Pod grlo je zubim' uhvatijo.
Ispod grla krvca udarila.
To začula dizdaraginica
U mutvaki pitu kuhajući.
Tevsijom je o tli udarila,
Oklagiju na dvoje slomila, 14
Pa potrče uz bijelu kulu, R. 3020
Pa povika mostarskog dizdara:
"Sram te bilo, mostarski dizdare!
Seb toga si prelo sakupijo,
Da ti ljubiš sumbul udovicu!"
Pa uhvati sumbul udovicu,
Zafrdlja je niz bijelu kulu.

Ibrahim Hrustanović, Gacko (Text 6315)
April 20, 1935

[1] Each line is preceded by "*haj*" ("*hej*" in stanza 3). The first four syllables, preceded by "*haj*" ("*hej*" in stanzas 3, 9, 11–16, 19–21, and "*ej*" in stanza 10) are repeated after each line.

33[1]

The prefect's wife gave a party.
She invited all Mostar to the party.
Last of all she invited the Widow Hyacinth.[2]
They played all kinds of games,
And in the end they played wolf and sheep.
The prefect of Mostar was the gray wolf,
And the Widow Hyacinth was the white sheep.
The prefect of Mostar caught her.
His teeth marked her throat,
And blood flowed from the wound.
The prefect's wife heard of this
As she was making pastry in the kitchen.
She threw her pan to the ground
And broke her rolling pin in two.
Then she ran upstairs
And called out to the prefect of Mostar:
"Shame upon you, prefect of Mostar!
That is why you gave this party;
That you might kiss the Widow Hyacinth!"
Then she took the Widow Hyacinth
And threw her out of the house.

[1] Of the twelve other texts of this song in the Parry Collection, only two are noteworthy here, because their endings are unusual. In No. 4721 from ninety-year-old Biba Mustajbegović the prefect gives the widow three necklaces after kissing her and takes her for his true love. Similarly, in No. 1745 from Almasa Zvizdić, the prefect quiets the widow by promises of gifts and of taking her for his true love.

[2] "Sumbul," Persian word meaning "hyacinth." Under "sumbulj-udovica" in the glossary of Matica, Vol. IV, we read "about the same as *berber-udovica*—one who is young and beautiful, but will not marry."

34[1]

1. Knjigu piše srpski knjaže, *hej*, A_1 R. 605
A na ruke Salih paši: A_3
"Salih paša, majko naša! A_4
Prodaj nama Himzibega F
2. Il za srebro, il za zlato, A_1
Il za koje hoćeš blago!" A_2
Salih paša otpisuje: A_2
"Srpski knjaže, svetla kruno! A_2
Ne mogu ga ja prodati A_2
Ni za srebro, ni za zlato, A_2
Ni za koje hoćeš blago." F
3. Divan čini Salih paša A_1
A na svoje borozane: A_2
"Borozani, deco moja! A_2
Svirajte mi Himzibega! A_2
Neka uzme dva buljuka, A_2
Dva buljuka Harnauta, F
4. A nek ide sad na Raču, A_1
Baš na Raču raz tajine!" A_2
Borozani zasviraše, A_2
Himzibega dozivaše: A_2
"Himzibeže, carski sine! A_2
Tebe zove Sali paša, A_2
Da ti uzmeš dva buljuka, A_2
Dva buljuka Harnauta, A_2
Pa da ideš sad na Raču, A_2
Baš na Raču raz tajine!" F
5. Borozani zasviraše, A_1
Himzibega dozivaše: A_2

[1] The capital letters in the column following the verses refer to the musical motifs distributed throughout the text; A_1, A_2, and so forth, are related motifs; F is the final motif.

34[1]

1. The Serbian prince wrote a letter
To the hand of Salih pasha:
"Salih pasha, our mother,
Betray to us Himzibeg,
2. For silver or for gold,
Or for any other treasure!"
Salih pasha wrote in answer:
"Serbian prince, shining crown,
I cannot betray him to you,
Neither for silver nor for gold,
Nor for any other treasure!"
3. Salih pasha gave orders
To his trumpeters:
"Trumpeters, my children,
Play and summon Himzibeg to me!
Let him take two companies,
Two companies of Albanians,
4. And let him go now to Rača,
Directly to Rača for provisions!"
The trumpeters played,
And they summoned Himzibeg:
"Himzibeg, son of the sultan,
Salih pasha calls you
To take two companies,
Two companies of Albanians,
And to go now to Rača,
Directly to Rača for provisions!"
5. The trumpeters played,
And they summoned Himzibeg:

[1] This song was a favorite of Professor Parry, and those who were fortunate enough to hear him translate it, as he did occasionally for small informal gatherings, will recall it. He never committed the translation to writing, but I have very probably been influenced by it in preparing my own. He first heard the song at the hotel in Gacko from an itinerant Gypsy band. I myself first heard it on the eventful day on which we recorded at Bare, southeast of Sarajevo, the day when King Alexander was assassinated in Marseilles. Hajdar Đozo started the song, but was unable to finish it. Mustafa Goro then took it up and sang a complete version for us. Later, by several months, when we were in a coffee house in Plevlje, another itinerant Gypsy band played it for us at my request.

Of the eighteen texts of this song in the Parry Collection, four are recorded. Three of these are published here. The fourth (No. 557, from Hajdar Đozo) is incomplete. Of the fourteen remaining texts, six are fragmentary. The three published texts are good examples of the type of variation to be found. Two songbook texts of this song loom large in its tradition: (1) Pertev (see bibliography) and (2) Odobašić, IV, 32.

	"Himzibeže, carski sine!	A_2	
	Tebe zove Sali paša,	A_2	
	Da ti uzmeš dva buljuka,	A_2	
	Dva buljuka Harnauta,	A_2	
	A da ideš sad na Raču,	A_2	
	Baš na Raču raz tajine!"	F	
6.	Himzibeg je muška glava,	A_1	
	Te okrenu svome dvoru,	A_2	
	Svome dvoru bijelome,	A_2	
	I pripasa britku sablju,	A_2	
	I uđaha kusa ata,	A_2	
	I *j*on uze dva buljuka,	A_2	
	Te povika belim grlom:	A_2	
	"Čuješ mene, Sali paša!	A_2	
	Ako mene Bog pomogne,[1]	A_2	
	Te se zdravo s Rače vratim,	A_2	
	Haj, na tebi glave nema!"	F	
7.	Kad je bijo na sred polja,	A_1	R. 607
	Na sred polja zelenoga,	A_2	
	Trefi njega stara baba,	A_2	
	I za babom mlado Srpče.	A_2	
	Stara baba progovara:	A_2	
	"Himzibeže, carski sine!	A_2	
	A ćeš ludo poginuti.	A_2	
	Izašla je silna sila,	A_2	
	Silna sila Šumadija,	A_2	
	Šumadija i Rusija,	A_2	
	I bosanska Srbadija."	F	
8.	Himzibeg je odgovara:	A_1	
	"Od' otalen, stara babo!	A_2	
	Evo tebi zlatan dukat!	A_2	
	Volim muški poginuti,	A_2	
	Neg se ženski povraćati."	F	
9.	Kad je bila prva klasa,	A_1	
	Prva klasa Lajkovića,	A_2	
	Tu je beže udarijo,	A_2	
	I tu beže sretan bijo,	A_2	
	Pa ni rane ne dobijo.	F	
10.	Kad je bila druga klasa,	A_1	
	Druga klasa Brankovića,	A_2	
	I tu beže udarijo,	A_2	
	I tu beže sretan bijo,	A_2	
	Pa ni rane ne dobijo.	F	

[1] Sung as "pomoge."

34 (continued)

"Himzibeg, son of the sultan,
Salih pasha calls you
To take two companies,
Two companies of Albanians,
And to go now to Rača,
Directly to Rača for provisions!"
6. Himzibeg is a manly hero,
And he returned to his castle,
To his white castle,
And girded on his sharp sword,
And he mounted his clipped-tail horse,
And he took two companies
And cried out from his white throat:
"Listen to me, Salih pasha!
If God aid me,
And I return safely from Rača,
Then you will be headless!"
7. When he was in the middle of the plain,
In the middle of the green plain,
An old grandmother met him,
And behind the grandmother a young Serb.
The old grandmother said:
"Himzibeg, son of the sultan,
You will perish foolishly.
A mighty force has been assembled,
A mighty force from Šumadija,
From Šumadija and Russia,
And from Bosnian Serbia."
8. Himzibeg replied:
"Go away, old grandmother!
Here is a golden ducat for you.
I would rather die like a man,
Than turn back like a woman."
9. When he came to the first pass,
The first, the pass of the Lajkovići,
There the beg attacked,
And the beg was fortunate there
And received no wound.
10. When he came to the second pass,
The second, the pass of the Brankovići,
There, too, the beg attacked,
And there, too, the beg was fortunate
And received no wound.

34 (continued)

11. Kad je bila treća klasa, A_1
Na eškiju udarijo, A_2
Sedam topa osvojijo, A_2
A osmi ga udarijo. F
12. Ranjen beže progovara: A_1
"Ibrahime, dragi brate! A_2
Evo tebi kusa ata, A_2
Pa ga prati Bajnoj Luci, A_2
Bajnoj Luci staroj majci! A_2
Neka gleda kusa ata, A_2
A viš' nikad Himzibega!" F
13. Opet beže progovara: A_1
"Ibrahime, dragi brate! A_2
Evo tebi zlatna sablja, A_2
Pa je prati Bajnoj Luci, A_2
Mome bratu Muharemu! A_2
Nek on gleda zlatnu sablju, A_2
A viš' nikad Himzibega!" F
14. Opet beže progovara: A_1 R. 608
"Ibrahime, dragi brate! A_2
Evo tebi zlatan sahat, A_2
Pa ga prati do Stambola, A_2
Mome bratu Fehimagi! A_2
Nek on gleda zlatan sahat, A_2
A viš' nikad Himzibega!" F^2

Ibrahim Mašinović, Kulen Vakuf (Text 521)
Sept. 24, 1934

34 (continued)

11. When he came to the third pass,
He attacked the enemy,
And seized seven cannon,
But the eighth struck him.
12. Wounded, the beg spoke:
"Ibrahim, dear brother,
Here is my clipped-tail horse.
Take him to Banja Luka,
To Banja Luka to my old mother.
Let her look upon my clipped-tail horse,
But never again upon Himzibeg!"
13. Then again the beg spoke:
"Ibrahim, dear brother,
Here is my golden sword.
Take it to Banja Luka,
To my brother Muharem!
Let him look upon my golden sword,
But never again upon Himzibeg!"
14. Again the beg spoke:
"Ibrahim, dear brother,
Here is my golden watch.
Take it to Stambol,
To my brother Fehimaga.
Let him look upon my golden watch,
But never again upon Himzibeg!"

35

1. Knjigu piše knjaz Milane, A R. 855
Knjaz Milane, kopiljane*j*, F_1
Na koljeno Salih paši: B
"Salih pašo, majko našo! F_1
Daj nam, prodaj Himzibega, B
Jal' za srebro, jal' za zlato, F_1
Jal' za žute madžarije!" F_1
2. Njemu piše Salih paša, B
Na koljeno knjaz Milanu: F_1
3. "Knjaz Milane, srpski care! B
Ne mogu ti Himza dati. F_1
4. Himzibeg je muška glava. B
Za Himza nam i car znade*j*, F_1
I carevi svi veziri. F_1
5. Već ti skupi silnu vojsku, B
Silnu vojsku i *j*ordiju, F_1
6. Svu Srbiju i Rusiju, B
I bosansku Njemadiju, F_1
7. Pa ti hajde na bogaze, B
Na bogaze ravnoj Rači! F_1
8. Ja ću Himza opremiti. B
Neka Himzo erzag prima!" F_1
9. Car nazove borozana: B
"Borozane, z Bogom brate! F_1
10. Hajde, skupljaj tri buljuka, B
Tri buljuka sve momaka, F_1
11. Jedan buljuk Arnauta, B
Drugi buljuk Bosanaca, F_1
Treći buljuk Albaneza, F_1
12. Pa ti hajde na bogaze, B
Na bogaze ravnoj Rači!" F_1
13. Tako Himzo učinijo, B
Pa otalen pokrenuo. F_1
14. Na po puta kad je bijo, B
Sreti njega stara baba, F_1
I sa babom mlado Srpče. F_2 R. 856
15. "Himzibeže, carev sine! B
Da si soko, ne bi prošo. F_2

35[1]

1. Prince Milan wrote a letter,
Prince Milan, the misbegotten,
To Salih pasha.
"Salih pasha, our mother,
Betray to us Himzibeg,
Either for silver or for gold
Or for golden imperial ducats!"
2. Salih pasha wrote to him,
To prince Milan:
3. "Prince Milan, Serbian emperor,
I cannot betray Himzi to you.
4. Himzibeg is a manly hero.
Even our sultan knows about Himzi,
And all the sultan's vezirs.
5. But gather a mighty army,
A mighty army, a powerful host,
6. All Serbia and Russia,
And Bosnian Germany,
7. And go to the pass,
To the pass at level Rača.
8. I shall send Himzi.
Let Himzi take the provisions!"
9. The emperor called his trumpeter.
"Trumpeter, brother in God,
10. Hasten, gather three companies,
Three companies of young men—
11. One company of Arnauts,
A second company of Bosnians,
And a third company of Albanians.
12. Then hasten to the pass,
To the pass at level Rača."
13. This Himzi did,
And departed from that place.
14. When he was at the midpoint of his journey,
An old grandmother met him,
And with the grandmother, a young Serb.
15. "Himzibeg, son of the sultan,
Even if you were a falcon, you could not escape.

[1] See No. 34 and footnote 1 to the translation.

35 (continued)

16.	Na Rači je silna vojska,	B	
	Silna vojska i *j*ordija.	F_1	
17.	Izišla je sva Srbija,	B	
	Sva Srbija i Rusija,	F_1	
	I bosanska Njemadija."	F_1	
18.	Himzo babi dukat dade.	B	
	"Maj to tebi, stara baba!	F_3	
	Pa ti hajde svome dvoru,	F_4	
	A ja odo' kud sam pošo."	F_5	
19.	Na prvi je bogaz bijo,	B	
	Prvi bogaz knjaz Milana.	F_1	
20.	Na njeg puče sto topova.	B	
	Sve je Himzo osvojijo,	F_1	
21.	I u vodu potopijo.	B	
	Nigdi rane ne dobijo,	F_1	
22.	Ni na sebi, ni na atu,	B	
	Ni na svoja tri buljuka.	F_1	
23.	Na drugi je bogaz bijo,	B	
	Drugi bogaz Smiljanića.	F_4	
24.	Tude puče sto topova.	B	
	I taj bogaz prolomijo,	F_5	
	Topove im potopijo,	F_4	
25.	Nigdi rane ne dobijo,	B	
	Ni na sebi, ni na atu,	F_4	
	Ni na svoja tri buljuka.	F_4	
26.	Na treći je bogaz bijo,	B	
	Treći bogaz Vukovića.	F_4	
27.	Na njeg puče osam topov'.	B	
	Sedam hi je osvojijo,	F_5	
	Osmi Himza pogodijo.	F_6	
28.	Pade Himzo z belog ata,	B	R. 857
	Pa doziva svoga brata:	F_4	
29.	"Borozane, z Bogom brate!	B	
	Ufati mi belog ata,	F_1	
30.	Pa povedi Banjoj Luci,	B	
	Banjoj Luci mojoj majci!	F_1	
31.	Neka hrani belog ata!	B	
	Nek spominje Himzibega!"	F_1	
32.	Opet Himzo povikuje,	B	
	Borozana dovikuje:	F_1	
33.	"Borozane, z Bogom brate!	B	
	Otpaši mi zlatnu sablju,	F_1	

35 (continued)

16. A mighty army is at Rača,
A mighty army, a powerful force.
17. All Serbia has assembled,
All Serbia and Russia,
And Bosnian Germany."
18. Himzi gave the grandmother a ducat.
"Here, this is for you, old grandmother.
Get you home!
I shall go whither I set forth."
19. He attacked the first pass,
The first, the pass of prince Milan.
20. There a hundred cannon roared.
Himzi seized them all
21. And sank them in the water.
Nowhere did he receive a wound,
22. Neither himself, nor his horse,
Nor his three companies.
23. He attacked the second pass,
The second, the pass of Smiljanić.
24. There a hundred cannon roared,
And he destroyed that pass
And sank their cannon.
25. Nowhere did he receive a wound,
Neither himself, nor his horse,
Nor his three companies.
26. He attacked the third pass,
The third, the pass of Vuković.
27. There eight cannon roared.
He seized seven of them;
The eighth struck Himzi down.
28. Himzi fell from his white horse
And called his brother:
29. "Trumpeter, brother in God,
Take my white stallion
30. And lead him to Banja Luka,
To Banja Luka to my mother.
31. Let her feed my white stallion!
Let her remember Himzibeg!"
32. Again Himzi cried out,
And called the trumpeter:
33. "Trumpeter, brother in God,
Unfasten my golden sword

35 (continued)

34.	Pa ponesi mome bratu!	B
	Neka *j*ima zlatnu sablju!	F_3
	Nek spominje Himzibega!"	F_1
35.	Ranjen Himzo povikuje,	B
	Pobratima dovikuje:	F_1
36.	"Borozane, mijo brate!	B
	Otpaš'der mi zlatan ćemer,	F_1
37.	Pa ponesi mojoj ljubi!	B
	Neka troši madžarije,	F_3
	Nek spominje Himzibega!"	F_1
38.	To je Himzo izustijo,	B
	Pa je dušu ispustijo.	F_1

Mustafa Goro, Bare (Text 559)
Oct. 10, 1934

35 (continued)

34. And take it to my brother.
Let him have my golden sword!
Let him remember Himzibeg!"
35. Wounded, Himzi cried out
And called his blood brother:
36. "Trumpeter, dear brother,
Unfasten my golden purse
37. And take it to my love.
Let her spend my imperial ducats!
Let her remember Himzibeg!"
38. This Himzi uttered,
And gave up his spirit.

36

1.	Knjigu piše srpski knjaže,	A_1	R. 519
	Aj, na ruke Salih paši:	A_2	
	"Salih pašo, lala naša!	A_1	
	Daj nam, prodaj Himzibega	A_3	
	Jal' za srebro, il' za zlato,	A_1	
	Jal' za koje pusto blago,	A_2	
	Oj, il' za pare, *aman*, carevine!"[1]	B_1F	
2.	*Oj*, otpisuje Salih paša:	A_1	
	"Srpski knjaže, zlatna kruno!	A_2	
	Ne mogu ti Himze prodat',	A_1	
	Ni za srebro, ni za zlato,	A_3	
	Ni za koje pusto blago,	A_1	
	Jer za Himzu i car znade,	A_3	
	I sve lale i veziri,	A_1	
	Da je Himzo, *aman*, muška glava!"	B_2F	
3.	*Aj*, divan čini Salih paša,	A_1	
	Ah, na svoje borozane:	A_2	
	"Borozani, djeco moja!	A_1	
	Zasvirajte, zapivajte,[2]	A_3	
	Himzibega, *aman*, dozivajte!"	B_2F	
4.	*Aj*, borozani zasviraše,	A_1	
	Himzibega zavikaše:	A_2	
	"Hajde, Himzo, carski sine!	C	
	Tebe zove, *aman*, Salih paša."	B_3F	
5.	*Aj*, a kad čuo Himzibeže,	A_1	
	On opasa oštru sablju,	A_2	
	A pojaha belog ata,	D_1	
	Koji valja hiljadu dukata,[3]	A_1	
	Pa *j*eto ga Salih paši.	A_2	
	Kada dojde Salih paši,	B_2	
	A veli mu Salih paša:	A_1	
	"Himzibeže, carski sine!	A_3	
	Hajde, *j*uzmi dva buljuka,	A_1	
	Dva buljuka, sve Bošnjaka,	A_3	
	I četiri Arnauta!	A_1	
	Hajde, beže, baš na Raču,	A_2	
	Jer na Rači, *aman*, rata ima!"	B_2F	R. 520

[1] Lines 7, 15, 20, 24, 37, 45, 52, 64, 75, 91 are repeated with the omission of the italicized words; "il' " is changed to "jal' " in line 7.

[2] Ikavski dialect for "zapjevajte." Note also "Di," l. 40; "osić', " l. 52; "srite," l. 55.

[3] Dekasyllabic line. The third word sung as "hiljada."

36[1]

1. The Serbian prince wrote a letter
To the hand of Salih pasha:
"Salih pasha, your Highness,
Betray to us Himzibeg,
Either for silver, or for gold,
Or for any untold treasure,
Or for the coin of the realm."
2. Salih pasha wrote in answer:
"Serbian prince, golden crown,
I cannot betray Himzi to you
Neither for silver, nor for gold,
Nor for any untold treasure,
Because even the sultan knows,
And all the nobles and vezirs,
That Himzi is a manly hero."
3. Then Salih pasha gave orders
To his trumpeters:
"Trumpeters, my children,
Play, sound your trumpets!
Summon Himzibeg!"
4. And the trumpeters blew
And summoned Himzibeg:
"Hasten, Himzi, son of the sultan!
Salih pasha calls you."
5. When Himzibeg heard this,
He girded on his sharp sword
And mounted his white horse,
Which was worth a hundred ducats.
Then he went to Salih pasha.
When he came to Salih pasha,
Salih pasha said to him:
"Himzibeg, son of the sultan,
Go, take two companies,
Two companies, all Bosnians,
And four of Albanians!
Go, beg, directly to Rača,
Because there is a battle at Rača!"

[1] See No. 34 and footnote 1 to the translation.

6.	*Aj*, a veli mu Himzibeže:	A_1	
	"Salih pašo, murtatine!	A_2	
	Di ću ići ja na Raču,	A_3	
	Aj, na Raču ratovati,	A_1	
	Kad je Rača napujnjena	A_2	
	Sa Srbijom Šumadijom,	A_3	
	Silnom vojskom svom Rusijom,	A_1	
	I bosanskom, *aman*, svom eskijom."	B_2F	
7.	*Aj*, a veli mu Salih paša:	A_1	
	"Himzibeže, carski sine!	A_2	
	Ja što reko', ne poreko'!"	A_3	
	A veli mu Himzibeže:	A_2	
	"Dobro, dobro, Salih pašo!	A_1	
	Ako li se-i[4] ja živ vratim,	A_2	
	Ja ću tebi, *aman*, osić' glavu!"	B_2F	
8.	*Aj*, ode Himzo niz tirnjake.	A_1	
	Kad je na sred polja bijo,	A_2	
	Srite njega stara baka,	A_3	
	Stara baka Srbijanka.	A_1	
	Ona nosi mlado Srpče.	A_2	
	Ona veli Himzibegu:	D_2	
	"Vrat' se, sine, Himzibeže,	A_4	
	Jer ćeš ludo poginuti!	D_2	
	Izašla je sva Srbija,	A_1	
	Sva Srbija Šumadija,	A_2	
	Silna vojska sva Rusija,	A_1	
	I bosanska, *aman*, sva eskija!"	B_2C	
9.	*Aj*, a veli joj Himzibeže:	A_1	
	"Ajd' otalen, stara bako,	A_2	
	Stara bako, Srbijanko!	D_2	
	Evo tebi žuti dukat,	A_4	
	Pa ti hrani mlado Srpče!	D_2	
	Ja se neću povratiti,	A_2	
	Cara hizlah učiniti.	A_3	
	Nisam žensko da se krijem,	D_1	
	Vet sam muško da se bijem.	A_2	
	Volim muški poginuti,	C	
	Vet se ženski, *aman*, povratiti!"	B_2F	R. 521
10.	*Aj*, ode Himzo nis to polje.	A_1	
	Kad je klancu prvom bijo,	A_2	
	Na njeg beže udarijo.	A_3	
	Tude Himzo sretan bijo,	A_3	

[4]"se i," sung as one syllable.

36 (continued)

6. Then Himzibeg said to him:
"Salih pasha, traitor!
Why should I go to Rača,
To fight at Rača,
Since Rača is filled
With the men of Serbia and Šumadija,
The mighty army of all the Russias
And all the soldiery of Bosnia?"
7. Then Salih pasha said to him:
"Himzibeg, son of the sultan,
What I have said, I shall not change."
And Himzibeg said to him:
"All right, all right, Salih pasha!
If I return alive,
I shall cut off your head."
8. Himzi went through the thorn bushes.
When he was in the middle of the plain,
An old grandmother met him,
An old Serbian grandmother.
She carried a young Serb.
She said to Himzibeg:
"Turn back, my son, Himzibeg,
For you will perish foolishly!
All of Serbia has assembled,
All Serbia and Šumadija,
The mighty army of all the Russias,
And all the soldiery of Bosnia."
9. Himzibeg said to her:
"Go away, old grandmother,
Old Serbian grandmother!
Here is a yellow ducat for you!
Find food for your young Serb.
I shall not turn back
And be a traitor to the sultan.
I am not a woman to hide myself,
But I am a man to fight.
I should rather die like a man,
Than turn back like a woman."
10. Himzi went on across the plain.
When he came to the first pass,
The beg attacked it.
There Himzi was fortunate;

Bijel klanac osvojijo. A_1
Tude rane ne dobijo. A_3
I na drugi udarijo, A_2
I tu Himzo sretno projde, A_3
Bijel klanac osvojijo. A_1
Kad je trećem klancu bijo, D_1
Tude vojska Lajkovića Đoke.[5] A_3
Na eskiju udarijo, D_1
Sve ćuprije oborijo, A_2
Na Drinu *j*i nagonijo, A_2
Sedam topa osvojijo, D_1
A osmi ga, *aman*, pogodijo! B_2F
11. Ranjen beže s ata pada, A_1
I dozivje svoga brata: A_2
"Slatki brate, Ibrahime! D_1
Ufati mi đogu moga! A_2
Pošalji ga Bajnoj Luci, A_3
A na ruke našoj majci! A_1
Neka majka đogu gleda, D_1
Himzibega nek ne gleda!" A_3
*J*opet bežĕ progovara: D_1
"Ibrahime, slatki brate! A_2
Otpaši mi oštru sablju, D_1
Pa je pošlji Carigradu, A_3
A na ruke bratu mome, D_1
Bratu mome Fehimagi! A_3
Neka bratac sablju gleda, D_2
Himzibega nek ne gleda!" A_1
Opet beže progovara: D_1
"Ibrahime, slatki brate! A_2
Skini meni almas prsten, A_4
Almas prsten s desne ruke! D_1
Pošalji ga Dojnoj Tuzli, A_2
A na ruke mojoj ljubi! A_3
Nek se ljuba preudaje! D_2
A ja sam se oženijo, A_1
S crnom zemljom sastavijo." A_2
To izusti Himzibeže, D_2
To izusti, *aman*, dušu pusti. B_2

Meho Jarić, Livno (Text 502)
Sept. 21, 1934

[5] Another dekasyllabic line.

36 (continued)

He seized the white pass.
There he received no wound.
And he attacked the second,
And there Himzi passed unharmed,
And seized the white pass.
When he came to the third pass,
There was the army of Đok Lajković.
He attacked the army,
Destroyed all the bridges,
Drove the men to the Drina,
And seized seven cannon,
But the eighth struck him down.
11. Wounded, the beg fell from his horse,
And called his brother:
"Sweet brother, Ibrahim,
Take my white horse!
Send him to Banja Luka,
To the hand of our mother!
Let mother look upon my horse!
Let her not look for Himzibeg!"
Then, again, the beg spoke:
"Ibrahim, sweet brother,
Unfasten my sharp sword
And send it to Carigrad,
To the hand of my brother,
To my brother Fehimaga!
Let my brother look upon the sword!
Let him not look for Himzibeg!"
And again the beg spoke:
"Ibrahim, sweet brother,
Take from me my diamond ring,
The diamond ring from my right hand!
Send it to Donja Tuzla,
To the hand of my true love!
Let my true love marry again,
For I have wed
And united with the black earth!"
This Himzibeg uttered,
This he uttered, and gave up his spirit.

37

1. Odbi, odbi, lađo, od kraja![1] R. 3562
Sad se dragi z dragom pozdravlja.
2. Stade, stade lađa kretati,
Stade moja mala plakati.
3. "Nemoj, nemoj, mala, plakati!
Opet će se lađa vraćati,
4. Opet će se lađa vraćati.
Mi ćemo se dvoje sastati."
5. "Ostala mi žuta marama,
Đe sam sinoć, dragi, stajala.
6. Svu noć me je majka karala:
'Đe je, šćeri, žuta marama?'
7. Daj mi, dragi, žutu maramu,
Da ne pravi majka galamu!"
8. "Ne dam tebi žute marame.
Neka pravi majka galame!"

Ibrahim Hrustanović and Hajrija Šaković
Gacko (Text 6481), May 21, 1935

[1] The last three syllables of each line are repeated at the end of the line; every two lines, together with the repeated last three syllables, are repeated.

37[1]

1. "O ship, leave these shores!
Now two lovers say farewell.
2. The ship begins to turn,
And my little one begins to weep.
3. No, no, little one, weep not!
For the ship will return,
4. The ship will return,
And we two shall meet again."
5. "I left my yellow kerchief lying,
Where I stood last night, beloved,
6. And all night my mother scolded:
'Where, my daughter, is your yellow kerchief?'
7. Give me my yellow kerchief, beloved,
That my mother may be quiet."
8. "I shall not give you your yellow kerchief.
Let your mother say what she will."

[1] There is also a shortened version of this song, which is found in ten of the sixteen other texts of it in the Parry Collection. The short version stops after line 8 of the published text. Between lines 8 and 9 some of the variants insert lines such as:

I u medna usta ljubiti, I bijelo grlo grliti, Za lijepo zdravlje pitati. (No. 6294)	And kiss your honey-sweet lips, And embrace your white throat, And inquire tenderly of your health.

or:

Što na mome srcu i tvome, Ti ne kazuj, draga, nikome. Kad nas dvoje mlado nestane, Nek nam lijep spomen ostane! (No. 8024)	What is in your heart and mine, Tell to no one, my dear. And when we two are gone, May a beautiful memory remain!

38

Čiji je, čiji je, ono tonobil[1] R. 3566
Crvenom, crvenom, farbom nafarban,
Što vozi, što vozi, braću Gačane
Od Gacka, od Gacka, pa do Mostara?
Auto karaca Toma Relovca.
U njemu, u njemu, šofer Milica.

Ibrahim Hrustanović, Gacko (Text 6484)
May 21, 1935

39a

1. "O Almasa, dušo rajska, krasan pogled tvoj! R. 3157
Sve zbog tebe ja izgubi' mlađan život svoj."[2]
2. To izreče mlad vezire, ode brez glasa;
Mrtva glava progovara: "Z Bogom, Almasa!"
3. "A da znadeš, mlad vezire, što ja sada znam,
Ti bi dao po Bagdata i Misir i Šam.
4. Kaži pravo, mlad vezire, amana ti tvog,
Ko ti dade zlatne ključi od harema mog?"
5. "Dala[3] mi hi seja tvoja, i poljubca dva,
A do zore kolko bješe, ni sam ne znam ja!"

Almasa Zvizdić, Gacko (Text 6378)
April 24, 1935

[1] Each line is repeated.
[2] Note the rhymes.
[3] Sung as "jola"—a slip of the tongue.

38[1]

Whose is that automobile,
Painted red,
Which carries our Gacko brothers
From Gacko to Mostar?
The auto is Toma Relovac's.
In it is chauffeur Milica.

39a[2]

1. "O Almasa, heavenly soul, beautiful is thy glance!
All for thy sake did I forfeit my young life."
2. Thus spoke the young vezir, then his voice was whisked away.
But his severed head made answer: "Farewell, Almasa!"
3. "If you knew, my young vezir, what I too know now,
You would give half of Bagdad, and all Egypt and Syria.
4. Tell me truly, my young vezir, on your solemn oath,
Who gave to you the golden keys to my harem door?"
5. "'Twas your sister gave them to me, with two little kisses,
And how many more 'til dawn came, I myself don't know."

[1] This bit of wit is an original song of Gacko life composed on the model of the song "Čija je ono đevojka, Što rano rani na vodu?" (Whose is that maiden, Who rises so early to fetch water?). Toma Relovac and his brother had come to America years ago and worked in the Middle West. Toma married an American wife, and after having accumulated a small fortune, he and his brother returned to Gacko with their families. Among other projects which they undertook was the purchase of one or more automobiles and the inauguration of automobile service from Gacko to Mostar. The Milica who is referred to in the poem as the chauffeur is Toma's wife.

[2] See also No. 42 in this book. These two are typical of all the other texts of the poem in the Parry Collection. Nos. 999, 5695, and 11670 belong to the 39a version; and Nos. 4026, 7036, and 8712 (all beginning with the same first line as 39a) together with Nos. 1607, 3656, 4418, 5509, 5893, 7427, 7523, 8268, 8412, 9717, 10916, 11020 (all beginning with the same first line as 42) belong to the 42 version. Some of these texts are very good, while others are corrupt and defective. This song, with its fixed stanzaic form and its rhymes is dependent upon songbook texts. Although it has passed into tradition, it has not been completely assimilated.

39b

U bašči mi sumbul cvati, al ga ne berem;[1] R. 2938
Pod sumbulom slavul peva, al ga ne slušam;
Na prozoru luče sjedi, al ga ne gledam.
Pred kućom ti bunar voda, ladna, ledena,
U bunaru morna riba, mlada, debela.
I bunar je voda ladna, al je ne pijem;
U njemu je morna riba, al je ne bijem.

Zejnil Sinanović, Bihać (Text 1981a)
April 13, 1935

40

Sve ptičice propjevale, jedna ne pjeva.[2] R. 3075
"Da je šćela moja majka, da joj ja pjevam,
Ne bi mene staru dala, da joj jadujem,
Ved[3] bi mene mladu dala, da joj carujem.
Kad ja pođem u al bašču, star mi ne dade:
'Vrn' se, Fato, vrn' se, zlato, viđeće te mlad!'
Nek me vidi, nek ne vodi, staru ne trebam!" R. 3076

Halima Hrvo, Gacko (Text 6342)
April 22, 1935

[1] Each line is repeated.
[2] Each line is repeated. The very first line, the first time, is preceded by "*Həj*," most of the other lines by "*ə*."
[3] Sung thus for "Vet."

39b[1]

In my garden a hyacinth grows, but I do not pluck it.
Beneath the hyacinth a nightingale sings, but I do not listen.
At the window my doll sits, but I do not look at it.
In front of the house is a well of water, cold as ice.
In the well is a big fish, fat and young.
In the well is cold water, but I do not drink it.
In it is a big fish, but I do not catch it.

40[2]

All the little birds began to sing, but one sang not.
"If my mother had wished me to sing,
She would not have given me to an old man, that I should always be sad.
But she would have given me to a young man, that I might live like a queen.
When I would go to the bright garden, the old man will not let me.
'Come back, Fata! Come back, my treasure! Some young man will see you.'
Let him see me and let him take me away! I am no use to an old man."

[1] The four other texts (6106, 7611, 3755, 5942) in the Parry Collection which begin with this same first line vary in detail, but not in spirit, from the published text, and make an important addition. "In my garden a spring flows, but I do not drink from it. Beside the spring is a rose bush, but I do not pick the roses. On the rose bush is a nightingale, but I do not listen to it. My beloved is not here to listen to it. He has gone marching off far, far away!" (No. 6106) Nos. 3755 and 5942 go on from this point into what is essentially a floating theme: "I write him a short letter: 'Come back, beloved!' and he answers sadly: 'I shall not return for three years. I have a loved one beside me who is more beautiful than you.' But I answer him still more sadly: 'I have a better lover than you with me. Whatever roses I pick I give to him!' " For another version see Mirković, No. 159, p. 104.

[2] After the first line the three other texts of this song in the Parry Collection add "Pitala je jaranica; 'Što ti ne pjevaš?' " ("Her friend asked her: 'Why do you not sing?' "). No. 5279 is slightly longer than the published text and lacks the garden episode. In its stead are two similar themes: "When I go to the window the old man won't let me." and, "I have a fine satin dress, but I do not wear it. When I want to put it on, the old man will not let me. 'Stop, stop, you she-devil! A young man will see you and take you away, because I am old!" Nos. 2469 and 3851 add eleven lines to the published text. The burden of these additional lines is that while the old man is preparing for bed, his young wife puts a pillow in her place in the bed, and after the old man has gone to sleep, she runs away. When he awakes, he kisses the pillow.

41

"Trepetljika trepetala puna bisera,[1] R. 3077
Ovi naši beli dvori puni veselja."
"Kakvo vam je to veselje, što se veselje?"
"Ovo[2] majka sina ženi, pa se veseli.
Svak se tome veseljaše, majka najviše.
Veselje joj sretno bilo, amin da Bog da!
U dvoru joj sretna snaša, amin da Bog da!
Svekra baba poslužila verno i ljepo,
A svekrvi podranila, kahvu ispekla, R. 3078
Z đeverim' se milovala, zaovam' vezla!"

Almasa Zvizdić, Gacko (Text 6343)
April 22, 1935

[1] Each line is repeated, with "*aj*" prefixed.
[2] Mr. Bartók hears "ova," which is feasible too.

41[1]

"The poplar is quivering full of pearls.
Our white houses are full of joy."
"What is the cause of your rejoicing?"
"A mother is marrying off her son, and there is celebration.
Everyone was joyful, his mother most of all.
May happiness and good fortune be hers, with God's blessing!
May her daughter-in-law be happy in her new home, with God's blessing!
May she serve her father-in-law well and loyally!
May she rise early and brew coffee for her mother-in-law!
May she love her brothers-in-law, and knit with her sisters-in-law!"

[1] Most of the eleven other texts of this song in the Parry Collection are shorter than the published text, rarely going beyond line 6. The protagonists in them, however, vary considerably: in four texts it is the mother who marries off her son; in one, the father. In two texts the father is marrying off his son, and in one the father marries off his son, and the mother, her daughter. Two of the texts add a new element to the basic six-line song. No. 8247a (the other is No. 8446) is the better of the two. "A golden thread came from heaven and encircled my son's fez and his bride's veil. It was not a golden thread, but it was good fortune sent by a loving God." A note by Nikola Vujnović in the journal states that "this is the first song at the beginning of a wedding."

42[1]

A

1. Kraj potoka bistra voda, šuma zelena, R. 529
Nevesela-*i*[2] zabrinjena sjedi devojka.[3]
2. Potok teče i protiče, vrelo žubori,
A devojka zamišljena kroz plač govori:
3. "Povrati se, mili strančе, strančе mlađani,
Da na tvoj'ma grud'ma umrem, grud'ma vatrenim!"

B

1. Na prestolu[4] sultan sjedi, Abdulah Džemil,
A do njega mlad vezire, Abdul Alidah.
2. "O Boga ti, mlad vezire, amana ti tvog,
Ko ti dade zlatne ključe od harema mog?"
3. "Dala mi je tvoja seja, i poljubca dva, R. 530
A do zore što bijaše, ni sam ne znam ja!"
4. "Šuti, more, mlad vezire, našao te jad,
Jer će dželat tvoju glavu odrizati sad."
5. "Još da znadeš, moj sultane, šta no noćas bi,
Trista glava da imadem, halal bijeli!"
6. To izusti mlad vezire, osta bez glasa.
Mrtva glava-*i*[2] progovara: "Z Bogom, Abasa!"
7. "Oj, Abaso, dušo rajska, mil mi miris tvoj,
Milija mi duša[5] tvoja, neg sav život moj!"

Meho Jarić, Livno (Text 506)
September 21, 1934

[1] Compare text 39a in this book. The rhymes seem to indicate an art poem.
[2] Pronounced as one syllable; the repeat has no "i."
[3] The second line of each stanza is repeated.
[4] Sung as "prestolju."
[5] In the repeat, changed to "miris."

42[1]

A 1. Beside the crystal waters of a brook, in the greenwood,
Sits a young maiden, forlorn and troubled.
2. The brook flows on, the spring babbles,
And deep in thought the maiden speaks through her tears.
3. "Come back to me, dear stranger, young wanderer mine,
That I may pass away in your arms, in your passionate embrace!"

B 1. On his throne the sultan sits, Abdullah Džemil,
And beside him stands the young vezir, Abdul Alidah.
2. "I pray you, young vezir, on your solemn oath,
Who gave to you the golden keys of my harem door?"
3. "'Twas your sister gave them to me, with two little kisses,
And what happened 'til the dawn came, I myself don't know."
4. "Silence, pray, my young vezir, misfortune be thine!
For now the executioner will sever your head from your shoulders."
5. "Were you to know, O sultan mine, what else took place last night,
Had I three hundred heads to give, they would be given gladly!"
6. Thus spoke the young vezir, and his voice was whisked away.
But his severed head made answer: "Farewell, Abasa!
7. O Abasa, heavenly soul, dear to me is thy fragrance!
Dearer far is thy soul[2] to me than even life itself!"

[1] Compare No. 39a. Although parts A and B of this text seem to be two separate songs, they are always found (in the Parry Collection texts, at any rate) as one song. It would appear that the folk singers consider them one song, perhaps drawn to that conclusion by the fact that they are sung to the same melody. This has undoubtedly accounted for the inclusion of more than one song in a single rendition in other instances also. Part B of this text is better narrative than text number 39a, because the story emerges more clearly. For A compare also Odobašić, II, 95, and for B, *ibid.*, II, 11.

[2] In the repeat, "fragrance."

43

"Ljepše cveče u proljeće, vet na Jurjev dan[1] R. 3174
Svi se momci oženiše, a ja osta' sam.
I ja ću se o jeseni, ako budem zdrav.
Konu imam sprema dvoru, ja je dobro znam.
Prevodim je o jeseni, majka mi ne da.
'Nemoj, majko, nemoj, jatko, umret ću ti ja!' "
Pa pristupi staroj majci, stade moliti.
Sažali se stara majka, da joj ne umre,
Pa dozvoli milu sinu, da je dovede. R. 3175
Skoro joj je prsten dao, da je dovede,
Al' se momak razbolijo, nije je doveo.

Almasa Zvizdić, Gacko (Text 6388)
April 26, 1935

[1] Each line is repeated.

43[1]

"The flowers are more beautiful in the spring, and on St. George's day
All the young men married, and I remained alone.
I myself shall marry in the fall, if I am well.
There's a girl living nearby whom I know well.
I would marry her in the fall, but my mother would not let me.
'Please, mother, please, or I shall die!'
Then he went to his old mother, and began to beseech her.
His old mother felt sorry for him, and didn't want him to die.
Finally she allowed her dear son to marry.
He had just given her the ring to take her in marriage,
When the young man fell ill, and he never married her.

[1] The four other texts of this song in the Parry Collection follow the published text as far as line eight. To this base three of the texts add "I gave her a golden ring, so that it might be known that she is mine. She gave me an embroidered handkerchief and two kisses" (Nos. 1293, 3059, and 10870). The other text (No. 2143) adds to this "I would take the girl now, but my mother will not let me. Be quiet, mother, be quiet, or I shall kill myself!"

44a

Zaplakala stara majka Džaferbegova:[1] R. 3034
"Džaferbeže, ludo dete, šta mi dovede?
Dovede mi ludo mlado, neće da radi,
Vet se beli i bakami, da ašikuje."
Naljuti se Džaferbeže, ode na čardak.
Na namazu verna ljuba selam predaje.
"Deder, ljubo, deder, dušo, selam predaji!" R. 3035
Sablja zveknu, ljuba jeknu, čedo proplaka.
Pa ga uze Džaferbeže na bele ruke,
Pa ga nosi staroj majci u donje boje.
"Da viš, majko, da viš, jatko, ove grehote!"

Hajrija Šaković, Gacko (Text 6322)
April 22, 1935

44b

Zaplakala stara majka Džaferbegova:[2] R. 2936
"Džaferbeže, ludo deto,[3] što nam dovede?
Dovede nam ludu mladu, ludu od tebe.
Moja[4] ljuba, tvoja[5] snaha,[6] neće da sluša."
On se fati silne sablje sa čiviluka.[7]

Zejnil Sinanović, Bihać (Text 1980)
April 13, 1935

[1] Each line is repeated; most lines are preceded by an "ə."
[2] Each line, except line 5, is repeated (recording breaks off).
[3] In the repeat sung as "det'."
[4] Error; in the repeat changed to "tvoja."
[5] Error; in the repeat changed to "moja."
[6] Sung as "snah'."
[7] Incomplete; see No. 44a in this book.

44a[1]

The old mother of Džaferbeg began to weep:
"Džaferbeg, my foolish child, what have you brought me?
You have brought me a foolish young thing who will not work.
Instead she powders and paints and thinks of love-making."
Then Džaferbeg was angry, and he went up to his room.
His true love was on her knees at prayer.
"Yes, pray, my love, pray, my soul's desire!"
His sword whirred, his love screamed, and the newborn child cried out.
Then Džaferbeg took it in his white arms,
And he carried it downstairs to his old mother.
"See, mother, see, unhappy one, what a sinful thing has been done!"

44b[2]

The old mother of Džaferbeg began to weep.
"Džaferbeg, my foolish child, what have you brought us?
You have brought us a foolish young thing, more foolish than you.
Your wife, my daughter-in-law, will not heed me."
He took his mighty sword from its peg.

[1] This is a very well-known song. There are 45 other texts of it in the Parry Collection. Of these two are defective, and fourteen are the same as the published text, but the remainder exhibit considerable variety. Two of the texts (Nos. 1136 and 754) begin the song differently. Džaferbeg asks his mother for the hand of Adem Kada. His mother refuses, but he marries the girl anyway. Then the song as published begins. In several texts (e.g., Nos. 3036, 9061, 9133) after the mother's complaint, that her new daughter-in-law will not work, she tells Džaferbeg that his wife is in their chamber kissing his brother Mehmedbeg. The wife overhears this and tells Mehmedbeg about it: "And God knows, and you and I, that it is not true!" At this point Džaferbeg comes home from the market, takes off his boots, and asks his mother where his wife is. She tells him that she is in the chamber with his brother. Then be hecomes angry, and the story continues along the usual lines. Three texts (Nos. 5156, 8021a, 9323) show Džaferbeg confronting his wife with the accusation that she is carrying on with his brother. In spite of her denial, he draws his sword and kills her. Nos. 4204 and 10151 give as the reason why the mother does not like her daughter-in-law the fact that she has no children. A number of texts add to the published version the statement by Džaferbeg's mother that she was "only joking." In others, the mother, after news that he has slain his wife, says she will get another one for him, but he, in deep remorse, says that he will not take her. Seven of the texts have him slaying his mother because she started all the trouble. In No. 8766 Džaferbeg shoots himself, and in Nos. 1136 and 4431 he leaves home to wander sadly throughout the world. For other versions see Odobašić, IV, 86, and Mirković, No. 36, p. 32.

[2] This text is unfinished. For a discussion of the story see footnote 1 to the translation of No. 44a.

45

Niti spavam, niti dremam, niti sna imam,[1] R. 3541
Vet to vazdan na[2] tužna, što suze proljevam.
Kako koja tica leti, ja je oplačem,
Kako koji putnik najde, ja ga upitam:
"Oj, putniče, namjerniče, viđe l' mi dragog?" R. 3542
"Sve da sam ga ja vidijo, ne znam koje je!"
"Lasno ga je poznavati, dobar je junak:
Crna oka, plava brka, staza[3] visoka!"

Hajrija Saković, Gacko (Text 6470)
May 20, 1935

[1] Each line is repeated.
[2] Sic; "a" for "na" in the repeat. See notes on the music examples, for No. 45.
[3] Sung thus for "stasa."

45[1]

I sleep not, I doze not, nor do I dream,
But all day I am sad and shed tears.
At every bird that flies by, I weep,
And from every traveler who happens by, I ask:
"Oh traveler, oh wanderer, have you seen my loved one?"
"If I had seen him, how would I know him?"
"It's easy to know him, for he's a great hero:
His eyes are black, his beard is dark, and he is wondrous tall."

[1] There is only one of the twenty-five other texts of this song in the Parry Collection which deserves special mention. All the others are pretty close to the published text. However, No. 10809 from forty-eight year old Đula Tanović of Gacko is unique. In answer to the girl's question, the wanderer says he knows her beloved. They were together in the tavern last night. When he went out into the street to see his girl, he found her with someone else. Then the girl says that he swore that he would always be true to her and would never love another the rest of his life. Four texts (Nos. 2092, 2566, 7942, 12254) begin with the same line as 45, but are different songs. They are versions of No. 39b in this book. For another version see Mirković, No. 40, p. 36.

46

Zaprosijo[1] Zajim Osmanaga[2] R. 3192
A u Livnu lijepu Eminu.
Često beže alkatmere sprema,
Oku zlata i dve oke svile.
Brzo mu se dari povraćali,
Al mu majci dara ne bijaše.
Ljuto kune Zajimova majka:
"Nit' mi došla, ni suđena bila,
Nit' po mome dvoru pohodila!"
Za to čuo Zajim Osmanaga.
"Šuti, majko, dugo jadna bila! R. 3193
Ja da što sam kulu napravijo,
Da dovedem ljepoticu Emu!"
Razbolje se Zajim Osmanaga.
Bolovao devet godin dana.
Sve ga čeka u Livnu Emina.
Knjigu piše iz Livna Emina:

[1] The first four syllables of every line are repeated.
[2] Every line (except 6 and 27) is repeated, with the repetition in Note 1.

46[1]

Zajim Osmanaga sought in marriage
Beautiful Emina in Livno.
He sent many red carnations,
A bushel of gold, and two bushels of silk.
He promptly received gifts in return,
But there were no gifts for his mother.
Zajim's mother cursed bitterly:
"May she never come, nor be destined for us!
May she never walk beneath my roof!"
Zajim Osmanaga heard that.
"Quiet, mother, may misfortune befall you!
Why else have I built a house,
Except to bring beautiful Ema into it?"
Zajim Osmanaga fell ill.
He was ill for nine years.
Emina waited for him in Livno.
Emina wrote a letter from Livno:

[1] This is a fairly good representative text of the common version of this song, of which there are seventeen good texts and fourteen defective, fragmentary, and short texts in the Parry Collection. It could, however, be somewhat fuller in certain places. *a*) After line 26 some texts give more details of the wedding. There is an exchange of letters with wedding instructions, the gathering of the wedding guests, their entertainment at the bride's house, and their departure are fully described. *b*) After line 31 Ema sometimes explains to the chief of the wedding guests that she wants to see Zajim to return to him the gifts which he had given her and to receive his blessing. *c*) Line 33 and following would be clearer if the first part of this theme had not been omitted. Ema goes into the house, and sits at the head of Zajim's bed. She weeps, and one of the tears falls on Zajim's cheek and rouses him. He thinks that his house is leaking. *d*) In many texts, after line 43, Zajim tells Ema to keep the gifts, and then from beneath the bed he brings out a golden apple as a parting gift. *e*) After line 45, Zajim requests his mother or a servant to raise him a little that he may see the wedding guests. They do so, and he dies. Then the band strikes up so that Ema may not hear the wailing, but she does. *f*) Finally, a number of the texts add that the two lovers were buried together and that a well was built on the spot. One text even says that their hands were left above ground and that a golden apple was put into their hands for them to play with.

No. 11640 is an elaboration of a short text of the common version. In it the mother tries to dissuade Zajim from marrying Ema, because she has neglected to send her gifts. Zajim is sure that she will bring fine gifts for her when he brings her home as his wife, but his mother shakes her head and says that she has heard that Ema sings a song about him: "My beloved, when you go into the army, you must not pass my house without coming in. Come to the courtyard gate, open it, and wave your handkerchief. Confusion to all our enemies!" This will be recognized as a floating theme. Compare lines 5–7 of No. 48 in this book.

Finally, No. 12039 is unique. It follows the common version through line 24. Ema then goes to visit Zajim. Follows the theme of the dropping tear and the leaking house. When Zajim sees Ema, he starts to rise and asks her why she has not married. She says that she is waiting for him. He embraces her and recovers his health.

46 (continued)

"Zajimaga, iza gore sunce!
Il ćeš umret, il ćeš preboljeti?
A da znadem, da ćeš preboljeti,
Čekala bi još devet godina."
A on njojzi tužno odgovara:
"Udaji se, ljepotice Emo, R. 3194
Udaji se, ne uzdaj se u me!
Boljeg sam ti mušteriju našo.
Evo tebi Hasan Osmanaga!"
Kad su bili poljem zelenijem,
Kad primaše Zajimovu dvoru,
Progovara ljepotica Ema:
"Stan'te malo, kićeni svatovi,
Da ja vidim Zajim Osmanagu!"
Kad je došla Zajimovu dvoru,
Progovara Zajim Osmanaga:
"Kula moja, kad si prokapala, R. 3195
Nijesam te davno popravljao,
Kad sam stijo veselje praviti
I dovesti ljepoticu Emu."
Progovara ljepotica Ema:
"Nije tvoja kula prokapala,
Vet je došla iz Livna Emina.
Što no imam ruha bijeloga,
Sve je tvoje, i zlato i svila.
Jal da platim, jal da mi halališ?"
"Fala tebi, ljepotice Emo!"
Ode Ema kićenim svatovim'.
Kad su bili poljem zelenijem, R. 3196
Zamlatiše bande i borije.
Odma se je Ema ovizala.
Pade Ema u zelenu travu.

Hajrija Šaković, Gacko (Text 6394)
April 26, 1935

46 (continued)

"Zajimaga, shining sun over the mountain-tops,
Are you going to die or will you get well?
If I were sure that you would get well,
I would wait another nine years."
But he answered in sorrow:
"Get married, lovely Ema,
Get married, do not wait for me.
I have found you a better suitor,
Even Hasan Osmanaga."
When they were on the green plain,
When they neared Zajim's house,
Beautiful Ema said:
"Wait a moment, wedding guests,
While I see Zajim Osmanaga."
When she arrived at Zajim's house,
Zajim Osmanaga said:
"My house, why do you leak?
It is not long since I repaired you,
When I wanted to hold a feast,
And to bring beautiful Ema."
Beautiful Ema said:
"Your house is not leaking,
But Emina has come from Livno.
Whatever possessions I have,
Are all yours, both gold and silk.
Shall I give them back or will you give me your blessing?"
"Many thanks, beautiful Ema."
Ema went with the wedding guests.
When they were on the green plain,
The bands and trumpets were muffled.
As soon as Ema heard this,
She fell to the green grass.

47

"Oj, Omere[1] Beograđanine,[2] R. 3170
Ustaj, more, Beograd izgojre!"
"Neka gori i kako mu drago!
Nije meni sve do Beograda,
Vet je meni do moije jada.
Sinoć mene oženila majka,
A jutros mi pobjegla devojka
Sa jastuka i sa beli ruka.
Oj, Hasane, na Savi vozare,
Jesi l' koga jutros prevozijo?" R. 3171
"Jesam jednu garavu devojku."
"O ja, O ja, garavušo moja!
Umrijet' ću, preboljet' te neću.
Kolko ti je vozarine dala?"
"Nešto malo, hiljadu dukata."
"Kolko si je poljubijo puta?"
"Trista puta u sedam minuta."

Almasa Zvizdić, Gacko (Text 6385)
April 24, 1935

[1] The first four syllables of each line are repeated.
[2] Every line is repeated, with the repetition in note 1.

47[1]

"O Omer of Belgrade,
Arise, my friend, Belgrade is in flames!"
"Let it burn, if it likes!
I care not for Belgrade.
I have my own troubles.
Last night my mother married me off,
And this morning my bride ran away
From my pillow and from my white arms.
O, Hasan, boatman of the Sava,
Have you ferried anyone across this morning?"
"Yes, a little nut-brown girl."
"Yes, O yes, my little nut-brown one!
I shall die. I shall never get well.
How much did she give you for the ferrying?"
"A little something, a thousand ducats!"
"How many times did you kiss her?"
"Three hundred times in seven minutes."

[1] There are twenty-two other texts of this song in the Parry Collection. Seven of them are defective. The remaining fifteen texts all belong to the common version. Some of them tell that the girl stole various things when she ran away—money, a watch, a horse, rings, and so forth. And the ferryman is usually asked three questions: 1) Did you ferry her across? 2) How much did she pay you? 3) How many times did she kiss you? In the songs in which the girl steals three bags of gold, the ferryman says that she gave him one bag for the fare, one for having kissed her, and one as a bribe that he should tell no one about it. Some texts hint that the girl has run away with someone else to be married, as there is a mention made of wedding guests who accompany her. For other versions see Odobašić, IV, 73, and Vuk, Vol. V, No. 371, p. 246.

48

Tri livode,[1] niđe lada nema,[2] R. 3568
Samo jedna ruža kalem bela.
Tu je ružu kalemijo Hilme,
Kalemijo kad je momak bijo.
"Čuješ, Hilme, ka' u vojsku pođeš,
Nemoj moju avliju da projdeš,
Vego meni na pozdrav da dojdeš!"
Sinoć mi je dolazijo Hilme,
Donijo mi tri kutije fine,
Kad u jednoj šećer čikolada, R. 3569
A u drugoj slatka marmulada,
Kad u trećoj puder i pomada.
Puder podaj mojoj jaranici,
A pomadu mojoj dušmanici!

Hajrija Šaković, Gacko (Text 6486)
May 21, 1935

[1] Sung thus for "livade."
[2] The first four syllables of each line are repeated. Then the whole line is repeated, with the refrain "slatko lane" added after the fourth syllable instead of the repeat of syllables 1–4.

48[1]

Three meadows and no shade
Except a single white rose bush!
Hilme planted the rose.
He planted the rose when he was a young man.
"Listen, Hilme, when you go into the army,
Don't pass my yard
Without coming in to greet me."
Last night Hilme came to me.
He brought me three fine boxes.
There was sweet chocolate in one,
Marmalade in the second,
And powder and rouge in the third.
Give the powder to my girl friend[2]
And the rouge to my enemy!

[1] There are twenty-five texts of this song in the Parry Collection. Ours is the most common variant (15 texts): it is distinguished from the others by the theme of the three boxes. For another published version see Odobašić, II, 23.

[2] Cf. No. 27e B, ll. 11–13.

49

Kraj Sarajva jedna bašča zelena,[1] R. 3505
U toj bašči jedno vrelo provrelo,
Kraj tog vrela jedna ploča mermera,
Na toj ploči ostajrela maštrafa,
U maštrafi tri cvijeta procvala.
Da mi daju tri cvijeta s te bašče,
Jedno šeboj, i karanfil, i ružica rumena,
Ni ću šeboj, ni karanfil, vet ružicu rumenu.
Da mi daju tri đevojke ljubiti, R. 3506
Jedno Emu, i Fatimu, i Hajriju devojku,
Ni ću Eme, ni Fatime, vet Hajriju devojku!

Hajrija Šaković and Almasa Zvizdić
Gacko (Text 6455), May 20, 1935

[1] The first four syllables of lines 1–6, 9 are repeated, and the whole line, including repetitions, is again repeated. In lines 7, 8, 10–11 the line is simply repeated.

49[1]

By Sarajevo there's a green garden,
In that garden there's a well of cold water,
By the well, a marble stone,
On the stone, an aged vase,
In the vase three flowers bloomed.
Were you to give me the three flowers from that garden,
A wallflower, a carnation, a red rose,
I'd not take the wallflower, nor the carnation, but the red rose.
Were you to give me three girls to kiss,
Ema, Fatima, and Hajrija,
I'd not take Ema, nor Fatima, but Hajrija!

[1] Although there are forty-three other texts of this song in the Parry Collection, most of the variations are unimportant, or at least not striking. Three texts add: "Fatima is like the golden moon when it rises; Emuša is the morning star beside the moon; but Habiba is the rising sun!" Hamdija Šaković has written down from Emina Šaković two texts which differ somewhat one from the other, but which are real variants of this song (Nos. 2324 and 2002). They begin with the usual opening (to line 5 of the published text), and then go on: Three girls came to the spring. A young man arrived on a horse, and greeted them. One of the girls received his greeting in silence, and he thought she was dumb. He said to her: "I do not want you, nor Emina, but I do want Bisera!" Compare also footnote 1 to the translation of No. 51.

50

1. "Šta je uzrok, moj dragane, R. 3234
Što me mladu ne voliš?[1]
2. Il' ti nisam čusta staza,[2]
Il' gosposka plemena?
3. Il' da mlada majke nemam,
Te sam jadna sirotna?
4. Ja sirota majke nejmam,
Tajnu ljubav otkrivam.
5. Ćela sam ti venac plesti
Od rumeni ružica,
6. A sada ću ti ga oples'
Od grkoga pelina.
7. U kafezu bumbul pjeva,
Ja ga mlada ne slušam,
8. Jer zbog toga, moj dragane,
Što me mladu ne voliš.
9. U avli mi bunar voda,
Ja je mlada ne pijem,
10. Sve uzroci, moj dragane,
Što me mladu ne voliš.
11. Ja ću svoju majku kleti,
Na žau mi je,
12. Ja ću svoju majku kleti,
Na žau mi je,
Što me dala nedragome,
Koga nisam volila,
13. Što me dala za nedraga,
Koga nisam volila."

Almasa Zvizdić, Gacko (Text 6412)
April 27, 1935

[1] Lines 1–2 are repeated in stanza 1.
[2] All the following stanzas, except stanza 12, are sung to the second half of the melody.

50[1]

1. "What is the reason, my beloved,
That you do not love me?
2. Am I not the right height?
Is my family not good enough?
3. Or is it because I have no mother,
And am a poor orphan?
4. I am poor, I have no mother,
I disclose a secret love.
5. I wanted to plait a wreath for you
Of red roses,
6. But now I shall weave one for you
Of bitter wormwood.
7. In my room a nightingale sings,
But I hear it not;
8. All for this my dear beloved,
That you love me not.
9. In the yard's a well with water,
But I drink it not;
10. This the reason, my beloved,
That you love me not.
11. I shall curse my own dear mother,
Ah, how sad am I.
12. I shall curse my own dear mother,
Ah, how sad am I,
That she gave me away to someone,
Whom I did not love,
13. That she gave me away to someone,
Whom I did not love."

[1] Almasa has included in this song many floating themes. The number of variations in the eight other texts in the Parry Collection indicates that the song is unstable and has no really fixed form. The first four lines are fairly constant, but from there on divergence is great. As in the published text, lines and themes which are familiar from other songs in this book appear. For example, lines 13–18 remind one of Nos. 39b and 45.

51

Kad ja pođem na Bimbašu na vodu,[1] R. 3487
I povedem belo janje za sobom,
Sve devojke s prozora me gledaju.
Na vratima moja draga bijaše.
Sve devojke jaglucima mahaju,
Moja draga sa belijem rukama. R. 3488
"Pričekaj me, da ja idem sa vama!
Belo ćemo ludo janje gojiti!"

Almasa Zvizdić, Gacko (Text 6449)
May 20, 1935

52

Vino pili age Sarajlije[2] R. 3523
Na Ilidži, pokraj Željeznice.
Služila i Sarajka devojka.[3]
Kako kome čaše dodavaše,
Svaki joj se lica prihvaćaše,
Omer hodža za grlo bijelo.
Progovara Sarajka djevojka:
"Ako morem biti svakom sluga,
Ja ne morem biti verna ljuba, R. 3524
Osim jednom, agi Hasanagi:
Hasanagi i sluga i ljuba."

Hajrija Šaković, Gacko (Text 6462)
May 20, 1935

[1] After the first four syllables, "aman" is added; then the four syllables are repeated, this time with the addition of "đanum" (from Turkish "canĭm," equivalent of "dušo moja"). Finally the last seven syllables are sung, and the whole stanza, including "aman" and "đanum" and repetitions, is repeated.

[2] Between syllables four and five "nane" is interpolated and then these six syllables are repeated before the line is completed. Each line is then repeated with this interpolation and repetition.

[3] Sung as "djevojka" in the repeat.

51[1]

When I go to the river Bimbaša,
I lead a white lamb with me,
And all the girls watch me from their windows.
My beloved was at the door.
All the girls wave their kerchiefs.
My beloved waves her white arms.
"Wait for me, and I shall go with you
And we'll tend the little white lamb."

52[2]

The agas of Sarajevo were drinking wine
In Ilidža beside the Željeznica.
A maid of Sarajevo served them.
As she gave to each his glass,
Each touched her on the cheek,
But Omer, the Hodža, on her white throat.
The maid of Sarajevo said:
"Although I can be a servant to each of you,
I cannot be true love to anyone,
Except to Hasanaga alone.
To Hasanaga I am servant and beloved."

[1] This text is not truly representative of the song as found elsewhere. The story of the majority of the texts is that the lover is leading a lamb and sadly seeking a glimpse of his beloved. Three girls stand in a doorway, but his beloved is at the iron-grilled window. This is the basic song. The seven other texts in the Parry Collection show some variations. No. 2188 does not mention the beloved, but brings in a floating theme familiar from our No. 49. "Three girls were at the door. They had a mother-of-pearl cup in their hands, in which were three flowers. Would that God would grant that I smell the three flowers!" Two texts (2511 and 4534a) omit lines 3–6 entirely. The maiden calls to the boy and tells him to go away from the well. No. 2687 is different. The girl is pictured weeping at the window. The boy greets her and asks why she is crying, and she tells him that she is going to marry someone else in a faraway land. They say a fond farewell. Finally No. 3691, after describing the girl at the window waving her kerchief, tells that the boy catches the kerchief and goes to fetch his tambura. He sings a song to her, and she breaks the window and jumps into his arms. They run home to his mother. A version of this song can be found in the Sonart Album M-6 entitled *Southern Slav Song Gems*, sung by Mme Zinka Milanov, and issued by the Sonart Record Corporation of New York under the direction of Dr. Lujo Goranin. Compare also *Omladinka*, p. 107.

[2] This is a good representative text of the common version of this song; it is comparatively stable and very popular. There are twenty-three other texts of it in the Parry Collection. Compare also Odobašić, II, 42, *ibid.*, IV, 80, and Matica, Vol. V, No. 53, p. 73.

53

1. "Grana od bora cvala kraj mora;[1] R. 3512
Ej, joj, Marice, divna krčmarice,
Dođi, sjedi kraj mene!
2. Grana od jele cvala kraj mene;
Ej, joj, Marice, i srce i dušo,
Sjedi[2] kraj mene!"
3. "Kami ću ti doć' sjesti kraj tebe,
Ej, jer mehana kraj Morića hana?
Ne mogu ti doć'!
4. Pala je rosa, ne mogu bosa,
Ej, pala tama, ja ne mogu sama,
Šta ću nevoljna?"
5. "Sazuj nalune, obuj sandale!
Ej, d' ak' i meni jaki Bog pomogne,
Kupit' ću ti cipele. R. 3513[3]
6. Jagluk ću ti dat', duvak uzeti,
Ej, ako Bog da, svom bijelu dvoru
Tebe[4] odvesti!"

Almasa Zvizdić, Gacko (Text 6458)
May 20, 1935

[1] The first line of each stanza is repeated, and lines two and three are repeated together (except in stanza 1).
[2] In the repeat, changed to "Dođi, sjedi."
[3] This record is poor; the music cannot be transcribed.
[4] In the repeat, changed to "Brže."

53[1]

1. "A fir branch blossomed beside the sea.
O, Marica, lovely wife of the tavern keeper,
Come and sit beside me!
2. A pine branch bloomed beside me.
O, Marica, my heart, my soul,
Come and sit beside me!"
3. "How can I come to sit beside you?
The tavern is by the inn in Morić,
And I cannot come.
4. The dew has fallen, and I can't come barefoot.
A mist has fallen. I can't come alone.
Ah me, what shall I do?"
5. "Put on your clogs, put on your sandals,
And if Almighty God helps me,
I'll buy you shoes.
6. I'll send you a kerchief to make a veil,
And with God's help, to my own white house
I'll carry you."

[1] Nos. 6459 and 1736 in the Parry Collection, also from Almasa Zvizdić, are the only other texts of this song which I have found in the Collection. The songs which begin with the line "Grana javora cvala kraj mora" are entirely different from the published text and are not even remotely related.

54

Ono ondi što—*gi—ga—no* R. 3224
Što no moje dragi—*ga—no*
Što no ondi sje—*gi—ge*—li
Što no u me gle—*gi—ge*—li
Što no meni ve—*gi—ge*—li
"Ti l' moja draga,
Nagigaj mi[1] se,
Navigaj—*gaj* mi,
Da malo sjedem,
Da malo ležem,
Da malo, dušo, počinem!"[2]

Halima Hrvo, Gacko (Text 6407)
April 27, 1935

[1] Sung as "me."
[2] This line is repeated.

54[1]

It is there
That my beloved
Sits
And looks at me,
And he says to me:
"My beloved,
Grant to me,
O, grant to me,
That I sit with you a while,
That I lie down a while,
That I rest a while, my soul!"

[1] I know of no other texts of this song either in the Parry Collection or elsewhere. Like the first text in this book, this too is somewhat difficult to translate.

Works Cited in Part Two

Bartók, Béla, *Turkish Folk Music from Asia Minor,* ed. by Benjamin Suchoff, Princeton University Press, 1976.

Clapier, Génina, *La Serbie Légendaire.* Paris, 1918.

Karadžić, Vuk Stefanović, *Srpske Narodne Pjesme,* Beograd, 1932 and 1935. Vols. I, V.

Matica Hrvatska, *Hrvatske Narodne Pjesme,* Vol. V (*Ženske Pjesme*), ed. by Dr. Nikola Andrić, Zagreb, 1909.

Mirković, P., *Srpske Narodne Pjesme iz Bosne,* Pančevo, 1886.

Odobašić, Salih, *Velika Nova Narodna Pjesmarica* (Zagreb, n.d.), Vols. II-IV.

Omladinka, Nove i Najpopularnije Ljubavne i Narodne Pjesme. Chicago, Palandech's Publishing House, n.d.

Pertev, *Junačka Smrt Hivzi-bega Džumišića, Boj pod Banja Lukom, i Junaštvo Duralagić Meha.* Sarajevo, 1927.

Ristić, Kosta H. *Srpske Narodne Pjesme.* Beograd, 1873.

Stanoyevich, B. Stevenson, *An Anthology of Jugoslav Poetry.* Boston, 1920.

Vitezica, Vinko, *Antologija Narodne Poezije.* Beograd, 1937.

Appendix One

WITHHELD PARRY TRANSCRIPTIONS

In his enumeration of types of source materials contained in the Parry Collection (pp. lxiii, 21, above) Bartók mentions "approximately 205 Serbo-Croatian so-called 'women's songs' . . . and 16 instrumental pieces" and, in a marginal note, 30 songs sung by an old woman whose unreliable intonation necessitated their exclusion from the study. The following concordance of record–melody designations of the transcriptions published on pp. 95–230, above, is given as a supplementary index.

Record No.	*Melody No.*	*Record No.*	*Melody No.*
519–21	36	3074	5
524–25	28b.	3075	40
526–28	20	3077–78	41
529–30	42	3079–80	12c.
532–33	28c.	3081–82	23a.
553–54	1	3086–89	31b.
606–08	34	3109–12	11
609	7	3116–17	27c.
855–57	35	3121	22
1538–40	28a.	3122	29
1547	13	3123–24	17
2934–35	27e.	3125–27	8a.
2936	44b.	3128–29, 3133	10b.
2938	39b.	3130–32	25
3019–20	33	3137–41	10a.
3031–33	32	3153–55	6a.
3034–35	44a.	3156	8b.
3050–51	19	3157	39a.
3052–53	12b.	3161	21a.
3071–73	6c.	3163–64	12e.

Appendix One

Record No.	*Melody No.*	*Record No.*	*Melody No.*
3170–71	47	3505	49
3174–75	43	3509–11	31a.
3178–79	18	3512–15	53
3180–84, 3187	12a.	3519–22	27b.
3190–91	31d.	3523–26	52
3192–96	46	3527	31c.
3197–3200	9	3541–42	45
3206–07	30	3547–48	24
3211–12	27d.	3553–56	27a.
3213–14	15	3557–59	3
3215–16	14	3560–61	26
3224	54	3562	37
3225–26	12d.	3566	38
3232–33	16a.b.	3567–69	48
3234	50	3572–73	2
3468	23b.	3574–75	6b.
3487–88	51	3576–77	21b.
		3586	4

Related recordings, in which other texts are sung to previously-designated melodies are: 1514–15 (melody No. 53); 1541–46 (28a.); 3158–60 (31b.); 3142–44, 3217–20, 3489–93, 3498–3502 (6c.); 3158–60 (31b.); and 3549–52 (12a.).

The drafts of the withheld transcriptions are listed and discussed on pp. xxvi–xxvii, above. The following list is ordered on the basis of chronological Parry record numbers—the same order that Bartók himself used to file the original and the carbon copy of the MS.[1] The data given for each listing is for the convenience of the reader: they have been extracted from the transcriptions.

R. 9–10 Vocal piece from Dubrovnik. Sung by Nikola Vujnović (age 26), July 11, 1934.

R. 335 *Javaštansko kolo* from Topolčane (Macedonia). Played on the *gayde* (bagpipe) by Jovan Stojčević; September 5, 1934.

[1] Exception: R. 391 transcription which is editorially placed after R. 1473 for practical purposes.

R. 336 *Oro Zaromo kolo.* Same remark as to R. 335.
R. 337 *Svadbeno kolo.* Same remark as to R. 335
R. 338 Vocal piece from Topolčane (Macedonia). Sung by Marija Karabelović (voice of a young girl), September 5, 1934. The transcription is preceded by the skeleton form of the melody, and the text was transcribed by Professor Roman Jacobson.
R. 341 *Kolo.* Same remark as to R. 334. Bartók erroneously indicates 1941 (transcription date?) as the performance year.
R. 342a) Vocal piece from Topolčane (Macedonia). Sung by Vasa Slivojić (child?), September 5, 1934.
R. 342b) Same remarks as to R. 342a) 1941 *should read* 1934.
R. 343 *Kolo.* Same remark as to R. 335.
R. 344 *Starinsko kolo.* Same remark as to R. 335.
R. 379 *Kozačko kolo* from Aleksandrovo (Macedonia). Played on the *tambura* (see description on p. 239, above) by Ariđon Velyković, September 7, 1934.
R. 385 *Kolo "Kokuneste."* Same remark as to R. 379.
R. 386 *"Cojle Manojle."* Same remark as to R. 379.
R. 387 *Kozačko kolo.* Same remark as to R. 379.
R. 388 *Makedonska pajduška.* Same remark as to R. 379.
R. 389 *Kolo "Vranjanka"* from Aleksandrovo (Macedonia). Played on the *duduk* (beak flute) by Dimse Lazić, September 7, 1934.
R. 390 *Pravo Makedonsko Kolo.* Same remark as to R. 389.
R. 390bis *Kraljevo Kolo.* Same remark as to No. 389.
R. 1473 *"Čobansko"* (dance?) from Stolac (Hercegovina). Played on the *dvojela* (double-beak flute) by Stojan Raguž, December 14, 1934.
R. 391 *Kolo "Srbijanka."* Same remark as to R. 379.
R. 1538b) Vocal piece from Rotinja srez Stolac u Stocu (Hercegovina). See performer's data on p. 88, above. Cf. melody No. 28a., lower staff, which is recorded on R. 1538a; see also the notes to melody Nos. 13 and 28a.
R. 2937a) *Sviranje* from Bihać (Bosnia). Played on the *tambura* by Zejnil Sinanović. See performer's data on p. 88 and the description of the instrument on p. 239, above.
R. 2937b) Same remarks as to R. 2937a).
Total: 5 vocal and 18 instrumental pieces

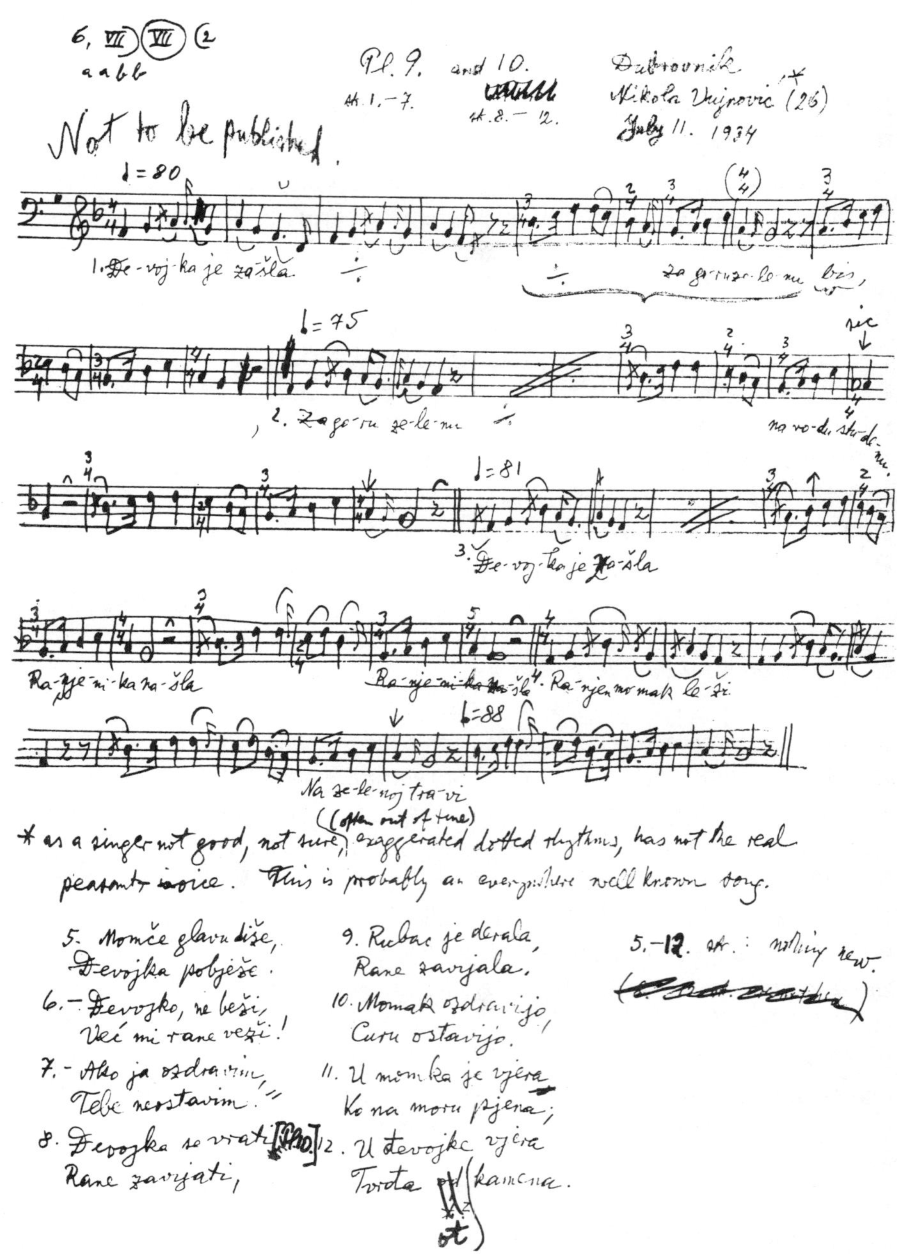
6, VI VII 2
aabb
Pl. 9. and 10.
st. 1.–7.
st. 8.–12.
Dubrovnik
Nikola Vujnović (26)
July 11. 1934
Not to be published.
♩=80
1. De-voj-ka je za-šla
♩=75
2. Za go-ru ze-le-nu
na vo-di stu-de-nu.
♩=81
3. De-voj-ka je za-šla
Ra-nje-ni-ka na-šla
Ra-nje-ni-ka na-šla
4. Ra-nje-nog mo-mak le-ži
Na ze-le-noj tra-vi
♩=88
* as a singer not good, not sure, (often out of time) exaggerated dotted rhythms, has not the real peasant voice. This is probably an everywhere well known song.
5. Momče glavu diže,
Devojka pobježe.
6. – Devojko, ne beži,
Već mi rane veži!
7. – Ako ja ozdravim,
Tebe neostavim."
8. Devojka se vrati
Rane zavijati,
9. Rubac je derala,
Rane zavijala.
10. Momak ozdravijo,
Curu ostavijo.
11. U momka je vjera
Ko na moru pjena;
12. U devojke vjera
Tvrda (od) kamena.
5.–12. st.: nothing new.

Pl. 335
Javaštansko kolo
Topličane (Macedonia)
Jovan Stojčević, Sept. 5.1934.
Gajde
fault?
(drone)
later
etc.
Pl. 336
Oro Zaromo (kolo)
Topličane (? .)
Jovan Stojčevic
IX. 5. 1934
Gajde
= 144
drone
later
etc.
= 160
several times
many times

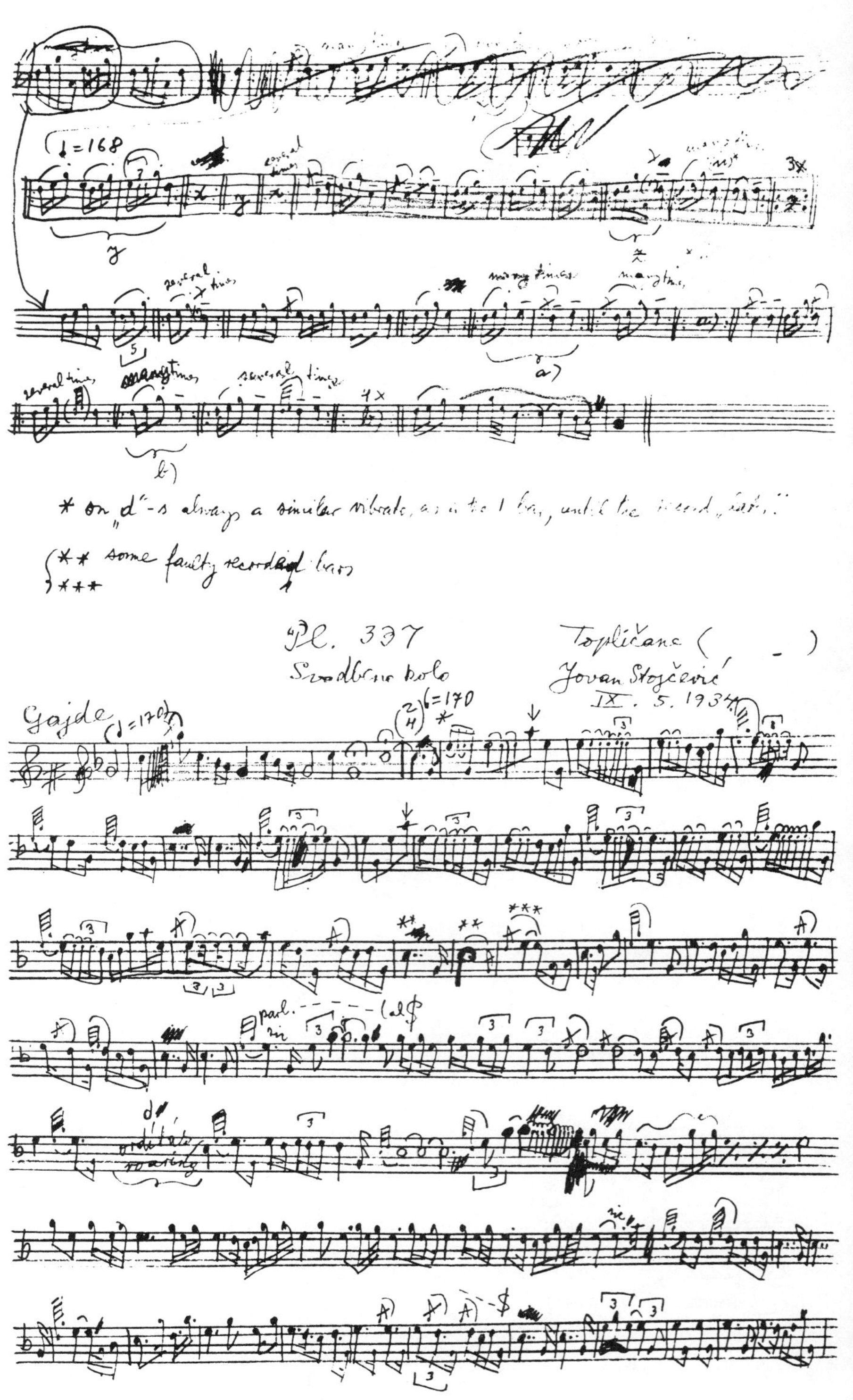

♩=168
several times
many times
4×
** some faulty recording bars
***
Pl. 337
Svadbeno kolo
Topličane
Jovan Stojčević
IX. 5. 1934
Gajde
♩=170

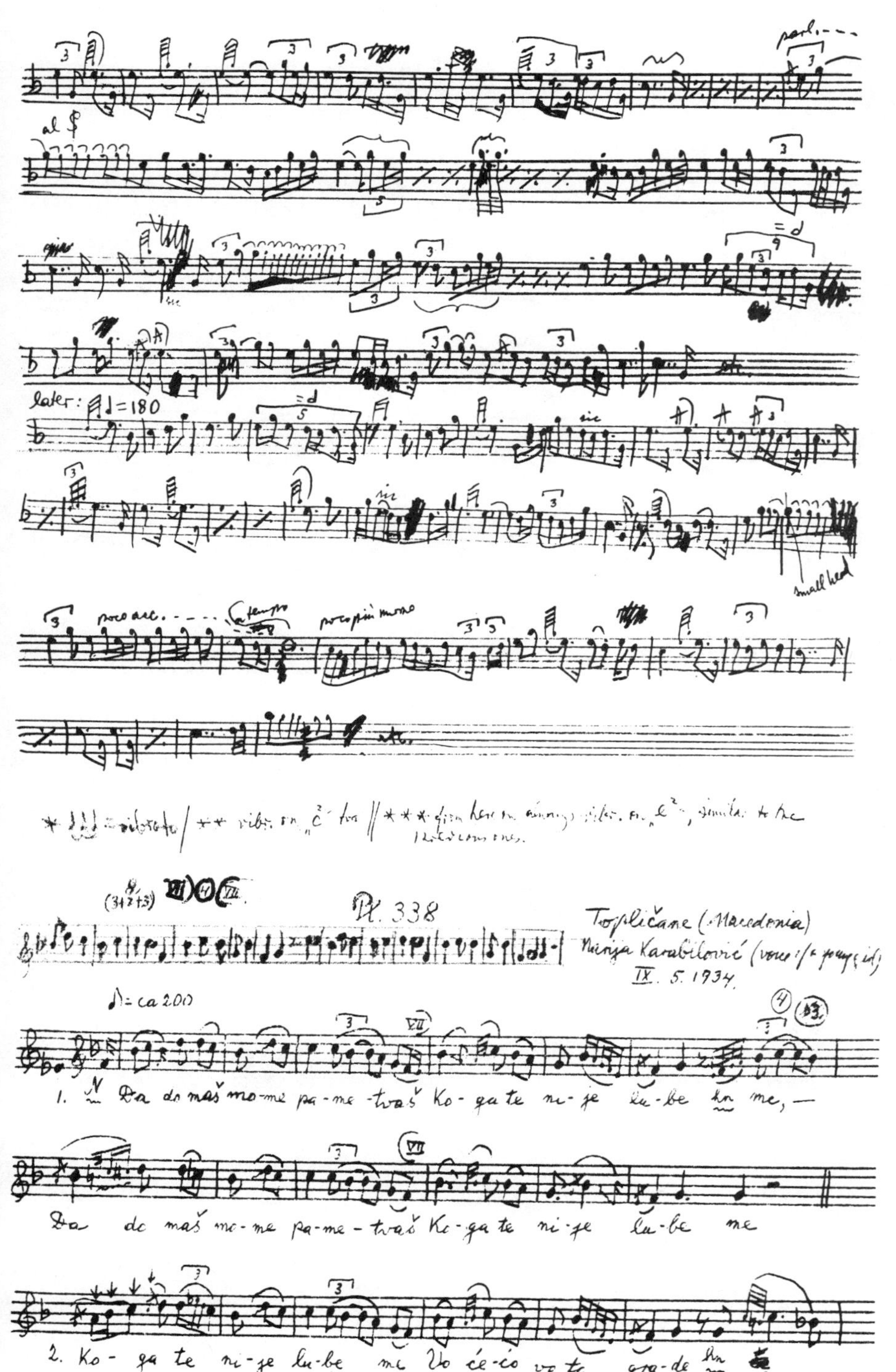

later: ♩=180
small head
Topličane (Macedonia)
IX. 5. 1934
♪= ca 200

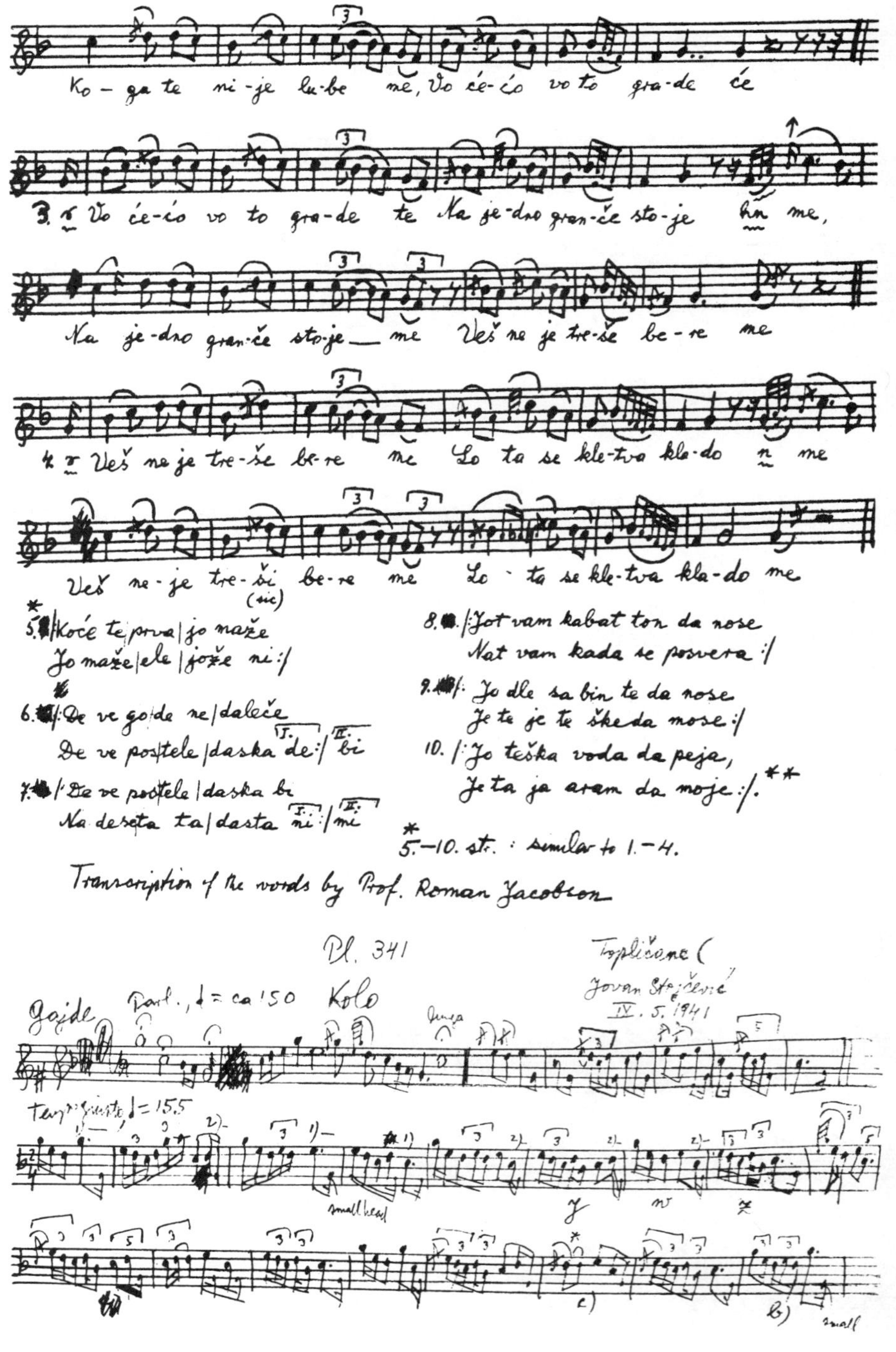
Ko – ga te ni - je lu-be me, Vo će-ćo vo to gra-de će
3. Vo će-ćo vo to gra-de te Na je-dro gran-če sto-je me,
Na je-dro gran-če sto-je — me Veš ne je tre-še be-re me
4. Veš ne je tre-še be-re me Lo ta se kle-tva kla-do me
Veš ne - je tre-ši be-re me Lo - ta se kle-tva kla-do me
(sic)
5. |Koće te prva | jo maže
Jo maže | ele | jože ni :/
6. /: De ve go|de ne | daleče
De ve postele | daska I. de :/ II. bi
7. /: De ve postele | daska bi
Na deseta ta | dasta I. ni :/ II. mi
8. /: Jot vam kabat ton da nose
Nat vam kada se posvera :/
9. /: Jo dle sa bin te da nose
Je te je te škeda mose :/
10. /: Jo teška voda da peja,
Je ta ja aram da moje :/. **
* 5.–10. str. : similar to 1.–4.
Transcription of the words by Prof. Roman Jacobson
Pl. 341
Topličane (
Jovan Stojčević
IV. 5. 1941
Gajde
Kolo
Tempo giusto, ♩ = 155
small head
small

* = vibr.

later:
etc.
from
I. groups.
(2.–4. line)
later:
II. groupe
(5.–6. line)
then again
I. groupe
and then from
II. groupe
2): rhythm sharper, sometimes almost
later too, in all similar groups,
at the end
parlando
squelette:

P. 342 a)
Topličane (Macedonia)
Slivojić
Vasa Slivojić child?
IX 5 1934
2. Kenetela mame nevada
3. Zagretila pate pa-te-na
4. out of tune
baran belena
bacila.
5.
vikom vikrajte
Jajdete mame latete

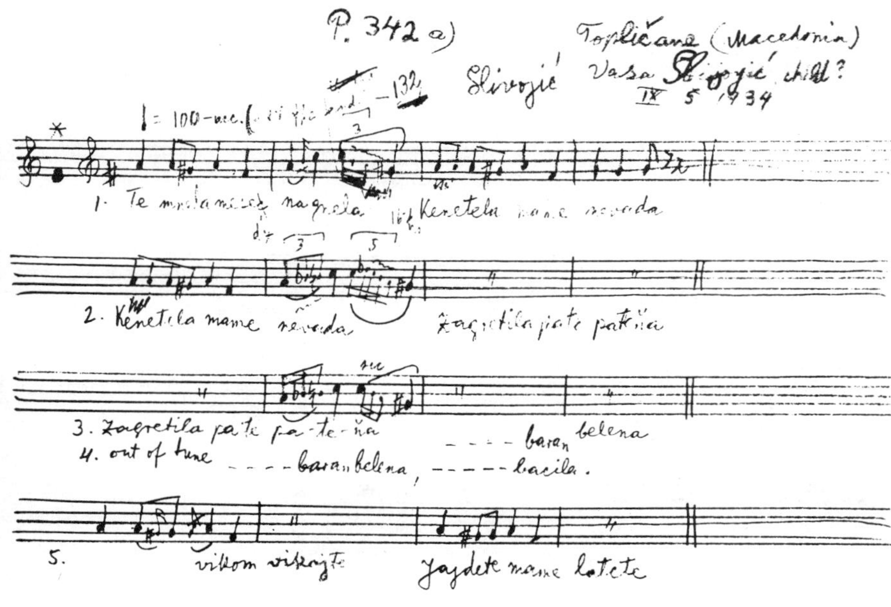

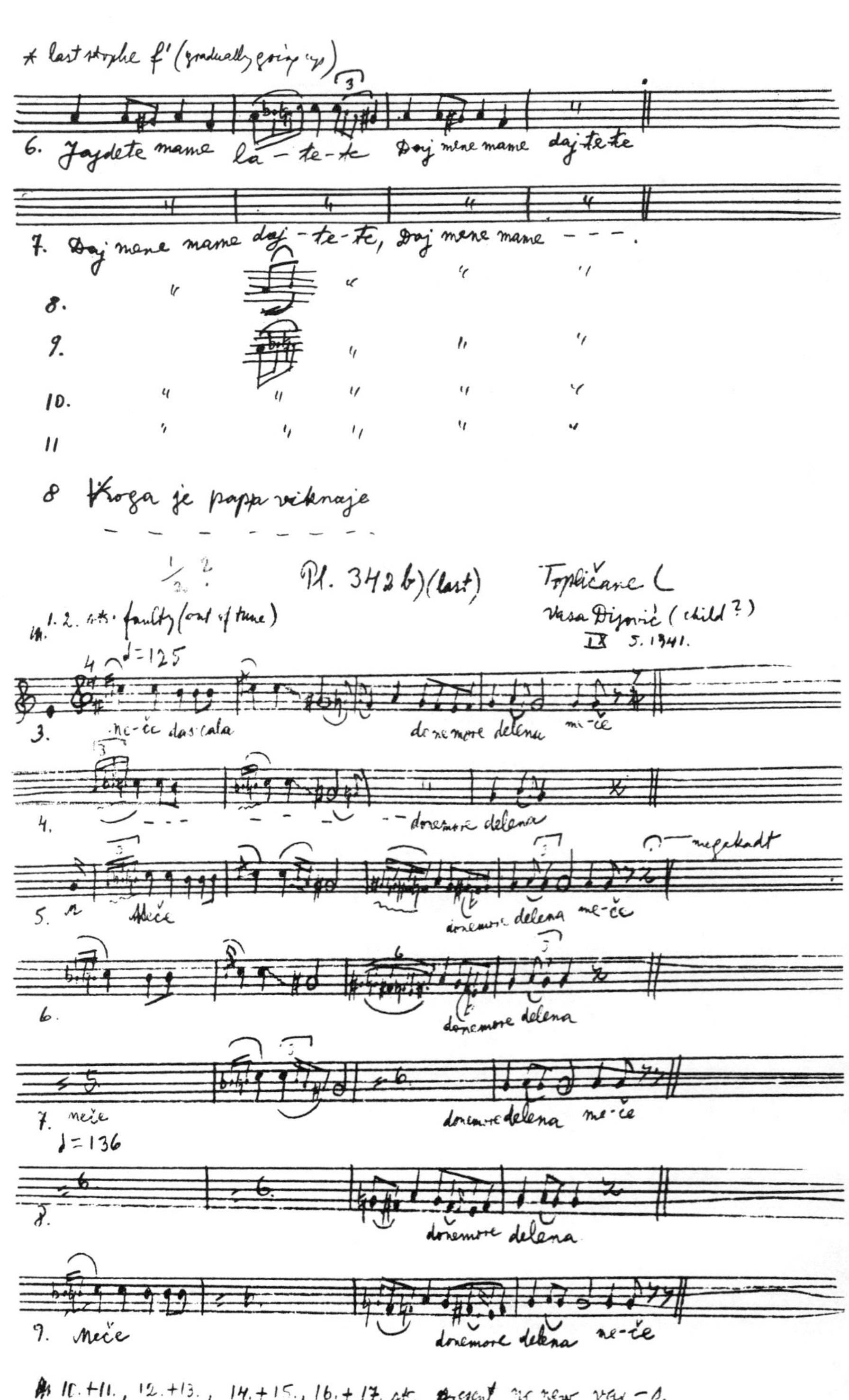
* last strophe f' (gradually going up)
6. Jajdete mame la - te - te Daj mene mame daj-te-te
7. Daj mene mame daj - te - te, Daj mene mame - - -.
8.
9.
10.
11
Pl. 342 b) (last)
Topličane
Vasa Dijović (child ?)
IX 5. 1941.
1. 2. str. faulty (out of tune)
♩=125
3.
donemore delena
4.
donemore delena
5.
donemore delena ne-će
6.
donemore delena
7. neće
donemore delena ne-će
♩=136
8.
donemore delena
9. Neće
donemore delena ne-će
10.+11., 12.+13., 14.+15., 16.+17. str. present no new var.

Pl. 343
Kolo
Toplićane
Jovan Stojčević
IX. 5. 1934
Gajde
d = 100
accel.
d = 104
16-ths
faulty
accel.
d = 112
d = 108
* vibr.

Pl. 343 (cont.)
meters change!
accel.
nothing!
faulty recorded
some more same bars, then

Pl. 344
Toplićane
Jovan Stojčinić
IX. 5. 1934
Starinsko Kolo
Gajde parlando
etc. simile
later:
end:
* slight accel.

Pl. 379
Aleksandrovo
Koračko kolo
Ariton Veljković
Tambura (some of the strings not well tuned!)
accel.
5.—13. str.-s in a similar way, no var.-s of importance.
In the last one, instead of the 6 last bars thus:

Pl. 385
Kolo „Kokuneśte"
Aleksandrovo
Tambura ♩=135
etc. Var. (upper voice)
N. B. the strings serving for the accompaniment seem to be out of tune, and some of them plucked frequently at haphazard.
Pl. 386
Aleksandrovo
Tambura ♩=144
acc.
sic.
volta:
10. volta:
no other new var.-s.

Pl. 389
Aleksandrovo
Kozačko kolo
Sept. 7. 1934
Tambura (some of the strings not well tuned!)
accel. — — — — — al
♩ = 112
♩ = 130
Var. (in some of the following str.-s)
5.—13. str.-s in a similar way, no var.-s of importance.
In the last one, instead of the 6 last bars this:

P. 388
Makedonska pajduška
Aleksandrovo
Ariton Veljković
Sept. 7. 1934.
Tambura
1. st. : beginning faulty ; otherwise no new var.

Pl. 387
Kolo „Vranjanka"
Aleksandrovo (Macedonia)
Dimše Lagić, Sept. 7. 1934.
Duduk* ♩ = 88
a few more notes (impossible to transcribe) as ending.
* kind of peasant flute (perhaps the „kaval"?); many unintentional „überblasen" notes
which sound generally as if in double stops in octaves, for instance the mostly sounds:
Pl. 390.
Pravo Makedonsko Kolo
Aleksandrovo (Macedonia)
Dimše Lagić, Sept. 7. 1934.
Duduk* ♩ = ca 180
n.b. 1) always too low
5.–13. (fine): no new var., except:
n.b. 2) 5.–13. presents 4-line structure
(1. part bis, 2. part bis)
* kind of peasant flute (kaval?)

Pl. 390a (why? not b suits) (better: 390 bis.
Kraljevo Kolo
Aleksandrovo
Dimše Lazić
Sept. 7, 1934
Duduk (= flute)
♩ = ca 170
x) or y many times; no important new var.s;
1) sometimes:
then:
many times c)+d)**; then:
many times
then again c) d)** many times, sometimes with these var.s:
*frequently „überblasen": in this case it sounds (rarely an octave) a duodecim heigher.
** frequently in this arrangement: d)+d) + c)+d) as a phrase (period).

Pl. 1473
Stolac
Dec. 14. 1934.
Dvojela
♩=165
next page
♩=138
♩=150

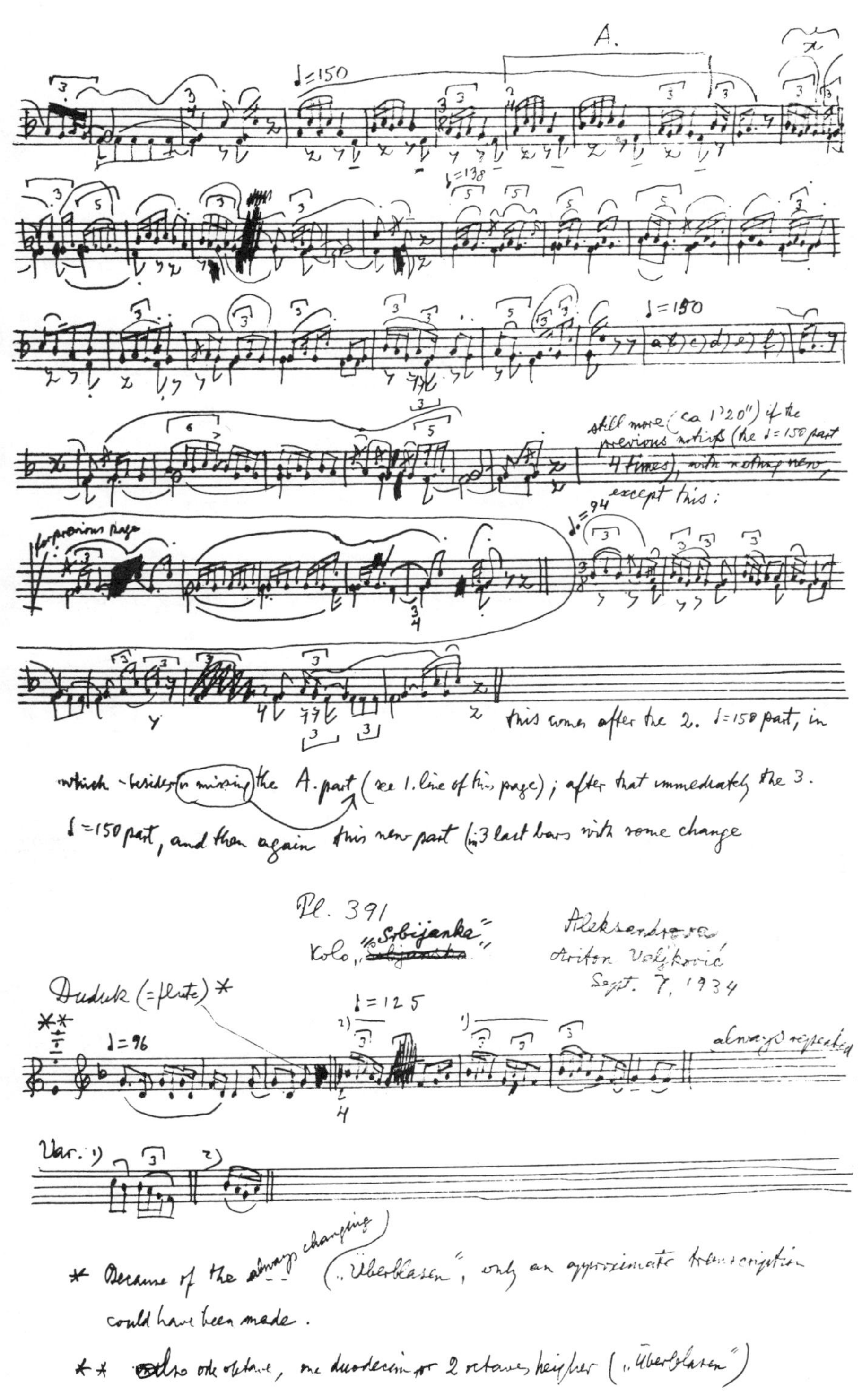

A.
♩=150
♩=138
♩=150
a) b) c) d) e) f)
still more (ca 1'20") of the previous motifs (the ♩=150 part 4 times), with nothing new, except this:
♩.=94
for previous page
this comes after the 2. ♩=150 part, in which – besides missing the A. part (see 1. line of this page); after that immediately the 3. ♩=150 part, and then again this new part (in 3 last bars with some change
Pl. 391
Kolo „Srbijanka“
Aleksandrovac
Ariton Veljković
Sept. 7, 1934
Duduk (=flute) *
**
♩=96
♩=125
always repeated
Var.: 1) 2)
* Because of the always changing („Überblasen“, only an approximate transcription could have been made.
** also one octave, one duodecim or 2 octaves higher („Überblasen“)

Pl. 1538 b)

Rotimje (srez Stolac u Stocu)
Naza Rokić (26–27)*
Dec. 15, 1934.

* She says: learnt it from her father who played it with gusle. But it can be performed as well without gusle.

** rest probably to take breath!

*** ♪ value perhaps because of coughing.

Pl. 2937 a)
Sviranje (?!) [title missing?]
Bihać
Apr. 13. 1935
Tambura
open strings?
accel.
più lento
a tempo
bis

Pl. 2937 B)

Sviranje (?!) [no title?]

Bihać
Zejnil Simarović
Apr. 13, 1935.

Appendix Two

SERBIAN FOLK MUSIC FROM THE BANAT REGION

The Banat region, formerly a Hungarian province, contains the southwestern Transylvanian (new Rumanian) counties of Timiș and Torontal. In March, 1912, Bartók collected nine instrumental and two vocal (with *tambura* accompaniment) pieces from Serbian inhabitants of the village of Mănăștur (Serbo-Croatian designation: Temešmonoštor; Hungarian: Monostor), Timiș (Temeš; Temes) County. The same year, in November, he added to his Serbian folk music collection seven instrumental and three vocal pieces from Saravale (its former Rumanian name was Sarafola; Hungarian: Sárafalva), Torontal County.

In 1935 Bartók prepared a fair copy, on transparent master sheets, of those twenty-one pieces plus seven Bulgarian folk songs from the Banat). He then had copies printed and sent them to colleagues abroad.

I have recently noted down some of my own Serbian and Bulgarian phonogr. recordings dated 1912, or rather I have revised my earlier, not altogether accurate, notations made from these recordings. I think the Serbian material will interest you, so I am sending you a copy of the notations. It's true that some of the Serbian pieces are well-known melodies, but nowhere have such accurate recordings and notations been published. In fact, I think this is the only Serbian material so far to have been taken down (with the greatest possible accuracy) from phonograph recordings; for, as far as I know, no phonograph has been used hitherto in your country for folk-song collecting; or at any rate, no material collected in this way has been published. The figures marked M.F. refer to cylinders owned by the National Museum in Budapest, the (sole) figure marked F. refers to a cylinder owned by myself.[1]

[1] Letter from Béla Bartók (Budapest) to Vinko Žganec (Zombor), dated December 23, 1935, as published in *Béla Bartók Letters* (ed. János Demény), Faber and Faber, London, 1971, pp. 244–245. See also the editorial commentary on pp. xii, xviii–xix, xxxi–xxxii, above.

Appendix Two

The five Serbian folk songs are listed in "Tab. of Mat." (Vol. II of the present publication) and are published in Bartók's later, skeleton-form draft in the Source Melodies (Vols. III–IV) as Nos. 39d., 1020a., 1223, 1259b., and 1602b.

The following list of pieces and their extracted data is given for the convenience of the reader.

1. *"Malo kolo,"* played on the violin by Mihaj Skitović, a gipsy.
2. *"Malo kolo,"* played on the *tambura* by Milan Marković (age 22).
3. *"Veliko kolo,"* played on the *tambura* by Milan Marković.
4. *"Veliko kolo,"* played on the violin by Mihaj Skitović.
5. *"Srbkinja,"*played on the *tambura* by Milan Marković.
6. *"Seljančica,"* played on the *tambura* by Milan Marković. Cf. No. 15.
7. *"Zaplet,"* played on the *tambura* by Milan Marković. This tune is the thematic source for No. 39 in Bartók's 44 Duos for Two Violins (see p. xlvi, above).
8. *"Oj djevojko rukoko,"* played on the *tambura* by Milan Marković.
9. *"Djurdjevka,"* played on the *tambura* by Milan Marković.
10. Vocal piece with *tambura* introduction, interlude, and postlude. Performed by Milan Marković, Ima Jović, and Dimja Urnaz.
11. Vocal piece (part song) with alternating *tambura* solo. Performed by Milan Marković and Ima Jović.
12. *"Malo kolo,"* played on the *gajde* (bagpipe) by a man.
13. *"Veliko kolo,"* idem.
14. *"Banatsko kolo,"* idem.
15. *"Seljančica,"* idem. Cf. No. 6.
16. *"Srpski madjarik,"* idem.
17. Song melody, idem.
18. Song melody, idem. Cf. No. 19.
19. Vocal piece, sung by the bagpiper (of Nos. 12–18). Cf. No. 18.
20. Wedding song, idem.
21. Vocal piece, idem.
Total: 5 vocal and 16 instrumental pieces

The nineteen pages of transcriptions that follow below are facsimile reproductions of a Bartók-corrected copy of the original MS.

1

„Malo kolo" (violino) [danse]

1. Tempo giusto, ♩ = 186 – (acc. sin al fine) – 202

2

M.F. 2026 a, Temešmonoštor (Temeš), Mihaj Skitović, ciganin, III. 1912.
2. Tempo giusto, ♩ = 184
Malo kolo (tambura)
* ~~~ = colla I. parte

3

4

M.F. 2027, Temešmonoštor (Temeš), Milan Marković, III. 1912.
3. Tempo giusto, ♩=148
„Veliko kolo" (tambura) [danse]
poco a poco accel.
al ♩=164

5
M.F. 2028, Temešmonoštor (Temeš), Milan Marković, III. 1912.
4.
„Veliko kolo" (violino) [danse]
Tempo giusto, ♩ = 144 - (acc. al fine) - 160
2. v.
3. v.
4. v.
M.F. 2026 b, Temešmonoštor (Temeš), Mihaj Skitović, cigan, III. 1912.

6
5.
„Srbkinja" (tambura) [danse]
Tempo giusto ♩(=124-(acc. al fine)-136
M.F. 2029b, Temesmonoštor (Temeš), Milan Marković (22), III.1912.
„Seljančica" (tambura) [danse]
6. Tempo giusto, ♩ = 150-(acc. al fine)-160
sempre simile
M.F. 2030 a, Temešmonoštor (Temeš), Milan Marković (22), III.1912.
Cf. N°15.

7

„Zaplet" (tambura) [danse]
7. Tempo giusto, ♩=160 - (acc. al fine) - 170
sempre simile
2. v.
3. v.
M.F. 2031 a; Temešmonoštor (Temeš), Milan Marković (22), II. 1912.
„Oj djevojko rikoko" (tambura) [danse ?]
8. Tempo giusto, ♩=110 - (acc. al fine) - 120
2. v.
sempre sim.

8

M. F. 2031 b), Temešmonoštor (Temeš), Milan Marković (22), III. 1912.

9. „Djurdjevka" (tambura) [danse]

M. F. 2030 b, Temešmonoštor (Temeš), Milan Marković (22), III. 1912.

9

10.
Un chant (joué et chanté alternativement)
(tambura: introduzione)
attacca:
1. Pe-vaj pe-tle, pe-vaj pe-tle, Pe-vaj pe-tle na du-du ja-lov-cu, Na du-du ja-lov-cu.
(interludio, tempo I.)
attacca:
attacca
2. str.
attacca:
(postludio, tempo I.)
M.F. 2029 a, Temešmonoštor (Temeš), Milan Marković (22), Ima Jović, Dimja Urnaz. III. 1912.
2. Devojka se dopala udovcu.
3. Zora rudi, majka sina budi:
4. – Ustaj, sine, prolazu devojke!
5. – Nek prolaze, moja proći neće. – e ?
ne jöjjön erre

2. Dobro jutro, moje luče!
Za tobom mi srce puče.
Pa ga lečim rujnom vinom,
Sa najboljom medicinom.

~~E 1601~~, Temešmonoštor (Temeš), Milan Marković, tamburaš (22), Ima Jović, III. 1912.

M.F. 3690

12

12. „Malo kolo" („gajde") [danse, - cornemuse]

M. F. 2058 a, Sarafola (Torontal), un homme, XI. 1912.

M.F. 2058 b, Sarafola (Torontal), un homme, XI. 1912.

14. „Banatsko kolo" („gajde") [danse, — cornemuse]

Tempo giusto, ♩ = 150 – acc. al – 168

15
M.F. 2059, Sarafola (Torontal), un homme, XI. 1912.
15.
„Seljančica" („gajde") [danse, - cornemuse]
Tempo giusto, ♩= 138 - acc. al fine - 144
1.
2.
M.F. 2060b, Sarafola (Torontal), un homme, XI. 1912.
Cf. n°6.

M.F. 2061 a, Sarafola (Torontal), un homme, XI. 1912.

1.F. 2061b, Sarafola (Torontal), un homme, XI.1912.

18.
18
Melodie d'un chant („gajde") [cornemuse]
quasi parlando, ♪=132
1.
♪=140
2.
cf. № 19.
M.F. 2060 a, Sarafola (Torontal), un homme, XI. 1912.
19.
Parlando, ♪=120
(11), 8, 6, 8, 6, 2 b3 2
1. O-tvo-ri mi, mi-le pi-le, Vrat- - ni-ce, Vrat-ni- - ce,
O-tro-vo-ri mi, mi-le — pi-le, — Vrat-.ni-ce, aj, vrat-ni-ce,
2. Da ti lju-bim, mi-le pi-le, o-či-ce, — o- - či- - ce,
Da ti — lju-bim, mi-le — pi-le, — o- - či-ce, aj, — o-či-ce!
cf. № 18.
M.F. 2060 a, Sarafola (Torontal), le joueur de la cornemuse, XI. 1912.

Elszakadt a gyöngyág

Chant de noces

20. Parlando, ♪ = 142 — 8, 5, [1]

1. Od-bi-se bi--- ser- gra---na Od— jor--go---ve-[na],
2. I— le-pa,— le--pa zmi---la- Ot— svo--- je— majk?
3. Ot- svo--je— mi--le- maj---ke, Od— bra--tje—drag?

M.F. 1712 a, Sarafola (Torontal), le joueur de la cornemuse. XI. 1912.

mindenki sorban

21. Tempo giusto ♩ = 116 ♩ = 132 — 8, [4] [4] [2]

1. Le-pu zmi-lu do-ve-do-še, Sa svir-čemje do-pra-ti-še, Svi je— se-dom iz-lju-bi-še,
Sa-mo svir-cu ne-da-doš? A-lje svi-rac i-tar bi-o,— Pa je pr-vi po-lju-bi?
2. Ta ta-ka je no-va mla-da, Sa-dje nje na vla-da, Ta ta-ka je no-va mla-da
Sa-dje nje na vla-da, Suk-nja joj se vu--če Nu me-da je vu-če.
3. A ki-ke-ljac ot šest po-la, Nu me da ga— ro-lja, A-ki—
ce--ljac ot šest po-la, Nu me— da ga— ro--lja.—

M.F. 1712 b, Sarafola (Torontal), le joueur de la cornemuse, XI. 1912.

görög, gördül

6-levelű

Appendix Three

SERBO-CROATIAN REFRAINS

In Vol. III (Texts) of Bartóks *Rumanian Folk Music*[1] is a list of Serbo-Croatian refrains which the author placed there for comparison with those of his Rumanian material. For the convenience of the reader, the list of Serbo-Croatian refrains is published here, in facsimile of Bartók's holograph, together with abridgements of the author's discussion (*R.F.M.* III, pp. lxxii-lxxxi) and, where necessary, editorially constructed explanatory material.

Early in his ethnomusicological career Bartók found that the Rumanians of southern Transylvania made more frequent use of refrains than their countrymen in other parts of that area. He hypothesized that such use resulted from contact with Yugoslavs in adjacent areas: the latter people also use refrains lavishly. But he later found marked differences between the Rumanian and Yugoslav refrains, the most essential being the lack of alternating refrains in the latter; moreover, rhyme-giving and transitional pseudo-refrains also seem to be characteristically lacking in the Yugoslav material.

Bartók's conclusion, then, is that there is a link between Rumanian folk song material from the southwest part of Transylvania (the Banat region) and adjacent Yugoslav areas in terms of frequency of use of refrains and, to a lesser degree, the use of refrain lines common to both materials (see *R.F.M.* III, pp. lxxxi and xcix-c).

The definition of a text refrain in Yugoslav folk song is given in the author's discussion on pp. 32–33 and 41, above. It is opportune to add here a preliminary-draft sentence missing from the beginning of marginal note 38 (p. 41, above) published in this volume, since the sentence is present in all three preliminary versions of Part One. Referring to the repetition of line fragments which are themselves the result of text

[1] Publication details will be found in note 8 on p. xi, above.

splitting at a main or secondary caesura, Bartók asserts that: "To call such line-fragment repeats 'refrain-like', as some scholars do, is completely erroneous."

The frequency of occurrence of refrains in the 3,449 "Tab. of Mat." melodies, in geographic distribution (the eastern material stems from areas contiguous with Rumanian ones), is as follows:

Refrain Subgroups	*Eastern Material* *Kuba* B.H., *XI–XIV;* Pred. Srb.; *Juž. Srb.;* Nar. Pev.; *Bosiljevac; Kačerovski;* Iz Levča; *Parry*[2]	*Western Material* *Kuba* IX–X; *Kuhac*[3]	*Total*
A. *II.*	95	29	124
A. *III.*	11	8	19
B. *I.*	197	87	284
B. *II.*	55	13	68
B. *III.*	50	21	71
B. *IV.*	13	11	24
B. *V.*	6	1	7
B. *VII.*	5	1	6
B. *IX.*	7	3	10
Total	**439**	**174**	**613**

According to the above figures, there is an occurrence of refrains in *17* per cent of the melodies (eastern: *20* per cent; western: *13.5* per cent) as compared with the *25* per cent average for the Rumanian material. And in the Banat and adjacent Rumanian areas, *45* per cent. Subgroups A. *I.*, B. VI., B. VIII., and Group C are lacking in the Serbo-Croatian material.

Though the grouping system is self-explanatory by the designations of the single groups and subgroups on pp. 476–491, the following tabulation presents a survey of them as a compendium:

[2] See the listings on pp. 22–23, above. The material of these collections comes from the eastern part of the Serbo-Croatian territory; that is, Old Serbia, Bosnia, Hercegovina, and Montenegro—called together "autochthonous" territory (cf. p. 46, above).

[3] See the listings on pp. 22–23 above. This material comes chiefly from the western part, that is, Slavonia.

Appendix Three

A. Refrains without definite sense

I. Transitions from pseudo-refrains to refrains
None

II. Refrains consisting of words with no definite sense
Nos. 1–61

III. Refrains consisting of words with indefinite sense as well as of words with definite sense
Nos. 62–78

B. Refrains with definite sense

I. Consisting of one line
Nos. *79–136*: two to four syllables
Nos. *137–174*: five to six syllables
Nos. *175–198*: six to eight syllables
Nos. *199–214*: nine to sixteen syllables

II. Double refrains, each consisting of one line (in the last four: one of one line, the other of two lines)
Nos. *215–253*; *254–257*

III. Refrains consisting of two lines
Nos. *258–263*: five-syllable lines
Nos. *264–266*: six to seven-syllable lines
Nos. *267–274*: eight-syllable lines
No. *275*: thirteen-syllable lines
Nos. *276–290*: heterometric structure **Z z**
Nos. *291–309*: heterometric structure **z Z**

IV. Refrains consisting of three lines
Nos. *310–312*: five to eight-syllable lines
Nos. *313–314*: heterometric structure **Z Z z**
Nos. *315–320*: heterometric structure **z z Z**
No. *321*: heterometric structure **z Z Z**
No. *322*: heterometric structure **z Z z**
Nos. *323–327*: other heterometric structures

V. Triple refrains, each consisting of one line
Nos. *328–330*

VI. Double refrains, each consisting of two lines
None

VII. Refrains consisting of four lines
Nos. *331–335*

VIII. Double refrains, each consisting of four lines
None

IX. Refrains consisting of more than four lines
No. 336

C. Rhyme-giving refrains
None

Appendix Three

General remarks:

In the list of Serbo-Croatian refrains that follows below, variants are placed into variant groups under a common Arabic figure even if some of the variants have a structure different from that of the respective groups or subgroups. The single members of such variant groups are distinguished by small letters (12a., 12b., 12c., and so forth).

Certain data follow the source melodies: figures in brackets indicate the current number in the "Tab. of Mat." (Vol. II) and Source Melodies (Vols. III–IV); after this entry as figures indicating syllabic structure and symbols designating section structure (caesuras) of the source melodies involved. **Z** letter symbols are added in the case of heterometric structures. { at the left side of lines or words (word groups) indicates alternatives.

The leading principle of the classification was to establish an order going from less to more and from simpler to more complicated.

Serbo-Croatian Refrains

A. Without definite sense

II. Refrains consisting of words with no definite sense

1.[1] Kuba B.H. 270 [819 d.]; 10,6,6, OC
Ahmo.

2 a. Đorđ. Pred. Srb. 16, 19, 72, 74 [261 a. c. d. e.]; 10, O
dos, dos.

2 b. Đorđ. Pred. Srb. 3, 18 [739 a. b.]; 6, 5, 6, OC
dos.

3. Đorđ. Pred. Srb. 180 [504]; 8, 6, O
le le.

4. Kuba B. H. 869, Kuhač 1142 [962 a. b.]; 7, 7, 13, ƆO
{|: hop hop hop :|[3x] [2]
{hop hop hop [2]
{cup cup cup
{hop hop hop

5. Kuba B. H. 81, 272 [577 a. b.]; 12, 9, O
Euhajha(j).

6. Kuba B. H. 243 [963]; 7, 7, 13, ƆO
|: jupajdaj :|[3x] [2]

7. Kuhač 757 [1076]; < 5, ƆaC
Ej more.

8. Đorđ. Pred. Srb. 441 [30]; 11,
vajkupo.

9. Kuhač 590 [1084]; 5, ƆOC
[agigo].

10 a. Kuba B. H. 162 [455 e.]; 12, O
a vaj vaj vaj.

10 b. Kuba XII 18 [828]; 12, 8, 8, OC
haj haj haj haj.

11. Kuhač 301 [1609]; 8, 7, 8, 7, ƆOC
|: Legre tam tam.

12 a. Kuba B.H. 42, 68, 69, 116, 117, 152, 231, 292, 328, 359, 629, 646, 648, 708, 844, 1016, XIII 36, Kuhač 388, Juž. Srb. 422 [125 b., 149-150, 357, 572, 576, 581, 605, 607 b., 907, 911, 997, 1066, 1077 a., 1619 a. c. d. e. f., 1737 b.]; various structures
Aman {aman.
{neman

12 b. Juž. Srb. 409, 421, Kuba XIV 10 [966 a. b., 1651 a.]; 8, 8, 10, ƆO; < 8, 5, 5, 5, ƆOC
aman.

12 c. Kuba B.H. 183, 246, 344, Kuhač 478, Đorđ. Pred. Srb. 101 [164 a., 872 a. b., 974, 1651 b.]; various structures
{Bre aman aman.
{jel'
{Jor
{sir
{Vaj

12 d. Kuba B.H. 43, 44 [738 a. b.]; 11, 11, 10, OC
{sir aman aman aman.
{šik aman aman.

12 e. Kuba B.H. 475 [1023]; 8, 7, 5, ƆO
1. aman aman.
2. krux aman aman.

12 f. Kuba B. H. 71 [1737 a.]; 6, 6, 9, 10, ƆOC
1. Dort paša.
2. aman aman.

13. Kuba B.H. 75, Kuhač 255 [1079 b. c.]; < 5, ƆOC
Kuba B.H. 1078 [1267]; 8, ƆOC
{Džanim aman.
{Džanum aman.
{Džanum benum.

14 a. Kuba B.H. 76, 77, 141, 614, XIV 23, Đorđ. Nar. Pev. p. 122, 1st mel. [724 b, 813, 920-921, 1332 a. b. c.]; various struct.
{Jandim aman.
{jangin
{popal
{aman

14 b. Đorđ. Pred. Srb. 99 [992]; 11, 6, 11, ƆO
jandin aman aman.

15 a. Kuba X 35 [642]; 8, OC
Džanom fendum.

15 b. Kuba B.H. 23 [1392 a.]; < 17, 17, [?] 17, ƆOC ?
1. fendum.
2. oj vaj.

16 a. Kuba B.H. 609, Bosiljevac 50 [1672 b. c.]; 8, 8, 8, 5, ƆOC
Aman gel aman.

16 b. Kuba B.H. 356 [562]; 11, 8, O
Sen gel aman, zarif aman.

---

1) The Nos. of the respective publications come first; the following Nos. in brackets refer to the so-called Tabulation of Material (see Serbo-Croatian Folk Songs); after these are placed the data concerning the structures of the respective melodies.

2) The repeats do not follow each other; each of them appears after a different main text-line section.

17. Kuhač 759 [1062]; 5, ƆOC
Ej džindžil more.

18a. Kuhač 865, 866 [1058 a.c.]; 5, ƆOC
Bre djidi deli.

18b. Kuhač 864 [1058 b.]; <5, ƆOC
1. /: Brej djidi brej :/.
2. Brej djidi brej deli.

18c. Kuhač 758, 863 [1054 f.d.]; (<) 5, ƆOC
{Ej / Brej} djidi.

19a. Kuba B.H. 390 [882 a.]; 13, 14, 12, OC
Haj vaj cakumbak.

19b. Bosiljevac 13 [882 b.]; 13, 14, 12, OC
Aj aj tikatak

20. ~~Đord.~~ Nar. Pev. p. 184, 1st mel. [1503-1504]; 8, 5, 8, 5, ƆOC
Didu lidu di.

21. Kuhač 87 [1633]; 10, 5, 10, 5, ƆOC
Djumlalela lom.

22a. Kuhač 601 [853 a.]; 9, 8+8, 5, OC
/: kukurikuku :/.

22b. Kuba IX 36 [853 f.]; 9, 8+8, 1, OC
ku.

23. ~~Đord.~~ Pred. Srb. 80 [1768]; 11, 11, 6, 7, ƆOC
Haj haj haj de de de.

24. Kuba IX 35 [505]; 8, 6, O
Hoja joj, hoja joj.

25. Kuba B.H. 60 [1366]; 5, 5, 6, 5, ƆOC
Berzivor, berzivor.

26. ~~Đord.~~ Pred. Srb. 386 [585]; 6, 7, O
Granumo, manumo.

27a. Kuba B.H. 713 [512]; 8, 7, O
Džido, džido, dzidijo.

27b. Kuba B.H. 38 [916]; 12, 8, 5, OC
1. dzido džido.
2. more džidijo.

28. Kuhač 855 [742]; 9, 8b, 9, OC
Dilber ber Andjo, liljo le.

29. ~~Đord.~~ Nar. Pev. p. 114, 1st mel. [1448 a]; 10, 10, 13, 13, ƆOC
Of neka neka neka.

30. Kuba B.H. 281 [1752]; 8, 8, 7, [?], ƆOC
Aj vaj rindiri baba.

31. Kuhač 1127 [1567a.]; 8, 6, 8, 6, ƆOC
Ei draj la la fidri bum bum.

32. Kuhač 231 [1386]; < 8, 8, 10, 8, ƆOC
Aulum saulum salfadelo.

33. ~~Đord.~~ Pred. Srb. 189 [597 a.]; 8, 9, O
Oj dudo, oj dudo, dodole

34. Kuhač 671, 1427 [1271 a.]; 8, ƆOC
/: Huma huma {duldi [duldi] duja :/. / djil djil [djil djil]}

35. ~~Đord.~~ Nar. Pev. p. 162, 1st mel. [166!]; 7, 7, 7, 10, ƆOC
Vas gidelam ajde sas gudelam.

36. Kuba XI 57 [1686]; 5, 5, 5+5, 5, ƆOC
Ej ler mi begler beg paša zada.

37. Kuhač 852 [1785]; 8, 7, 13, 13, ƆOC
/: Džin džin džinarata
džinarata tatata :/.

38a. Kuba B.H. 120, ~~Đord.~~ Pred. Srb. 554 [886 a., 141-142]; 9, 8, 3, OC; 8, O
1. hm.
2. {more / mori} bre.

38b. ~~Đord.~~ Pred. Srb. 448 [886 b.]; 9, 8, 3, OC
1. haj.
2. more de.

38c. ~~Đord.~~ Pred. Srb. 344, Kuba XII 42 [886 c., 617]; 9, 8, 3, OC, 9, 11, O
1. bre.
2. bre {le le. / bre bre.}

38d. Kačerovski 22 [886 d.]; 9, 8, 7, OC
1. oj.
2. more bre zangine.

39. Kuhač 638 [830]; 8, 9, 9, OC
1. Fendon.
2. Haj vaj.

40. Kuba B.H. 606 [941]; 11, 11, 8, ƆO
1. aj vaj.
2. haj demka.

41. Kuhač 1531 [433 e.]; 11, O
1. perdivoj.
2. perdimoj.

42a ~~Đord.~~ Nar. Pev. p. 191, 2nd mel. [409]; 11, O
1. dudo dudo.
2. dudo.

42b. ~~Dord.~~ Pred. Srb. 39 [342]; 10, O
Dude.

43. Kuba B.H. 507, 688, Kuhač 178 [1010 a. b. c.]; 8, 7, 9, ↄO
1. {bir / Al} {efendum. / efendi.
2. {aj / haj} vaj.

44. Kuhač 405 [579-580]; 14, 12, O
1. nina nena.
2. nena.

45. Kuba B.H. 283 [726]; 11, ↄO
1. Ej vaj, ej vaj.
2. ajdi mi haj.

46-47. ~~Dord.~~ Pred. Srb. 504 [691 a.]; 8, ↄO
1. Sajgu najgu.
2. Izur vezur.

48. ~~Dord.~~ Pred. Srb. 505 [407 a.]; 11, O
1. tandara trup.
2. tandara truptrup trup.

49. Kuba XII 54 [1427]; 14, 14, 10, 10, ↄOC
1. lumajde lumajde.
2. |: Andal mandal lumajde lumajde :|.

50. Kuba B.H. 513 [1817]; 11, 12, 6, 7, ↄOC
1. Štoj benum vaj sen aman vaj gin amanun.
2. jadu.

51. Kuba B.H. 635. [1780]; 8, 7, 7, ↄOC
Taj bron |: bronga :| tiri [rin] ru
Ririrata brontajta] bron.

52 a. ~~Dord.~~ Pred. Srb. 310 [815 a.]; 8, 7, 7, OC
Lemperi lempeperi
Kajlari kajzlatari.

52 b. ~~Dord.~~ Pred. Srb. 237 [815 b.]; 8, 7, 7, OC
Lemparu lempataru
Kozlaru kozlataru.

52 c. ~~Dord.~~ Pred. Srb. 376 [815 c.]; 8, 7, 7, OC
Lejleri lepiperi
Vojzari vojzatari.

53 a. Kuba B.H. 580 [1797]; 8, 7, 7, 6, ↄOC
Na djuzel karadjuzel
Vaj kozol vaj vajgiga.

53 b. Kuba XII 1, ~~Dord.~~ Pred. Srb. 85 [1367 a. b.] 5, 5, 6, 5, ↄOC
{Benum / Benam} kara džuz {li. / le.

54. Kuhač 600 [728-729]; 8, 8, 7, OC
Šil bir Barka žošnum dele
Šil bir rada za meštra. Z z (8, 7)

55. Kuba B.H. 228 [431]; 11, O
[Turhan aman aman aman Z z
Čikmi šeni sevdaha.] (8, 7)

56. Kuba B.H. 709 [1678]; 9, 9, 9, 5, ↄOC
Sumbul bijara sulvan ulvan
Ulvan gilan hajr. Z z (9, 5)

57. Kuba B.H. 445 [1747]; 8, 8, 6, 10, ↄOC
Šandudle šandudle z Z
Ora ora dudle šam nedrbu. (6, 10)

58. Kačerovski 55 [1786]; 12, 10, 8, 8, ↄOC
Aman aman kamo ti demana
Eske gelgi djul hanuma
Djul hanuma gel gel aman.

59 a. Bosiljevac 2 [1815 c.]; < 9, 5, 6, 7, ↄOC
davallah
Zveče dabillah
Zveče zveče vallal
Zveče billah zveče ja
[ah ah ih ih juh juh].

59 b. Kuba B.H. 342, ~~Dord.~~ Nar. Rev. p. 28, 1st mel. [1815 a. b.]; 9, 5, 6, 7, ↄOC
Zveče {davala / tavala / da bila / ta}
Zveče zveče {valja / vala}
Zveče {valja / bila} zveče ja
[{a i / a a ju ju} {ujuja / ih ih ju ju}].

60. Kuba B.H. 333 [1813-1814]; 8, 6, 13, 12, ↄOC
Džule džule džuleraj
džuleriarara
Dija diju indži džiju
džulesareraj.

61. Kuba B.H. 512 [1819]; 12, 14, 9, 10, ↄOC
bir na nume
Ofe ofe jeleč
bir tan aman aman
Kaoleri aj kuzum džuleri
Divan nejleri beni a beni.

III. Refrains consisting of words with definite sense, as well as of words with no definite sense

62. ~~Dord~~. Pred. Srb. 560[820]; 10, 6, 6, ◯ C
Smilj bere dilbere.

63. Kuhač 1101[905e.]; 10, 6, 6, [?], ◯ C
iha miha lengera

64. Kuhač 210[1807]; 8, 6, 7, 6, ⊃◯C
Šadi radi rum pum pum.

65. ~~Dord~~. Pred. Srb. 194[744]; 5, 7, 5, ◯ C
Vaj bedo karadjuzle.

66. Kuba B. H. 792[11]; 10,
Jedna dajna dao, vida nojlo.

67. Kuhač 306[601]; 8, 10, ◯
Vajam aman naman vaj dušice.

68. Kuba B. H. 824[890]; 10, 7, 5, ◯ C
Čimber bane, čim sana ruža rumena.

69. ~~Dord~~. Pred. Srb. 437[1451]; 10, 10, 14, 14, ⊃◯C
|: Dumaj, Jelo, dum dum dum,
dumaj, dušo, dušalaj.

69 bis. Iz Levča 49[923]; 8, 8, 5, ⊃◯
Bum Andelko, bum Nedeljko,
Bum sulum bum bum.

70. Kuba B. H. 405[839]; 10, 9+8, 10, ◯ C
Šeftu dertu ne budi dertu
sija mladi dela dragi.

71a. Kuhač 374[881a.]; 10, 12, 8, ◯ C
Oj traninu trajninenu trajnenune
Zelena mala dubrava.

71b. Kuba IX 16[588]; 7, 9, ◯
Trajnani naj naj nam.

72. Kuba B. H. 668[1660]; 7, 7, 7, 10, ⊃◯C
nejdelu
Ne bil Kajder nakaj ser
Cuj di bere voj di der.

73. Kuhač 1011[1793]; 8, 7, 8, 5, ⊃◯C
Saj legum begum begum,
Bebe Jure nosi bilje
Alaj biljure.

74. Kuhač 684[1473]; 7, 6, 7, 6, ⊃◯C
[Tana tana tani nena
nena tani tani |: nena :|
Niti tani tani nena,
sreća je zgubljena.]

75. Kuhač 1446[1021c.]; 14, 11, 11, 11, ⊃◯C
čavrole čavrole
Čavroljuške jato tinje čavrole
Ao lele djukar lele djukarle
Djuka pende crno lele ternine

76. Kuba B. H. 987[1826]; 10, 7, 5+5, 6, ⊃◯C
Najzlez aman, džel aman
Džej Jela Ivo
džej Jela dušo
Džujler aman aman.

77. ~~Dord~~. Nar. Pev. p. 182, 1st mel. [1769];
12, 12, 10, 9, ⊃◯C
alaj bela
Sultijani ćilim vezi bela alaj,
Banju kanju oj kinju kiti oj
I ju joj, djerdan moj, blagonjoj.

78. Kuba B. H. 527[1823]; 8, 7+7, 6+5, 5, ⊃◯C
Tam bugi gusi muri
ta tari dari beri
Beri ben, deti hoj
hej zema karsum
Hajde gorom haj.

B. Refrains with definite sense

I. Consisting of one line

79. ~~Dord~~. Pred. Srb. 224[36d.]; 5, ◯
dilber.

80a. Kuba B. H. 210, 269, 944, 945, IX 12, Bosiljevac 38, ~~Dord~~. Pred. Srb. 412, 436 [75b., 618, 666a., 819a. b. c., 818a. b.] various structures
{Jano.
{janjo.

80b. ~~Dord~~. Pred. Srb. 391[611]; 8, 10, ◯
Jano rano.

80c. ~~Dord~~. Nar. Pev., p. 80, 1st mel. [867]
Oj Jano, Jano 10, 5, 6, ◯ C

80d. ~~Dord~~. Pred. Srb. 374[448i.]; 12, ◯
1. Jano, Jano.
2. Oj Jano.

80e. ~~Dord.~~ Pred. Srb. 470, Iz Levča 43 [454 a. b.]; 12, O
1. Jano, Jano.
2. Ej, [mori,] Bozano.

81a. ~~Dord.~~ Pred. Srb. 423 [1653]; 8, 6, 6, 6, ↄOC
Jelo.

81b. Kuba B. H. 312 [1789 b.]; 8, 5, 8, 10, ↄOC
1. jelo.
2. dušo jelko.

82. ~~Dord.~~ Pred. Srb. 462 [309 b.]; 10, O
ježo.

83. Kuhač 454 [1095 d.]; 7, 7, 7, 6, ↄOC
leljo.

84. ~~Dord.~~ Pred. Srb. 223 [183 i.]; 8, O
Leno.

85a. Kuba B. H. 410 [596]; 7, 14, O
Lazo.

85b. Kuhač 302 [876]; 7, 10, 4, OC
Lazo, ej.

86. ~~Dord.~~ Pred. Srb. 430 [253]; 9, O
nane.

87. ~~Dord.~~ Pred. Srb. 309 [815 e.]; 8,
Jerido.

88. ~~Dord.~~ Pred. Srb. 411 [1484 a.]; 7, 6, 7, 6, ↄOC
Avrame.

89. ~~Dord.~~ Pred. Srb. 15 [554]; 10, 7, O
Lazare.

90. ~~Dord.~~ Pred. Srb. 399, 452, 484 [553 a. b. d.] 10, 7, O
Petrole(ro).

91. ~~Dord.~~ Nar. Pev., p. 130, 2d mel. [444]; 11, O
Radule.

92a. Kuhač 569 [873]; 7, 10, 9, OC
Jelena.

92b. ~~Dord.~~ Pred. Srb. 64 [477]; 8, 5, O
Jelenke.

93a. ~~Dord.~~ Pred. Srb. 383 [101]; 7, O
koledo.

93b. Kuba X 41 [801]; 8, 6, 6, OC
Koledo, koledo,
Veselo, veselo.

94a. ~~Dord.~~ Pred. Srb. 394 [243 g.]; 8, 6, O
Devojko.

94b. Kuhač 71 [748]; 8, 4, 4, OC
|: Oj djevojko :|.

94c. Kuhač 448 [24 b.]; 10,
aj devojko.

94d. Kuhač 284 [905 a.]; 10, 8, 6, OC
Oj divojko.

94e. Kuba XI 14 [938 b.]; 10, 10, 7, ↄO
Daj, djevojko, daj daj daj.

94f. Kuhač 1080 [31]; 11,
1. djevojko.
2. djidjio.

95a. ~~Dord.~~ Pred. Srb. 360, Kuba B. H. 88 [627, 891 c.]; 7, OC; 10, 7, 6, OC
švaler moj.

95b. Kuba B. H. 865, 221 [986 a. b.]; < 10, 6, 10, ↄO
{šever moj.
{šaver

96. ~~Dord.~~ Pred. Srb. 335, Kuba B. H. 139 [981, 988]; < 10, 6, 10, ↄO
mile moj.

97. ~~Dord.~~ Pred. Srb. 289 [215]; 8, 6, O
Mil' kume.

98. Kuhač 363 a) b), 422 [892 a. b. d.]; 10, 7, 6, OC
rodjena.

99. ~~Dord.~~ Pred. Srb. 545 [1472 bis]; 7, 6, 7, 6, ↄOC
berberče.

100. ~~Dord.~~ Pred. Srb. 133, Kuhač 22, 276 [28, 270 e., 595]; 11, ; 10, O; 7, 13, O
zoraje.

101a. ~~Dord.~~ Pred. Srb. 515 [781 b.]; 8, 6, 6, OC
lado, lado.

101b. ~~Dord.~~ Pred. Srb. 53, 184, 232, 349, 373, 381, 382, 402 [252 a. b., 349 b., 448 d. f. j. n.]; 12, O; 10, O; 9, O
1. lado, lado.
2. lado.

101c. ~~Dord.~~ Pred. Srb. 282, 314 [448 l., 35]; 12, O; 11,
ladojlo.

101d. ~~Dord.~~ Pred. Srb. 262, 283, 284, 287 [448 a. e. h. k.]; 12, O
1. Lado, Lado.
2. Ladojlo.

102a. Kuba B. H. 793, 958 [455 e., 321]; 12, O 10, O
jadi, jadi.

102 b. Kuba B.H. 448 [926]; 8, 8, 6, ↄO
1. Jadi, jadi.
2. Ej ej.

103. Kuhač 605, 606, 607, 608, Kuba B.H. 848, IX 6 [897 a., 898 a. b. c. d. e.]; 10, 8, 6, OC
ime moje.

104 a. Kuhač 118, 417, 488, 722, 819, Kuba IX 46 [94 a. b., 599, 610 b. d. e.]; 7, O; 8, 10, O
{janje / janješce} moje.

104 b. Kuba B.H. 826 [561]; 11, 7, O
Janje milo.

104 c. Kuba B.H. 93, 368 [957 a. b.]; 6, 6, 10, ↄO
Janje moje b'jelo. (jelo,)

104 d. ~~Dord.~~ Pred. Srb. [1539]; 8, 6, 5, 8, 6, 5, ↄOC
1. Janje bijelo.
2. Janješce moje.

104 e. Kuhač 957 [740]; 8, 5, 8, OC
Janješce moje,
Moje janješce bijelo.

104 f. Kuba B.H. 794 [870]; 10, 8, 9, OC
1. /: Janje moje :/,
2. dilber moj.

105 a. Kuhač 486, 1110 [513 b., 1783]; 8, 6, O; 8, 6, 10, 10, ↄOC
lane moje

105 b. Kuhač 602, Kačerovski 60 [853 c. d.]; 9, 8+8, 5, OC
/: Lane moje oj :/.

105 c. Kuba B.H. 728 [908]; 10, 8, 6, OC
lale moje.

105 d. Kuba 519, 520 [339 a.]; 10, O
Ej, lale moje.

105 e. Juž. Srb. 428 [799]; < 8, 6, 6, OC
rane moje.

105 f. ~~Dord.~~ Pred. Srb. 445 [23]; 10,
nano moja.

105 g. Kuba B.H. 558, 559, 689, Bosiljevac 11, ~~Dord.~~ Nar. Pev. p. 167, 2d mel. [1655 a. b. c. d. e.]; < 12, 6, 6, 6, ↄOC
1. {lane moje. / lale moje. / lan moj. / dragče moj(e).}
2. {Ej hoj, lane moje. / Haj, haj,} (Cf. N° 153)

106. Parry 48; (10) 8, 6, 8, 6, ↄOC
slatko lane.

107. Kuhač 1410 [730-731]; 10, 10, 4, OC
Roža moja.

108 a. ~~Dord.~~ Nar. Pev. p. 188, 1st mel. [1014]; 8, 6, 7, ↄO
zlato moje.

108 b. Kuhač 820 [825]; 11, 6, 6, OC
Zlato, zlato l' moje.

109. Kuhač 344 [569]; 12, 6, O
željo moja.

110. Kuhač 423 [1631]; 10, 4, 10, 4, ↄOC
srdce moje.

111. Kuba B.H. 207 [909]; 10, 8, 6, OC
srce Jovo.

112. Kuhač 1252 [934]; 8, 8, 7, ↄO
Belaj dude.

113 a. Kuhač 1444, 1445, ~~Dord.~~ Pred. Srb. 337 [1657 a. b., 895]; 8, 10, 10, 10, ↄOC; 10, 8, 6, OC
{bjelo / belo} lale.

113 b. Kuba B.H. 897 [608]; 8, 10, O
bjela lalo.

114. ~~Dord.~~ Pred. Srb. 246 [949]; 5, 5, 9, ↄO
Jano mori.

115. Kuba B.H. 285 [804 a.]; 8, 6, 6, OC
ludo mlado.

116. Kuhač 668 [603 a.]; 8, 10, O
oko ~~Đoko~~.

117. Juž. Srb. 400 [1092]; < 6, ↄOC
[mila nano.]

118. Kuhač 266, 293, 294, Kuba B.H. 563, 636, 874 [1011, 878 a. b., 27, 1579 b., 826]; various structures
mila moja. (Cf. N° 218)

119. ~~Dord.~~ Pred. Srb. 8 [34]; 12,
abo mila.

120. Kuba B.H. 155, Kuhač 942 [591 a. b.]; 7, 11, O
draga mila.

121 a. Kuhač 939 [593 a.]; 7, 11, O
milu milom

121b. Kuhač 940, 941, 943 [593 b. c. d.]; 7, 11, O
{dragi lubi.
{drage lubo.
{dragu ljubim.

122. Kuba IX. 22, Kuhač 13 [1006 a. b.]; 8, 6, 10, ↃO
Kato zlato.

123. Kuba B.H. 415 [732]; 10, 10, 4, OC
Rano Ano.

124. Kuhač 237 [1017 a.]; 12, 6, 10, ↃO
Curo rano.

125a. Kuba B.H. 306, 898 [281 b., 318]; 10, O
Grdna rano.

125b. Kuba B.H. 128 [927]; 8, 8, 6, ↃO
Aman aman grdna rano,
Ej, gidi.

125c. Kuba B.H. 843 [1383]; 7, 7, 8, 7, ↃOC
aman aman grdna rano,
Aman aman.

126. Kuba B.H. 148 [1371 b.]; 5, 5, 9, 5, ↃOC
komšo dušo.

127. Iz Levča 53 (texts 129, 130), Đord. Pred. Srb. 466 [32, 553 c.]; 11, ; 11, 7, O
varaj {Rado.
{Radu.

128. Kuba B.H. 966, 185 [435 c., 1077 d.]; 11, O
< 5, ↃOC
{zora Maro.
{zoro

129. Kuba B.H. 132 [1371 a.]; 5, 5, 9, 5, ↃOC
beg Ali beg.

130. Kuhač 665 [527]; 10, 4, O
Cviet zeleni.

131. Đord. Pred. Srb. 435 [391 b.]; 10, O
Oj golube.

132. Kuhač 69 [33]; 12,
O javore.

133. Kuhač 25 [270 d.]; 10, O
Oj Marice.

134. Kuhač 134, 287, 554 [1570 f., 327 c., 377 b.]
10, O; 8, 6, 8, 6, ↃOC
oj {žalosti.
{žalostna.

135a. Iz Levča 29, Đord. Pred. Srb. 259. [1561 c. d.]; 8, 4, 8, 4, ↃOC
Noć, {tamna, noć.
{tavna,
{Maro,

135b. Đord. Pred. Srb. 489, 406, 356 [123 ee. ff. gg.]; 8, 5, O;
Noć, noć, tamna noć. 8, 7, O

136. Kuhač 655 [1584 d.]; 8, 4, 8, 4, ↃOC
Spat, stari, spat.

137. Đord. Pred. Srb. 563 [1285 d.]; 8, 6, ↃOC
Ej, Jovo, Jovo.

138a. Kuba XII 25 [1082]; < 5, ↃOC
Oj, tugo, tugo.

138b. Đord. Pred. Srb. 425 [815 b.]; 8, 7, 7, OC
|: Ej, tuge tuge njene :|.

139. Kuba B.H. 694 [602]; 8, 10, O
Hoj, saba zora.

140. Đord. Pred. Srb. 594 [123 cc.]; 8, O
Čoče mi, čoče.

141a. Bosiljevac 4 [982]; < 10, 6, 10, ↃO
čuj, curo moja.

141b. Kuba B.H. 755 [1015]; 10, 5, 6, ↃO
Čuj, moja draga.

141c. Kuhač 603 [853 e.]; 9, 8+8, 7, OC
Čuj, dragi, čuj, dragi, čuj.

142. Kuhač 541 [939]; < 10, 10, 6, ↃO
Milčice moja.

143. Kuba B.H. 656, XI 62 a), Đord. Nar. Pev. p. 36, 1st mel. [312 c. d., 892 c.]; 10, O; 10, 7, 6, OC
{Milko, Milčice.
{Ja oj Milko,

144. Đord. Pred. Srb. 144 [928]; < 8, 8, 6, ↃO
nano, nanice.

145. Kuba B.H. 800 [749 c.]; 8, 5, 5, OC
|: Čuj mi ružica :|.

146. Kuhač 727, 728 [1022 a. b.]; 8, 6, 5, ↃO
Oj, oj, {tode moj.
{Bože

147. Đord. Nar. Pev., p. 42, 2d mel. [1532 b]; 8, 5, 8, 5, ↃOC
Oj, dragana, oj.

148. Bosiljevac 44, Kuba XIII 10, B.H. 1118 [1532 a. e. f.]; 8, 5, 8, 5, ⊃○⊂
Oj, čobane moj.

149. Kuba B.H. 238 [1672 a.]; 8, 8, 8, 5, ⊃○⊂
Dragi tvoja sam.

150. Iz Levča 14 (t. 36) [120 a.]; < 8, ○
Jao! kuku Arso.

151. Iz Levča 69 [673]; 6, ⊃○
Diko Peruniko.

152. Đord. Nar. Pev. p. 188, 3d mel. [1059] < 5, ⊃○⊂
Nane mila nane.

153a. Kuhač 545 [904 b.]; 10, 8, 7, ○⊂
Oj ti lane lane.

153b. Kuhač 744, 198, 756 [868 a. b. c.]; 10, 6, 7, ○⊂
Oj ti lane lane,
Žar ne mariš za mene.
(Cf. N° 105)

154. Đord. Pred. Srb. 135 [606]; 8, 10, ○
tugo mili Bože.

155. Kuhač 1219 [480 a.]; 8, 6, ○
Hajde, hajde, Maro.

156. Iz Levča 17 [972]; 7, 6, 7, ⊃○
Roso, magla pade.

157. Kuhač 1114, 270 [1435 a. b.]; 8, 8, 10, 10, ⊃○⊂
{Sedam tjedan dana.
{Sedem tjeden danak.

158. Đord. Nar. Pev. p. 154, 1st mel. [1599 a.]; 8, 6, 8, 6, ⊃○⊂
Ivan van, Ivan van.

159. Kuhač 1144 [1634]; 10, 6, 10, 6, ⊃○⊂
Joca joj, Joca joj.

160. Đord. Nar. Pev. p. 74, 1st mel. [1599 b.]; 8, 6, 8, 6, ⊃○⊂
Jovane, Jovanke.

161. Đord. Pred. Srb. 570 [508]; 8, 6, ○
Lade moj, lade moj.

162a. Đord. Pred. Srb. 292, 384, Kuhač 1008 [883 b., 123 j., 1598]; 8, 6, ○; 8, 6, 8, 6, ⊃○⊂
Paun moj, paun moj.

162b. Kuba B.H. 366, Kuhač 1007, 1006, 1005 [123 b. c. e. f.]; 8, ○
Paune moj, paune moj.

162c. Đord. Pred. Srb. 35 [123 k.]; 8, 6, ○
Moj paun, moj paun.

162d. Đord. Pred. Srb. 96 [123 g.]; 8, 7, 7, ○⊂
Paun, paun, paun moj.

162e. Kuhač 1004 [123 a.]; 8, ○
Moj paune, siv sokole.

163. Đord. Pred. Srb. 158 [509]; 8, 6, ○
Milano, Milano.

164. Kuba XIV 21 [1448 b.]; 10, 10, 12, 12, ⊃○⊂
Oj, lane, Milane.

165. Iz Levča 48 [552]; 10, 6, ○
aleno, maleno.

166. Kuhač 742, 772, Kuba IX 14 [800 a. b., 929]; 8, 6, 6, ○⊂; 8, 8, 6, ⊃○

167. Kuhač 155 [335 c.]; 10, ○
Oj diko, dikice.

168. Đord. Nar. Pev., p. 69, 1st mel. [1728]; 11, 11, 8+8, 6+6, ⊃○⊂
|: Jabuko, bedriko :|.

169. Kuba B.H. 19, 20 [1809 b. a.]; < 8, 6, 10, 6, ⊃○⊂
Rucica rumena.

170. Kuhač 298 [1827]; 10, 8, 7+6, 7, ⊃○⊂
Ristane, Salgane.

171. Kuhač 527 [1806]; 8, 5, 6, 5, ⊃○⊂
Lale sam, zumbul sam.

172. Kuhač 836 [1022 c.]; 8, 6, 5, ⊃○
Oj oj staj, ne spavaj.

173. Kuba B.H. 428 [938 a.]; 10, 10, 6, ⊃○
Sjaj goro zelena.

174. Kuhač 1469, Đord. Nar. Pev., p. 102, 1st mel. [1148 a. b.]; 6, ⊃○⊂
{Ha hm jel istina.
{Hm

175a. Iz Levča 55, 57 [891 a. b.]; 10, 7, 6, ○⊂
Oj dilbere, dilbere.

175b. Kuhač 769 [571]; 12, 7, ○
Ej, nedeljo dilbero.

175c. Parry 30; 8, 6, 5, ⊃○
Moj dilbere, moj.

176. Đord. Pred. Srb. 369 [523]; 8, 7, ○
Rano, rano, najrano.

177. ~~Dord.~~ Pred. Srb. 2[1630]; 8b, 7, 8b, 7, ↄOC
Tale, belo devojče.

178. ~~Dord.~~ Pred. Srb. 439[558–559]; 11, 6, O
dušice, dušo moja.

179. Kuhač 76[1800 c.]; 7, 6, 8, 6, ↄOC
Oj lepa devojako.

180. Kuba B. H. 925, 1125[1446 a. b.]; 10, 10, 13, 13, ↄOC
Čuj Anko Srbijanko.

181. ~~Dord.~~ Pred. Srb. 139[125 dd.]; < 8, O
Dodole, daj Bože dažd.

182. Kačerovski 61[1449–1450]; 10, 10, 14, 14, ↄOC
A oj Mile brgjanine.

183. Kuhač 545[904 a.]; 10, 8, 6, OC
Oj ti luče, moje luče.

184. ~~Dord.~~ Pred. Srb. 26[169]; 8, O
Oj, dodole, mili Bože.

185. Kuba B. H. 665[735]; 10, 10, 8, OC
Ej, bor zelen, bor nad rodom.

186. Kuba XII 31[745]; 7, 8, 7, OC
Dilber Andjelijo lele.

187. Iz Levča, 44, 63[422 a. b.]; 11, O
Dimitrole ruse kose.

188. Kuba B. H. 814[570]; 12, 7, O
došo zlato, zlato moje.

189. Kuhač 804[1380]; 6, 6, 8, 6, ↄOC
Lipa bila golubica.

190. Kuba B. H. 653, XI 2[724 a., 1762]; 11, ↄO
Biserrosa magla pala. 10, 10, 8, 6, ↄOC

191. ~~Dord.~~ Pred. Srb. 294[666 b.]; 6, 8, 6, ↄO
Ler, lero, lepa mi Maro.

192. Kuba B. H. 189[694]; 8, ↄO
Hej, Maro, hej, hej, zašto to?

193. ~~Dord.~~ Pred. Srb. 420[1285 a.]; 8b, ↄOC
|: Todori oko šareno :|.

194. ~~Dord.~~ Pred. Srb. 240[708 a.]; 8b, ↄO
|: Gukaj mi, gukaj, golube.

195a. Kuba B. H. 657[995]; 6, 5, 8b, ↄO
Haj, haj, haj, ustaj, ne spavaj.

195b. Kačerovski 31, ~~Dord.~~ Nar. Pev. p. 76, 1st mel. [973 a. b.]; 8, 5, 8, ↄO
sele žetva je!
Haj, haj, haj, ustaj, ne spavaj.

196. ~~Dord.~~ Pred. Srb. 256[203]; 8b, O
Napi se ljutu rakiju.

197. ~~Dord.~~ Pred. Srb. 496[708 e.]; 8b, ↄO
Sam sedi, beri, devojko.

198. ~~Dord.~~ Pred. Srb. 203[831]; 8, 11, 11, OC
|: Hej danga, dej danga vojnole :|.

199a. ~~Dord.~~ Pred. Srb. 127, 153, 164, 173, 215, 258, 301[123 l. m. n. o. p. r. s.]; 8, 9, O
{Gospodi, Gospodi pomiluj.
{Gospode, Gospode

199b. ~~Dord.~~ Pred. Srb. 288, 478, Iz Levča 72 [123 t. u. v.]; 8, 6, O
{Gospodi pomiluj.
{Gospode

199c. ~~Dord.~~ Pred. Srb. 23[123 y]; 8, 6, O
Gospode zaraduj.

199d. ~~Dord.~~ Pred. Srb. 138, 233, Juž. Srb. 399 [123 z. aa. bb.]; 8, 6, 6, OC
Gospode, Gospode
Pomiluj, pomiluj.

199e. ~~Dord.~~ Pred. Srb. 146[1067]; 5, ↄOC
Gospode Bože
Pomiluj polje.

200. ~~Dord.~~ Pred. Srb. 387[254]; 9, O
Jagodo,
Jagodo devojka, Jagodo.

201. ~~Dord.~~ Pred. Srb. 385[964]; 8, 8, 9, ↄO
U rumen medno vino, lerje.

202. ~~Dord.~~ Pred. Srb. 317[349 c.]; 10, O
Oj ubava, ubava devojko.

203. Kuhač 61[423 b.]; 10, 11, O
Spavaj, spavaj i o meni sanjaj.

204. Kuba B. H. 159[280 d.]; 10, O
Ankice moja, draga ljubezna.

205. Kuba XII. 16[722–723]; 10, O
Žalosti moja, dangubo moja.

206. ~~Dord.~~ Pred. Srb. 400[597 b.]; 8, 10, O
Da dođe, da dođe, da ne dođe.

207. Kuhač 838[961 a.]; 7, 7, 10, ↄO
Jelene, plemenite gospoje.

208. Kuba XII 39, B. H. 53[880 a. b.]; 8, 11, 6, OC
Čuj. {Ivane dilbere, željo moja.
{Marice grančice,

209. ~~Dord.~~ Pred. Srb. 5[1442]; 10, 10, 11, 11, ↄOC
|: Vančice, dušice, lečiću te ja :|.

209 bis. Iz Levča 71[422 c.]; 11, O
Todoro,
Oj, Todoro, grčko cveće ubavo.

210. Bosiljevac 28 [1428]; 14, 14, 12, 12, ⊃○⊂
|: Hajde nek ide lanac i pô livade :|.

211. Kuba B.H. 957 [1446 c.]; 10, 10, 13, 13, ⊃○⊂
|: Hej, Anko Srbijanko ladju od Merdzana :|.

212. Kuhač 1082 [1447 c.]; 10, 10, 13, 13, ⊃○⊂
Oj devojko, devojko, materino mleko.

213. Kuhač 520, Kuba B.H. 14 [1439 a. b.]; 8, 8, 13, 13, ⊃○⊂
|: Duna, Duna, Dunave tiha vodo hladne :|.

214. Kuhač 1091 [1447 d.]; 10, 10, 16, 16, ⊃○⊂
|: Eto ljudi tulipana,
ljubi seku u poldana :|.

II. Double refrains, each consisting of one line
(in the last four: one of one line, the other of two lines)

215. Đord. Pred. Srb. 431 [670]; 6, ⊃○
1. haj haj.
2. lale.

216. Parry 25; 6, 6, 10, ⊃○
1. ago.
2. bego.

217. Kuba B.H. 67 [725]; 11, ⊃○
1. majko.
2. Lejla.

218. Kuba B.H. 74 [823]; 10, 8, 8, ○⊂
1. mila.
2. Mila moja. (Cf. N° 118)

219. Kuba B.H. 936 [919]; 13, 10, 5, ○⊂
1. Jovo.
2. Jovo na novo.

220a. Kuba XII 40 [958 b.]; 7, 7, 10, ⊃○
1. haj haj haj.
2. baš nekaj.

220b. Đord. Nar. Pev. p. 23, 1st mel., Kuba B.H. 866, Kačerovski 25 [954 a. c. b.]
{aj. haj haj.
{hej
{ču

220c. Bosiljevac 15 [958 a.]; 7, 7, 10, ⊃○
1. uhaha.
2. baš neka.

221a. Kuba B.H. 50 [958 e.]; 7, 7, 10, ⊃○
1. Anuša.
2. jagoda.

221b. Kuba B.H. 640 [958 g.]; 7, 7, 10, ⊃○
1. Hanio.
2. jagodo.

221c. Kuba B.H. 639 [958 d.]; 7, 7, 10, ⊃○
1. Ilija.
2. jado.

221d. Kuba B.H. 446 [959 a.]; 7, 7, 10, ⊃○
1. milje moj.
2. jagodo.

221e. Kuba XI 9, Đord. Nar. Pev. p. 14, 1st mel. Kačerovski 1, Đord. Pred. Srb. 357 [1778 a. b. c., 959 b.]; 7, 8, 6, 6, ⊃○⊂
1. {jagoda. < 7, 7, 6, ⊃○
{jagodo.
2. jagodice.

222. Kuba B.H. 907 [958 c.]; 7, 7, 10, ⊃○
1. Alija
2. sevlija.

223. Đord. Pred. Srb. 336 [958 f.]; 7, 7, 10, ⊃○
1. brelele.
2. tugole.

224. Đord. Pred. Srb. 434 [594]; 7, 11, ○
1. lej lele.
2. tužnole.

225. Đord. Pred. Srb. 181 [418]; 11, ○
1. Lepole.
2. Dragole.

226. Kuba B.H. 140 [1019]; 7, 10, 4, ⊃○
1. Ivo moj.
2. Oj, Ivo hej.

227. Iz Levča 46 [874]; 7, 8, 6, ○⊂
1. Duduce.
2. dušo moja.

228. Đord. Pred. Srb. 497 [452 b.]; < 12, ○
1. gungule.
2. gungulice.

229. Kuhač 595 [914]; 11, 8, 5, ○⊂
1. šarinom.
2. Žuti lilijom.

230. Kuba B.H. 3 [869]; 13, 6, 7, ○⊂
1. što mi što.
2. Neka neka o hoho.

231. Đord. Pred. Srb. 333 [1021 b.]; 10, 18, 5, ⊃○
1. Srbijanke.
2. Hoj haj.

232. Đord. Pred. Srb. 396 [456]; 12, ○
1. Miljo, Miljo.
2. milome.

233a. ~~Dord.~~ Nar. Pev., p. 7, 2d mel., Kuhač 1460, 726 [566c., 567a., 401a.]; 11, 10, O; 10, O
1. lako, lako.
2. lagano.

233b. Kuba B.H. 215, 407, 536 [566a.b., 567b.]; 11, 10, O
1. lako {lale. / lane.
2. lagano.

233c. Kuhač 164 [912]; 11, 7, 6, OC
1. tako lako.
2. Lagano, lagano.

234. Kuhač 850 [1303b.]; <8, ƆOC
1. Dojka Fira.
2. Frandafil.

235a. Kuhač 591 [458]; 12, O
1. vaj vaj vaj vaj.
2. daj dušo daj.

235b. Kuhač 771 [645]; 8, OC
1. Haj ha ha haj.
2. Dej dušo dej.

236. Kuba XII 5 [1334]; 11, ƆOC
1. Ej vaj ej vaj.
2. ajde mi haj.

237. Kuba B.H. 737, 738 [877 a.b.]; 8, 10, 6, OC
1. {Neno / Lenko} moja.
2. {Ružo / Vamdzo} moja.

238. Kuba B.H. 908 [965]; 8, 8, 10, ƆO
1. jalak neno.
2. dockan dušo.

239. ~~Dord.~~ Pred. Srb. 443 [1205]; 8, ƆOC
1. E karavilj.
2. Karavilj - vilj.

240. ~~Dord.~~ Pred. Srb. 486 [452 a.]; 12, O
1. Nedo, Nedo.
2. jadna mi Nedo.

241. Iz Levča 30 [1555b.]; < 8, 6, 8, 6, ƆOC
1. pile rajsko.
2. Oj oj, zora je.

242. Juž. Srb. 411 [1754]; 8, 8, 10, 4, ƆOC
1. jagnje moje.
2. Aman aman devojčice mlada.

243. Kuba B.H. 693 [879]; 9, 10, 4, OC
1. Djete molim te.
2. lale Lazo.

239bis. Kuba B.H. 485 [449]; 12, O
1. moj rode moj.
2. gajtane moj.

244. ~~Dord.~~ Pred. Srb. 405 [407b.]; 11, O
1. ~~zorole zoro.~~
2. aj zorole.

245a. Kuba B.H. 521 [1789c.]; 8, 5, 8, 8, ƆOC
1. Dangubo moja.
2. milo i drago.

245b. Kuba XI 41 [460]; 13, O
1. dangubo moja.
2. dojdi do veče.

245c. Kuba B.H. 73, 815, 816 [1789a.d.e.] 8, 5, 8, 10, ƆOC
1. Dangubo moja.
2. Drago je meni {mladoj miloje. / i milo.

245d. ~~Dord.~~ Nar. Pev. p. 14, 2d mel. [746]; 7, 5, 5, OC
Dangubo moja,
Žalosti moja.

246. Kuba B.H. 173 [385]; 10, O
1. vajvaze moja.
2. vaj bolan dragi.

247. Kuba B.H. 403 [1632]; 10, 5, 10, 5, ƆOC
1. lele skafrere.
2. za nevenčić moj.

248. ~~Dord.~~ Nar. Pev. p. 191, 1st mel. [1359]; 14, ƆOC
1. lele Duneranke.
2. |: Duneranke :|, kato Piroćanke.

249. Kuhač 1308 [1352 a.]; 13, ƆOC
1. viv la kompagnija.
2. |: viv la :|, vivlala, viv la kompgnia.

250. Kuhač 174 [1415]; 10, 10, 6, 6, ƆOC
Two alternating refrains:
1. Mehmede, Mehmede.
2. Zelene nevene.

251. ~~Dord.~~ Pred. Srb. 210 [402 a.]; 10, O
1. tedeno, tedeno.
2. ledeno, ledeno.

252. Kuhač 460 [893]; 10, 7, 6, OC
1. Longer baša, kum baša.
2. [bielo lale].

253. Kuhač 321 [917]; 12, 8, 6, OC
1. divojčice, divojčice.
2. ruža moja.

254. Kuhač 324 [1791]; 8, 6, 8, 7, ƆOC
1. bela lalo.
2. Aj oj, Iso, sitno piso.
Za devojkom uzdiso.

238 bis. Iz Levča 43 [454b.]; 12, O
1. Jano, Jano.
2. oj Bojano.

255. Kuhač 11, 10, 12 [1795 a. b. c.]; 8, 6, 6, 7, ɔOC
1. lane moje.
2. A ja ju! ja bi tu,
Poljubio Tasiku.

256. Kuhač 200 [1565]; 8, 6, 8, 6, ɔOC
1. lane moje.
2. U proleće beri cvieće,
Beri pa se ženi.

257. Kuba B. H. 742 [833 b.]; 8, 6+5, 8, OC
1. Zvjezdan i Danica
moj mio dragi.
2. ne ma Danice.

III. Refrains consisting of two lines

258. Kuba XI. 35 [817]; 10, 5, 5, OC
Marice moja,
Ljuba, ne vjerna.

259. Kuhač 548 [1779]; 8, 6, 5, 5, ɔOC
Kato, Katice,
dušo i srdce.

260. Đord. Pred. Srb. 345 [766 b.]; 8, 5, 5, OC
Oj le Manojle.
Ditla, divitla.

261a. Kuba B. H. 476 [1013]; 9, 5, 10, ɔO
sad je zora je,
Sad je svanula.

261b. Kuba B. H. 561 [1821]; 8, 6, 5+5, 11, ɔOC
Sad je zora je,
sad se svanulo,
Sad se moje kat mer cvjece razmeće.

262. Kuba B. H. 741, Đord. Nar. Pev. p. 150, 1st mel., Bosiljevac 31, Đord. Pred. Srb. 467 [833 a. e. g.] 8, 5+5, 8, OC
Zvjezdane dane,
moj mio {brane.
{brale.

263. Đord. Pred. Srb. 353 [760 a.]; 8, 5, 5, OC
Karanfile moj,
Frandafile moj.

264. Đord. Pred. Srb. 236, 221 [802 d., 807]; 8, 6, 6, OC
Dojde da ne dojde,
Pošla će da dojde.

265. Đord. Nar. Pev. p. 190, 1st mel. [1781]; 8, 6, 7, 7, ɔOC
Hajd' pole, hajd' polako,
Hajd' laga, hajd' lagano.

266. Kuhač 724 [1179 a.]; 7, ɔOC
Sem biser sermo moja,
Stani veli dilbere.

267. Iz Levča 20 [691 b.]; 8, ɔO
Cane jane moj dragane,
Oj devojko, vita jelo.

268. Đord. Nar. Pev., p. 153, 1st mel. [1270]; 8, ɔOC
Oj vi jadi, moju jadi,
Šta moj dragi sada radi?

269. Kuhač 1139 [1692 b.]; 8, ɔOC
Srdce moje ranjeno je,
Od ljubavi stopljeno je.

270. Kuba B. H. 550 [630]; 8, OC
Stoj, stoj Drino vodo hladna,
Stoj, stoj devojko rode moj.

271. Đord. Pred. Srb. 495 [701 a.]; 8b, ɔO
Oko treni, kolo kreni,
Za gorom, džanom a džanom.

272. Đord. Nar. Pev. p. 139, 1st mel. [1279 a.]; 8b, ɔOC
Oj jagnje belo, prebelo,
Povedi kole veselo.

273a. Đord. Pred. Srb. 561 [650]; 8, 8b, 8b, OC
Za gradom, za vinogradom,
Za lozom, za ne rezanom.

273b. Kuhač 35 [863]; 8, 6, 9, OC
Za gradom, za gradom,
Za Legradom, za vinogradom.

274. Kuba B. H. 531 [647]; 8b, OC
Žalosti moja, žalosti,
Asime dušo za tobom.

275. Kuba XI. 12 [1447]; 10, 10, 13, 13, ɔOC
Dunaj, Dunaj, Dunave, tiha vodo hladna,
Mare, Mare, Maruško, lepa ti si mlada.

276. Kuhač 1217 [480 b.]; 8, 10, O
Hajdte, hajdte druge,
Hajdte druge. **Z z** 6, 5,

277. Iz Levča 51 [857]; 10, 6+5, 6, OC
Čuješ momče dilber,
oj, dušo drago. **Z z** 6, 5,

278. Đord. Pred. Srb. 293 [883 a.]; 8, 6 5, OC
Ježole, dragole,
Dragi brate moj. **Z z** 6, 5,

279. Kuba 836, Đord. Nar. Pev. p. 175, 2d mel. [1744 a. b.]; 8, 8, 6, 5, ↄOC
Veselo, veselo, Z z 6, 5,
Veselo je to.
|: Veselo je ovo selo :| ovo.

280. Đord. Pred. Srb. 243 [884]; 8, 7, 5, OC
Je l' Jelo, je l' Jeleno, Z z 7, 5,
Je l' je veće noć.

281. Kuhač 1103 [889]; 10, 7, 5, OC
Znam da znaš, prsten moje, Z z 7, 5,
Drage da mi daš.

282 a. Kuhač 96, 95 [1750 a. c.]; 8, 8, 7, 6, ↄOC
Čaj čirom, sedi s mirom, Z z 7, 6,
U seku ne diraj.

282 b. Kuhač 1115 a) [1750 b.]; 8, 8, 7, 6, ↄOC
Čaj čiro perlengiro, Z z 7, 6,
U pile ne diraj.

283. Kuba B.H. 984 [885]; 8, 7, 6, OC
Moj Aljo, moja dušo, Z z 7, 6,
Moj šećer Alibeg.

284. Đord. Pred. Srb. 368 [901]; 10, 8, 6, OC
Oj Todoro, željo moja, Z z 8, 6,
Ružo uz prozore.

285. Kuhač 269 [1674]; 8, 8, 8, 7, ↄOC
Kaži meni, sjajna zvierzda, Z z 8, 7,
Gdje je moja ljubezna.

286 a. Kuba B. H. 1020 [888 a.]; 9, 8, 7, OC
Stoj Drina, vodo ladna, stoj, Z z 8, 7,
O djevojko, rode moj.

286 b. Đord. Nar. Pev. p. 121, 1st mel. [888 b.]; 11, 8, 7, OC
Oj, Drino, stoj, stoj, Drino vodo ladna, stoj,
Stan' devojko, rode moj.

287. Kuba B. H. 806 [1755]; 8b, 8b, 10, 4, ↄOC
Tra na nina uroke ti voda Z z 10, 4,
Od ni jela.

288. Kačerovski, 72 [1419]; < 10, 10, 9, 9, ↄOC
Milčice moja, šećer usta tvoja, Z z 11, 9,
Milko moja, al te volim ja.

289. Đord. Nar. Pev. p. 15, 1st mel. [1755 bis]; 8b, 8b, 12, 5, ↄOC
Srmi djeni grani mami čez nem, se nem, Z z 12, 5,
Sane dragane.

290. Kuba X 38 [1771]; 12, 12, 13, 11, ↄOC
Nijega, nijega nego doma nijega, Z z 13, 11,
Nego doma nijega, sutra će doć.

291. Iz Levča 45 (text 120) [420 a.]; 11, O
Kalino, z Z 3, 11,
Kale vile vito pero zeleno.

292. Iz Levča, 71 [422 c.]; 11, O
Todoro, z Z 3, 11,
Oj Todoro, grčko cveće ubavo.

293. Đord. Pred. Srb. 520 [1398 b.]; 8, 8, 4, 7, ↄOC
Čik, Božo, čik, z Z 4, 7,
Čik djavolo, čik, čik, čik.

294 a. Kuhač 447 [967]; 8, 8, 10, ↄO
eto tako, z Z 4, 8,
Čuješ li me mila majko

294 b. Đord. Nar. Pev. p. 4, 2d mel. [1585 c.]; 8, 6, 8, 6, ↄOC
eto tako.

295. Kuba B. H. 1041 [130 c.]; 8, O
|: Hoj' vamo, hoj :|, z Z 4, 8,
Djevojčice, da spavamo

296. Kuba XIV 28, B. H. 638, 637 [1388 a. b. c.]; 7, 7, 5, 7, ↄOC
Haj vaj Bože daj, z Z 5, 7,
Pri je curu, negoraj.
Prvo
Ili curu, ili raj.

297. Kuhač 432, 433 [1017 b.]; 12, 6, 12, ↄO
Varaj, nevaraj, z Z 5, 7,
varaj curo jošt malo.

298 a. Kuba B. H. 710 [856]; 10, 5+7, 6, OC
Ej lala dragane, z Z 6, 7,
neday zori da svane.

298 b. Kuba B. H. 659 [1811]; 10, 6, 13, 10, ↄOC
|: Hasane :|, dragane,
Hoće zora |: da svane :| cf. No 340.

299. Kuba XIV 11 [1745-1746]; 8, 8, 6, 7, ↄOC
Ej lano plameno z Z 6, 7,
I sa šerbet bojeno.

300. Đord. Pred. Srb. 34 [855 b.]; 8, 8+6, 7, OC
i ju ju redom re, z Z 6, 7,
Redom redi Jovane.

301. Iz Levča 38 [865]; 8, 6, 7, OC
Stevano, Stevano, z Z 6, 7,
Rosno cveće na rano.

302. Kuhač 702 [866]; 8, 6, 7, OC
Za gorom, za vodom, z Z 6, 7,
Za zelenim javorom.

303. Kuhač 546 [904 c.]; 10, 6, 8, OC
Oj Maro, Marica, z Z 6, 8,
Zišla je danica biela.

303 bis. Kuba B. H. 829 [1553]; 8, 6, 8, 6, ↄOC
[Eno, ojoj, nena,] z Z 7, 8
ojoj nena rano moja.

304a. Kuba B.H. 796[741]; 8, 7, 8b, ⊃ O C
Magla, maglica moja,
Razvijaj nam se, razvijaj — z Z 7, 8b,

305. Kuhač 1462[1723]; 8, 8, 8+8, 10, ⊃ O C
[Upalo tu, fika fuku,]
žagrebem, potrčim, poljubim tu. — z Z 8, 10,

306. Kuhač 1291, 1292, 1290[1764a.b.c.]; 10, 10, 8, 11, ⊃ O C
Stani {de / der}, dušo, stani {de / der}, — z Z 8b, 11,
Stan' počekaj, {drago srdce, / samo malo} {kraj / kod} mene.

307. Kuba XII 21[1331]; < 10, ⊃ O C
Nevene, nevene daj džuzel daj.
Jagodo, jagodo, propiću se ja. — z Z 10, 11,

308. Dord. Nar. Pev. p. 126, 1st mel. [1774]; 14, 14, 10, 13, ⊃ O C
Lele, lele, izgore za tebe,
Izgore mi, džanum Sano, srce za tebe. — z Z 10, 13,

309. Kuhač 1247[1437]; < 8, 8, 12, 12, ⊃ O C
Der der pile moje, der koho moja,
Sviraj mi kumu mome, kumu debelome. — z Z 11, 13,

IV. Refrains consisting of three lines

310. Kuba B.H. 717[1820]; 8, 6, 5+5, 5, ⊃ O C
O Rade, Rade,
jelen na rane,
Oj draga spava.

311. Dord. Pred. Srb. 557[833h.]; 8, [6,] 6+6, 8, ⊃ O C
Dođi, Jelo, dođi,
Kako ću ti doći,
kad nemogu proći.

312a. Kuhač 36[1690b.]; 8, 8, 8+8, 8, ⊃ O C
Po čem sam ja lane moje,
duša tvoja, lane moje,
Aman aman duša tvoja.

312b. Kuhač 37[1690c.]; 8, ⊃ O C
Po čem sam ja džanum fendum
Duša tvoja, duša tvoja.

313. Kuba B.H. 831[1709]; 10, 10, 6+6, 4, ⊃ O C
O zelena travo,
koj' na tebi spavo, — Z Z z 6, 6, 4,
Kaži pravo.

314. Iz Levča 54[1824]; 10, 6, 7+7, 3, ⊃ O C
Dika veli jabuko,
ajd' za nama, devojko, — Z Z z 7, 7, 3,
Devojko.

315. Kuhač 689[1732]; 16, 16, 5+5, 9, ⊃ O C
Draga ružica,
mila ružica, — z z Z 5, 5, 9,
Zapet ću te ljubit od srdca.

316. Kačerovski 20[1724], 10, 10, 6+6, 7, ⊃ O C
|: Varaj curo mala
još godinu dana, — z z Z 6, 6, 7,
Varaj curo još malo :|.

317. Kuhač 743[860c.]; 10, 6+6, 11, O C
Čuj curice curo,
birtašice gulo — z z Z 6, 6, 11,
Al što točiš siljer vino jeftino.

318. Kuhač 874, 875, 872[1722 a.b.c.]; 8, 8, 6+6, 15, ⊃ O C
Moja lepa {Milko, / Jano,} — z z Z 6, 6, 15,
moja {Severinko / sevdelinko}
Moja {črno / carna} - oka ubava, {Milko mi djevojko. / Jano / ja ljubim}

320. Kuba B.H. 201[1727]; 5+5, 5+5, 8+8, 12, ⊃ O C
Svije svati ispratiše,
samo svircu ne dadoše. — z z Z 8, 8, 12,
|: Ja sam cura mlada, sad je moja vlada :|

319. Kuba B.H. 661, 664[860a.b.]; 10, 7+7, 11, O C
Šučkaj, bučkaj, garava,
a što laju za nama, — z z Z 7, 7, 11,
Valjda n' ješmo ni mi, lole, najgore.

304b. Kuhač 948a) b) [1784]; 8, 7, 5, 5, ⊃ O C
Maglo, maglice moja,
Razvijaj mi se,
Maglo razvijaj.

321. Kuba B.H. 549[1792]; 8, 6, 8, 7, ⊃ O C
Aj nevene, - vene,
Daj do |: mene :| ne varaj, — z Z Z 6, 7, 7,
Daj mi ruku, djevojko.

322. Kuhač 613[1810]; 10, 6, 8, 6, ⊃ O C
Ljubiš mene Maro,
Ljubiš mene, siv sokole, — z Z z 6, 8, 6,
Draga duša moja.

323. Kuhač 394[942b.]; 10, 11, 8b, ⊃ O
Ljubi me diko,
ne čekaj toliko — z z Z 5, 6, 8b,
Ne čekaj dušo i srdce.

324\. Kuhač 236[942 a.]; 11, 11, 8б, ⊃O
Ljubi me Jelo, zZZ 5, 6, 8б,
moje čedo belo,
Jelice dušo i srdce.

325\. Kuba B.H. 739, 740[833 c. d.]; 8, 5+6, 10, OC
Mamice {moja, / mama, zZZ 5, 6, 10,
mene boli glava,
Jablane, tjeraj grane na strane.

326\. Kuhač 739[864]; 10, 8, 17, OC
Buki az ba, buki ez be, ZzZ 8, 7, 10,
Slovo ljudi mišljete,
mislis diko volim te, nevolim.

327\. Juž. Srb. 410[913]; 11, 8, 5, OC
jablane,
Jablanove divne rese zZZ 3, 8, 5,
Neronite se.

V. Triple refrains, consisting each of one line.

328\. Kuhač 346[956]; < 6, 6, 10, ⊃O
1\. Maco.
2\. Marice.
3\. Šefteli.

329a. Kuba B.H. 25, 26[1385 a. b.]; 7, 7, 10, 7, ⊃OC
1\. {mamice. / mamo.
2\. {tatice. / mamice.
3\. Moja mila mamice.

329b. Kuba B.H. 926[1659 g.]; 6, 6, 11, ⊃O
1\. mamo.
2\. mamice.

330a. Kuba B.H. 835[1759]; < 9, 9, 10, 6, ⊃OC
1\. Sojko djevojko,
2\. Sojčice djevojčice.
3\. arano, parano.

330b. Kuba B.H. 554, 555[1018 a. b.]; 9, 11, 10, ⊃O
1\. Sojko {djevojke. / djevojko.
2\. sojčice djevojčice.

325 bis. Kuba B.H. 1009[1326]; < 5+5, ⊃OC
[Ne luduj, ne budali, zZZ 7, 8, 9,
ostani se ludo mlado,
Ne zadaj se sevda golema.]

VII. Refrains consisting of four lines

331\. Kuhač 1295[1764 e.]; 12, O
[Tjeraj vodu na polje, 8, 6, 8, 6,
Pa zatvori vrata,
S vinom doć ćeš najdalje
Braći oko vrata].

332\. Kuba B.H. 696[1712]; 11, 11, 8+8, 3, ⊃OC
Zumbul Sava, dika plavo, 8, 8, 6, 7,
širi dragi bjele ruka,
Tvoja sam, [dojdi mi,
doj do veče, sama sam].

333\. Kuba B.H. 253, Đord. Nar. Pev. p. 112, 1st mel. 10, 10, 17, 18, ⊃OC
Boga mi Bog mi {je dao, / ih dade, 9, 9, 10, 8б,
duše mi majka {mi ih rodi. / ih
Osta ćeš ludo mlado ne luduj,
ne pravi sevda golemih.

334\. Đord. Nar. Pev. p. 157, 1st mel. [1725]; < 10, 10, 6+7, 7+7, ⊃OC
Pilence mamino, 6, 7, 8б, 8б,
gugulence tatino,
Ej, djidi, bela nimena,
ej, djidi, tanka, visoka.

335\. Kuba B.H. 239[1772-1773]; 12, 12, 16, 23, ⊃OC.
Daj da ga gledněm, daj da pogledněm tako živa) bila!
Daj da mu dam, daj da nedam, 16, 8, 8, 7,
hoću da ti kako neću,
hoću da ti rekla sam.

IX. Refrains consisting of more than four lines

336\. Kuba B.H. 663[1152]; 6, ⊃OC
[O moj dragi dilber drag
Jado, jadole
Dete djavole,
Djevojko dušo,
Djavole, djavole].

337. Kuba B.H. 1011[1830]; 17,13,8+11,7, ↄOC
aj džidi aj, na kormanu vaj,
Ima ljepših djevojaka jol dašo kaldaš.
Sizum bizum never nejak
a svi džuzli; tlapi džuzli jok torjok
Imam ljepu djevojku.

338. Kuhač 598[1794]; 10,16,10,5, ↄOC
Daj da ga budim
i da ga ljubim
i da mu govorim
Da ide kuči
šorom sa zorom
S Bogom djevojko!

339. Dord. Nar. Pev. p.40, 1st mel. [977]; <10,6,10, ↄO
[Dara se ponosi,
neće venac da nosi,
Ta nemoj se srditi
ja ću tebe ljubiti.]
Čuj, Jovo, vraže,
šta ti Dara kaže.

340. Kuhač 1088[1729]; 12,12,7+7,13, ↄOC
Oj Katice, Katice,
na mom srdcu ranice,
Je si l' majki kazala,
da si sa mnom igrala?
Asane, dragane,
hoće zora da svane.
cf. N° 298.

336 bis. Dord. Pred. Srb. 507[701b.]; 8,8,8b, ↄO
[I ja ja i ja Mija,
i nojkoj adžamija
pusti plot trnjeviti,
Ćau mene pci izesti
Kod one dobre devojke.]

341. Dord. Nar. Pev. p.151, 1st mel. [861a.] 8,8+8,6, OC
[Šibljani, Šibljičani,
Kratljani, Kratljičani,]
Kratko ajte, kratko noste,
kratko grane savijate.
[Čuvajte, ne salomte]
Grane jablanove.

342. Dord. Pred. Srb. 523[1812]; 14,17,12,14, ↄOC
majka Mar-, majka Mar-,
Majka Maru Margito
tijo govori sitno u pleće:
Ne moj, Maro, Margito isti u vorje,
U vorju je šušter Petar
Stepan ban Marijan.

343. Kuba IX 17[1726]; 10,10,6+6,18, ↄOC
Ja sam cura bela
svoj dragog zanela
Ruža cvati, dika pati
ja ću ruku drugom dati, šalaj!
Ruža cvala, i odcvala
ja sam ruku drugom dala, šalaj!

344. Dord. Nar. Pev., p.159, 1st mel. [861b.]; 8,5+5,10, OC
[Ver meni meni
Ver meni tebi
Ver meni janje
Tamo moje drago.]
Ne lomi sana,
ne gubi dana,
[Ne da mene moja mila nana,]
Ne da mene za godinu dana.

Index of First Lines

SERBO-CROATIAN TEXTS[1]

[1] Page numbers 95–230 refer to words with music. For a list of the singers and the regions and villages from which they come, see p. 89.

ENGLISH TRANSLATIONS

Index of First Lines

General Index

GENERAL INDEX

General Index

General Index

General Index

General Index

AUSTRIA
GRAZ
Villach
Klagenfurt
R. DRAVA
R. SAVA
Dravograd
POHORJE Mts.
Maribor
Murska Sobota
Lendava
BUDAPEST
Jesenice
Bled
Radovljica
KAMNIK Alps.
Mt. Triglav
Kranj
Kamnik
Ptuj
Tolmin
Celje
Rogaška Slatina
Varaždin
ITALY
Gorizia
Ljubljana
SLOVENIA
MILAN
Ajdovščina
Kalce
Postojna
Klanjec
Durdevac
Mt. Sljeme
Bjelovar
Trieste
Novo Mesto
Zagreb
Dugo Selo
Vitrovitica
VENICE
Piran
Koper
Portorož
Metlika
Umag
Buje
Crnomelj
Daruvar
Novigrad
Karlovac
Kutina
Opatija
Rijeka
Sisak
CROATIA
Istria
Pakrac
Poreč
Pazin
Crikvenica
Glina
Vršac
Ogulin
Novi Vinodolski
Vojnić
Novska
Rovinj
Labin
KRK
Krk
R. UNA
Bos. Dubica
Bos. Gradiška
Cres
Senj
Bos Novi
Prijedor
Pula
KVARNER
CRES
RAB
Rab
Otočec
Plitvice Lakes
Bihać
Bos Krupa
Osor
Sanski Most
LOŠINJ
Mali Lošinj
PAG
Karlobag
Gospić
Banja Luka
SUSAK
Bos. Petrovac
Ključ
Udbina
ADRIATIC SEA
Drvar
Gračac
ANCONA
Zadar
Bos. Grahovo
Jajce
DALMATIA
Benkovac
DUGI OTOK
Biograd
Knin
Donji Vakuf
Drniš
Livno
Šibenik
Sinj
Trogir
Ugljane
Split
Omis
Posušje
Imoski
Brela
ŠOLTA
BRAČ
PESCARA
Makarska
Ljubuški
HVAR
Ploče
VIS
BISEVO
Blato
Orebić
Korčula
KORČULA
LASTOVO
MLJET
0 kms 40 80
0 miles 25 50
N

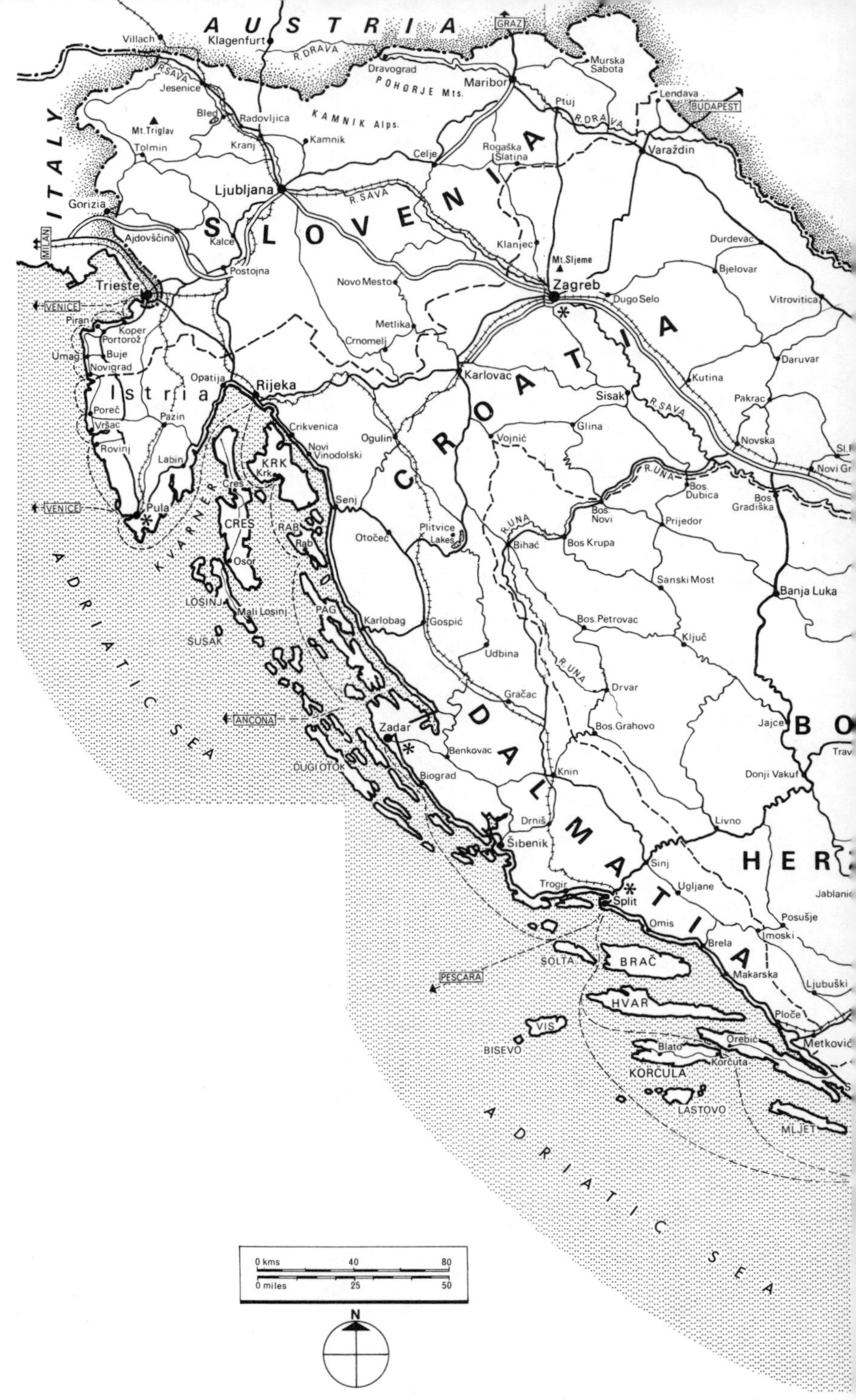

YUGOSLAVIA

KEY

Motorways
Main roads
Other roads
Railways
Car ferries
Cities
Large towns
Other towns
Airports

HUNGARY
RUMANIA
BULGARIA
ALBANIA
GREECE
VOJVODINA
Bačka
Banat
Srem
SERBIA
KOSOVO
MONTENEGRO
MACEDONIA

BUDAPEST
Szeged
Palić
Subotica
Senta
Kikinda
Ada
Sombor
Timisoara
Srbobran
Vukovar
Vinkovici
Bački Petrovac
Novi Sad
Zrenjanin
Plandište
Alibunar
Vršac
Ruma
Sremska Mitrovica
R. DANUBE
R. TISA
R. SAVA
R. DRINA
Brčko
Bijeljina
Šabac
Pančevo
BELGRADE
Kovin
Ve. Gradište
Iron Gate (Dam)
Kladevo
Smederevo
Požarevac
Tuzla
Loznica
Zvornik
Vlasenica
Mladenovac
Smed. Palanka
R. MAVA
R. MORAVA
Petrovac
Gornjak Gorge
Topola
Valjevo
Negotin
Žagubica
Bor
Rogatica
Kragujevac
Titovo Uzice
Požega
Čačak
Ćuprija
Paraćin
Zaječar
Goražde
Priboj
Foča
Kraljevo
Ćićevac
W. MORAVA R.
Maglić
Vranjačka Banja
Knjaževac
Nova Varoš
Kruševac
S. MORAVA R.
Prijepolje
Ušće
Pljevlja
Brus
Blace
Niš
Bela Palenka
Žabljak
Raška
Prokuplje
Pirot
Novi Pazar
Kuršumlija
Babušnica
DURMITOR Mts.
Šavnik
Lescovac
SOFIA
Kos. Mitrovica
Nikšić
Kolašin
Ivangrad
Priština
Surdulica
Risan
Kotor
Tivat
Cetinje
Titograd
Peć
Lipljan
Dakovica
Uroševac
Kjustendil
L. Skadar
Prizren
Bar
Vratnica
Stracin
Kumanovo
SAR PLANINA Mts.
Mt. Popova Sapca
Tetovo
Skopje
R. VARDAR
Ulcinj
BRINDISI
TIRANE
Kočani
Dulčevo
Gostivar
Titov Veles
Pehčevo
Štip
Mavrovo
Mt. Solunska Glava
Grasko
Radoviš
Kičevo
Brod
Stobi
Negotino
Debar
Izvor
Kavadarci
Kruševo
Strumica
Prilep
Velešta
Struga
L. Dojran
Ohrid
Resen
SALONICA
Bitola
Otesevo
Mt. Pelister
Heraclea
L. Ohrid
L. Prespa